Popped Culture

Popped Culture

A Social History of Popcorn in America

Andrew F. Smith

Smithsonian Institution Press
Washington and London

Library of Congress Cataloging-in-Publication Data
Smith, Andrew F., 1946–
Popped culture : a social history of popcorn in America / Andrew F. Smith
p. cm.
Originally published : Columbia, S.C. : University of South Carolina Press, 1999.
Includes bibliographical references and index.
ISBN 1-56098-921-1 (alk. paper)
1. Cookery (Popcorn). 2. Popcorn—History. 3. Popcorn—Social aspects. I. Title.
TX814.5.P66 S62 2001
641.6'5677—dc21 00-53347

British Library Cataloguing-in-Publication Data is available

A Smithsonian reprint of the edition published by University of North Carolina Press in 1999

Manufactured in the United States of America
07 06 05 04 03 02 01 5 4 3 2 1

♾ The paper used in this publication meets the minimum requirements of the American National Standard for Information Sciences—Permanence of Paper for Printed Library Materials ANSI Z39.48-1984.

This book is dedicated to popcorn children everywhere,

Charles, David, and James,

Tim, John, and Kelly,

and to future popcorn generations, especially Meghanne.

Contents

PART II: HISTORICAL RECIPES 165

Illustrations

Preface

About twenty years ago I addressed a conference of history teachers in Connecticut. As I was the luncheon speaker, I decided to build my presentation on the concept of food as a vehicle for understanding history. Specifically, I examined how the food that had just been consumed affected history and, conversely, how historical events influenced those foods. The audience, expecting a twenty-page treatise on some significant but boring topic, greeted the unorthodox approach with surprise and enthusiasm.

Subsequently, I received invitations "to do the food thing" at other meal functions. These requests prompted me to prepare histories of foods and drinks commonly served on the lecture circuit. I found extensive literature on the histories of some foods and beverages, such as sugar, chocolate, potatoes, wine, beer, and spices. Other foods had received almost no attention. Little, for instance, had been written about the history of the tomato—one of the more commonly eaten foods in the world. This dearth of information prompted me to delve further into its history. In this quest I visited libraries with excellent culinary collections, such as the New York Public Library, the Library of Congress in Washington, D.C., and the American Antiquarian Society in Worcester, Massachusetts. Librarians directed me to culinary historians. These were individuals seeking to answer some part of the question: who ate what, when, how, and why? The field was also concerned with culinary dynamics: how and why do culinary systems change over time? It was a broad-based and eclectic field and counted scholars in such diverse disciplines as sociology, anthropology, women's studies, history, culinary arts, and sciences related directly to food production, consumption, and nutrition. In addition to academics, the field embraced professional chefs, food writers, independent scholars, cookbook authors, and just plain old foodies.

While the field of culinary history is of recent vintage, interest in food's past goes back hundreds of years. In the last five hundred years thousands of works have been published on food history. However, much of what has been written consists of twice-told myths. Undocumented food stories are the grist of newspapers, magazines, cookbooks, and even works which purport to be true histories. Myths gain reality through repetition, and unfortunately almost all modern food writers from James Beard to Waverly Root have colluded by repeating them.

A major change in the approach to food history began in the United Kingdom in the 1960s. This and subsequent changes were sparked by the works of three people. The first, Elizabeth David, whose works include such titles as *Mediterranean Food* and *Harvest of the Cold Months: The Social History of Ice and Ices,* offers good writing coupled with a clear attempt to locate appropriate support for her historical statements. The second, Reay Tannahill, published *Food in History* in 1973. This ambitious work taps into extensive sources and offers a broad overview of culinary history throughout the world. While some scholars have rightly criticized specifics in Tannahill's work, her book legitimized a broad field and provided a fresh framework for understanding the history of food. The third person to influence the field is Alan Davidson, a former British ambassador, who wrote several culinary works including the soon-to-be-released *Oxford Companion on Food.* His most important contributions are exemplified by his founding of Prospect Books, his editing of the journal *Petits Propos Culinaires* (*PPC*), and his participation in and encouragement of the Oxford Symposium on Food and Cookery. Prospect Books is the single largest publisher of British cookery facsimiles and other works related to food. *PPC* includes essays on culinary topics and reviews of cookery books. The Oxford Symposium serves as an annual meeting place for those interested in culinary history. Both *PPC* and the Oxford Symposium are major communications vehicles for individuals interested in culinary history throughout the world.

In the United States the field of culinary history has unfolded within the past two decades. One observer has claimed that the field was created by Karen Hess. This may be an exaggeration, but not by much. With her husband John Hess she co-authored *The Taste of America,* published by Viking Press in 1977. She edited *Martha Washington's Booke of Cookery,* a facsimile edition of Mary Randolph's *The Virginia House-wife,* and other works. They are all well researched and well written—characteristics that make her books unique among culinary history works. When I started my research into the tomato, I phoned her on the off-chance that she might be willing to respond to some questions. She had never heard of me, of course, yet she was still extremely helpful—a characteristic consistently reflected in her contact with others. Her insistence on accurate scholarship has strengthened the culinary history field throughout the United States, and she has identified high standards for us all.

American culinary historians were assisted by the publication of the *Journal of Gastronomy,* starting in 1984, by the American Institute of Wine and Food which began in 1984. The journal served as an outlet for articles on culinary history and provided a communication mechanism among those working in the field. Unfortunately, this periodical was discontinued in 1991. However, by that date culinary history was firmly rooted in the United States. This is reflected by the growth of academic courses and programs such as those offered by Radcliffe College, Boston University, New York University, and the New School in New York. The number of books published on culinary history has also mushroomed. Two university presses—the University of Iowa and the University of South Carolina Press—have developed extensive lists of culinary history books. Several newsletters devoted to culinary history have been introduced during the past decade, the most important of which is *Food History News,* published by Sandra Oliver in Isleboro, Maine. Organizations of culinary historians are now thriving in Boston; New York; Houston; Los Angeles; Washington, D.C.; Chicago; Philadelphia; Toronto; and Ann Arbor, Michigan.

My research into culinary history has resulted in the publication of four books to date. When I completed *Pure Ketchup: A History of America's National Condiment,* Rebecca Kameny, the wife of the associate director of the University of South Carolina Press, Fred Kameny, suggested that I write a book on the history of popcorn. It so happened that as a child I was fascinated by popcorn, but initially I questioned whether the topic merited a book. My concerns were twofold: Was enough information available to write a history? and Was the topic significant enough to warrant a book? After all, I thought, popcorn is just a trivial snack food. Despite misgivings, I agreed to look into it and report back.

The initial exploration was unpromising. I visited several libraries and checked their catalogs and periodical guides. This search turned up a couple of agricultural pamphlets, a few corporate histories, several cookbooks, a dozen or so children's books, and numerous articles in popular magazines related to popcorn and popcorn products. The historical American cookbooks featured few popcorn recipes. The modern sources offered a series of myths frequently presented as "popcorn history." As few stories cited primary sources for their assertions, I explored the myths. While it is impossible to disprove myths, I can report that no archaeological or historical evidence was uncovered to support the following frequently repeated statements:

- Columbus found popcorn in the Caribbean;
- Pilgrims ate popcorn on the proverbial first Thanksgiving in Plymouth in 1621;
- Amerindians attached religious significance to popcorn;
- Native Americans living in what is today the eastern United States or southern Canada ate popcorn in pre-Columbian times;
- Popcorn or maize was cultivated outside of the Americas before Columbus's arrival;
- Colonial Americans ate popcorn as a snack.

Many other frequently repeated popcorn statements are clearly inaccurate or misleading. For instance, a report indicates that core samples containing maize pollen from a lake bed near Mexico City are eighty thousand years old. Some secondary sources conclude that this is popcorn pollen. Further study on the original core sample site indicates that the pollen is only twenty-two hundred years old. Popcorn histories frequently mention the estimate of eighty thousand years and fail to report the revised estimate. Furthermore, it is not possible today to determine the variety of maize from pollen samples; hence those who claim popcorn's existence at any historical period based on pollen samples are mistaken.

Unfortunately, debunking myths does not make a book. However, my exploration did generate enough interest to redouble my research efforts. By necessity I altered my research strategy to concentrate on nontraditional culinary sources. This strategic shift paid off. While few popcorn recipes were published in general cookery books, I located thousands of recipes in agricultural bulletins, popcorn processors' pamphlets, and specialty cookbooks. Few libraries or historical societies saved these ephemeral materials, but private collectors and some popcorn processors had preserved many documents and memorabilia. With the help of processors, culinary historians, archivists, librarians, collectors, and booksellers I slowly pieced together popcorn's history.

When it finally became clear that information about popcorn is abundant, I pondered whether popcorn is a suitable topic for a book. Several friends were surprised that I even considered writing about a "joke food." From an agricultural perspective, popcorn is indeed a minor crop. While maize is the second largest cereal grain crop in the world and the largest in the United States, popcorn production hovers around two one-thousandths percent of the total crop.

Of all the types of corn raised in the United States, however, none is more commonly recognized than popcorn. Americans eat popcorn in movie theaters, amusement parks, and sports arenas and around campfires. At home we pop corn in microwave ovens, through hot-air poppers, or in covered frying pans on stovetops. We snack on ready-to-eat savory and candied popcorn confections. Over two hundred million boxes of Cracker Jack alone are crunched and munched annually, and today Cracker Jack is outsold by Franklin Crunch 'N' Munch. Our intake of popcorn in all forms has more than doubled during the past two decades, and consumption abroad has expanded at an even faster pace. As trivial as popcorn may appear when compared to the total maize crop, Americans annually devour eleven billion popped quarts, which averages out to about forty-four quarts per person. By volume popcorn is America's favorite snack food.

It was not just consumption statistics or today's popularity that convinced me to write this book. Popcorn exploded onto the American mainstream in the nineteenth century. Unlike other fads that quickly passed from the culinary scene, popcorn has thrived and become enshrined in our national mythology. To many outside the United States popcorn is almost a defining component of American culture. How popcorn was introduced and why the mainstream embraced it is a story about broader historical trends that have influenced us over the past fifteen decades.

While I am concerned with what popcorn can tell us about larger social and historical issues, I remain fascinated by popcorn itself, as fascinated as when I was a child. Popcorn's story is an exciting tale of unexpected twists and turns that are even more amusing than the frequently regurgitated popcorn myths. It is peopled with archaeologists and anthropologists, street vendors and merchants, seedsmen and farmers, processors and grocers, nutritionists and health-food nuts, scientists and salespersons, poets and songwriters, and just plain Americans. It is a story filled with hot-shot inventors, high-flying promoters, risk-taking growers, efficiency-conscious processors, hard-hitting advertisers, and lip-smacking consumers—all of whom have contributed to popcorn's transformation into an American icon. As important, the popcorn story is interwoven with significant events, inventions, and social movements in American history, such as the Depression and World War II; the inventions of movies, television, and the microwave; and the rise of health-food consciousness in America. It is a story worth telling.

A word about the extensive documentation. My reasons for documentation are multifold. First, many books which purport to be culinary histories are really collections of myths and twice-told stories which have captured the fancy of writers and readers alike. Frequent repetition of myths does not change their accuracy or truthfulness. As many food stories are inaccurate or false, their repetition does not improve our understanding of culinary matters or of broader historical contexts. Second, some who write about food history make broad, sweeping statements unsupported by factual evidence. Others claim that they have deep insight into culinary history. Still others have specific ideological positions and present their opinions as facts. While insight, ideology, and opinion are significant and play an important role in culinary history, it is imperative that readers be aware of the factual basis for a writer's statements and conclusions. If the field of culinary history is to thrive, it must promote higher evidentiary standards. Failure to do so will result in culinary history's relegation to the arena of fiction, myth, and trivia.

Third, many conclusions presented in this book differ dramatically from those presented by previous writers and challenge cherished popcorn myths. As no serious history of popcorn has previously been written, it is likely that future researchers will uncover additional information that may lead in new directions or contradict the conclusions I have presented here. Future culinary historians and writers will make better judgments if they can easily check the sources upon which I have relied. I hope this book encourages others to revise, challenge, and improve the story of popcorn and the social history in which it is embedded.

Acknowledgments

This book could not have been completed without the help of many others. Special thanks go particularly to four people who have been helpful throughout the process of researching and writing:

- to Karen Hess, culinary historian, for her review and comments on an early draft of the first five chapters and the historical recipes
- to George K. Brown, former president of Wyandot Popcorn Company and current president of the Wyandot Popcorn Museum in Marion, Ohio, for his willingness to open the museum's files, for his constant encouragement for this book, and for his review and comments, particularly with regard to sections on popcorn processors
- to Kenneth E. Ziegler, popcorn researcher at Iowa State University, for his review and comments on the entire book, particularly those sections connected with the technical and scientific aspects of popcorn
- to Joe Carlin, proprietor, Food Heritage Press, for his constant encouragement and forwarding of popcorn-related materials.

For their assistance on the culinary history sections I thank the following people: Jan and Dan Longone, proprietors of the Food and Wine Library, Ann Arbor, Michigan, for identification of early popcorn recipes and the permission to hunt popcorn references in their cookbook collection; Jackie Williams, culinary historian, for location of early popcorn recipes; Sandy Oliver, editor of *Food History News,* Isleboro, Maine, for publication of my request for information; Alan Davidson, editor of *Petits Propos Culinaires,* London, for his publication of my request for information regarding popcorn cookery outside the United States and Canada, and for the publication of "The Pop Corn Polka: or How Maize Popped into the American Mainstream"; Millie Delahunty, editor of the newsletter of New York Culinary Historians, and Ann Woodward, editor of the newsletter of Culinary Historians of Ann Arbor, for their publication of "A True History of Popcorn"; Laura Wasowicz, reference specialist for children's literature, American Antiquarian Society, for locating the children's pamphlet *Old Pop Corn;* Barbara Kuck, curator, Johnson & Wales University, Culinary Archives and Museum, Providence, Rhode Island, for kind assistance examining their archives and cookbooks; Carley Robison, librarian, Seymour Library, Knox College, Galesburg, Illinois, for locating material about Olmsted Ferris; and Cara de Silva, writer and culinary historian, for identifying early popcorn sources and for her support and encouragement.

Thanks to the following individuals at historical societies or museums: James W. Baker, vice president and chief historian, Plimouth Plantation, Plymouth, Massachusetts; Brian Jensen, exhibit specialist, National Museum of American History, Washington, D.C.; Hans J. Bosig, director, Jasper County Historical Museum, Newton, Iowa; Ann Billesbach, head of reference services, Nebraska State Historical Society, Lincoln, Nebraska; Martha E. Wright, librarian, Indiana State Library, Indianapolis, Indiana; Elizabeth H. Ernst, librarian, Grinnell Historical Museum, Grinnell, Iowa; Mary Ann Townsend, collection manager, Floyd County Historical Society, Charles City, Iowa; Susan Kinsey, Genesee Country Museum, Geneseo, New York; and Steph McGrath, senior curator, DuPage County Historical Museum, Wheaton, Illinois.

For the information about microwave ovens, thanks to: Robert Buderi, author of *The Invention that Changed the World: How a Small Group of Radar Pioneers Won the Second World War and Launched a Technological Revolution;* William Hall, formerly of Raytheon Company, Concord, Massachusetts; Norman B. Krim, archivist, Raytheon Company, Lexington, Massachusetts; and John Osepchuk, formerly of Raytheon Company, Concord, Massachusetts.

Thanks to the following popcorn processors, breeders, professors, promoters, and manufacturers of poppers for their interviews and information forwarded: William Smith, executive director, Popcorn Institute, Chicago, Illinois; Charles Bowman, president, Chester, Inc., Valparaiso, Indiana; James Watkins, founder, Golden Valley Microwave Foods, Minneapolis, Minnesota; Herbert Gettelfinger, founder and former president, Gettelfinger Popcorn, Palmyra, Indiana; Wrede Smith, president, and Brian M. Clarke, American Popcorn Company, Sioux City, Iowa; Charles Sing, professor, University of Michigan, Ann Arbor; Roger Moery, president, Vogel Popcorn, Marion, Ohio; Kelly Modisett, founder, Kel Pop, Inc., Lafayette, Indiana; Robert F. Ware, president, W. F. Ware Company, Trenton, Kentucky; Bernard Schwarzkopf, retired popcorn processor, Wall Lake, Iowa; Charles D. Cretors, president, C. Cretors Company, Chicago, Illinois; James A. McCarty, retired president of Colonial Gardens, Evansville, Indiana; Fred Childers, president, Bromwell Housewares, Inc., Michigan City, Indiana; and Jim Iverson, research director for popcorn, Crookham Company, Caldwell, Idaho.

For their help with the archaeological sections, thanks to Walton C. Galinat, professor emeritus, University of Massachusetts, Waltham; Deborah M. Pearsall and Ed Buckler, Department of Anthropology, University of Missouri, Columbia; Gayle Fritze, University of Washington, Saint Louis, Missouri; Anna Roosevelt, Field Museum of Natural History, Chicago, Illinois; and Janice B. Klein, registrar, Field Museum of Natural History, Chicago, Illinois.

For their assistance with the sections on Cracker Jack, thanks to Larry White, author of *Cracker Jack Toys,* Rowley, Massachusetts; Roberta Bowen, editor, *The Prize Insider,* Cracker Jack Collector's Association, Tempe, Arizona; John Vavra, Cracker Jack collector, Fairfax, Iowa; Harriet Joyce, Cracker Jack collector, DeBary, Florida; and Ronald Toth Jr., Cracker Jack collector, Rochester, New Hampshire.

Thanks also go to the many librarians at the Historical Society of Iowa Library, Des Moines, Iowa; the Henry Ford Museum and Greenfield Village Library and Archives; the Chicago Historical Society; the American Antiquarian Society; the Library of Congress; the National Agricultural Library; the New York Public Library; the Brooklyn Public Library; and particularly Joseph Benford, librarian, Print and Picture Collection, Free Library of Philadelphia, Pennsylvania.

Finally, special thanks to Michael Beiser for his assistance with editing versions of this manuscript.

While I appreciated all interviews, materials, and advice, not all information or suggestions were included in this book. The final decisions for inclusion and exclusion were mine, and I accept all responsibility for any errors or significant omissions.

Part I

History

Chapter 1

The Pop Heard 'Round the Americas

Almost every schoolchild has heard the story of how Native Americans introduced the Pilgrims to popcorn on that famous first Thanksgiving feast held at Plymouth in 1621. At the end of the feast Quadequina (in other accounts, Massiott) poured upon the table a bushel of popcorn, "a dainty hitherto unseen and unknown by most of the Pilgrims." John Howland hastily gathered up a portion upon a wooden plate and carried it "to the Common house for the delectation of the women, that is to say, for Elizabeth Tilley, whose firm young teeth craunched it with much gusto." Or so the American novelist Jane Adams wrote in *Standish of Standish: A Story of the Pilgrims* published in 1889.[1]

It is a fascinating story that magazine writers have perpetuated. Some even revised it: Syd Spiegel, a Canadian popcorn distributor, claimed that popcorn had been given at the "First Thanksgiving," which was celebrated in Jamestown in 1630. Other writers expanded the original story, assuming that if Quadequina had introduced popcorn to the Pilgrims, then other Native American leaders—Tecumseh, Red Jacket, and Powhatan—also did so to other colonists. Likewise, other Native American tribes—the Mohawks and the Iroquois—have also been credited with popping corn and giving it to European colonists.[2]

The story is also of the stuff that children's writers love. For instance, in *Farmer Boy* Laura Wilder celebrates popcorn as an American creation. "Nobody but the Indians ever had popcorn, till after the Pilgrim Fathers came to America. On the first Thanksgiving Day, the Indians were invited to dinner, and they came, and they poured out on the table a big bagful of popcorn." Wilder at least had the good sense to hypothesize that the popcorn purportedly eaten by Native Americans would not have been very tasty: "they didn't butter it or salt it, and it would be cold and tough after they had carried it around in a bag of skins." Whatever the potential objections to the story, writers of children's books have latched on to it.[3] In addition, the tale has been a standard part of the elementary school curriculum, especially around Thanksgiving time, when students portray Native Americans proudly offering popcorn to the starving Pilgrims.

Other observers have conjured up a religious symbolism for Native Americans and popcorn: "Indian tribes believed popcorn contained spirits who were released when the corn exploded." Popcorn therefore "had special religious significance, and was used to symbolize fertility in religious ceremonies." Promoters and marketeers have utilized stories that connect popcorn with Native Americans, Pilgrims, and early American colonists. These stories have been frequently mentioned in promotional advertisements and more recently in Web sites on the Internet. Popcorn promoters have deducted logically that if Native Americans ate popcorn, the English colonists surely would have had the good sense to pop corn themselves. Several twentieth-century renditions assert that colonial housewives did just that, serving it as a snack as well as at meals. Still others have reported that American colonists used popcorn as a Christmas decoration. In 1980 the *Washington Star* reported an even more unique use of popcorn: "Indians who often brought deerskin bags of popped corn to peace negotiations with English colonists, offered popcorn to Pilgrims at their first Thanksgiving dinner, and apparently it was a big hit. Colonial settlers often ate it for breakfast with cream and sugar." In 1984 an article in *Reader's Digest* claimed that an Indian brought popcorn to the first Thanksgiving "as a demonstration of good will." George Plimpton announced in the *New York Times* in 1997 that some chronicles of the first Thanksgiving reported that the Indians gave the Pilgrims popcorn balls made of maple syrup.[4]

Unfortunately for the above stories, no evidence has emerged indicating that the Pilgrims "craunched" popcorn at the proverbial first Thanksgiving. Only one account of the event survives. *Mourt's Relations,* attributed to Edward Winslow, mentions only fowl and deer. William Bradford's account of the harvest period mentions cod, bass, waterfowl, turkeys, and Indian corn. According to James W. Baker, vice president and chief historian for Plimouth Plantation, no trace of popcorn has been uncovered in regional archaeological excavations. Several sources delighted in reporting that the whole story is a myth.[5] While absence of popcorn in archaeological sites is not proof that it was not grown, it does suggest as much. Of all the types of maize, popcorn has the hardest kernel and would have been the most likely variety to survive.

The inability to locate popcorn in eastern America is surprising, particularly when popcornlike plants were grown in the American Southwest centuries before the arrival of Europeans to the New World. To understand why popcorn was not cultivated in eastern America in pre-Columbian times requires some botanical, archaeological, and historical background.

Botanical Maize

Popcorn is a type of maize—a member of the Maydeae tribe in the large natural order of grasses called the Gramineae. There are two genuses of Maydeae: *Tripsacum,* which grows wild in Central America; and *Zea,* which has two major species—*Zea mays,* which is what Americans call corn, and *Zea diploperennis,* a perennial type of teosinte. Teosinte is a colloquial name applied to all sorts of plants native to Mexico and Central America. An annual variety of teosinte—Zea *mays mexicana*—is corn's closest botanical relative. By the time Europeans encountered the New World in the late fifteenth century, maize was already a domesticated plant that did not grow in the wild. Without human cultivation, maize did not survive.

Although varieties of maize are highly diverse, all are members of the same species. The first serious effort to classify maize was attempted in 1884 by the director of the New York Agricultural Experiment Station, E. Lewis Sturtevant. His system was based on the kernel's size, shape, and composition.[6] Popcorn kernels, like those of all cereals, have three major structural components: the germ (or embryo), the endosperm, and the outer hull called the pericarp. The endosperm is made up of soft starch granules (also called floury or opaque), and hard starch granules (also called corneous, horny, or translucent). Different types of maize contain varying amounts of soft and hard starch granules. The endosperm is enclosed in the pericarp, which laypersons know well because hulls often get stuck in their teeth. The pericarp and underlying layers can be of various colors, but the endosperm is either white or yellow inside.

Based on his analysis, Sturtevant identified six major maize types: pod corn, sweet corn, flour corn, dent corn, flint corn, and popcorn. Pod corn is a mutant form of maize with soft, leaflike flaps known as glumes covering each kernel. Several observers, including Sturtevant, speculated that pod corn might have been the ancestral form of cultivated corn. Sweet corn is characterized by a shriveled, horny, and translucent appearance—a condition resulting from the failure of its soluble sugar to be converted into starch. Its kernels are therefore higher in sugar content than any other corn. Sweet corn is consumed almost exclusively by humans. Dent corn is characterized by a depression on the crown caused by uneven drying of the hard and soft starch in the kernel. Dent corn resembles sweet corn but is tough to chew. Americans and Europeans harvest more dent corn than any other type of corn, but it is mainly fed to livestock. Flour corn generally has a rounded or flat crown but contains virtually all soft endosperm. Also known as squaw corn, it is usually similar to flint corn but differs in the soft texture of the kernels, which are easily chewed or ground. Flint corn contains a hard endosperm and little soft starch, and hence does not become dented upon drying. It is often called Indian corn and comes in a rainbow of colors.[7]

The final type of maize noted by Sturtevant was popcorn, an extreme form of flint corn with small and particularly hard kernels. Its pericarps are multicolored, but the most common are yellow and white. The popcorn plant is prolific as most stalks produce more than one ear, but its ears are smaller, and its total yield is less per acre than other maize varieties. Popcorn's thinner and weaker stalks tend to have standability problems. Its endosperm contains a much greater ratio of hard starch to soft starch. Its kernels differ from those of other maize types in that they are smaller and have a thicker pericarp. Extrinsically popcorn kernels come in three basic shapes: rice types, which are long and slender with a sharp point at the top; pearl types, which are oval with a smooth top; and South American types, which are larger and round. Today the majority of commercial popcorns are pearl types.[8]

The major common trait shared by all varieties of popcorn is the ability to explode and produce a flake when raw kernels are subjected to heat. This ability to pop is not unique to popcorn. Many flint and some dent corns also pop, but their flakes are relatively small by comparison. Neither is the popping phenomena limited to maize. Popping grains from the Old World include some varieties of rice, milo, millet, and sorghum. In the New World some varieties of Quinoa (*Chenopodium quinoa*), a sacred Incan food employed to thicken soups, pop just like popcorn. So do varieties of amaranth (*Amaranthus caudatus*), which was first domesticated in Peru about four thousand years ago and was consumed extensively in South and Central America before Columbus's arrival in the New World.[9]

Of all the major cereal grains in the world, maize is the only one to have a disputed point of origin. One theory hypothesizes that corn originated from a wild form of maize which subsequently died out and was unrecorded. Although not the first to expound this theory, Paul Mangelsdorf, who had grown up in northeastern Kansas and studied agriculture at Kansas State Agricultural College, was its major proponent.

He became a graduate assistant at Connecticut Agricultural Experiment Station in New Haven while simultaneously completing his doctoral studies at Harvard University. Upon completing his doctorate, Mangelsdorf was hired by the Texas Agricultural Experiment Station. At College Station he met Robert Reeves, and they both began experimenting on corn.[10]

Mangelsdorf's roommate during his first year at Harvard was Edgar Anderson. After graduation Anderson was hired by the Missouri Botanical Garden in Saint Louis but maintained his friendship with Mangelsdorf. On one visit to Texas, Anderson asked if teosinte might be a hybrid of corn and *Tripsacum.* At first Mangelsdorf ridiculed the idea, but Mangelsdorf and Reeves began to explore the relationships among maize, *Tripsacum,* and teosinte. Eventually Mangelsdorf and Reeves concluded that Anderson was right. In May 1939 Mangelsdorf and Reeves published a massive study titled *The Origin of Indian Corn and Its Relatives.* They hypothesized that domesticated maize derived from an extinct wild type of maize. Through mutation a wild pod popcorn emerged. Its seeds were small, hard, and stony and were completely covered by separate husks. By accident, theorized Reeves and Mangelsdorf, Amerindians heated the ears and "caused the seeds to burst from their enveloping glumes and converted the flinty endosperm to an easily masticated and palatable food." After maize was domesticated, *Tripsacum* hybridized with it, and teosinte was one of the results, claimed Mangelsdorf and Reeves. North American dent corn and some varieties of flint and flour corn were also derivatives.[11] Shortly after the publication of the book, Mangelsdorf was offered a position at Harvard University as a professor of botany and assistant director of the Botanical Museum.

Edgar Anderson deduced that if Mangelsdorf's theory were correct, popcorn was the key to understanding the origin of maize. Like Mangelsdorf, Anderson believed that popping was the first way pre-Columbian Indians prepared corn to eat. He also hypothesized that if wild corn had survived, it was likely growing somewhere as a popcorn. As popcorn had been so closely associated with carnivals and circuses, scientists had not seriously studied it, and consequently little information was available. In 1942 Anderson began to investigate popcorn. He wrote letters seeking answers and traveled throughout Mexico and South America. While he did not locate the illusive wild maize, he did amass information about popcorn.[12] Based on this historical and botanical information, Anderson concluded that popcorn was indeed the original corn. As important as Anderson's theoretical speculation was, however, what was really needed was archaeological evidence. It soon emerged.

Archaeological Maize

In 1948 Herbert W. Dick, a graduate student in anthropology at Harvard University, convinced the Peabody Museum to support an archaeological dig in an abandoned rock shelter in New Mexico. Students from Harvard and the University of New Mexico launched their investigation at a site known as Bat Cave, which was actually a series of caves about 165 feet above the level of an ancient lake floor. The largest cave evidenced few signs of human habitation, but the excavation of the smaller tunnel-like caves turned up a considerable number of kernels and corncobs. The kernels in the two lower levels of the site were small and corneous. Based on their location in the excavation, the students concluded that the oldest maize in Bat Cave was a popcorn type, just as Mangelsdorf and Anderson had predicted.

The first estimate on dating the specimens retrieved from the Bat Cave was determined by geological considerations. Subsequently, radiocarbon dating of some plant remains was conducted. Radiocarbon dating techniques are based on the fact that all living things absorb carbon. Carbon is constantly present in the atmosphere. Plants inhale atmospheric carbon, including some radioactive isotope ^{14}carbon, which decays into ^{12}carbon at a constant rate of 50 percent every 5,700 years. In about 40,000 years the ^{14}carbon is very small and difficult to measure. Hence the age of material from an archaeological site can be calculated from the material's ration of ^{14}carbon to ^{12}carbon. The age of once-living plants and animals can therefore be determined by the amount of residual ^{14}carbon. During the 1950s using this test required relatively large amounts of carbon, much more than the amount in small maize kernels. The Bat Cave study made the assumption that specimens found at the same level were also the same age. Radiocarbon tests on charcoal surrounding the oldest corn in the cave suggested that the Bat Cave maize was from 4,000 to 5,000 years old. These graduate students had located the earliest known maize specimens!

Since the 1948 expedition had excavated only one section of Bat Cave, Herbert Dick made a second expedition in 1950 in hopes of finding more specimens. More maize remains were indeed uncovered. Of 299 kernels found in the refuse, 6 were partly or completely popped. Dick gave the collection to Mangelsdorf. After careful inspection Mangelsdorf announced that his 1939 theory regarding the origin of maize had been proven correct. The earliest maize had small slender ears, which were not completely enclosed by husks. It was both a pod corn and a popcorn—the popped flakes proved that the Amerindians ate popcorn. To make sure of this conclusion, Mangelsdorf placed 10 of the unpopped kernels from Bat Cave "in a petri dish with a piece of moist paper towel for 48 hours. When dropped into hot oil, all of these popped in varying degrees, providing dramatic proof that primitive corn was a popcorn."[13]

Since maize could scarcely have existed as a wild plant in the region in which Bat Cave was located, archaeologists deduced that it had been introduced into the Southwest as a cultivated plant from Mexico. Richard MacNeish, a Canadian archaeologist credited with finding more maize remains than any other individual, located 24,186 specimens at sites in the Tehuacán Valley of Mexico alone. Mangelsdorf visited the valley in 1962 and declared that some specimens were definitely examples of wild maize as he had hypothesized. The oldest known remains were about seventy-two hundred years old, and their cobs were small and soft. About one thousand years later harder cobs appeared, presumably caused by their hybridization with teosinte. Then about three thousand years later, asserted Mangelsdorf, teosintoid maize entered the valley. Hybridization produced more vigorous and productive hybrids. A slender popcornlike kernel became predominant. Subsequently, improved races made maize "the most important staple food plant, first of Mesoamerica and later of the New World."[14]

The discovery of maize cobs and kernels in the prehistoric deposits at Bat Cave and Tehuacán set the stage for a long and productive collaboration between Paul Mangelsdorf and numerous archaeologists. When *Races of Maize in Mexico* was published in 1952, the National Research Council and the National Academy of Sciences established a committee to collect, classify, and preserve maize germplasm throughout the Western Hemisphere. Mangelsdorf participated in eleven studies that followed, all of which were based on his theory about corn's origin.[15] Mangelsdorf's conclusions were regularly cited in journal articles, dissertations, and textbooks.

There were some problems with Mangelsdorf's popcorn origin. As pre-Columbian Amerindians did not use oil as a cooking medium, if they had popped corn, they had not done so in the way that Mangelsdorf had posited. To accommodate this fact, Mangelsdorf conducted another experiment. As many cobs were slightly scorched or charred, he proposed that the original inhabitants popped corn over the open fire. To test his new belief, he put a stick through a cob, held the ear over the coals, and slowly rotated it. Some kernels exploded and remained on the ear. Other kernels shot onto the ground where they could easily be retrieved and eaten.[16] Mangelsdorf concluded that as popcorn could be popped in such a manner, this was the way Amerindians had prepared it. However, no archaeological evidence indicated that the Bat Cave inhabitants had popped corn purposely; for instance, the corn cobs were not pierced. While the remains of maize at other sites in the Southwest were extensive, no other ancient remains of popped corn or pierced corncobs were uncovered. Had this been the way Amerindians had prepared popcorn for consumption, it would have been logical to assume that further evidence would have been located. The popped corn in Bat Cave may well have been accidental.

Despite a few dissenters questioning some tenets, Mangelsdorf's theories remained unchallenged for almost twenty years. One reason for the dearth of criticism typical of most academic dialogue was that the monograph describing the Bat Cave expeditions was not published until 1965. When it was released, several problems surfaced. In 1967 when Paul Mangelsdorf, Herbert Dick, and Julián Cámara-Hernández admitted that the dating of the Bat Cave maize was solely based on two ^{14}carbon tests: one on a sample consisting only of cobs; and the other using a combination of cobs and wood from Bat Cave. These two tests yielded dates respectively of 1,752 and 2,249 years old, far less than the 4,000- to 5,000-year-old dates announced previously. While surrounding material was indeed thousands of years older, many factors might have caused maize kernels and cobs from a later time period to settle at a lower level. In addition the provenance controls for the samples were challenged as were the sampling techniques. After carefully reviewing the procedures employed at Bat Cave, Michael S. Berry concluded that it "was a poorly excavated site that can be interpreted nearly any way one pleases by juggling the data." When Michael Berry reexamined evidence from all the sites in the Southwest, he concluded that the oldest known maize in the Southwest was only about 2,430 years old. Likewise, the dating of the maize at the Tehuacán Valley sites was challenged. Using the accelerator mass spectronomy (AMS) method of dating, Austin Long et al. concluded that the oldest maize in the Tehuacán Valley was only 4,700 years old.[17] Bruce Smith maintains that the best evidence is that the oldest maize specimens are about 4,000 to 4,500 years old.[18]

As other underpinnings of Mangelsdorf's theory were questioned, anthropologists began to suspect that maize may well have been domesticated from teosinte, which grew wild in Mexico, Honduras, and Guatemala. Teosinte unmistakably is the closest relative of maize. Mangelsdorf had maintained that teosinte could not have been the progenitor of maize because it was "so unpromising as a source of food that it seems unlikely that it would ever have been domesticated." Its seeds were enclosed "in hard bony shells from which they cannot be removed by ordinary threshing operations."[19]

George W. Beadle, a biologist, Nobel Prize winner, and president of the University of Chicago, led the opposition to the Mangelsdorf's wild maize theory. As a graduate student Beadle had studied teosinte.

After reviewing the evidence presented by Mangelsdorf, Beadle was convinced that maize could have derived from wild teosinte. One of Mangelsdorf's arguments against teosinte was his belief that it was inedible. Beadle acquired some seeds and tried to figure out how to consume them. As a boyhood lover of popcorn, he wondered if perhaps teosinte would pop. To Beadle's surprise, teosinte seeds, when subjected to heat, exploded out of their fruit cases. The resulting popped teosinte flakes were physically indistinguishable from today's popped corn. Beadle surmised that Amerindians placed the kernels "on a fire, on glowing embers, on hot rocks or on heated sand." The kernels popped out of their indigestible shells and could be retrieved with sticks and tongs. The flakes were admirably suited for human consumption. Based on this experiment, Beadle hypothesized that prehistoric Amerindians had also discovered that popped teosinte could be consumed and had cultivated it. Over hundreds of years, speculated Beadle, Amerindians selected the combination of the five or more major genes and chromosome mutations that distinguished domesticated maize from its wild ancestors.[20]

Mangelsdorf, who had offered the same argument with regard to popcorn, dismissed Beadle's extension of the same case to teosinte. While agreeing that it was possible for teosinte to be popped out of its indigestible shell, Mangelsdorf fired back that there was no evidence that the Amerindians had so prepared it in this manner. Few teosinte shell fragments were located in ancient fecal matter, suggesting that it was not consumed by early Amerindians. Mangelsdorf countered by popping *Tripsacum* seeds. This proved that the ability to pop was probably common among all starchy seeds that are small and corneous. Popability could not be the basis determining whether or not teosinte had been the original source of domesticated maize. Then Mangelsdorf questioned whether humans could tolerate ingesting 50 percent or more roughage present in the teosinte seeds. Beadle responded by consuming 75 grams of whole teosinte seeds on two successive days. He then increased his intake to 150 grams per day for two more days. He completed the regimen with no ill effects whatever. Beadle prepared the seeds in a variety of ways. He ground, pounded, and dried them with a *metate*—a flat stone mortar—and a *mano*—a handheld stone used to grind maize and other grains. He also soaked teosinte seeds until they became soft enough to chew. He suggested, presumably with a twinkle in his eye, that teosinte may have been ground and made into teo-tortillas. He concluded that it was possible to feed a small family on teosinte seeds. Mangelsdorf struck back by countering that Amerindians did not possess food-preparation implements at the time when maize was thought to have been domesticated. Indeed, New World ceramics did not emerge until thousands of years later. Mangelsdorf further claimed that teosinte was too difficult to harvest and had limited nutritional value. Beadle's teosinte diet was deficient for he received only one-sixth of the minimum daily caloric requirement. Amerindians would not have domesticated teosinte when other more promising grasses were readily available in pre-Columbian America. Mangelsdorf proclaimed that teosinte was never grown extensively as a crop nor was it ever domesticated.[21]

Beadle shot back with a salvo in *Scientific American,* reporting that teosinte-like seeds had been recovered from an undisturbed preceramic site dating back seven thousand years about twenty miles southeast of Mexico City. He also stated that early Spanish accounts reported that teosinte had been cultivated. As only two mutations were necessary to convert teosinte into a productive plant, he claimed that a teosinte of some eight thousand to fifteen thousand years ago was the direct ancestor of maize. Indeed, in the nineteenth century teosinte was cultivated extensively in the United States as a forage plant for animals, particularly in southern states. Evidently neither Beadle nor Mangelsdorf was aware that teosinte was also used for culinary purposes in America. Thomas Murrey's *Salads and Sauces,* for instance, employed teosinte shoots to make a salad. This usage raises the possibility that the leaves, and not the seeds, were eaten by early hunter-gatherers.[22]

Contact with teosinte leaves as a source of food perhaps led to the accidental positioning of teosinte seeds in or near fire, with the resulting pop heard around the Americas. Popping likely caused surprise and amusement, just as it does to modern-day Americans. To the pre-Columbian Amerindians the explosion was even more important. Popping meant that teosinte seeds could easily have been eaten. Mangelsdorf's proposition that teosinte was not eaten because by itself it would not provide enough calories is ludicrous. Amerindians ate anything and everything. There is no need to believe, as Mangelsdorf proposed, that teosinte was the only food eaten by Amerindians at any time. At first it was likely a supplemental food that hunter-gatherers collected and consumed along with many other New World fungi, plants, animals, and insects. When hunter-gatherers became more sedentary, perhaps due to the extinction of their traditional animal-based food supply, protofarmers experimented with the plants they already knew. Their potential consumption of leaves and the popped teosinte flakes would have been sufficient reason for planting teosinte seeds. It is likely that advantageous mutations accidentally developed and that Amerindians encouraged them, leading to domesticated maize.

While the above scenario is speculative, today most anthropologists believe that maize was domesticated more than once from wild forms of teosinte in central Mexico, Guatemala, or Honduras beginning about eight thousand years ago. The earliest maize consisted of pop-type varieties. Early on, these pop-type corns accompanied migrants to South America, where they developed in isolation from the maize domesticated in Mesoamerica. During the 1950s and 1960s the National Research Council and the National Academy of Science's studies of maize were published. Reviewing these studies, Major M. Goodman and Robert Bird concluded that at least 219 races of maize grew in South America, 18 of which were popcorns. Goodman and Bird reported that the relationships among the South American popcorns were obscure, but they had many common characteristics, such as white pointed kernels, tapering ear shapes, and hairy plants with few tassel branches.[23] As South American popcorns had developed in isolation, they differed dramatically from those that evolved in Central and North America. One important difference was that the popcorns in Chile, Brazil, and Paraguay were daylight neutral. As the maize plant originated in tropical areas, it required equal lengths of days and nights. The popcorns grown in the southern part of South America had to survive long summer days and short nights. No evidence has been located to indicate that early popcorn cultivated in Central America or in the American Southwest developed this crucial characteristic.

From Central America maize was disseminated into what is today the United States. As previously mentioned, it was cultivated in the American Southwest more than twenty-five hundred years ago, but due to environmental, botanical, and cultural factors it did not rapidly spread into northern and eastern parts of the North American continent. The vast, largely unsettled, arid areas of New Mexico, Arizona, and Texas served as a barrier impeding corn from easily migrating northward or eastward. Likewise, the Rocky Mountains provided a barrier northward and westward. In the Midwest poor soil conditions were also a factor. Sod, which blanketed much of the area, was inhospitable to maize. Conditions in the Midwest did not become generally favorable to maize until the sod had been broken up by the steel plow introduced in the nineteenth century. Maize was cultivated in the alluvial floodplains of rivers, but its northward advance was delayed until day-neutral varieties became available.[24]

The best evidence indicates that only two races of maize populated eastern America prior to European colonization. Dent corn was disseminated from the American Southwest to the southern states. In the American South dent corn was not generally cultivated until about one thousand years ago, and it may not have been grown in southern Florida at all prior to the European conquests in the New World. The second maize type to enter eastern America was a race of eight-rowed flint corn (Maíz de Ocho), which was cultivated from North Dakota to New

England and parts of southern Canada. This was probably not cultivated in New England until about nine hundred years ago. French and British colonists found flints when they settled in northern North America, but maize was a recent addition to the diets of Native American groups inhabiting New England's coast.[25]

Historical Maize

If maize is important in our lives today, it was even more so in the lives of pre-Columbian Amerindians. Murdo MacLeod estimated that maize in various forms made up 80 percent of Amerindian diets in Central America. Because of its importance Aztecs, Mayas, and most other Amerindians considered maize a "sacred thing."[26] When Europeans arrived in the New World five hundred years ago, they found maize growing in the Caribbean and all through the area from southern Canada to central Chile. Numerous varieties of maize were grown in the Americas before the European conquest, including the major varieties noted previously by Sturtevant.

From a culinary standpoint, maize was an especially versatile food. Amerindians roasted it over a fire and ate it on the cob. Many types of corn could be heated and dried. The process of parching preserved kernels for long periods of time. Parched corn was then pounded to make corn flour. Coarse flour was employed to make hominy, samp, gruel, or porridge. Fine flour was combined with water, then rolled and baked on stones to make bread or tortillas. Some tortillas were large, thick, and white; others were small, delicate, and colored. Steamed under a hot cloth or warmed on stones, they were served open or folded. Filled with fish or fowl and flavored with chiles and herbs, tortillas had versatility that equaled that of any bread produced elsewhere.[27]

Amerindians also popped corn. Archaeologists found pop-type varieties in diverse locations in Central and South America. Ricardo E. Latcham, director of the Mueso in Santiago, Chile, unearthed popcorn in twelfth-century burial sites in Calama, Chiu Chiu, and Quillagua. According to Thomas H. Goodspeed, the pre-Incan inhabitants of northern Chile had placed little bowls or cotton bags filled with popcorn flakes and midget cobs beside mummified bodies. Latcham gave Goodspeed a cob and a few unpopped kernels. After his return from Chile, Goodspeed heated them on his stove to see if they would pop. Although harvested nearly a thousand years previously, the maize "popped as readily as did last year's crop that had come from a box from the shelves of the neighborhood cash-and-carry."[28]

Popcorn was also extracted from burial sites in Anchon, Peru. When Latcham compared them to the popcorn he had located in Chile, he announced that the corn *morocho* of Peru and *curagua* of Chile were originally the same variety. Directly translated, morocho and curagua referred to a popcorn with small round grains, a thin pericarp, and a dark red to purple color. When ground, this popcorn flour was extremely white. Latcham reported that when it popped, "the kernels characteristically exploded into the shape of a four point star." Subsequently, some Christians reportedly believed that curagua, called Valparaiso popcorn in the United States, was a religious symbol "on account of the grains, when roasted, splitting regularly into the form of a cross."[29]

In addition, popcorn was illustrated on ancient sculpture and mentioned in early Spanish texts. Garcilaso de la Vega, who was born in Cuzco in 1539, reported in his *Royal Commentaries of the Incas* that the Incas ate toasted maize called *camcha,* which was pounded, not ground, and used in porridges. Bernabé Cobo, a Jesuit missionary in Peru between 1609 and 1629, reported that Peruvians toasted "a certain kind of corn until it bursts." It was called *pisancalla* and was consumed as a confection. In Paraguay two early references to popcorn found their way into print. The first was by Martin Dobrizhoffer, who was a missionary from 1749 to 1767. Dobrizhoffer reported that the Guarani of Paraguay had a kind of corn "called *bisingallo,* the most favored of all, the grains of which are angular and pointed." Popcorn of a very different type was located by Félix de Azara in the late eighteenth century. He reported locating a variety whose grains when boiled in fat or oil burst "without becoming detached, and their results [were] a superb bouquet fit to adorn a lady's hair at night without anyone's knowing what it was." He reported that the burst grains were also edible and tasted very good.[30]

On October 16, 1492, Columbus reported seeing millet (*panzio*) growing in the Bahamas. A later description reports "a prolific kind of grain, as large as the lupine and round as chick-pea, from which a flour of a very fine texture is produced. It is ground like wheat and makes bread of admirable flavor." As no millet grew in the Caribbean at the time, observers have concluded that this was the first European reference to maize. In accounts of subsequent voyages the word *maize* was mentioned.[31] The term is thought to derive from the Taino word for "life-giver." Its importance throughout the Caribbean is well documented. It is also clear that Taino and other Caribbean groups planted different types of maize. Despite the fact that popcorn kernels have been found at archaeological sites that approximate the location and time period that Europeans first scouted the Caribbean, neither Columbus nor other explorers mentioned popcorn in their diaries or logs. No other early Spanish settlers and explorers made any reference to it prior to the conquest of Mexico.

While the preeminence of maize in the New World diets has been well established, no historical evidence has surfaced indicating that popcorn was an important foodstuff. Relatively few accounts have been uncovered which even mention it. One was written by Bernardino Sahagún, a Franciscan, who came to Mexico from Spain in 1529. He learned Nahuatl, and under his direction Aztec scholars compiled materials in their native language. As the Aztecs had no written alphabet, Nahua words ended up as phonetic approximations based upon Spanish pronunciations. Sahagún then translated the Nahuatl into Spanish. Before 1580 he completed his final manuscript, titled "General History of the Things of New Spain." The narrative was enriched with extensive treatment of the customs of the common people. Sahagún offered many comments about maize but only one about popcorn. He reported that the Tlalocs, one of the Aztec tribes, had a god named Opochtli for those who lived on the water. When Opochtli's feast was celebrated, the Tlalocs "strewed toasted [pop] corn grains [*mumuchitl*] like hailstones, or like scattered dice." Sahagún also mentioned *izquitl,* translated as "parched corn," which was included in the list of food prepared for the bathing ceremony. Parched corn was also identified in another Aztec text as part of the birthing process.[32]

Another early Spanish reference, which may have been a description of popcorn, was written by Joseph de Acosta, who came to the New World seventy years after the conquest. While discussing maize, Acosta reported that the "Moroche" variety was small and hard but that there was another "round and bigge" variety that the Spanish ate "toasted." Other references were absolutely clear. Juan de Torquemada, a friar and the provincial of the Franciscan order who lived in Mexico, published his three-volume *Monarquía indiana* in 1615. He reported that in an Aztec celebration "in honor of the god of war, the virgins who served in his temple painted their cheeks, decked their arms to the elbows with richly colored plumes," and "placed over their heads, like orange blossoms, garlands of parched maize, which they called *mumuchitl.*"[33]

The above accounts indicate that some Amerindians did pop corn, but the paucity of references suggest that it was insignificant in the pre-Columbian New World. Popcorn continued to be used in Hispanic America. In Ecuador, W. S. Steere and W. H. Camp found popcorn growing in the highlands around Quito. In Peru twentieth-century botanists found *Cancha*. For its preparation Peruvians used a baked clay vessel called a *tiesto*. It was mound shaped and slightly rounded on the bottom with a small opening on the side. The tiesto was similar to vessels that had been unearthed in the Peruvian tombs. After popping, the flakes were ground into a fine meal. Modern researchers also found popcorn employed in an American marriage ceremony during the mid twentieth century. Peruvians threw popped corn into the air like rice and shouted "Vivan los novios," which translates as "Long live the sweethearts!"[34]

In Mexico a reference to popcorn appears in an unpublished manuscript in the public library in Guadalajara, Mexico. According to this 1776 account, a town in Sonora named San Miguel de Sahuaripa employed *maiz reventador* (exploder corn) to make *pinole,* "which was made by toasting and grinding the aforesaid maize and was the common food of the land." In the nineteenth century Professor Dugès described *Mais rosero*—a popcorn in Guanajuato, Mexico. In the mid twentieth century popcorn was sold in western Mexico as loose flakes, but more frequently it was converted into popcorn balls by the addition of *panocha*—a crude brown sugar syrup. Also, the unpopped kernels were employed in the manufacture of thin sweet cakes known as *ponteduro.* Popcorn necklaces were found on statues of the Virgin Mary in out-of-the-way chapels in Mexico. In modern Guatemala popcorn balls were sold in markets.[35] Popcorn clearly survived the colonial period and thrived in modern Central and South America.

Pops Heard 'Round the World

Shortly after maize's discovery Spanish explorers introduced it into Spain and Italy. It was disseminated to Turkey. The Ottoman Turks in turn introduced maize to other parts of Europe: "Turkish Corn" was the original name for maize in several European languages, including British English. Maize was almost exclusively used in Europe for animal feed, but there were some exceptions, such as in southwest and southeastern France, Italy, and Romania. In northern Italy corn replaced mashed grains or legumes in making the traditional dish polenta. Based on descriptions of maize seeds mentioned in European herbals, popcornlike seeds were transported from the New World to the Old World. Curiously, no evidence has been uncovered revealing that Europeans popped corn, with the exception of nineteenth-century rural Romanians.[36]

Popcorn received a different reception in Asia. The Spanish planted maize from South America in Guam and the Philippines. Subsequently maize (including popcorn) was disseminated to Asia during the sixteenth century. Popcorn may have appeared in China as early as 1578 when Li Shih-chên wrote his herbal *Pê ts'ao Kung ma.* According to Walter T. Swingle, the herbal has a paragraph on maize, which Li Shih-chên reports came "from western lands." The paragraph reports that the ears had numerous seeds which could be "boiled or roasted and eaten. When roasted they broke open into white flakes glutinous in appearance."[37] While some botanists claim that this was a description of an unusual type of millet, it is certainly possible that popcorn could have reached China by this early date. As previously mentioned, the Ottoman Turks acquired maize shortly after its introduction into Europe, and the Turks disseminated it to other countries. Since overland trade routes continued to flourish between Turkey and China during the sixteenth century, maize was likely disseminated by the Turks into China and other parts of Asia.

Despite its early and widespread introduction, popcorn all but disappeared except in various ethnological back corners. Popcorn was served to Sir Joseph Hooker, the first British explorer of Sikkim, in July 1849. He reported it as roasted "in an iron vessel, when it splits and turns partly inside out, exposing a snow-white spongy mass of farina." Hooker stated that it looked "very handsome, and would make a beautiful dish for dessert." In a later edition of his work he reported that this foodstuff was "called pop-corn in America."[38]

During the early 1940s Henry Stevenson reported that the Burmese people prepared *Vainiim kan,* roasted maize, by popping it in an iron pot until it burst. It was then pounded with honey or salt and converted into lumps which could be easily transported. Stevenson reported that occasionally bananas were "pounded into the grain as a change of flavor." Other botanists found popcorn frequently consumed among groups living in Assam, a part of India that today borders Myanmar and Tibet. They reported that some tribes prepared popcorn by placing the kernels "with some sand, in the cooking-pot, and heating it over a fire." Another tribe used an earthenware vessel to pop the corn. Still another tribe put "the grain into the glowing embers of the fire" and picked the popped kernels out with bamboo tongs. H. H. Bartlett, a professor at the University of Michigan, located a small pearl popcorn from Sumatra that "even has a ceremonial name, which would ordinarily indicate considerable antiquity."[39] Asians adopted popcorn quickly perhaps because the process of popping was well known to them. Varieties of rice, sorghum, and millet will pop and were integrated into the cuisine of many Asian peoples. Popcorn simply was a better popper than native grains.

Popcorn in North America

Parched maize played a significant culinary role for Native Americans in Canada and the United States. Many accounts of parching corn appeared in early European observations of Native Americans. In *Mourt's Relations,* Edwin Winslow's account of the early life at Plymouth published in London in 1622, the author disclosed that "at this towne Massyots wee brought about a handful of Meale of their parched Corn." Shortly after the Puritans arrived at Plymouth, they bought "about a handful of Meale of their parched Corn" from the local Native Americans. Roger Williams, the founder of Rhode Island, divulged that Indians ate "Nocake," which was "nothing but Indian corne parched in the hot ashes; the ashes being sifted from it, it is afterward beaten to powder, and put into a long leatherne bag, truffed at their backe like a knapsacke; out of which they take thrice three spoonefulls a day, dividing it into three meales." According to Williams, parched cornmeal was a wholesome food that the Indians ate after adding a little water. He once traveled with about two hundred Indians almost one hundred miles through the woods and observed that every man carried "a *little Basket* of this at his *back,* and sometimes in a hollow *Leather Girdle* about his middle sufficient for a man three or foure daies." Williams continued, "With a *spoonfull* of this *meale* and a *spoonfull* of water from the *Brooke,* have I made many a good dinner and supper."[40]

The Iroquois living in western New York, Pennsylvania, and southern Canada probably did not cultivate maize until the fourteenth or fifteenth century. In New York the Iroquois parched corn and carried it in bear- or deerskin pockets for sustenance. George H. Loskiel described twelve ways that the Iroquois parched corn in Pennsylvania. One was to roast it in hot ashes till it became thoroughly brown, after which it was pounded into flour, mixed with sugar, and stuffed into bags.[41] Loskiel makes no mention of any popped corn.

Further south other observers mentioned similar use of parched cornmeal by Native Americans from Virginia to Florida. In California, Native Americans parched corn. In the Southwest, while observing the Zuni, Frank Hamilton Cushing wrote that the most primitive way to parch corn was to bury kernels in hot ashes and constantly stir. The Zuni's favorite process was to fill a shallow roasting pot or pan halfway with clean, dry sand, which was then heated. When the sand was hot, the kernels were poured in and constantly stirred with hardwood sticks. When the kernels were browned and swollen, the pot was shaken. As the parched kernels surfaced, they were removed from the sand. The Zuni cracked the grains, retoasted them, and then ground them into flour.[42]

Of the many primary source descriptions of corn in colonial times, only three describe what appear to be popping corn. John Winthrop Jr., son of the first governor of Massachusetts, reported to the London's Royal Society in 1662 that a common way the Native Americans prepared maize was to parch it among the ashes by putting the kernels among the hot embers. The embers were stirred to parch the corn thoroughly without burning them. When heated they became tender and "turned almost inside outward, which wilbe white and flowry."

These were sifted "very leane from the ashes, and then beate . . . in their wooden Morters with a long Stone for a pestle, into fine meale." This constituted a regular meal both at home and during travel, when it was placed into a bag "for their Journey, being at all times ready, and may be Eaten either drie, or mixed with water; they find it strengthening and wholesome diet." This was also "the food which their souldiers Carry with them in time of Warr." Winthrop also reported that this cornmeal was sometimes purchased by the English as a novelty. They added milk, sugar, or water, which made it "much more pleasant."[43]

The second account was written by Benjamin Franklin. In 1785 Franklin reported that Native Americans filled an iron pot with sand and placed it on the fire. When the sand was very hot, two or three pounds of kernels were mixed with the sand. The popped kernels were sifted from the sand with a wire sieve, while the sand was returned to the pot and reheated. Native Americans pounded the parched grain into flour in mortars. Franklin claimed that warriors could subsist on only six to eight ounces of meal per day when traveling.[44]

The third account was written by John G. E. Heckewelder, who reported that Native Americans in Pennsylvania ate *Psindam can* or *Tassimanáne* made from a blue sweetish maize. The Iroquois heated kernels in clean hot ashes until they burst. Then they sifted, cleaned, and pounded them into flour. For a special treat, Heckewelder reported, the flour was mixed with some sugar. When in camp they boiled the flour to make a thick pottage. When traveling the Iroquois consumed small quantities and hence were not burdened with a heavy load of provisions. The Iroquois placed a tablespoonful into their mouths and chased it down with river water. If they had a cup, they combined the flour with water, "in the proportion of one table spoonful to a pint." Heckewelder considered Psindam can a "most nourishing and durable food" but advised those unacquainted with it to consume only one or two spoonfuls at any one time for it was "apt to swell in the stomach or bowels, as when heated over a fire."[45]

The secondary accounts that claim Native Americans consumed popcorn prior to its adoption by mainstream America appear to be based solely on the above reports. As there have been no reports of popcorn kernels found at archaeological sites east of the Mississippi, the above reports likely refer to popping flint corn, which was abundantly grown by Native Americans in northeastern America. Flint corn would pop under proper conditions, but its flakes were tough, half-popped corn. Flint corn when popped does resemble the flakes described by Franklin: "Each Grain bursts and throws out a white substance of twice its bigness."[46]

The absence of popcorn among Native Americans living in eastern America should come as no surprise. Native Americans would not have favored popcorn and would not likely have grown it intentionally. Raw popcorn kernels are hard and can break a tooth when bitten. While this hard kernel, associated with a thick pericarp, was advantageous in that it permitted storing kernels for long periods of time with less likelihood of damage by mold and insects, the unpopped kernels were too hard to grind using stone or wooden mortars and pestles. To grind popped popcorn was also extremely difficult using wooden mortars and pestles or stones. As the twentieth-century agronomist A. T. Erwin pointed out, popping popcorn "hinders rather than expedites the process of pulverizing." Another problem was that popcorn grown near other varieties of corn quickly lost its ability to pop. It must be grown in isolation. While Native Americans could easily have done this, it is unlikely that they would have done so. Popcorn was less productive than other varieties of maize in terms of yield per acre. It has smaller kernels and yields less than other varieties. And popcorn requires more work to harvest. It is no wonder that when Erwin asked Snow Bird of the Elbow Woods Reservation about popcorn, Snow Bird told him that popcorn was "white man corn."[47]

During the nineteenth and twentieth centuries other accounts connecting popcorn with Native Americans were published. For instance, in 1850 Lewis Morgan described an Iroquois "pop corn sieve." His description was poor and confusing, and he likely misnamed it. Arthur Parker subsequently reidentified Morgan's "pop corn sieve" as a melon basket. In the early twentieth century M. R. Harrington examined corn and its preparation among one of the Iroquois nations—the Seneca—and made no mention of popcorn, but he did report that the Seneca were quickly discarding their old ways. Arthur Parker reported that the Iroquois of the early twentieth century did pop corn "in a metal or clay kettle and then pulverized [it] in a mortar and mixed with oil or syrup." Parker also observed Iroquois making "Popcorn Pudding" with modern poppers and chopping machines. They ate the resulting cornmeal with sugar and milk or cream. The Canadian anthropologist F. W. Waugh observed Iroquois popping corn "by throwing it on the hot coals in an open fire-place, stirring it quickly, then pulling it out as it popped." He also described how the Iroquois prepared "Popcorn Mush or Pudding," composed of cornmeal, sugar, and milk, cream, or sour milk, and two recipes for "Popcorn Soup or Hominy," one version of which was eaten with milk.[48] Needless to say, neither sugar, milk or cream were New World ingredients, nor were poppers and chopping machines traditional cooking implements. All recipes include ingredients or cooking implements that were clearly of modern derivation.

Even west of the Mississippi little evidence suggests that popcorn was cultivated by Native Americans in pre-Columbian times. The exception is in the Southwest, where popcorn, as we have seen, was known to have been cultivated in ancient times but likely died out. Almost no references to popcorn have been found in modern anthropological literature on Native Americans in the late nineteenth and twentieth centuries. Where its existence was recorded, popcorn was a recent addition. The Papagoes, for instance, reported that popcorn arrived from Mexico about 1900. One potential exception was an early-twentieth-century account by Melvin Randolph Gilmore, who reported that Nebraska tribes cultivated all the general types of maize, including popcorn. These tribes did maintain the purity of these varieties "by selecting typical ears for seed and by planting varieties at some distance from each other." While popcorn seed was present in early-twentieth-century Nebraska, there was no clear idea how long it had been cultivated. Popcorn was probably not an ancient crop: again, no archaeological evidence has been uncovered indicating that popcorn was grown in Nebraska prior to the arrival of European Americans. Gilmore's popcorn was likely a recent introduction. A possible explanation for Gilmore's reference to popcorn was supplied by A. F. Yeager, who researched maize in North Dakota. Yeager reported that popcorn was unknown in North Dakota prior to the late nineteenth century. He believed that mainstream Americans had introduced popcorn to tribes further south, who in turn introduced it to Native Americans in North Dakota.[49]

Whether or not popcorn was cultivated in eastern North America, the above accounts clearly distinguish the ways maize was consumed by Native Americans from the ways popcorn was eaten by modern Americans. In all previous accounts Native Americans consumed parched or popped maize as ground flour. The most likely reason why Native Americans did not eat the popped corn directly was because it was tough, small, and possessed a hard hull. It did not resemble what we think of as popcorn today. While edible, it was more consumable if pounded into flour.

The myth of the Pilgrims receiving popcorn from the Native Americans, rather than depicting what actually happened during colonial times, was a reflection of what was under way in America during the late nineteenth century. Until the 1880s Native Americans were characterized as "primitive savages." This image helped mainstream Americans rationalize their settling of territories legally ceded to Native Americans, waging war on recalcitrant tribes, and converting them to Western religions. With the end of the Indian wars, mainstream white Americans shifted their perceptions of Native Americans from that of fierce, threatening savages to the noble natives who had helped starving immigrants from Europe survive during their early colonial years. Whether or not Native Americans actually ate popcorn did not matter to the mythmakers.

The late nineteenth century was also a period of vast immigration to the United States. National myths, such as those surrounding the "First Thanksgiving," were created and sanctified in magazines, newspapers, books, and in the curricula of America's schools. The Pilgrims were deified in these myths, although they did not constitute the first English colony: in Virginia, Jamestown had been settled almost fourteen years previously. The Pilgrims did take on a "founding" importance in New England. In other regions of America the Pilgrims only became important after the defeat of the South during the Civil War. Thanksgiving was not celebrated in many southern states until decades after the Civil War.

Finally, the specific association of popcorn with the "First Thanksgiving" and Pilgrim myths generated during the 1880s underscored popcorn's growing national significance. Popcorn was sold in grocery stores, popped at fairs, and peddled at sporting events. Popcorn and popcorn balls conquered the streets of the United States. Americans young and old enjoyed "craunching" on popcorn. The story of how popcorn really became a mainstream food fad is the topic of the next chapter.

Chapter 2

The Invention of Popcorn

Although American colonists parched corn, no historical evidence has turned up even hinting that colonists popped corn. Only one pre-nineteenth-century account has surfaced suggesting that popcorn was possibly grown by mainstream farmers. Joseph Cooper, a prominent New Jersey farmer, claimed that "about the year 1772 a friend of his lent him a few grains of a small kind of Indian corn, not larger than gooseshot, which produces from eight to ten ears on a stalk." While he described the kernels as popcornlike, Cooper made no comment about popping them. The first clear identification of popcorn does not appear until well after the turn of the nineteenth century. By the mid 1820s seedsmen sold it under the names Nonpareil, or Pearl. Boston seed seller George Barrett considered it "curious and beautiful." Popcorn quickly migrated south. John Jay Janney, a Virginia farmer, reported that, while he had previously parched common corn, popcorn did not arrive in his region until about 1825.[1]

If popcorn was not grown by Native Americans in eastern North America, the question emerges as to its derivation. Popcorn may have been introduced into America from Africa. The New Jersey farmer Joseph Cooper, mentioned previously, reported that his popcornlike seeds had been imported from Guinea in West Africa. Maize was disseminated to Africa shortly after the discovery of the New World. It grew easily in the tropical climate and quickly blossomed into an important food crop. While no early evidence of popcorn in Africa has been located, popcorn might well have been introduced there from South America. American slavers or slaves could easily have brought it to the English colonies. From New Jersey these seeds might well have been introduced into New England. In 1817 the Massachusetts Agricultural Society mentioned Cooper and small maize kernels just before the listing of popcornlike seeds in the catalogs of Massachusetts seedsmen.[2]

While introduction from Africa was possible, a more likely point of origin for New England's popcorn was southern South America. Popcorn clearly survived in Chile where American traders, sailors, or whalers likely came across it. Popcorn expanded to a much greater extent than did flint corn and would have been a real sensation. Intrigued, American sailors may have brought it back to New England. Popcorn from Chile would have been daylight neutral and could easily have grown in the long days and short nights of summer. Some evidence supports this possibility. One frequently mentioned New England popcorn was called Valparaiso, or curagua in South America. The American name presumably derived after the city in Chile, where perhaps New England sailors or explorers first encountered it. Other early varieties probably originated in South America. Lady Finger, for instance, was similar to Argentinian and Paraguayan popcorn, and clearly was not initially a North American variety. Still another variety, referred to as Brazilian popcorn, was a sensation that received extensive press coverage during the 1860s.[3]

Whatever its initial origin, popcorn quickly spread throughout the eastern United States. Jesse Buel, editor of the *Cultivator,* an agricultural journal in Albany, published the first reference to popcorn in 1838. It was a rice popcorn with four-inch ears. By the 1840s popping corn had become a popular recreational activity. This new food fad certainly caught the attention of American writers. In 1842 American transcendentalist Henry David Thoreau reported in his journal that popcorn was "only a more rapid blossoming of the seed under a greater than July heat." Enthralled, he believed that popcorn was "a perfect winter flower, hinting of anemones and houstonias." Popped corn was mentioned in the *Yale Literary Magazine.* Another reference appeared in the *Knickerbocker,* a prestigious New York literary magazine. By 1848 the word *popcorn* was important enough to be noted in John Russell Bartlett's *Dictionary of Americanisms.* According to Bartlett, popcorn acquired its name from "the noise it makes on bursting open."[4]

Research into popcorn commenced during the late 1840s. Daniel Browne reported that "Pop-corn" had small ears. The kernels were of various colors and had more oil and less starch than any other kind of maize. Browne published the first known recipe for popping corn: "Take a gill, a half pint, or more of Valparaiso or Pop Corn, and put in a frying-pan, slightly buttered, or rubbed with lard. Hold the pan over a fire so as constantly to stir or shake the corn within, and in a few minutes each kernel will *pop,* or turn inside out." Browne reported that as soon as the popping was completed, sugar or salt could be added while the corn was still hot. In 1848 the New York State Agricultural Society awarded three hundred dollars to J. H. Salisbury for the best submission of an article on maize. Salisbury's 196-page prize-winning essay, "History and Chemical Investigation of Maize or Indian Corn," borrowed whole sections from the works of Daniel Browne as a preamble to an exhaustive chemical analysis. Of the twenty varieties of maize examined by Salisbury, three were identified as "pop" corns. During the following year Ebenezer Emmons described even more varieties.[5]

During the following decades popcorn's popularity expanded. According to Susan Fenimore Cooper, daughter of James Fenimore Cooper, acres of "popping Corn" were raised near large northern towns by 1850. During the Civil War an advertisement appeared in the *Country Gentleman* soliciting five hundred bushels of "Popping Corn," which reflected the vast increase in the demand for popcorn. In 1863 seedsman and gardener Fearing Burr described five varieties and estimated that popcorn was "somewhat extensively cultivated for commercial purposes" in some parts of Massachusetts and New Hampshire. Two years later he revised his assessment upward, stating that popcorn was cultivated extensively for commercial purposes throughout New England.[6] By the end of the Civil War popcorn had spread throughout the nation.

During the late 1860s popcorn companies started up. Recipes were incorporated into many cookbooks, particularly in sections on confectionery or candy. According to the British *Cassell's Dictionary of Cookery,* by the early 1870s popcorn was a "much relished" food in America. It was sold at special events and near stadiums and other large public buildings and parks. For instance, an illustration of a "Pop Corn" store next to the entrance to Boston's coliseum was published in 1872. By 1875 the *American Cyclopedia* reported that popcorn's preparation was "one of the small industries which in the aggregate amount to a respectable sum." By this date it was a common item sold in grocery stores and at concession stands at circuses, carnivals, and street fairs.[7]

At the Philadelphia Centennial Exposition in 1876, popcorn helped celebrate the nation's one hundredth anniversary. President Ulysses Grant opened the exposition on May 19, 1876. Before it closed six months later, over ten million visitors had attended. A single popcorn vendor, I. L. Baker, paid the huge sum of eight thousand dollars for the exclusive popcorn concession throughout the grounds. Baker set up several of the "curious and attractive furnaces and selling-booths" around the exposition with a major exhibit in the Machinery Hall where the process of manufacturing red and white popcorn balls was demonstrated. In this exhibit men and women roasted popcorn over a gas furnace, mixed it with sugar syrup in large bowls, pressed it into the popcorn-ball shape, piled baskets with the finished product, and then sold them to visitors. According to an article in *Frank Leslie's Illustrated Newspaper,* the booth "was crowded all day, and thus showed the attractiveness of the exhibitor's peculiar wares and machinery." An advertisement for "Excelsior Pop Corn" promoted nickel bags of "Sugar Coated" corn prepared expressly for the Centennial Exposition.[8] Other dealers sold popcorn outside the grounds, taking advantage of the large crowds drawn to the exposition without having to pay exhibition fees.

Wire-over-the-Fire Corn Poppers

During the early nineteenth century mainstream Americans practiced several methods for popping corn, none of which was particularly efficient. One method was simply to strew kernels in hot ashes and stir. When the kernels exploded, some flew onto the fire or embers and had to be quickly removed with tongs before they burned. Others popped onto the floor. This method resulted in burnt, smoky, and dirty popped flakes. Another method placed the kernels on pierced iron sheets, shovels, or wire mesh positioned over a fire or coals.[9] The mesh prevented kernels from falling into the fire, but most flakes absorbed smoke. The iron sheets and shovels prevented the popped corn from becoming smoky, but many flakes still burned. After the kernels had popped, the flakes still had to be collected from the floor or ground.

Still another way of popping corn placed the kernels into a kettle filled with fat or lard. When the popped kernels surfaced, they were skimmed off. Covered frying pans were also used.[10] They were filled with a cooking medium, and the kernels were poured in. To pop properly, popcorn needed high heat for a short duration. Before the advent of the gas range, it was difficult to control the heat. Provided that the stove was hot enough, the heavy frying pan then had to be shaken back and forth above the surface of the stove to prevent burning. All in all these early popping methods were arduous.

Several popping mediums were tried. Butter burned before the popcorn was heated sufficiently to pop. Lard was the most common popping medium, but observers were unhappy with the lard-soaked popcorn which resulted. Robert Trall's *New Hydropathic Cook-book* referred to it as "dyspepsia corn" because it was heavily seasoned with salt and was very greasy. Lard did not bother others. The editor of a California newspaper wrote that as corn was "good to fatten hogs," he knew "of no good reason why 'pop-corn' should not lard a man."[11]

One reason why popcorn became so popular during the second half of the nineteenth century was the invention of corn poppers. The first "Wire-over-the-fire" poppers were reportedly constructed by Francis P. Knowlton of Hopkinton, New Hampshire. According to the *People and Patriot,* Knowlton purchased wire netting from a hardware vendor named Amos Kelley in 1837. Knowlton fashioned the wire into the shape of a box and added a long handle. He was unable to sell his corn poppers, but Kelley took over sales. He and his son were successful in marketing their wire corn poppers.[12]

While no pre–Civil War corn popper has been located, descriptions have survived. Daniel Browne praised the corn popper as a "very ingenious contrivance" consisting of a wire-gauze box "with the apertures not exceeding one twentieth of an inch square." Early poppers were made of thin wire with their edges secured by a rim of folded sheet metal. Wires connected the rim to the basket. Iron supports along the bottom held the basket together. A wooden handle was attached to the basket.[13]

The advantages of poppers over previous methods were numerous. Poppers contained the exploding corn in the basket. Poppers were composed of low-cost materials and could be constructed by anyone. Wire baskets weighed less than heavy skillets and were therefore more maneuverable. With their long handles poppers could be heated over open fires without exposing hands to the flames. Poppers did not burn the popcorn as readily as did other methods and did not require a popping medium; therefore they required less preparation and popped grease-free flakes. This invention set the stage for the vast increase in popcorn consumption that struck America during the latter half of the nineteenth century.

Although the early poppers were successful, they were not without structural weaknesses. The wire gauze permitted smoke from the fire to permeate the popped corn. If the popper were not shaken vigorously enough, the popcorn still charred. However, often the basket did not survive the constant horizontal shaking motion over the hot fire. Likewise, the handle often disengaged from the basket. Some handles were too short, and the fire singed fingers. Fingers were threatened again as the user unfastened the latch holding down the lid.

After the Civil War inventors across the nation set their creative genius in motion to solve popper problems. Many were resolved by inventors who looked at similar devices for roasting other products, such as coffee and nuts. The first patent was issued for a corn popper in 1866. William Orberton of Haverhill, Massachusetts, concluded that rather than a boxlike basket, a round basket would permit a circular hand motion, thus avoiding the rough back-and-forth shaking. George

D. Dudley of Lowell, Massachusetts, invented a popper with a crank at the bottom of the basket that when turned could prevent burning. Daniel A. Denison of Troy, Michigan, placed iron strips at the bottom of the basket permitting it to be placed on top of the stove without the basket coming in contact with the burner. L. A. Warner of Freeport, Illinois, developed a popper intended to be held with one hand while the other turned a crank in the handle and stirred the kernels in the basket. Warner also installed a hand guard to protect fingers from the heat. He subsequently improved this by including a spring latch for discharging popcorn, which avoided burning the fingers. J. H. Bigelow of Worcester, Massachusetts, created a wire attachment that improved the connection of the handle of the popping box and made it possible for the handle to be easily detached and packed for shipment.[14]

The frantic pace of corn-popper development continued throughout the nineteenth century. In 1874 William Wood of Olmstead, Kentucky, invented a corn popper with two pans separated by a wire mesh big enough for raw kernels to fall through. The corn was placed in one pan and popped on the stove. When a portion of the corn was popped, the machine was turned upside down and the unpopped kernels fell through the mesh into the second pan. The popped corn remaining on top could be removed or retained until the rest was popped. This patent was subsequently acquired by Cincinnati's Bromwell Brush and Wire Goods Company, which sold it as Wood's Patented Novelty Reversible Corn Popper throughout the late nineteenth and early twentieth centuries. According to the company's catalog, this "Novelty" was an established favorite in the trade. Bromwell regularly lowered the price during successive seasons until it was "within the reach of all." The poppers cost retailers $3.50 for a gross. Dealers sold them for a quarter apiece and still made a handsome profit. According to a Bromwell advertisement, wherever these poppers were introduced, they ran "the common poppers out of the market."[15]

Not all corn-popper inventors were men. The popper designed by Alice B. Wood of Beaver Dam, Wisconsin, featured two hemispheres which formed a round ball. The kernels were placed into one hemisphere, and the other was closed over the first to make a ball. It was positioned over the fire; the wooden handle was grasped with one hand while the ball was rotated with the other hand. A bolt in the handle opened the ball, thus avoiding burnt fingers or soiled hands. The wooden handle was four or five times as long as the diameter of the ball so that "the person holding the popper need not have his fingers near the fire." This device could be used over the round opening in the kitchen or parlor stove. Its weight was supported by an arm which rested on the top of the stove beyond the fire.[16]

A commentator in the *Country Gentleman* argued for a popper that was three inches long, four inches wide, and five inches deep with a handle three feet long. W. E. Watkins, an amateur popper from River View Farm, Tennessee, described the best popper as a sheet-metal box six inches wide, eight inches long, and three inches deep. The top opened back toward the handle, which was made of light wood, such as an old broom stick. The handle was fitted into a socket four or five inches long and fastened at right angles to the back end. *Knight's American Mechanical Dictionary* published the first known illustrations for poppers. The dictionary described one as a gauze cylinder turned by a crankshaft with a sleeve handle and screen plate for the supporting hand. This was the prototype for large cylindrical poppers manufactured for commercial use. The Bartholomew Company's Jumbo Factory Roaster, for instance, was almost five feet long and could handle one-hundred-pound bags at a single popping.[17]

Beginning in the 1870s commercial companies began manufacturing corn poppers. Chester F. Wickwire of Cortland, New York, who received a patent for strengthening the wire basket on a popper in 1875, began manufacturing them with his brothers. Wickwire Brothers advertised corn poppers in magazines, such as *Iron Age,* whose audiences were proprietors of hardware stores. By 1887 *Iron Age* advertised several different corn poppers in almost every issue and also announced the release of new poppers.[18]

Poppers were also marketed through mail-order catalogs. The U.S. Stamping Company distributed two types of poppers. Both were sold in one-, two-, four-, and eight-quart sizes. Sears, Roebuck and Company also listed popcorn and poppers in their sales catalogs. The 1897 catalog charged 5¢ for twenty-five pounds of rice popcorn on the cob and $2.25 for forty pounds of shelled popcorn. A one-quart popper sold for 8¢, while a two-quart popper cost 14¢. As more manufacturers produced corn poppers, their price declined. Sears later reduced its heavy wire one-quart popper to 6¢ and its two-quart container to 10¢.[19]

Magazines published articles brimming with advice and comments by popper users. One observer recommended covering the bottom of the pan with corn and holding the popper over a bright coal fire. He instructed the user to hold the popper some distance from the fire, but to shake it constantly to permit uniform heating of all the kernels. When the kernels commenced popping briskly, the popper should be moved closer to the coals. When the popping became infrequent, the popped kernels were turned out and a little salt was sprinkled over them. Other advice was offered by Gussie Thomas, who reported that her family popped corn during winter evenings. While she was sewing and her husband was reading, her father built a large hardwood fire in the stove and shelled some popcorn. When the fire was blazing, he put kernels in the wire popper and shook it gently until it began to snap. After the first kernel burst, he shook the popper rapidly until no more popped. Then he removed the flakes and placed them in the oven while another batch was prepared. Thomas preferred using an open fire to pop corn. Popping did not commence until the fire burned down to a bed of coals. The advantage, claimed Thomas, was that coals emitted less smoke.[20]

W. E. Watkins preferred a blazing wood fire. If he had a coal fire, he removed the freshest coal to lessen the smoke and placed kindling on top. He held the popper at the top of the blaze and shook it to prevent sticking or burning. Watkins preferred poppers made of sheet iron for two reasons: sheet iron prevented the popcorn from absorbing the smoke from the fire; and he could add a little grease and salt, which he believed greatly improved the flavor of the popped corn.[21]

One of the more unusual ways of popping corn was offered by a reader in *Good Housekeeping* who reported that she took the globe off her round burner lamp and placed the lamp on a paper to catch falling kernels or chaff. Putting a handful or two of corn into a small wire-cloth popper with a long handle and supporting the popper with a stick held in the left hand, she popped the corn over the lamp. She reported that the heat was so fierce and concentrated that it took lively shaking to keep the corn from scorching, but several batches could be popped in a few minutes.[22]

Literary Corn

This explosion of interest in popcorn was not lost on the literary world. In the 1850s popping corn was anything but commonplace, as the following tract demonstrates. Described by an unidentified woman from the Female Academy in Rochester, New York, the act of popping corn was more than just a pleasant activity. "Entertaining it certainly is, but far *more so,* and *highly exhilarating,*" she wrote. Popped corn "rushes forward with convulsive gasp" and "darts out of sight." Then the air was "white with ascending and descending curious little forms." She continued:

> Snapping here, there, *everywhere;* hither and yon; *into* our aprons; *under* our aprons; into the wood box; on the table; behind the dresser; through the crack in the pantry door, frosting the stove like a huge fruit cake, clicking the windows, deriding the clockcase, battering the firebox, oh Ceres! Was *ever* pop corn *whiter,* thicker, fresher or fuller!
>
> Pop! Pop! Pop! Into your eyes! Into your ears! Into our mouths! Delicious! Not a particle burnt!
>
> Pop! Pop! Thicker than ever, better than ever! Falling in sparkling showers, gold and silver intermingling! Heaping our pans full; darting

in tangents, springing on cork soles, covering the floor like a deep snow bank, drifted in from the silent meadows.[23]

In 1853 *Harper's Magazine* published the first known poem about popcorn, a portion of which appeared in the second edition of Bartlett's *Dictionary of Americanisms.* Charles Stewart penned the second poem, which stresses the romantic side of popcorn with a couple sitting by the fire popping corn. In part it reads:

We were popping corn
    Sweet Kitty and I;
It danced about,
    And it danced up high.
The embers were hot,
    In their fiery light;
And it went up brown,
    And it came down white.
White and beautiful,
    Crimped and curried.
The prettiest fairy-dance in the world![24]

Perhaps inspired by Stewart's poem, Benjamin Russell painted a watercolor showing a man and woman seated romantically by a fire popping corn. Born to a wealthy New Bedford family in 1804, Stewart usually sketched and painted ships. When his family lost their wealth, Stewart painted anything that would sell. Presumably his popcorn watercolor fell into this category. This painting was later used to illustrate John S. Barrows's poem "Popping Corn" and was published in *Good Housekeeping* magazine. Barrow's poem depicts a maiden with a swain:

Their eyes meet; the words are spoken—the story sweet and old,
Which so long he has been learning, now with tenderest grace
    is told,
And at once beside the fireplace, happy love is born,
And forgotten is the world outside, amid thoughts of
    Popping Corn.

While popcorn did not sustain its romantic allure into the twentieth century, remnants have survived. *Parents* magazine and other sources have recommended Valentine's Day treats such as popcorn shaped in the form of a heart, that promoted togetherness and "happy memories."[25]

Along with the literary explosion, popcorn inspired tall tales. Kate Sanborn related that once a farmer had stored one thousand bushels of popcorn in a barn. Unfortunately, the barn caught fire and the kernels popped, covering a ten-acre field. In the field was an old mare with defective eyes. The mare, claimed Sanborn, thought the popcorn was snow and froze to death. Sanborn titled the book in which this story appeared, presumably tongue-in-cheek, *A Truthful Woman in Southern California*.[26]

Why Does Popcorn Pop?

Not only did popcorn capture the imagination of the literary world, it was also of burning interest to scientists. Trying to understand why popcorn popped challenged British and American observers for a century and a half. Explanations revolved around four different popcorn components: oil, water, the pericarp, and the starch granules in the endosperm. One of the first to discuss this phenomenon was agricultural expert Daniel Browne, who believed that popping depended on the oil. This was reasonable since previous experiments had demonstrated that popcorn kernels contained more oil than did other types of maize. Browne believed that when the kernels were "heated to a temperature sufficiently high to decompose the oil" an explosion occurred in which every cell ruptured due to "the expansion of gaseous matters arising from the decomposition of the oil, and the formation of carburetted hydrogen gas." This explosion completely "evoluted" the grain, turning it inside out.[27]

In 1851 British chemist James F. W. Johnston, a frequent visitor to America, concluded that popping was due to two factors: oil and the hard outer covering of the kernel. When heated, explained Johnston, the oil expanded and tore "asunder every little cell"; burst "the epidermis of the top or side of the seed with a slight report, like that of a popgun"; and forced back the "swollen and now white and spongy mass." Johnston reported that the expansion was so great that one barrel of popcorn produced sixteen barrels of popped corn: rice popcorn, with its smaller kernel, converted into "thirty-two barrels of popped corn." Similar opinions were expressed by many other nineteenth-century observers in horticultural journals, dictionaries, encyclopedias, and cookbooks.[28]

The view that oil caused popping was discarded toward the end of the nineteenth century. Others subscribed to the view that corn popped when the moisture in the kernel converted to steam and that steam was the driving force to produce the internal pressure. Experiments determined that the amount of water in the kernel was important. Popcorn soaked in water for twenty-four hours popped very little. Alternately, seven-year-old popcorn popped if soaked in water and allowed to dry.[29] Popping expansion was directly correlated with moisture in the kernels. Maximum popping expansion was produced when kernels had between

13 percent and 15 percent moisture. However, as important as moisture was to popping, it was clear that water alone was not the full explanation. Other types of corn possessed similar percentages of water but did not pop.

Other factors contributing to popcorn's ability to pop were soon identified. William Brewer argued in his *Report on the Cereal Production of the United States* that popping was due to the bursting of individual starch granules. When the pericarp was no longer able to contain the pressure, it exploded. Popcorn does have a hard pericarp, but several observers pointed out that pieces of popcorn also popped, suggesting that the pericarp was not essential. F. H. Storer, a professor of agricultural chemistry, removed the pericarp from kernels and concluded that the pericarp exerted a decided influence on the process of popping. Henry Kraemer, editor of the *American Journal of Pharmacy,* examined the endosperm of the popped kernels, noting that considerable alteration in the starch granules and cell walls had occurred. Just before the explosion starch was converted into a soluble form. Paul Weatherwax reported that the ability to pop was based on the relative proportion of hard to soft endosperm. The starch granules were embedded in a tough, elastic colloidal material, which confined and resisted the steam pressure generated within the granule until it reached explosive force. Agreeing with Weatherwax, John Willier and Arthur Brunson concluded that kernels with the least soft starch had the greatest popping volume. In a later study Brunson found that just before a kernel popped, it swelled to two or three times its normal size.[30]

Roger M. Reeve and H. G. Walker Jr. took another crack at unveiling the mystery of popping. They compared a variety of different cereal grains and concluded that the endosperms expanded by popping showed different degrees of starch granule gelatinization. In barley and wheat, which do not expand greatly when heated, starch granules gelatinized without appreciable granule expansion, while other granules expanded and fused. When the kernels split open, the cell walls ruptured. Localized cell-wall rupturing also occurred in expanded endosperms of popped sorghum, milo, dent corn, and popcorn, but the expanded endosperm formed a "soap bubble" structure, which was less extensively developed in all poorly popped kernels. Reeve and Walker concluded that the "differences in distribution of horny and floury endosperm, and differences in their protein content influence the capacity to expand when different cereals are popped."[31]

Popcorn researchers Kenneth Ziegler of Iowa State University and Bruce Ashman of Purdue University summarized the research on why popcorn pops. They concluded that when heated, the moisture inside the kernel rapidly expands to a point where the pericarp is unable to contain the explosion. Just before the internal steam is released, starch granules gelatinize. During the explosion the starch granules rapidly expand and quickly dry in a three-dimensional network. The soft starch granules undergo little change by popping except to spread further apart.[32]

Connected with the question of why popcorn pops are the related issues of popcorn's taste and texture. Taste relates to many different sensory perceptions. Texture, an important element, includes the kernel's tenderness, crispness, and the lack of hulls that stick in teeth. Among all varieties of maize, popcorn has the thickest pericarp. Hulls vary considerably in thickness among different varieties. Larger kernels tend to have thicker hulls than smaller ones. Thin, light-colored pericarps are less visible and on casual inspection may appear hull-less. As the pericarp is necessary for popping, it cannot be eliminated. Popcorn breeders have developed varieties in which the pericarp shatters into small pieces when the kernels pop.[33]

Writers in *Consumer Reports* tried to define popcorn flavor as "rather delicate—a slight to moderate baked-corn flavor, a whiff of toasted grain, a hint of heated oil." If salt were present, it was the most obvious taste. They believed that a moderate level of salt was appropriate. If a butter flavor was present, "it should suggest a dairy origin, not a chemist's beaker." Popcorn should not have a burnt taste or a "cardboardy" taste of oil. They also believed that texture was important in popcorn because of its delicate flavor. Popcorn should be crisp, not tough. It should be easily swallowed, "leaving few crumbled bits in the mouth."[34]

Freshly popped corn does have a noticeable, appealing flavor. Unfortunately, this quickly dissipates, and most commercial popcorns provide a bland base for additives. Flavor has been essentially bred out. As Kenneth Ziegler and Bruce Ashman have pointed out, popcorn hybrids were selected on the basis of samples popped in oil. Flavor is strongly influenced by the popping medium used and by toppings, such as butter and salt. The varying flavors of popcorn have been evaluated with only a few experimental hybrids, and these tests have not been conducted by professional tasters. This has created a problem. Consumers, for health reasons, prefer dry-popping popcorn to avoid added oil and salt, and present-day popcorn hybrids—without additives—tend to have a bland flavor.[35]

Popcorn's most appealing advantage over other snack foods is its aroma when freshly popped. Aroma is more complex than flavor. From a chemical standpoint, popcorn aroma is produced by the release of particular pyrazines, furans, pyrroles, carbonyls, and phenols when popped. In 1991 a study by Peter Schieberle revealed twenty-three odorants among which 2-acetyl-1-pyrroline (roasty, popcornlike) and two others predominated with the highest aromas.[36] Whatever the chemical causes of its aroma, popcorn vendors have long known that sales increase when popcorn can be smelled. Although popcorn's aroma quickly dissipates after popping, it can be extended by heating the popped corn in a warmer. As popcorn is frequently an impulse item when purchased from vendors, its aroma is a distinct advantage not shared by most other snack foods.

One reason why the smell of popcorn may be particularly agreeable to Americans is its association with enjoyable occasions. As children, most Americans were introduced to popcorn at family gatherings, movies, circuses, and baseball games. Smells are retained in the brain and can be recognized years later, even though the person may not have been exposed to them for decades. Smell functions as a kind of "starter motor" that evokes all kinds of forgotten experiences and events, as well as the moods associated with events.[37]

The Healthy Snack

Popcorn recipes were published in many late-nineteenth- and early-twentieth-century health food cookbooks. Ella Kellogg reported in 1892 that popcorn was "an excellent food, the starch of the grain being well cooked." However, she urged readers to eat popcorn "in connection with other food at mealtime, and not as a delicacy between meals." She was particularly enthusiastic about popcorn pudding. Her husband, John Harvey Kellogg, health-food guru of the sanatarium at Battle Creek, Michigan, was even more impressed with popcorn, which he reported to be "one of the most wholesome of cereal foods." It was "easily digestible and to the highest degree wholesome, presenting the grain in its entirety, and hence superior to many denatured breakfast foods which are found in the market."[38]

William Evans of Amherst, Virginia, went one step further when he applied for a patent for "Medicated Pop-Corn." Evans's creation was composed of popped corn saturated with metheglin, which acted "as a mild tonic, assisting and strengthening the stomach to overcome or prevent indigestion." It was covered with honey, which offered additional healing powers and acted "to heal inflamed conditions of the mouth, throat, bronchial tubes, and stomach." One great advantage, claimed Evans, was that honey's healing powers were "perfectly and slowly brought in contact with the mouth, throat, and stomach." The concoction was formed into balls, bars, or sticks and then was flavored with wintergreen, peppermint, sassafras, horehound, or other flavoring extract. Combined with saliva formed by eating popped corn, said Evans, his medicine cured bad cases of dyspepsia.[39] Thankfully, this product does not appear to have been widely prescribed.

The belief that popcorn was nutritious encouraged many other writers to proclaim its excellence. Mrs. Chambers, a Brooklyn teacher of domestic science, lectured her students: "Popcorn is one of the best foods we have; people don't begin to appreciate its value. Let your children eat all the popcorn they want. It contains a valuable oil, has high calorific power, and is mostly starch, cooked thoroughly by high pressure of steam." She also believed that popcorn balls were "a very good food." A writer in *Good Housekeeping* proclaimed popcorn nutritious but only "if not used to overindulgence." Health-food advocate Harvey Wiley proclaimed popcorn as "a delicacy, and with sugar and cream as a dessert." Wiley reported popcorn to be composed of soft, delicate edible material and highly prized.[40]

Popcorn products were also touted as healthful. Advertisements proclaimed that Cracker Jack was "a healthful, nourishing food-confection." A writer in *American Cookery* advised readers to "eat more pop corn as a food—not as a lunch but as a cereal or vegetable, and reap the benefits of its coarseness and vitamin content." During the 1930s a popcorn salesman in Alabama urged consumers to "eat it for your health's sake." Bernard Fantus of the Department of Pharmacology and Therapeutics at the Illinois College of Medicine asserted that popcorn "has the same food value as other corn or maize." The fiber, Fantus continued, adds "a certain amount of roughage which has a laxative tendency." The editor of the *Kernel,* a magazine for popcorn processors and marketeers, was delighted with these findings and urged the industry to educate the public about popcorn's healthful benefits.[41]

Chapter 3

Popcorn Children

The connection between popcorn and children was highly predictable. The magical, mysterious, and surprising explosion of the kernels was a child's delight. The pop sound was associated with children's toys such as popguns and the jack-in-the boxes that played the song "Pop Goes the Weasel," which were popular about the time popcorn became a food fad in the United States. The pop was an attention getter associated with fun times, circuses, fairs, and campfires that mesmerized children. It was a low-cost snack, easily accessible to children of all economic classes. The wild fascination of children with popcorn began almost from the advent of its popularity in the United States. In 1850 Susan Fenimore Cooper observed, "The children delight so much" in popcorn.[1]

The first known popcorn poem, published in *Harper's Magazine* in 1853, described children's reaction to popping corn. The poem reads in part:

> Pop, pop! and the kernels, one by one,
> Come out of the embers flying;
> The boy held a long pine-stick in his hand,
> And kept it busily plying;
> He stirred the corn, and it snapped the more,
> And faster jumped to the clean-swept floor.
> Part of the kernels hopped out one way,
> And a part hopped out the other;

Some flew plump to the sister's lap,
Some under the stool of the brother:
The little girl gathered them into a hap,
And called them "a flock of milk-white sheep."[2]

During the 1870s the *American Cyclopedia* reported that popcorn was "much prized by children." In 1879 the McLoughlin Brothers, publishers of children's books, released an eight-page illustrated pamphlet titled *Old Pop Corn.* When old Pop Corn—an anthropomorphized corn-ear caricature—went out for a walk, he wore a spotless tie and had an umbrella in his hand and monocles in both eyes. Reflecting the gruesome nature of many children's stories written during the nineteenth century, naughty boys and girls in this story scraped off old Pop Corn's kernels:

That night, when old Pop Corn got home,
A worthless cob was he;
And all those naughty boys and girls,
Had Pop Corn after tea.[3]

In 1883 The *Grocer's Companion* described popcorn as "a special favorite with the children throughout the Union." In 1893 an observer in the *Country Gentleman* reported that in her family "the little folk" were exceedingly fond of popcorn balls. The younger children shelled the corn and assisted in popping it. Pails were filled with the exploded flakes, and with the contents popcorn balls were formed with molasses. One young girl was proud of her skill in making them. The editor of the *American Grocer* believed that Americans had not yet begun to appreciate popcorn's value and urged Americans to permit their children to "eat all the popcorn they want." Other grocers revealed that during winter seasons customers purchased vast quantities of popcorn for Christmas decorations.[4]

Holiday Corn

Due to children's fascination, popcorn became increasingly associated with holidays such as Halloween, Thanksgiving, Easter, and particularly Christmas. In the 1850s popcorn appeared in accounts of Christmas celebrations. Ralph Waldo Emerson believed that popcorn was a good means of diverting young people during the "weary" Christmas holidays. In the 1870s William Emerson, author of the *History and Incidents of Indian Corn and Its Culture,* heralded popcorn as "capital for Christmas parties."[5]

Drawing largely on her youth in Nebraska during the late nineteenth century, Willa Cather described popping corn as a social event at

Christmastime in *My Ántonia*. Popped kernels were strung on string and used as decorations for Christmas trees. For these decorations others favored coloring different batches of popcorn and alternating various colors on the strings. Food columnist Barbara Allen endorsed popcorn strings as "pretty garnish for Christmas trees" that gave "employment to the small people anxious to assist in the ceremonies." Children eagerly scrambled afterward to consume the popcorn strings even though their "candy bags consisted largely of the same viand."[6]

Charles Hartley and John Willier's "Pop Corn for the Home," published by the United States Department of Agriculture, proclaimed that some people considered popcorn decorations "a necessary adjunct to the Christmas festivities." The authors believed that if farmers kept a supply of popcorn and poppers convenient, "fewer nickels would be spent for less wholesome knickknacks and more enjoyable evenings would be spent around the family hearth." The authors specifically advocated Little Tom Thumb and Eight-Rowed popcorn varieties for Christmas decorations.[7]

Clemence Haskin, who grew up on a Kansas farm, vividly remembered her family's popcorn-rich Christmas celebrations. According to Haskin, her father considered popcorn and Christmas closely associated. For a week before each Christmas the family popped and prepared popcorn. The first job was to string popcorn on their Christmas tree. Red and green popcorn kernels punctuated periodically with a plumb cranberry were threaded with big needles onto three-foot lengths of string. For longer garlands they tied shorter lengths together. During later years crumpled cellophane was added. In addition to the strings of popcorn, Haskin's family threaded pieces of popcorn on thin wire and shaped them into "funny fellows," flowers, and wreaths, the latter of which were spotted with red cranberries and tied with green bows. Their Christmas popcorn balls were "special" because hidden inside each was a present wrapped in wax paper. White popcorn "snowflakes" were pinned to the tree. At the tree's base popcorn snowballs wrapped in white paper were piled high: "Anyone who dropped in Christmas week was invited to help himself and 'take a few along for the folks.'"[8]

Haskin's Christmas days started off with popcorn cereal composed of ground "old maids and the old bachelors" with sugar and cream. Old maids and old bachelors were the kernels that did not pop after exposure to heat. (Today these terms have been deemed politically incorrect: the proper substitutions are "duds," "unpopped kernels," "pooped corn," or "flopcorn.") At dinner crisp buttered popcorn sprinkled with paprika and celery salt was scattered over the cream soup. Nut baskets were molded of popcorn using sugar syrup as the binding agent. Candied popcorn was "shaped into hollow nests, big ones for the center of the table or little ones, over-grown thimble size, for individual holders." Waxed paper lined each basket before goodies were heaped inside. The thick white frosting of the Christmas cake was covered with big popcorn flakes. Popcorn flowers were positioned on the top of the cake, and others were stuck to bonbons. "A lot of work?" Haskin asked. "Well maybe—but we did it just for fun!"[9]

Recently Diane Pfeifer recommended making "Christmas Candy Cane Corn" composed of the usual ingredients plus peppermint extract and food coloring. According to Frances Towner Giedt, popcorn cakes were traditional housewarming gifts in Charleston, South Carolina. Herbalist Linda Flemming received several the first year she resided in Charleston. After Flemming moved to Connecticut, she carried on the tradition by serving popcorn cakes at Christmastime.[10]

Popcorn sculptures were commonly created throughout the early twentieth century. After the United States entered into World War I, Alice Bradley encouraged Americans to shape popcorn into cannons and soldiers. Similar advice was given during World War II, but an article in *House and Garden* also advocated molding popcorn into the shapes of children, baskets, and animals "if the fancy strikes you." After World War II, Lynn Parsons advocated fashioning popcorn into Christmas trees with red and green gumdrop ornaments. The trees were pierced by a wooden skewer grounded in an apple at the base. Parsons's Christmas popcorn balls were speared with candy canes, wrapped in cellophane, and tied with red ribbons and holly. Popcorn was formed into the shapes of cats with whiskers made of red cellophane straws and into clowns with candy mouths and gumdrops eyes. Parsons also made "Popcorn Pops," which were fashioned in the same way as popcorn balls but with wooden skewers inserted like Popsicle sticks. Popcorn Pops were covered in cellophane and hung on trees as ornaments or stuffed into Christmas stockings. For fireside snacking Popcorn Pops were easier to eat than traditional popcorn balls, and the skewers prevented the hands from becoming sticky.[11]

For the party table popcorn sculptures were constructed in the forms of animals, birds, and decorations including bouquets, favors, and bonbons. *House Beautiful* proposed that popcorn be formed into Christmas wreaths and tiered trees. As if this gallery were not enough, Sue Spitler and Nao Hauser developed a recipe for "Tree Trimmer's Popcorn," as well as instructions for constructing popcorn and candy houses. Syd Spiegel, a Canadian popcorn distributor-manufacturer, reported that popcorn had been molded into every conceivable shape from Howdy-Doody to Santa Claus.[12]

Popcorn sculpture was revived during the 1970s. In 1976 two books were published with instructions for numerous popcorn sculptures.

Carolyn Vosburg Hall's book, *I Love Popcorn,* included tips to shape popcorn into a Valentine heart, a snowman, and a gingerbread man. Barbara Williams's *Cornzapoppin'!* offered directions for making Christmas popcorn wreaths, stars, snowballs, and snowmen. Patricia Fox Sheinwold's *Jolly Time Party Book* presented directions for constructing a popcorn Christmas tree, Santa, and snowman. Orville Redenbacher, who claimed that he got "a little corny at Christmas," developed recipes for Christmas garlands, ornaments, candle holders, and other decorations in his *Popcorn Book.* Frances Towner Giedt reported that her family's favorites were swags composed of popcorn, fresh cranberries, cinnamon sticks, and air-dried oranges, lemons, and apples, which made fragrant as well as attractive Christmas decorations. Today popcorn swags are back in vogue, at least among environmentalists who recommend setting out popcorn and cranberry garlands for birds after the holidays are over.[13]

The Christmas connection was certainly not lost on the business world. In their 1891 seed catalog V. H. Hallock & Son on Long Island, New York, heralded their California Golden variety of popcorn, which they claimed had been discovered recently among a tribe of Indians in Lower California. They reported that California Golden was valuable and "highly esteemed for making mantel ornaments, Christmas decorations" and round, white balls that looked "like miniature balls of snow." Christmas and winter images sparkled on popcorn boxes and advertisements. The Albert Dickinson Company of Chicago, for instance, trademarked Santa Claus and Snow Ball brands of popcorn. The A. A. Berry Seed Company of Clarinda, Iowa, named a brand Mistletoe and trademarked a wreath with a ribbon on which appeared the words "Christmas Time All The Time." Early advertisements for Jolly Time popcorn, produced by the American Pop Corn Company in Sioux City, Iowa, highlighted the statement "Popcorn Brings Christmas Cheer." The first Jolly Time label depicted three small children, seated on the floor with toys scattered around them, digging into a huge bowl of popcorn.[14]

Popcorn sculptures were modeled for many other occasions in addition to Christmas. Patricia Fox Sheinwold's *Jolly Time Party Book* included directions for styling popcorn pigtails or ponytail holders, candleholders, and turkeys and for Indian corn centerpieces. Larry Kusche's *Popcorn* published recipes for making Poppo the Clown. Books also included recipes for other holidays, including New Year's Day, Valentine's Day, Mardi Gras, Lincoln's Birthday, Columbus Day, and, of course, Thanksgiving. Connie Evener and MarSue Birtler developed intriguing ideas for using popcorn to create collages, apples, trees, a gardening hat, hot air balloons, jack-o'-lanterns, unicorns, and posies, as well as a string bird feeder. For Independence Day popcorn firecrackers and cannons have been ingeniously contrived.[15]

The strongest and most prolific advocate for popcorn sculpture was Barbara Williams. She published instructions for forming popcorn sculptures for nearly every holiday. For January, Williams recommended popcorn ball fondue as well as a popcorn string bird feeder. She continued through the calendar with creative applications of popcorn for specific holidays: for Lincoln's Birthday, "Popcorn Log Cabins"; for Valentine's Day, "Cinnamon Popcorn Hearts"; for Washington's Birthday, "Cherry Popcorn Balls"; for Saint Patrick's Day, a green castle and shamrocks; for Easter, "Popcorn Baskets"; for Mother's Day, table decorations; for Independence Day, popcorn cannons; for Halloween, "Creamy Orange Witches," "Cat Lollipops," and "Scarecrows"; for Thanksgiving, a "Cornucopia Centerpiece"; and for New Year's, popcorn clocks. For birthdays Williams shared theme popcorn recipes for each month. Perhaps her most unusual contribution was the November treat—"Popmen from Outer Space." Since the 1980s popcorn sculpture has disappeared from the culinary horizon, but there have been a few glimmerings. Recently *Parents* magazine recommended making eggs out of popcorn and marshmallows for inclusion in Easter baskets.[16]

The American Pop Corn Company asserted that their popcorn was "Just Fine for Halloween Parties." Others also linked popcorn with Halloween. For instance, the *Good Housekeeping Cookbook* recommended that Halloween popcorn be shaped, wrapped, and tied to look like ears of corn. Also for Halloween, *Sunset* recommended filling an apple basket with popcorn and candied popcorn, dipping popcorn balls into chocolate, as well as fashioning popcorn into lollipops, jack-o'-lanterns and "Gum Drop Popcorn Squares." *House Beautiful* promoted making Halloween sculptures such as clowns, owls, and "Gobblin' Cats." During the 1970s Patricia Fox Sheinwold's *Jolly Time Party Book* gave tips for sculpting popcorn bowls, popcorn balls on sticks, "Jack O'Lantern Sandwiches," and "Pumpkin Place Holders."[17]

Popcorn Boys

Initially popcorn was cultivated "chiefly in gardens in very small patches." As the amount of popcorn grown was small compared with other varieties of maize, gross profits on sales were limited. Farmers often encouraged their sons to raise and sell it to neighbors or local grocery stores. In urban areas boys sold popcorn balls and other ready-to-eat products on streets and at train stations.[18]

George Stockwell reported that many boys regarded cultivating popcorn as their own domain. The young farmer with popcorn plots hacked weeds in the morning, and "night often overtook him as he ministered to the wants of his pop-corn plants." When the time came, these youngsters harvested the crops, husked the corn, and removed the silk. The popcorn was frequently dried in attics. When cured, some was fried—for example in the same kettles of fat used for frying doughnuts. The popped kernels came to the surface and were removed with a skimmer. When the corn was combined with milk or cream this mixture was considered "one of the great luxuries—one of the daintiest luxuries—of this life." Surplus popcorn was sold. Such sales often generated more money than the young men had ever possessed for their own use.[19]

An unidentified correspondent in the *Country Gentleman* described the process in greater detail. Enterprising boys purchased flat paper boxes that required construction. Each boy was then encouraged to acquire a printing press and illustrate the box with popcorn and its price, along with his name. The correspondent proclaimed: "Bright and attractive packages sell goods!" These packages could "be sold by the dozen to village storekeepers, of whom a great many will be found in a radius of a dozen miles." Popcorn was sold shelled or on the ear, "for people like to pop it over their own fires and have it fresh." Alternately, the popcorn could be packaged in attractive "little white, pink or yellow tissue bags, with 'Fresh Pop Corn' printed on them in colors." In addition, some popcorn was molded into popcorn balls, "those delicious globes that everybody likes, and that nearly everyone is at least tempted to buy when he sees them offered for sale." The observer recommended selling bags for five cents and the popcorn balls at one cent each, or ten cents for a dozen. The correspondent believed that this would teach boys "some of the principles of doing business, while earning pocket money at the same time."[20]

The A. A. Berry Seed Company of Clarinda, Iowa, channeled the same belief into a way to sell popcorn. In its 1902 catalog the company urged farmers to "give the boys an acre to raise pop corn for the market." The belief was expressed that it was "better to give the boys an acre to raise a crop to furnish them some spending money" because the money earned from selling popcorn, which was generally in demand at profitable prices, would be more "appreciated, and cultivates a business habit in the boy that might always stay down."[21]

Popcorn Parties

As the twentieth century dawned, the popcorn party became an important form of entertainment. As one such party was described, a San Franciscan provided half a dozen corn poppers. When the bed of coals in the fireplace was just right, the children shelled, popped, and salted their own popcorn. The novel feature at this popcorn party "consisted of dainty little square-shaped bowls made from crepe paper of various colors, the shape being formed by gathering up the corners with a few stitches." These bowls were set on plates covered with dainty Japanese napkins. By the side of each lay a ragged-edged card with a question related to corn. In the center of the table was a large dish cloaked inside and out with pleated crepe paper. While the children filled the dish with hot popcorn, they answered the questions.[22]

Popcorn games for such parties were described in an article in *Good Housekeeping* written by E. M. Pine. Pine was in charge of a large country house where a number of young people had unexpectedly congregated on a cold evening. She brought out poppers and appointed two judges and a manager. The manager paired the group into couples, then asked them to pop a specified amount of corn. When the couples were finished, the judges emptied the good kernels and counted the unpopped kernels. The judges announced the winning couple and presented a booby prize for the couple with the greatest number of unpopped kernels. According to Pine, the "game caused much merriment, and all joined in eating the corn just popped with generous additions of apples and cider, voting the impromptu entertainment a great success."[23]

Other popcorn games included "hit the mask," in which children stood three feet away and tossed popcorn at the mask's mouth. Another was the "Pop Corn Balancing Race." Popcorn was placed on a table knife and children raced across the room without spilling. Then there was the "Pop Corn Eating Race," in which twenty-five pieces of popcorn were threaded on a string on both sides of a popcorn ball. Children on each side were required to eat the popcorn. The first child to arrive at the popcorn ball won. For a Halloween party Patricia Fox Sheinwold recommended pitching popcorn into a pumpkin and a popcorn bob.[24]

Of course, adults had popcorn parties as well, but apparently they were not as successful. When fishing was bad and conversation was worse, cookbook writer Allen Prescott's answer was a popcorn party. "Just suggest a good popcorn party to your friends when they are gathered for an evening," advised Prescott. If they were the right sort, they would fall in with these plans and "run around getting poppers and corn and burning themselves." If they were not the right sort, they would leave at once, "but it's just as well to know who your friends are," Prescott stated.[25]

Larry Kusche's *Popcorn* recommended sending out invitations to popcorn parties. At his parties a variety of butters and sweet powdered mixes were arranged buffet style at the end of each table. Mixes included powdered orange breakfast drink, powdered milk, powdered cocoa mix, instant coffee, cocktail mixes, and colored cake decorations. Heaping bowls of popcorn were placed at the other end of each table, with individual bowls for each guest. Pitchers with a variety of beverages were available, and guests were encouraged to make their own creations. Kusche proclaimed, presumably with a straight face, "Your Popcorn Party will be a topic of conversation for a long time."[26]

Twentieth-Century Popcorn Children

Whether or not Americans as a whole appreciated popcorn's value, children's book writers certainly did. Laura Ingalls Wilder's *Farmer Boy,* second in her Little House children's series, was a fictionalized biography of her husband, Almanzo Wilder. It was based on his recollections of the year 1866 in Melone, New York. Wilder wrote that when the family had settled down by the stove on a cold winter's evening, Almanzo opened the stove's iron door and "put three handfulls of popcorn into a big wire popper, and shook the popper over the coals. In a little while a kernel popped, then another, then three or four at once, and all at once furiously the hundreds of little pointed kernels." When the pan was full, melted butter and salt were poured on top. Popcorn's advantage was that "it was hot and crackling crisp, and deliciously buttery and salty, and everyone could eat all he wanted to." According to Wilder's fictionalized account, Almanzo examined every kernel before he ate it. He had eaten thousands of handfuls of popcorn and never found two kernels alike. Almanzo speculated about the relationship between milk and popcorn. One glass could be filled to the brim with milk and another glass filled with popcorn. When the kernels were put in one at a time, the milk would not run over. Almanzo concluded that popcorn and milk were "the only two things that will go into the same place."[27]

Carl Sandburg's juvenile book *Rootabaga Stories,* published in 1922, included one popcorn story: "The Story of Jason Squiff and Why He Had a Popcorn Hat, Popcorn Mittens and Popcorn Shoes." A second popcorn story appeared in a later edition: "The Huckabuck Family and How They Raised Popcorn in Nebraska and Quit and Came Back." While in Nebraska the Huckabuck family raised a large popcorn crop. But after it was harvested, according to the story, the barn burned down and the popcorn exploded all over the farm. After the popcorn was piled up to the windows, the family decided it would be best to move to Iowa and let the wind disperse the popcorn. Three years later they returned to Nebraska but refused to grow popcorn.[28]

The theme of stored popcorn exploding has continued to surface in literature. In Ruth Adams's *Mr. Picklepaw's Popcorn* Mr. Picklepaw stockpiled popcorn in a sheet-iron shed. When the temperature rose on a hot day, the town feasted on the results. In *The Biggest Popcorn Party Ever in Center County* Jane Hoober Peifer turned to popcorn to teach the importance of sharing. When two children refused to share their popcorn crop with friends, the barn burned down and the stored kernels popped. The children finally decided to have the grandest popcorn party ever. Needless to say, children's fiction does not always match reality. When a popcorn crib owned by the American Pop Corn Company burned down in 1931, "not only did the corn in that crib fail to pop, but every bit of it was totally destroyed."[29]

Children's magazines, such as *St. Nicholas,* published popcorn stories, poetry, and recipes. One short story, Mildred Stapley's "The K. & A. Company," related how two American children moved to Paris and discovered that Parisians had never seen popcorn. The children's grandmother sent some popcorn, and the American children demonstrated the process of making honeyed popcorn balls. The Parisians so prized this "new *confiscerie*" that the American children went into business selling popcorn. This theme of American children introducing popcorn to others around the world has endured. Emily Arnold McCully's *Popcorn at the Palace,* published in 1997, told the story of how Maisie Ferris traveled to England with her father, Olmsted Ferris, and introduced popcorn to Queen Victoria and Prince Albert in 1848. While Maisie Ferris is a fictitious character, Olmsted Ferris's trip to England with popcorn is evidently true, at least according to Earnest Elmo Calkins, a local historian of Galesburg, Illinois. That Ferris actually saw Queen Victoria or Prince Albert and demonstrated popcorn is extremely unlikely.[30]

Children's popcorn poetry has blossomed throughout the twentieth century. Nancy Byrd Turner's "A Song of Popcorn" was a favorite and was frequently reprinted:

Sing a song of popcorn
When the snow-storms rage;
Fifty little brown men
Put into a cage.
Shake them till they laugh and leap,
Crowding to the top;
Watch them burst their little coats—
Pop! Pop! Pop!

Sing a song of popcorn
In the firelight;
Fifty little fairies
Robed in fleecy white.
Through the shining wires see
How they skip & prance
To the music of the flames:
Dance, dance, dance.

Sing a song of popcorn—
Done the frolicing;
Fifty little fairies
Strung upon a string.
Cool & happy, hand in hand,
Sugar-spangled, fair;
Isn't that a necklace fit
For any child to wear?[31]

The "Popcorn Song" was composed by Sophia T. Newman, who was wild about the sound and sight of popping corn. She wrote:

In they drop with a click, clack, click
Kernels so hard and yellow;
Round they whirl with a hop, skip, hop,
Each little dancing fellow.
Up they leap with a snap! crack! snap!
Tossing so light and airy;
Out they pour with a soft, swift rush,
Snowballs fit for a fairy![32]

Elizabeth Gordon's *Mother Earth's Children* included a poem as well as a friendly illustration of popcorn children.

The Popcorn children are so dear
They stay with us all through the year.
They like to dance in dresses white
Around the open fire at night.[33]

An article titled "How Indians Popped Corn," published in *St. Nicholas* magazine, claimed that "Indian Children" were fond of popcorn. The article announced that Native Americans prepared popcorn in several ways. The first included heating sand until it was piping hot, after which popcorn was stirred into the sand. As the kernels burst, they surfaced and were gathered into bowls. Another way that Native Americans purportedly prepared popcorn was to heat a hollowed-out soapstone in which popcorn was placed and covered. The article reported that when the lid was lifted, the kernels shot out in every direction: "Imagine the fun the children must have had scampering after the runaways!" Alas, the article cited no sources for these statements.[34]

The children-popcorn connection continued to flourish. Many popcorn confections, such as Cracker Jack, targeted children and enclosed prizes to induce children to covet their product. From the late 1940s through 1957 Fawcett and National Group comics advertised Cracker Jack. Other popcorn products today are directly marketed for different age groups. Advertisements for Cracker Jack and Screaming Yellow Zonkers are aimed at consumers from fourteen to twenty years old. Smartfoods's white cheddar cheese popcorn targets college-age and young adults by capitalizing on two trends—New Wave and New Age. Marketeers shower samples at sporting events, beach parties, and other youth-oriented events. To counter the success of Smartfoods, Frito-Lay introduced Chee*tos Cheddar Cheese Flavored Popcorn and employed their cartoon character Chester Cheetah to appeal to preteens and teens.[35]

In September 1997 the Ramsey Popcorn Company introduced FunPop, targeted at children from six to twelve years old. Studies showed that children within this age group were the second largest "heavy users" of popcorn. FunPop came in two flavors, Lightly Sweet, and Big Butter. Packages are vibrantly colored on the outside and contain toys inside. FunPop's introduction was accompanied by an aggressive marketing campaign shown during prime-time children's programming on Nickelodeon.[36]

Juvenile fiction featuring popcorn as an important component has continued to expand. In Hazel Krantz's *100 Pounds of Popcorn* eleven-year-old Andy Taylor starts a popcorn business after finding a huge bag of unpopped popcorn. In Alice Low's *The Popcorn Shop* Popcorn Nell buys a large popping machine which pops day and night to keep up with demand. Popcorn is the secret weapon that restores a kidnapped princess to the royal household in Mary Wilkins's fairy tale *Princess Rosetta and the Popcorn Man*. Beatrice Schenk de Regniers's *Sing a Song of Popcorn,* a collection of poetry for children, and James Stevenson's *Popcorn* include popcorn poems.[37]

Many educational books aimed at elementary-school children have employed popcorn as a vehicle to improve understanding of history, math, sciences, and reading. Dave Woodside's *What Makes Popcorn Pop?* examines the history and science of popping. Rose Wyler's *Science Fun with Peanuts and Popcorn* incorporates popcorn into a number of children's science experiments. In the Modern Curriculum Press's Beginning to Read series, Phylliss Adams's *Popcorn Magic* permits students to plot their own stories. On a rainy day an older sister helps two younger children pass the time by heating popcorn. The young readers determine what happens next by turning to a specific page. Likewise, popcorn has been used in school curricula to teach particular concepts and even found its way into collegiate classrooms. At the University of Colorado at Denver, popcorn has been used to demonstrate the scientific method and introduce concepts in elementary statistics, significance testing, and measurement error.[38]

Kathleen Kudlinski's *Popcorn* describes the life cycle of a popcorn plant from its sowing by farmers until the kernels explode. Others have highlighted popcorn as an example to help children learn how vegetables grow and where food comes from. Clyde's Restaurant Group, which operates several restaurants in the Washington, D.C., area, has offered seed packets to young diners that "feature cartoon-type vegetables with kid-cool names." One packet is named "Col. Pop Corn."[39]

Perhaps the most extensive use of popcorn in the precollegiate and collegiate curricula is in the arena of setting world's records. In 1988 the Jones High School in Orlando popped 3,787.5 cubic feet of popcorn. The students of Fresno State University beat this record in 1991 with the accumulation of 3,791.8 cubic feet of popcorn. No sooner had they made it into *The Guinness Book of Records* when the students at Stanly County Community College in North Carolina popped 5,438.16 cubic feet of corn. The following year the world's record fell out of American hands and went to the citizens of Derby, United Kingdom, who popped 5,979.33 cubic feet of popcorn. Finally, American educators regained the initiative. For six days in October 1994 students at Beauclerc Elementary School in Jackson, Florida, popped corn. Teachers built their curricula around popcorn. In English classes students wrote stories about popcorn; in mathematics classrooms students calculated the amount of popcorn contained in a box. On the final day the school had popped 6,619 cubic feet of popcorn. It stood eight feet high, over twenty feet wide, and almost forty feet long. The school dubbed it the "World's Largest Box of Popcorn." *The Guinness Book of Records* agreed, and their feat was duly noted in the 1996 edition. But records are made to be broken. In October 1996 the students and teachers at Pittsfield Elementary School, Pittsfield, Wisconsin, built a container measuring forty feet long, twenty-eight feet wide, and six feet and eight inches high. It was filled with 7,466 cubic feet of popped corn.[40] But how long will this record stand?

Popcorn Children Revisited

The association of popcorn and children was less an accident and more an expression of forces that transformed other aspects of American culture. Specifically, it was part of a broader trend in America that made children the center of attention. As social historian Stephen Nissenbaum has pointed out, prior to the late eighteenth century Christmas was usually a period of lower-class drunkenness and was not celebrated as a religious or family holiday by most Americans. During the early nineteenth century Christmas was reinvented and focused on children—at the same time that popcorn became an American fad. Santa Claus became a commercial icon during the 1840s. Christmas trees, introduced during the mid nineteenth century by Pennsylvania German immigrants, became important national symbols.[41] Popcorn was one of

Santa's gifts to children and to America, and was also used to create Christmas tree decorations.

Commercial Christmas presents were luxury items that many Americans could not manage, but almost everyone could afford popcorn. By comparison to other possible gifts, it was extremely inexpensive. To anyone with a farm or garden, popcorn could easily be grown. If purchased in a grocery store, popcorn was among the least expensive snack foods. Due to its low cost, it was an ideal Christmas food and decoration. As Christmas became increasingly commercialized, popcorn processors and sellers frequently associated popcorn with Christmas through advertising techniques. The association of Christmas and popcorn continued through the 1950s but waned during the second half of the twentieth century.[42] As inexpensive commercial tinsel and other adornments became available, popcorn strings declined in importance. Affluent America could afford more expensive Christmas treats and baubles and many Americans were unwilling to spend the time to make the tedious decorations.

While the link between popcorn and Christmas has waned, the connection between children and popcorn has flourished. Since popping corn over an open fire or potbellied stove has been replaced by preparing popcorn in a convenient package in the microwave oven, the wonder caused by the explosion and the rapid expansion is lost. Today's advertising and marketing of popcorn target children, nurturing and exploiting the connection between the two.

Chapter 4

Pop Cookery

Popcorn erupted onto the American culinary landscape in the mid nineteenth century. At first it was just a novelty among upper- and middle-class Americans. Unlike other novelties, popcorn had staying power and easily cruised into mainstream cookery. Its pop was inherently mysterious, particularly to young people. It was extremely inexpensive, particularly when compared with other snack-type foods, and therefore was easily accessible to lower classes. Anyone could cultivate it in a garden plot. Popcorn or popcorn products could be easily marketed to generate small amounts of cash. Popcorn was also easily prepared by anyone with a fireplace or stove. Its flavor was essentially neutral and therefore mixed well with popular flavorings and additives. As the popularity of flavorings changed, popcorn remained a neutral platform for new taste sensations. As the century progressed common people fueled popcorn's conversion into a food fad.

Nineteenth-century cookbooks mainly catered to the middle and upper classes. Often these cookbooks reflected traditions that were decades behind cooking practices. Products commonly used often did not appear in cookbooks until well after they were established. This pattern did not hold true in the case of popcorn, which was duly noted in cookbooks almost simultaneously with its appearance in magazines and diaries. This suggests that popcorn was initially a top-down food fad, initiated or popularized by members of the urban middle and upper classes. Only later was it adopted by farmers and the less affluent.

The first cookbook found to mention popcorn was Catherine Beecher's *Domestic Receipt Book,* published in 1846. Beecher was the sister of Henry Ward Beecher, the famous agriculturalist and minister, and also the sister of Harriet Beecher Stowe, the author of *Uncle Tom's Cabin.* In a recipe for "Molasses Candy," Beecher parenthetically reported that "*Whole Popped* corn" could be made into excellent cakes when served with molasses or maple sugar. She also reported that some people ate it with milk.[1] Beecher clearly circulated among the rich and famous in New England. Her inclusion of this recipe supports the contention that the popcorn revolution began with the New England–New York establishment.

The first complete popcorn recipe was published in 1853 by an unidentified pupil in Mrs. Goodfellow's cooking school in Philadelphia, which catered to husbandless middle-class women. Her recipe recommended heating fresh lard in a pan, dropping in the kernels, and covering tightly with the lid to prevent kernels from popping out. While the lard drained off the popcorn in a colander, she prepared a syrup flavored "with either seville orange juice or lemon juice." When boiled down, she combined the syrup and the popcorn and simmered the mixture for ten minutes. It was then lumped onto buttered dishes to cool. This recipe was frequently reprinted in subsequent editions of the cookbook and was borrowed by other cookbook authors. In addition to orange and lemon juice, rose and vanilla were also endorsed as flavorings by subsequent cookbook authors.[2]

Shortly thereafter popcorn recipes were published in farming journals. Other recipes were published in prestigious cookbooks. Two appeared in E. F. Haskell's monumental work, *The Housekeeper's Encyclopedia,* published in 1861. After the Civil War, Maria Parloa, who had served as the cook for the prestigious Appledore House of Isle of Shoals in New Hampshire, recommended serving popcorn pudding in her *Appledore Cook Book.*[3] By the 1870s popcorn recipes regularly appeared in magazines and cookbooks devoted to candy making. Popcorn recipes were common in comprehensive cookbooks by the late nineteenth century. During the early twentieth century popcorn cookery exploded.

Many cookbook authors classified popcorn solely as a confection and placed the recipes in candy, dessert, or miscellaneous sections. Diversity and originality were manifest in the recipes. Charlotte Brewster Jordan offered popcorn recipes in verse, such as ones for "Hunky-Dories" and "Best Evers." Amelia Sulzbacher incorporated seven popcorn recipes into her article "Popcorn Dainties" in *Good Housekeeping,* featuring "Popcorn Brittle" and "Popcorn Marguerites." Riley M. Fletcher-Berry offered fifteen popcorn recipes in *Ladies' Home*

Journal, including ones for "Popcorn Cheese," "Coffee Pop-Corn Dainties," "Pop-Corn Biscuits," and "Pop-corn Balls for Clear Soup." The first entire chapter on popcorn cookery, titled "Pop-Corn Sweets," was published in 1915 by Mary M. Wright in her *Candy-Making at Home.* Wright's recipes encompassed such treats as "Snow Pop-Corn Balls," "Ice Pop-Corn Balls," "Maple Pop-Corn Bars," "Pop-Corn Almond Nougat," and "Pop-Corn Fudge."[4]

Alice Bradley, principal of the School of Cookery in Boston made famous by Fannie Merritt Farmer, incorporated a chapter on "Popcorn Candies" in her *Candy Cook Book.* This chapter featured thirteen popcorn recipes with unusual contributions for "Popcorn Nuggets," "Mock Violets," and "Popcorn Nests." This candy cookbook went through at least four editions and received widespread acclaim and distribution. After the United States entered into World War I, Bradley's article in *Woman's Home Companion* asserted that popping corn at Christmas was the patriotic thing to do. Americans, living in "wartime conditions," should substitute popcorn for confections composed of sugar and molasses. Her reasoning was simple: if Americans consumed less sugar and molasses, more would be available for English and French children.[5]

May B. Van Arsdale, Day Monroe, and Mary I. Barber's *Our Candy Recipes,* published in 1922, featured fifteen recipes, including ones for "Johnny Cake," "Amber Pop Corn," "Pop Corn Lace," and "Cornlets." Their recipe for "Dusky Maidens" called for adorning the faces with melted chocolate, and they were "appropriate for children's parties." Perhaps more important than the specific recipes was the affiliation of the authors. Van Arsdale was an associate professor and the other two were instructors in food and cookery at Teachers College, Columbia University, then considered to be the nation's premier school of education. Their connection with the college bestowed legitimacy to popcorn cookery.[6]

While cookbooks and magazines gave visibility to popcorn cookery, the most important contributions appeared in pamphlets and leaflets distributed by popcorn processors. The first located popcorn booklet was published in 1916 by Sam Nelson Jr.'s popcorn company in Grinnell, Iowa. It incorporated popped corn into omelets, hash, custard, macaroons, and pie as well as in combination with roasts, cutlets, parsnips, turnips, carrots, macaroni, potatoes, and, believe it or not, prunes. Popcorn was also recommended for soups, salads, and confections. Subsequently, other processors carried popcorn recipes in promotional brochures and newsletters and on and in popcorn packages. The Albert Dickinson Company of Chicago issued a broadside with recipes for crispettes and popcorn brittle. Unlike the traditional cookbooks which confined popcorn cookery to the confection section, the material published by processors and marketeers brimmed with multifaceted ideas for popcorn dishes served at breakfast, lunch, and dinner.[7]

Popcorn Pudding and Flour

Popcorn pudding recipes evolved from the original preparation created by Native Americans for parched corn. The pre-Columbian inhabitants of the Western Hemisphere ground down parched corn and added water. Shortly after the arrival of English colonists the water was replaced with milk and sugar was added. Subsequently, popcorn was substituted for parched corn and was eaten with milk as a breakfast food. European colonists also ate cornmeal mush at breakfast, which came to be known as hasty pudding.[8] Popcorn pudding was a simple adaptation of the hasty pudding recipe with popped corn substituting for parched corn.

In 1858 S. A. Cole of Gorham, New York, offered a recipe for popcorn pudding that included three pints of milk, two eggs, three pints of popped popcorn, and some salt; the mixture was then baked for half a hour. When served with rich cream, Cole considered it an excellent and delicious dessert. Another recipe was published the following year in the *Rural New Yorker.* It comprised similar ingredients but in drastically different quantities: one quart of milk, one cup of sugar, and four eggs to one quart of popped popcorn. This was flavored with nutmeg or cinnamon and a little salt. The mixture was poured into a dish lined with soda-biscuit paste and baked for an hour in a moderate oven. Similar recipes appeared after the Civil War. Maria Parloa's "Popcorn Pudding" called for baking popped corn with milk in a pudding dish and serving with sugar and cream. A more elaborate popcorn pudding recipe was developed by C. H. Crane of Ossawattomie, Kansas, who used crackers, an egg, salt, and sugar. The combination was soaked in milk for three hours and baked. This recipe was published in the *Kansas Home Cook Book,* which was printed at least a dozen more times.[9]

At a meeting of the Farmer's Club of the American Institute, Solon Robinson ground popped corn to make another pudding. Robinson believed that this flour was "superior to farina or any other known meal, as a vehicle for the usual condiments used in making puddings." The editor of the *Working Farmer* experimented with popcorn meal and agreed with Robinson's assessment. The editor reported that popcorn increased in bulk seventeen times when popped, and when crushed to meal it lost only half of its volume; thus it was "light, absorbent, superior to farina or any other known meal" and was "an admirable vehicle for the usual condiments used in the making of puddings."[10]

In Battle Creek, Michigan, Ella Kellogg, the wife of Harvey Kellogg and sister-in-law of the future cereal magnate William K. Kellogg, used popcorn meal as a key ingredient in pudding. If popcorn meal were not available, she recommended substituting finely rolled, freshly popped corn. She combined this with milk, sugar, and eggs and baked the mixture in a pudding dish placed inside another filled with hot water until the custard set. She topped it with a meringue made of egg whites, a teaspoonful of sugar, and a little popcorn meal. Almeda Lambert, a friend of the Kelloggs, reported in her *Guide for Nut Cookery* that ground popcorn was "excellent eaten with nut milk, and [could] be used in making mushes and puddings."[11]

Popcorn pudding flourished during the early twentieth century. Fannie Merritt Farmer recommended "Corn Pudding" as a food for the "Sick and Convalescent." Her recipe reduced the number of eggs and the amount of milk, sugar, and cream. She pounded the popcorn in a mortar and then added egg, butter, sugar, and salt. The pudding was baked in a slow oven and served with or without cream. Mary Hamilton Talbott's "Pop Corn Cream Pudding" used gelatine and a custard of milk, egg yolks, sugar, and salt as the base. Ground popcorn was added along with almond extract. Finally she blended in stiffly whipped egg whites, chilled the entire dish, and garnished it with popped corn and whipped cream. Her "Prune and Pop Corn Pudding" was similar but called for cinnamon and lemon juice along with the prunes. Canadian Iroquois also made popcorn pudding, which served as the basis of a number of dishes lauded as "highly in favour." Their version was "considered a great dainty, as well as a treat for visitors." The Iroquois made the pudding by popping, pounding, sifting, and boiling popcorn in water until it thickened. It was enjoyed with syrup, sugar, milk, cream, or sour milk. Other popcorn pudding recipes varied in the application of particular flavorings. Some included almond extract, lemon juice, pecans, and vanilla.[12]

This genre gradually disappeared after World War I, but popcorn flour revived shortly after the end of World War II, when wheat and other grains were desperately needed to support a prostrated Europe and prevent starvation. President Harry Truman ordered that conservation of essential grains be imposed. Bakers were only permitted to use 75 percent of the wheat that they had previously used. The H. Piper Company, a major retail baker in Chicago, explored alternatives. The obvious choices, rye for instance, were also in short supply. In April 1946 Piper announced that popcorn was the answer. Using popped popcorn as well as frozen and frostbitten kernels, Piper purchased special equipment to mill popcorn into flour. By a special treatment they made a mixture of 25 percent popcorn and wheat flour and produced bread.

The flour gave the bread "a higher protein content, a richer color, and a much better taste." Also, popcorn bread remained fresh twice as long as did ordinary bread due to a higher moisture content. By August, Piper had seven thousand retail stores within a short distance of Chicago selling popcorn bread. During the first two days of sale ten thousand loaves were sold in Milwaukee alone. Piper charged a one-cent royalty on each wrapper. Piper agreed to spend 25 percent of its royalties advertising its new product. These efforts were so successful that Piper came out with Popcorn Muffins and Popcorn Doughnuts. Piper proudly announced that popcorn bread was a permanent addition to the company's line. However, this announcement was premature. When a freeze destroyed a large portion of the popcorn crop in late 1947, the price of raw popcorn escalated and popcorn bread disappeared.[13]

Popcorn as a Breakfast Cereal

Although not thought of as a breakfast food today, popcorn was a forerunner of modern American cereals. Some early popcorn pudding recipes were simply popcorn immersed in milk with a sweetener. As the definition of popcorn pudding shifted toward a baked dish, popcorn cereal continued to be eaten well before the advent of other breakfast cereals. Popcorn cereal was cherished by many nineteenth-century Americans. George Stockwell exclaimed: "If any person lives who has never eaten pop-corn and milk, or better, pop-corn and cream, he or she has missed one of the great luxuries—one of the daintiest luxuries—of this life." Popcorn cereal may well have provided the model for commercial cereal that emerged at the end of the nineteenth century. Ella Kellogg proclaimed ground popcorn with milk or cream to be a "delectable dish" well before Kellogg's Corn Flakes were served at the Battle Creek sanatarium. Commercial cereal manufacturers may have focused on other grains simply because no one would buy popcorn in a box when they could easily make it in their own homes. Also, people were used to fresh popcorn, not popcorn that had been in boxes for months or even years. It is ironic that commercial cereal makers sold other popped cereals, such as puffed rice or "wheat shot out of a cannon," but failed to sell popcorn cereal. In any case, popcorn cereal was overshadowed by aggressive promotional campaigns of manufacturers who used other grains for their basic ingredients. Lack of commercial advertisement meant that popcorn was left out of the great American cereal revolution that commenced during the early twentieth century. As one observer lamented in 1917, the failure of popcorn as a breakfast cereal was due to the fact that it had not masqueraded under a "curiosity-compelling name" and bore "no pretty girl" on its container.[14]

During the late nineteenth and early twentieth centuries, popcorn cereal was served in many different ways. The simplest was in a bowl submerged in milk. In an article in *Good Housekeeping* May Belle Brooks proclaimed that children delighted in this novelty. She advised running the popped kernels through the food chopper and serving them with cream and sugar, fruit juices, plain fruit, raisins, or dates. Brooks pointed out that the corn could be popped at any time and reheated in the oven when needed. Even the U.S. Department of Agriculture weighed in by reporting in a 1911 *Farmers' Bulletin* that popcorn was frequently "eaten with milk, like other cereal preparations." In another issue of the *Farmers' Bulletin* published two years later, the authors recommended that cereal be made from ground up unpopped duds. This preparation made "a very good breakfast food for eating with cream and sugar or for boiling with water and serving like oatmeal."[15]

Several others made like-minded recommendations. J. I. Holcomb, proprietor of a popcorn machine manufacturing business, asserted in 1915 that there was nothing in the whole realm of edibles that was "more agreeable to the taste or more satisfying than pop corn with cream and sugar." It was a dish that made "the heart glad with pure joy of living." He doubted that there was any breakfast food that tasted better. Holcomb urged his salesmen to encourage luncheonettes to add popcorn and cream to their menus, as it was ideal "for a business man's quick lunch."[16]

Mary Hamilton Talbott published recipes for hot and cold popcorn cereal. For the hot version, she recommended that popped kernels should be covered the night before with cold water to soak overnight. In the morning the waterlogged kernels were cooked in milk and served with sugar and cream. She recommended adding dates, stewed apples, prunes, plumped raisins, fruit juice, or any kind of plain fruit. Her recipe for cold popcorn cereal blended popped kernels with a mild grated cheese. Cream or sugar could be added if desired. Another observer reported that popcorn cereal could be savored with syrup or butter, mingled with berries, or served with meat. It was a dish that could take the place of potatoes, rice, macaroni, or toast. It was a dish appropriately fit "for an American citizen." In a rousing climax the observer proclaimed: "Let the sound of the popper be heard in the land."[17]

It was only a matter of time before a commercial company tried to cash in on popcorn cereal. In 1938 Dixie French Fried Pop Corn introduced "a fine new substantial breakfast food or cereal served with cream and sugar." The Superior Pop Corn Company of Portland, Oregon, opened stores throughout the Pacific Northwest. Their Seattle store featured popcorn as a substitute for corn flakes and other cereals. Their Dixie French Fried Popt Corn served with cream and sugar purportedly was based on "a French Fried process that gives the corn a distinctive flavor." C. M. Littlejohn believed that it was "a delightful change in the matter of cereals to feast on breakfast fare of French Fried Popt Corn." He also believed that "an immeasurable market for pop corn looms in this new direction." Frank Prescott, vice president of an early manufacturer of electric popcorn poppers, predicted that popcorn would become a breakfast favorite because it was so easy to make.[18]

Alas, Littlejohn's and Prescott's predictions were not to be fulfilled. As few general cookbooks featured recipes for popcorn cereal, the idea almost disappeared when World War II commenced. In 1942 James Margedant refused to recommend popcorn cereal. He preferred a leisurely breakfast, and a popcorn dish with cream and sugar "has to be gulped in a hurry if you don't want the kernels to get soggy." Popcorn cereal was resurrected shortly after the war when a large portion of the American grain reserve was sent to Europe to prevent starvation. When a writer in the *Popcorn Merchandiser* recommended that popcorn be substituted for other grains in short supply as a breakfast cereal, the editor cautioned that too much milk should be avoided because the cereal became quite mushy.[19]

Again, this fashion did not thrive, and serving popcorn cereal as a breakfast food largely disappeared. It was again resurrected by popcorn boutiques in the late 1970s. In 1976 Carolyn Vosburg Hall reported that a popcorn breakfast was one of the healthiest ways to eat popcorn, assuring juvenile readers that this was the way the colonial women served it. The following year Larry Kusche also reported that colonial housewives served popcorn with sugar and cream as the first puffed cereal. His nine recipes for a popcorn breakfast included "Popcornmeal Cereal," "Overnight Popcornmeal Cereal," and "Popcorn Milk," as well as popcorn in granola, omelets, scrapple, and pancakes. Orville Redenbacher published a recipe for "Sweet 'n' Crunchy Cereal Snack" in 1984, and Len Sherman published one for "Fruit & Three Puff Breakfast Cereal" twelve years later. At least one popcorn processor, Wilfred Sieg Jr., president of the Ramsey Popcorn Company, maintains that his customers today still eat popcorn topped with milk as a cereal.[20]

Popcorn Balls

Popcorn balls were among the most popular confections in the late nineteenth and early twentieth centuries. Although references appeared as early as the 1840s, the first recipe seems not to have been published until 1861. This recipe was published in E. F. Haskell's *Housekeeper's Encyclopedia*. Her recipe was simple: "Boil honey, maple, or other sugar to the great thread; pop corn and stick the corn together in balls with the candy." In homes, making popcorn balls was usually the province of girls and women. A commentator in the *Country Gentleman* reported that in her family "the little folk" were exceedingly fond of popcorn balls. The younger children shelled the corn and assisted in the popping. A pail was filled with popcorn to which was added a boiling syrup composed of molasses, sugar, salt, and butter. When cooled sufficiently, balls were formed.[21]

After the Civil War popcorn-ball recipes proliferated. John D. Hounihan, a Virginia baker and confectioner, published a recipe employing one-half bushel of popped corn over which he poured a syrup of sugar in a thick solution of gum arabic. This concoction was quickly hand pressed into balls. *The Candy-Maker* published two recipes for popcorn balls. The first was similar to Hounihan's, but a solution of carmine was sprinkled on top for a red tint. The second used boiled molasses without any other flavorings, "as the excellence of this commodity depends entirely upon the united flavor of the corn, salt, and the sugar or molasses." Lafcadio Hearn, New Orleans chef extraordinaire, also published one and begged those making popcorn balls to do so "with clean hands."[22]

To keep up with increased demand, commercial popcorn-ball producers soon required professional equipment. In 1860 Russell Arnold of Hartford patented the first commercial molding machine. His invention formed six popcorn balls simultaneously and automatically ejected the balls from the cups. During the next few decades numerous popcorn-ball machines were manufactured. William M. Thompson of Moline, Illinois, patented a machine for "Forming Pop-Corn into Balls or Cakes." His creation consisted of a table for holding the prepared corn and a single cylinder with two semispherical cups. Popped corn with sweetener was heaped in one sphere while the other was compressed on top by the action of a foot lever. William Goodwin of Philadelphia patented a "Machine for Making Pop-Corn Balls." The plunger forced the popped corn into the shape of a ball. Most recipes called for whole popped corn, but E. H. Leland recommended grinding the popcorn down, adding syrup, forming balls, and covering the outside of the ball with pulverized sugar.[23]

Before the turn of the century, most cookbooks featured at least one recipe for popcorn balls. Sidney Morse offered four methods of making popcorn balls using sugar, molasses, butter, and soft water. The ingredients were combined with wooden paddles or were rolled with wet hands. Rolling popcorn balls also required skill. Morse instructed the cook to first dip her "hands into very cold water before forming each ball and work quickly before the candy hardens." He recommended laying the ball on a circular piece of waxed paper placed in a large pie plate. The edges of the paper were brought together and twisted at the top.

Popcorn balls needed to be stored in "a cold place to prevent the popcorn from becoming tough." They were made on ships at sea and sold in barrels by grocery stores. They were a mainstay along Midways at fairs and amusement parks. At Coney Island, an amusement park established in 1844 in Brooklyn, popcorn confections abounded. Coney Island Pop Corn Balls were favorites composed of the usual contents plus vinegar and butter. Dozens of recipes appeared in American cookbooks and cookery manuscripts.[24]

Popcorn balls were accented with various flavorings. Mary Wright created a recipe for "Chocolate Pop-Corn Balls." It was similar to other recipes except the balls were dipped into hot chocolate. Wright's "Snow Pop-Corn Balls" were flavored with vanilla and peppermint. Her recipe for "Ice Pop-Corn Balls" employed sugar crystals to simulate ice. For Mary Hamilton Talbott's "Honey Pop Corn Balls" the binder was honey. Many recipes resorted to maple syrup as an ingredient. African-American scientist George Washington Carver published a popcorn ball recipe which combined roasted peanuts with the popcorn. Professional candy maker W. O. Rigby used raisins, which he believed made "a good looking as well as a choice eating novelty." Other flavorings and additives employed were molasses, strawberries, dried fruits, hazelnuts, walnuts, pecans, and marshmallows.[25]

Popcorn balls were not unique to the United States. They were probably made in Mexico and Guatemala well before they appeared in the United States. The initial appearance of popcorn balls in the United States shortly after the Mexican-American War suggests the possibility that soldiers and sailors engaged in the war and occupation of Mexico brought the concept back. Whatever its source, the idea captured the imaginations of Americans and quickly spread throughout the land and to other countries as well. Shortly after their appearance in the United States popcorn balls were mentioned in British culinary works. The first known British recipe for popcorn balls was published in *Skuse's Complete Confectioner,* which instructed its British readers that "corn berries" needed to be roasted "over a smokeless fire in a corn-popper." The popped corn was then coated in a syrup. The candied popcorn was set aside to dry, after which the process was repeated, and the resulting sticky concoction was then formed into ball shapes using a lemon squeezer.[26]

The concept, at least, of making popcorn balls may have been introduced into Japan by Japanese students studying in American colleges. Koto Yamada, a student at Vassar College, who was born in Yamanashi, Japan, created a recipe for "Japanese Pop-Corn Balls." There is no evidence that at the time popcorn was grown or consumed in Japan. Hence, her recipe included no popcorn but used popped rice and brown sugar to make the balls.[27]

Despite the general triumph of popcorn balls, there were detractors. Popcorn balls were not easy to make, and skill was required to avoid a mess. Homemade balls were sticky and not as attractive as those produced by professionals at fairs and amusement parks, but they were "far more palatable." Confectioners' popcorn balls, notwithstanding their "white beauty," were otherwise tasteless and inferior to the homemade kinds. By 1903 popcorn balls were already described as an "old fashioned sweet" that was clumsy and sticky and left "molasses on cheeks and chin."[28]

Making popcorn balls declined as the century progressed. However, as the twentieth century nears its end, there are some indicators that a revival may be under way. In recent years the American Pop Corn Company put onto the market a handheld Jolly Time's Pop Corn Ball Maker composed of durable molded plastic. This device takes the mess out of constructing the balls. In another development, Rygmyr Foods in South Saint Paul, Minnesota, recently introduced Popit brand popcorn balls flavored with caramel.[29]

Another sign belying the twilight of popcorn balls has been in the arena of world records. The residents of Peekskill, New York, under the direction of Chef Franz Eichenauer, a professor of culinary arts, crafted a mega popcorn ball measuring twelve feet in diameter. It used more than 2,000 pounds of popcorn, 4,000 pounds of sugar, 400 gallons of water, and 280 gallons of corn syrup. Not to be outdone, Sac County in Iowa, which had long claimed to be the "Popcorn Capitol of the World," created a 2,225 pound, six-foot-high popcorn ball in April 1995. A year later the Boy Scout troop in La Crosse, Wisconsin, produced one that weighed 2,377 pounds and measured more than seven feet long and twenty-three feet in circumference. According to the 1997 *Guinness Book of Records,* this holds the world's record for the largest popcorn ball ever constructed. However, this record will soon be officially broken. Trails End, a subsidiary of Weaver Popcorn headquartered in Van Buren, Indiana, underwrote the creation of a popcorn ball by the Boy Scouts. During a tour of fifty-two cities Trails End trucks carted the popcorn ball around the nation, and about 25,000 Boy Scouts added to it at each stop. This corresponded with a Boy Scout drive to sell Trails End popcorn. By the time the popcorn ball reached Van Buren in November 1997, it weighed over 7,200 pounds and easily topped the current record.[30] But for how long?

Popcorn Cakes

Popcorn cake recipes were also abundant during the late nineteenth and early twentieth centuries. Most cake recipes included ingredients similar to popcorn balls. The first located recipe was published by

E. F. Haskell. Her "Pop Corn Cakes," a creation similar to macaroons, was made of popcorn with eggs and sugar. They were baked without browning. According to Haskell, the resulting cakes were not larger than plums. *The Candy-Maker* recommended chopping up the popcorn and spreading it evenly in the bottom of a pan. A thin, hot syrup was poured over the corn up to two inches thick. Small businesses flattened their mixtures with cider presses or clothes wringers set wide.[31]

May Perrin Goff placed the mixture in a milk pan. A syrup composed of gum arabic or molasses, water, and sugar was poured over the kernels. While warm, the concoction was placed in tins and pressed by rollers into thin sheets. *Good Housekeeping* recommended placing the mixture into deep pans and pressing down on it with a flatiron. It was then turned out of the pan and cut into thick slices. Alice Bradley recommended using a rolling pin to make it as thin as possible. Marion Harris Neil's recipe for "Popcorn Griddle Cakes" used popcorn put through a food chopper to make a product similar to a pancake. Syrup or honey was poured over the top after frying on a hot griddle.[32]

The consumption of popcorn cakes was not limited to the United States. In Mexico producers made sweet cakes out of ground, unpopped grains. *Skuse's Complete Confectioner,* published in London, included a recipe for popcorn cakes in 1890. They were prepared similarly to popcorn balls, but the candied popcorn was packed densely into strong, slightly oiled square tins. When the candy cooled, the sheet was cut with a sharp knife. Other British recipes were published in subsequent cookbooks.[33]

Unlike other ready-to-eat popcorn snacks, cakes have survived—at least in some form. Conrad Rice Mill, Inc., in New Iberia, Louisiana, manufactures Konriko Brand Popcorn Cakes. These are made of puffed corn and brown rice and can be eaten plain or with a variety of toppings, such as peanut butter, jelly, cheese dips, and other spreads. Likewise, the Quaker Oats Company produces Strawberry Crunch, White Cheddar, Banana Nut, and Butter Popped corn cakes. Other commercial popcorn cakes are flavored with caramel.[34] Most modern corn cakes, however, are not made of popcorn but are composed of other varieties of maize.

Popcorn Crisps and Crispettes

Popcorn crisps and crispettes were also popular at the turn of the twentieth century. Most were commercial products similar to popcorn cakes. Crisps and crispettes were made by placing the corn and syrup mixture on marble slabs or breadboards and rolling it very thin. The mixture was then cut into pieces. By the late 1890s crisp and crispette machines were manufactured by W. Z. Long in Springfield, Ohio. These machines made uniform crisps for commercial production. Despite the automation, experience was essential for making crisps. If the kettle containing the syrup was not heated long enough, the crispettes ended up too sticky; if the syrup cooked too long they became brittle. A heaping teaspoonful of baking soda was added to the syrup just before it was poured onto the popcorn.[35]

The C. E. Dellenbarger Company of Chicago, another manufacturer of crispette machinery, published a pamphlet composed almost entirely of crisp and crispette recipes. Their recipe for "Chocolate Crispettes" substituted grated chocolate for the molasses. Dellenbarger published recipes for "Maple Crisp," "Golden Crisp," "Vanilla Crisp," "Strawberry Crisp," and "Plantation Popcorn Crispettes." A recipe for "Puffed Rice Crispettes" based on rice did not contain any popcorn.[36]

Other creations called "crisps" were similar to Cracker Jack, although with a variety of flavors. For instance, Coney Island Crisp was a mixture of syrup and popcorn flavored with strawberry, maple, vanilla, chocolate, or molasses. The coated popped kernels were ejected from the tank onto tables and spread out to cool. This was combined with peanuts or coconut and was akin to New Wrinkle Crispettes, a commercial product produced by the manufacturers of Cracker Jack. Cherokee Crisp was made similarly but with molasses, salt, and vanilla flavorings. Recipes for crisps and crispettes continued to be published until the Depression, after which they disappeared from cookbooks.[37]

Popcorn Candy

Popcorn candy was another popular turn-of-the-century confection. It was widely disseminated throughout the United States. During the early 1850s settlers migrating west in covered wagons made popcorn candy. This was probably similar to the recipe published by A. M. Collins in her *Great Western Cook Book,* which simply added popcorn to a recipe for "Molasses Candy." Collins also suggested that nuts could be treated in a similar fashion. Similar recipes were published in the first California cookbook and the first cookbook published in the Pacific Northwest. A recipe for "Crystalized Popcorn" published in the 1880s instructed the cook to stir popcorn into a combination of sugar, boiling water, and butter. When the popped corn had absorbed the candy, each flake was separated. Mary Wright flavored the popped flakes with strawberry, orange, maple, or melted chocolate. They were then dried on greased or waxed paper. She suggested that these kernels could "be used to decorate other sweets or may be served in little baskets or odd receptacles."[38]

Popcorn candy ranked prominently among the first ready-to-eat commercial products. The first located popcorn trademark was issued to

George E. Clark of Cleveland, Ohio, in 1883 for "Sugar Coated Pop-Corn." His symbol was an elephant with the word "Jumbo" on its saddle, which was associated with the circus elephant of the same name. In New Orleans popcorn candy was covered in sugar or rolled into small balls while still hot. These were wrapped in dainty rolls of tissue paper and sold along the streets of the city.[39]

In January 1896 Chicago's Rueckheim brothers named their peanut and popcorn combination "Cracker Jack." The commercial product did not differ substantially from previously published recipes for popcorn candy, some of which encouraged adding nuts to the popcorn. Cracker Jack quickly became the rage, and recipes for homemade versions appeared in cookbooks shortly after the commercial product was first marketed. In 1897 Constance Wachtmeister and Kate Buffington Davis included two unusual popcorn candy recipes in their vegetarian cookbook: one, titled "Cracker Jack," mixed popcorn with just the sugar and molasses; the second was for "Choc-o-Pop," which mixed popped corn with sugar, molasses, and chocolate—a product similar to one produced by the Cracker Jack Company decades later.[40]

Other recipes titled "Cracker Jack" were dissimilar to the commercial product. The Knights of the Globe Home in Freeport, Illinois, published a recipe for "K. of G. Cracker Jack," which included popcorn and peanuts but was formed into small balls. Other recipes for homemade Cracker Jack employed butter, sorghum, soda, cream of tartar, and various almond extract and vanilla flavorings. A sister of the Church of the Brethren, J. W. Miller of Hereford, Texas, published a recipe titled "Cracker Jack" without any popcorn. It consisted of a syrup composed of sugar, vinegar, and the whites of two eggs mixed with rolled nuts (walnuts were preferred), which was poured on top of crackers.[41]

Soups, Salads, and Entrées

Throughout its history popcorn has been largely used as a confection. During the early twentieth century popcorn was also employed as an ingredient in foods. For instance, it was used in soups and salads. Fannie Merritt Farmer appears to be the first cookbook author to suggest that popcorn be added to soup. In her 1905 recipe for "Clam and Corn Soup" she recommended that popped corn be added to garnish the dish. Evidently the suggestion took hold: the following year Amelia Sulzbacher announced that it was "a pleasing conceit of today to sprinkle large and perfect grains of freshly popped corn over light, thin cream soups" just as each portion was served. Floating on the surface of the soup, the popped kernels were "certainly attractive" and were "also a most excellent substitute for wafers or croutons." A writer in *Good*

Housekeeping replaced crackers with popcorn for corn chowder because it was "a pleasing novelty." Evidently President Theodore Roosevelt enjoyed this novelty. Poppy Cannon and Patricia Brooks, authors of *The Presidents' Cookbook,* claimed that Roosevelt consumed his corn chowder with popcorn.[42]

Popcorn was used as a thickening agent in Mary Hamilton Talbott's recipe for "Pop-Corn Soup." Her recipe combined one quart of scalded milk with one can of corn. This was pressed through a sieve and seasoned with salt, pepper, and butter. A handful of popcorn was used to thicken the soup. It was topped off with a dollop of whipped cream and sprinkled with popcorn flakes just before serving. In another recipe Talbott recommended heating peas in a quart of milk and pressing them through a sieve, then adding popcorn mixed with a few bread crumbs. Before serving, a teaspoonful of popped corn was added to each bowlful of soup. A writer in *American Cooking* reported that crisp popcorn instead of croutons in soup was delicious. K. M. Palmer recommended popcorn be used to garnish cream of tomato soup. In his *Gentleman's Companion* world traveler Charles Baker asserted that garlic popcorn made excellent croutons for soup. He warned, however, to be sure to add the popcorn kernels "at moment of service, or they will be soggy and tough."[43]

While Native Americans may not have popped corn during the colonial period, they quickly adopted it after the mid nineteenth century. The Canadian anthropologist F. W. Waugh described how the Iroquois prepared "Popcorn Soup or Hominy." Popped corn was ground into meal and was boiled along with venison or beef. Another method was to sweeten the soup by adding maple syrup and eat it cold with milk.[44]

Several writers recommended popcorn in salads. In 1906 Amelia Sulzbacher, writing in *Good Housekeeping,* recommended "another clever idea," which was to serve fresh buttered popcorn with salad. The combination was, according to the author, "delicious and the corn should be tastefully arranged, encircling a mound of salad." Mary Hamilton Talbott offered a variety of salads with popcorn. In one recipe she sliced bananas into halves, scooped out the centers, and stuffed them with ground popcorn. The stuffed bananas were served on lettuce with mayonnaise dressing. In a second recipe she mixed chopped celery, raisins, and rolled popcorn and served it "on lettuce or any salad green with mayonnaise dressing." A third recipe combined apples with rolled popped corn and chopped celery. It was presented in apple cups or on lettuce leaves. Another consisted of boiled potatoes, chopped celery, and ground popcorn. Salt and pepper were sprinkled on top along with mayonnaise. Just before serving the salad was dressed with half a pint of whipped cream. Riley Fletcher-Berry simplified Talbott's salad recipes and recommended serving them with ground popcorn and grated cheese seasoned with paprika and mayonnaise.[45] Despite such creative élan, popcorn soup and popcorn salad disappeared from the American table.

Other recipes stuffed popcorn into dates and turkeys. Popcorn was folded into omelets, stuffed into sandwiches, and served with bacon. Popcorn products were served as main courses and with entrées. Popcorn was recommended for consumption at breakfast, lunch, and dinner, as well as for the between-meal snack. Popcorn was glued together with molasses or other sweetening and converted into containers for other confections. Others were concerned with how to serve popcorn. One source examined the possibilities of serving popcorn in corn cribs, cups, wooden baskets, and salad bowls.[46]

By the early twentieth century hundreds of popcorn recipes had appeared in women's magazines, government bulletins, and pamphlets published by corporations engaged in promoting their products. Assessing the impact of these recipes is difficult. The vast majority of recipes that appeared in nontraditional cookery ephemera were experiments that died quiet deaths. Some recipes reflected more enduring traditions. Popcorn pudding, balls, cakes, and candy, especially Cracker Jack, were themes that survived and thrived.

By the late 1930s popcorn was the queen of the confection world and was poised to become a mainstream staple. As promising as this potential was, home popcorn cookery abruptly declined. The major reason for this rapid demise of popcorn cookery in the home was ironically due to the overwhelming success of commercial ready-to-eat popcorn products and popcorn's conquest of movie theaters. By the late 1940s popcorn was again considered solely a confection or a snack food. The promotion of movie popcorn and prepopped snacks was so successful that most Americans continue to have difficulty conceiving of popcorn as an ingredient in soups, salads, or main dishes.

Chapter 5

Early Pop Pros

The first professionals on the commercial popcorn scene were seedsmen who purveyed raw popcorn kernels to growers. Seedsmen started selling popcorn seed at least as early as the mid-1820s. At first this was not a particularly lucrative trade as most farmers reserved their own seed stock for future use. Farmers were urged "to keep the variety as pure as possible by selecting slender and small-sized, but well-filled, ears for seed, and in no case to plant such as may have yellow or any foreign sort intermixed." In practice this advice was difficult to follow. Cross-fertilization easily occurred between field corn and popcorn, and contamination resulted. An increase of kernel size usually indicated deterioration. As kernels increased in size, popping expansion declined and the volume of unpopped kernels increased.[1] Since maintaining purity was difficult when other types of maize was cultivated in close proximity, growers found it easier to buy seeds directly from seedsmen rather than raise them in isolation for later planting.

Another factor encouraging farmers to purchase seeds was the increased availability of diverse popcorn varieties. One of the first descriptions of a popcorn variety appeared in John Russell Bartlett's *Dictionary of Americanisms* in 1848. The editor described it as "of a dark color, with small grain." The following year J. H. Salisbury identified three as "pop" corns: Blue Pop, Yellow Pop, and White Pop. Also in 1849 Ebenezer Emmons described three popcorns. Emmons was particularly taken with "a beautiful variety of maize" which he named

"Lady Finger." Its ear was "quite small, slender, delicate and white." It grew on a seven-foot high stalk that bore an ear or two with small kernels. Emmons considered Lady Finger "by far the best" variety. As previously mentioned, it probably originated in South America. A second variety, "Canada pop-corn" or "Egyptian corn," Emmons described as having a small reddish cob with yellow, blue, or dark purplish-red kernels. The third variety was rice popcorn, whose kernels came in both white and yellow varieties with pointed ends. Its ear was from four to six inches long, and it bore three to four ears on a stalk. Emmons considered it "a beautiful variety, and probably one of the richest and sweetest."[2]

Susan Fenimore Cooper mentioned two varieties of popcorn: rice-corn and Egyptian corn, "the last kind being a native of this country, like the others." Other varieties of popcorn included chicken corn and Valparaiso Corn. Another was called Brazilian Pop-corn, identified by Mississippi farmer M. W. Phillips. Its kernels were purple. Each ear was about three and one-half inches long and three-quarters of an inch at its largest diameter. The editor of the *Country Gentleman* believed that Brazilian Pop-corn was the "*prettiest* thing of its kind."[3]

Seedsman Fearing Burr identified two commercial popcorn varieties in 1863. One had a kernel that was "roundish, flattened, glossy, flinty, or rice-like, and of a dull, semi-transparent, white color." When popped, it was "of pure snowy whiteness, very brittle, tender, and well flavored." Growers planted it on hills three feet apart or in drilled rows three feet apart. It produced a similar quantity of bushels of ears that the same land would yield of shelled field corn. The second variety, according to Burr, was yellow in color. Its popped kernels were tender but not so mild flavored as the white variety. The yellow color was considered objectionable according to the taste of that time, and consequently it was cultivated only as a novelty.[4]

New popcorn varieties proliferated during the late nineteenth and early twentieth centuries. The 1875 edition of the *American Cyclopedia* reported, "Several varieties are known as pop-corn, of which there are white and yellow kinds, those with kernels pointed at the ends, and others with the grain of the ordinary shape." Three years later William D. Emerson noted seven, including Early Yellow Pop, Joint Pop, and Pearl Pop. In 1884 E. Lewis Sturtevant described ten varieties, including Nonpareil, Silver Laced, Twelve-Rowed White, Dwarf Golden, Golden, Miniature Maze, White Pearl, Red Pearl, Egyptian, and Bear's Foot. In 1890 Thomas J. Burrill and George W. McClure of the Illinois Agricultural Experiment Station tested thirteen, such as Blush, Monarch Rice, White Rice, Page's Striped Rice, California, Common White, Pearl, Mapledale Prolific, Silver Lace, and Tom Thumb. By 1899 Sturtevant had identified twenty-five varieties, including Small Pearl, Golden, Black Pop, Negro Pop, Blue Pearl, Lemon Pearl, Golden Queen, White's Variegated, Rice Pop, Amber Rice, Red Rice, and Yellow Rice. In 1900 a correspondent in the *Louisville Commercial* reported that he had tried over forty popcorn types. From a commercial standpoint, claimed the author, the only significant ones were the "eight-rowed large, smooth-grained, early flint sorts, the squirrel-tooth or rice sorts, and the miniature or the flower-garden sorts."[5]

By the turn of the twentieth century almost all seedsmen distributed popcorn seeds. In 1903 W. W. Tracy compiled an extensive list of vegetable varieties noted in seedsmen's catalogs. He noted fifty-two popcorn varieties:

Table of Popcorn Varieties Sold by Seedsmen in 1901–1902

Amber Rice	Pearl
Black Diamond	Pride of Hiram
Boy's Favorite	Red Beauty
Buckbee's Snowball	Red Rice
California Yellow	Rice
Cook's Improved Egyptian	Ruby Beauty
Dye	Salzer's Silver Ball
Early Amber Rice	Silver Ball
Early White Rice	Silver Lace
Egyptian	Small White Bow
Excelsior	Smooth White
German White Rice	Snowball
Golden Dwarf	Striped
Golden Queen	Striped Beauty
Golden Tom Thumb	Striped Rice
Golden Yellow	Tattooed
Illinois Snowball	Tattooed Yankee
Improved White Rice	Tom Thumb
Mapledale Prolific	Variegated
Miniature	White
Monarch	White Market
Monarch Red Rice	White Pearl
Monarch White Rice	White Rice
Nonpareil White	Wisconsin Eight-Rowed
Old Homestead White Rice	Wisconsin Prolific
Page's Striped Rice	Yellow Rice

Many popcorn names cited by Tracy, of course, were synonymous, and others were novelties. The most popular varieties, based on the number of seedsmen who carried them, were Golden Queen, Rice, White Rice, and Silver Lace, the latter of which was also called White Pearl.[6]

Until about 1925 White Rice, Queen's Golden, Japanese Hulless, and Spanish were the only varieties in commercial production, with White Rice the most popular. White Rice (also known as Snowball, Wisconsin Prolific) was an early commercial variety recognized by Fearing Burr in 1863. The plant was hardy and prolific, but the flakes were less crisp and tender than those of other varieties. As it was a tough flake, it was employed early on to make commercial popcorn candy. Queen's Golden was marketed in the 1880s by a gardener in Indiana named Mr. Queen, who claimed that it was so far ahead of all others "as to be beyond comparison in every respect, in yield, in sturdy growth, in size and in color when popped—being of a delicate golden yellow." When popped it was exceedingly tender with a delicious and delicate taste. Others agreed with Queen's assessment.[7]

Among the most significant new varieties to appear before World War II were the Japanese Hulless and the Spanish, whose names were misnomers. Neither the Japanese nor the Spanish cultivated popcorn early in the twentieth century and hence did not develop any varieties, hull-less or otherwise. How they acquired their names and where they originated are unknown. The term "hulless" is also incorrect: popcorn needs a hull (or pericarp) to pop fully. However, some hulls are thinner than others, and some are translucent. The hull of the Japanese Hulless was more translucent than that of other varieties at the time. The Spanish variety was the first used in the caramel popcorn industry. It was a flint corn with mediocre popping expansion. However, "the large kernel and the tough texture of the flakes adapted this variety well to caramel popcorn processing."[8]

During the 1930s several new varieties became significant. One of the most important was South American, which shared characteristics found in popcorn from Argentina and Paraguay. It was yellow in color. Its peculiar "mushrooming" shape caught the public's fancy. Its ability to withstand processing caught the attention of popcorn manufacturers, who used it in making caramel confections. How the South American variety arrived in the United States has been a matter of discussion ever since it miraculously appeared in Kansas City during the 1920s. Some maintained that a friend of Luther Burbank sent the seeds to him from South America. Burbank purportedly grew them, and the first year's production was stored in a vault "for safe keeping until it could be used or distributed in quantities to growers in other sections of the country."

Others doubted that the variety was in fact imported from South America. Whatever its source, it became one of the most popular pre–World War II varieties.[9]

Growers

The first major popcorn growing area was New England. After the Civil War commercial cultivation spread westward. By the 1870s and 1880s cultivating popcorn was still only a marginally profitable business for farmers near large markets. The editors of the *Country Gentleman* reported that a farmer near Buffalo, New York, raised an acre of popcorn. Its yield was similar to other varieties of yellow corn, but the grower had to plant twice as much popcorn. It therefore required twice the work to cultivate and harvest. In addition, extra time and expense were required for marketing popcorn. However, there was always a limited market for popcorn "at a higher price than field corn, in northern towns."[10]

Popcorn growing continued in New England on a declining scale, but it mushroomed throughout the Midwest before the turn of the twentieth century. The earliest known popcorn grower in the Midwest was Nathan Ferris, who planted about fifty acres in 1846 on his farm near Galesburg, Illinois. This produced from fifteen hundred to eighteen hundred bushels of popcorn. Ferris shipped one hundred barrels to New York and twenty barrels to England. Ferris followed his popcorn barrels (and other merchandise) to Europe where he tried to sell it. Through the U.S. ambassador in the United Kingdom, Ferris purportedly became acquainted with Prince Albert, the husband of Queen Victoria, and claimed to have exchanged letters with the prince. In some secondary accounts Ferris actually met Queen Victoria, who was amused with popcorn. Despite this allegation, no one in England was interest in buying Ferris's popcorn. As the popcorn that Ferris sent to New York failed to sell well, he grew no more.[11]

Despite Ferris's failure, others grew popcorn in the Midwest after the Civil War and were more successful. Chicago quickly became the hub of the industry. The most important popcorn-growing area prior to World War II was Iowa, particularly Sac and Ida Counties. C. W. Cook, founder of the Cook Ranch, introduced the first popcorn to Sac County during the 1870s. George O. Colton, originally from Illinois, planted popcorn in 1884. The soil and climatic conditions were ideal for cultivating popcorn. When popcorn sales increased, the industry thrived. One man leased a farm of 160 acres and bought equipment on time. He planted 45 acres of popcorn and increased this to 65 the second year. He grossed a total of three thousand dollars in two years, an extremely handsome income at the time. By the 1890s the Iowa State Agricultural

Society was awarding farmers and boys for the best popcorn grown in Iowa.[12] By the beginning of the twentieth century, popcorn growing occupied the attention of a good many farmers.

The first popcorn firm in Ida County was that of Reuber and Bruce, which was founded about 1893. By 1914 this firm shipped popcorn from coast to coast and "from Canada to the far-off Gulf." Soon other firms established operations in Odebolt, Iowa. So great was the demand for popcorn that competition bristled among dealers, and growers received the "best possible prices." One reason for the heightened demand for popcorn was that confectionery manufacturers were acquiring the bulk of the crop. Some ground the popcorn into flour and used it as an ingredient in chocolate candy. Popcorn flour permitted the chocolate candy "to stand up as no other ingredient will make it." Candy firms bought popcorn by the carloads. In 1912 a popcorn shortage hit the market. Confectionery houses reported great difficulty in acquiring an adequate supply. Popcorn manufacturers paid as much as $3.60 per bushel. Popcorn growers received up to $1.25, but some demanded $1.50. The difference was pocketed by popcorn processors.[13]

As the demand for popcorn increased, growers realized that almost any land which grew field corn was suitable for popcorn. As popcorn prices increased, growing areas in other states expanded. Even before the turn of the twentieth century popcorn was grown extensively in Valley County in central Nebraska and in four or five counties in northeastern Kansas. The autumn weather in these counties was more favorable for curing raw popcorn. During 1916 and 1917 the popcorn crop in Sac and Ida Counties failed to mature. The price skyrocketed. In 1918 nearly every farmer in these two counties planted popcorn. Some planted as much as 150 acres. This backlashed in oversupply: the price dropped to less than a dollar, and millions of pounds could not be sold at any price.[14]

During the Depression hard times hit Iowa, Nebraska, and Kansas. An unprecedented series of disastrous droughts created a dust bowl and devastated the traditional popcorn-growing areas. When popcorn prices increased, scattered growers in Illinois, Indiana, Kentucky, and Ohio jumped on the wagon. These growers found popcorn "very profitable during the years when the total production of the country was at a low ebb." This regional diversity in growing popcorn was a boon for the industry.[15] Popcorn with different characteristics could be grown in different climatic and soil conditions. This diversity supported the rapid growth of the industry and strengthened popcorn's commercial germplasm base. Although Iowa remained the dominant popcorn-producing state, its lead deteriorated. After World War II, Iowa relinquished its commanding position as other states predominated.

Processors

Growing popcorn was relatively easy. Launching a popcorn processing company was much harder. Special cribs for curing popcorn were needed. A considerable quantity of popcorn needed to be raised in one locality to make processing it financially worthwhile. Outlets for the popcorn needed to be developed, and then the popcorn needed to be transported to the vendors. It was difficult for a grower to perform all these tasks. About the 1880s popcorn processors emerged as middlemen between the farmers and the grocery stores, concessionaires, and manufacturers. Some processors grew their own popcorn, but most contracted with farmers for specific amounts. After farmers harvested their crop, processors stored, dried, processed, and marketed the grain in bulk quantities. Processors distributed it to grocery stores, vendors, and producers of ready-to-eat popcorn.

The Albert Dickinson Company had been launched by A. F. Dickinson in 1854. When his health failed in 1872, his son Albert Dickinson took over the seed business. The company later claimed that it was the "World's Oldest Popcorn Company," although exactly when Dickinson began selling popcorn is unclear. Unfortunately, the early records for the company have not been located. Ted Meland, a mid-twentieth-century Dickinson executive, concluded that the company commenced selling popcorn during the 1870s. The first located Dickinson advertisement that mentioned popcorn was published in the Chicago *Grocer's Bulletin* in 1882. Only "Pop Corn" appeared in large, bold print, suggesting that the Albert Dickinson Company already emphasized it as a major product. Throughout the 1880s and 1890s the company advertised extensively in *Grocer's Criterion, Grocer's Regulator,* and the national agricultural publication *Prairie Farmer.* Soon sales exceeded the company's ability to produce kernels. Dickinson contracted with farmers in Illinois to deliver popcorn at preset prices. In 1888 the company contracted with farmers in Odebolt, Iowa, and Ord, Nebraska. With its supply secured, Dickinson was able to meet increased demand, and business boomed. In 1891 the company sold 502 bags of popcorn for a total of $746, which is thought to have been the largest single sale of popcorn to that date.[16]

Processors initially sold on-the-ear corn in bulk quantities. During the 1890s grocers started to demand shelled popcorn. Ear popcorn in 100- or 150-pound burlap bags or barrels took up too much floor space, while boxes of shelled corn were smaller and easier to handle, and occupied less space. Shelled kernels were also sold in bulk barrels and sacks, but unless the volume of sales was high enough and the stock sold quickly, the kernels dried out and their ability to pop declined. In addition, popcorn cobs or kernels in barrels and burlap bags needed to be scooped out, placed in small bags, and weighed before selling. Boxes required no such procedures and were more convenient for the shopper as well as the grocer. Finally, open barrels and bags were easily accessible to insects and rodents. As sanitary and health conditions of the nation's food supply were under the spotlight of reformers around the turn of the twentieth century, small cardboard boxes became the containers of choice. While cardboard was not airtight and did not prevent kernels from drying out, the small boxes were usually sold more quickly than the large barrels, thus minimizing moisture loss and popping deterioration.

This simple shift to cardboard boxes launched another revolution in popcorn preparation and packaging. Unpopped popcorn had previously been sold as a generic item: it was identified usually only by its variety. Cardboard packaging presented an opportunity to change this. During the 1890s the Albert Dickinson Company became the first popcorn company to trademark brand names and place labels on its boxes. Its first brand name was Snow Ball Shelled Rice Pop-Corn, introduced in November 15, 1891. This trademark featured a representation of a popper filled with popped corn along with the company monogram "The A D Co." Their second brand name, launched in August 1892, was Yankee popcorn. A conventional picture of Uncle Sam decorated the label, and there were red, white, and blue stripes on the box. Dickinson sold shelled popcorn under the name Santa Claus. The company's visualization was a conventional Santa Claus with snowflakes. The Albert Dickinson Company subsequently trademarked other brand names including Danny Boy Hulless Pop Corn, Dickinson's Little Buster, and Dickinson's Big Buster Brand Yellow Pop Corn. Company advertisements proudly announced that its popcorn was "Guaranteed to Pop."[17]

As the demand for popcorn increased, new processors jumped into the field. Sam Nelson, born in Grinnell, Iowa, in December 1879, began vending popcorn as a child. Early on, Nelson recognized the need for a superior grade of popcorn and scientific cultivation. Within a few years he claimed to produce one of the finest grades of popcorn, which he named "Amber Rice Pop Corn." Nelson raised fifty acres of his selected seed and claimed that it was the best popping corn on the market. It yielded from four to five more bags of popped corn per pound than any other known brand. These results were so gratifying that Nelson subsequently planted three hundred acres, which yielded over seven hundred thousand pounds of Amber Rice Pop Corn. He sold it to grocery stores and confectioners for ten cents per pound. As Nelson's price was higher than his competitors', he decided to inform potential consumers about the high quality of his premium popcorn. To assist him in this task he created a special cartoon character known as "Kernel Pop." This legendary character charged into newspaper advertisements and gained a great deal of prominence. He figured in the "Who's Who" of famous advertising characters, *Printers Ink,* a trade newspaper advertising magazine. The opening announcement for the advertising campaign read:

> "Kernel Pop" salutes you. His army of Nelson poppers is at your service. Every man is a shooter—every shot a big, fluffy, white kernel. Just give 'em a chance to warm into action; they're eager to pop! The pick of Iowa's best, waiting to cheer your fall and winter evenings. When a heaping bowl of this delicious crisp, fluffy, white Nelson's pop corn, with melted butter and salt, is just about the best ever.

Kernel Pop championed the ability of Nelson's corn to pop. One heading on an advertisements was: "When Kernel Pop says 'Fire' you just bet they all shoot." Another read: "every man will do his duty, Kernel Pop knows his Nelson army—knows every man is ready and eager to shoot." This aggressive campaign paid off. Within a few short years Nelson's company occupied the forefront of popcorn production with customers from Maine to California and from Canada to the Gulf Coast. "Kernel Pop" became a household name across the country. Nelson assured readers that great care was taken in packing his popcorn, which was "stored in absolutely mouse and rat proof cribs." He reported that, while there were many grades of popcorn, his Amber Rice variety passed the "highest popping test," and was "free from that hard and objectionable center found in most grades of pop corn."[18]

Popcorn had long been looked upon solely as a snack food. Few processors realized its possibilities as an ingredient in general cookery. Popcorn had a recognized food value containing a high percentage of protein, claimed Nelson. He urged Americans to use popcorn "frequently in every home" because it was "nutritious, wholesome and appetizing." To enhance his beliefs and promote his company, Nelson hired Mary Hamilton Talbott—a well-known recipe writer for the leading women's magazines—to write a booklet, *Pop Corn Recipes,* which was published in 1916. The pamphlet urged readers to employ popcorn "with various dishes for regular meals, as well as for entertainment, for an evening by the fireside, or upon the occasion of 'company' to whom you wish to present something new, or at least unusual." And truly unusual were the recipes in this booklet. It included over thirty-five, categorized under such headings as breakfast dishes, desserts, salads, soups, sandwiches, pies, candies, meat substitutes, and vegetables.[19] Nelson is the first processor known to have published a cookery booklet.

By 1915 Nelson was one of the largest producers of popcorn in the United States. The following year he expanded his popcorn cultivation to five hundred acres and commenced building a processing plant. In July 1916 Nelson traveled to Chicago to interest Sprague, Warner & Company in retailing his popcorn. While on the trip, he died unexpectedly of pneumonia and a weak heart.[20] After Nelson's death the company declined and was liquidated by his family.

Although few enterprises ended as abruptly as Nelson's did, most early popcorn processors did not thrive long. Most either went bankrupt or were purchased by other processors. An example of the buy-out pattern was a popcorn company founded in 1920 by Carl Erne, a farmer, and August "Gus" Fischer, a barber who had emigrated from Germany to America before World War I. Residents of Wall Lake, Iowa, they founded Erne Fischer, which was subsequently renamed Popcorn Growers and Distributors. Erne and Fischer were known for their flamboyant style and outrageous products. One product was colored popcorn. They achieved this by boiling popcorn seeds in colored water. The trouble with the idea was that the color change was mainly external with only a slight tint inside. As a novelty, it survived and is still sold today, although not by Popcorn Growers and Distributors. In 1955 the National Oats Company bought the company out.[21]

There were many exceptions to the failure or sell-out patterns. One was the Bennett Popcorn Company in Schaller, Iowa. D. D. Bennett grew popcorn on fifteen acres in 1899. His son, D. J. Bennett, continued growing popcorn. Just before the outbreak of World War II he sold popcorn to an Omaha elevator operator, who unfortunately was having difficulty selling it. Bennett and his sons shoveled the kernels into a Ford pickup truck and delivered them to regional distributors and retailers. This gave them the idea to go into business for themselves as popcorn processors. In 1916 Bennett and his sons established the Bennett Popcorn Company. Business was slow in the early years, but they continually made progress. When the Depression hit, the Bennetts sold out to Leonard Blewitt, who renamed the operation the Central Popcorn Company. Blewitt expanded the facilities and marketed Bang-O brand popcorn. During the 1960s Central was renamed Consolidated Popcorn Company. Two stockholders in Central Popcorn Company in 1934 were Forest and Leona Wanberg. They had been involved in the popcorn industry since 1923. From the sale of their shares in 1958, they created the Wanberg Popcorn Company.[22]

Another exception was the American Pop Corn Company, founded by Cloid Smith and his son Howard Smith in 1914. Cloid Smith was raised in a farming family in Sac County, Iowa. Popcorn was grown in the county, and his family popped corn often when Smith was a boy. Smith managed a drugstore and in 1899 established the first local telephone exchange in Odebolt. In 1905 Smith became the general manager of the New State Telephone Company. When local exchanges were consolidated, the office was moved to Sioux City. The telephone system was sold to Bell Telephone Company in 1912. Smith remained general manager but sold his interest in the company. With part of the money from this sale, he bought land north of Odebolt, where a tenant farmer raised popcorn. The tenant farmer sold his popcorn to a buyer, but the price was low. Smith argued with the buyer. The buyer reportedly remarked: "If you don't like the way I do business, why don't you go into the pop corn business yourself?"[23]

Cloid Smith did just that. In 1913 he planted popcorn on his Odebolt farm. He harvested it by hand and transported it by wagon sixty miles to his home in Sioux City, where he shelled it—also by hand. Smith's wife and son washed it in large tubs. The first popcorn sold in 1914 was a twenty-five-pound shipment to a man in Council Bluffs. By the end of the first year Smith had sold over seventy-five thousand pounds of popcorn. How the name "Jolly Time" originated is unclear. Family tradition has it that Cloid Smith settled on the name while dining with a friend during the first year of operation. The American Pop Corn Company staff members are fond of saying (without apology) that the name just popped up. Jolly Time has been the flagship brand of the American Pop Corn Company ever since.[24]

On October 28, 1915, Cloid Smith resigned his position as manager of the New State Telephone Company to work full-time building the American Pop Corn Company. According to an article in the *Odebolt Chronicle*, the business had "assumed such proportions" that it was "imperative for him to give it all his attention." Rather than continuing to transport popcorn sixty miles from Odebolt to Sioux City, Smith decided to construct a storage crib in Sac County. The crib was especially designed to provide maximum ventilation for natural air drying. In 1916 the America Pop Corn Company began advertising Jolly Time. Its first advertisement, titled "Pop Corn That Pops," reported that Jolly Time gave the "smallest percentage of waste and greatest volume of popped corn." It was cured on the cob and packed in heavy jute bags.[25]

The American Pop Corn Company built another storage crib in Schaller, Iowa. Before completion, it was sold to James L. Bruce, formerly of Reuber and Bruce, who had incorporated the Iowa Pop Corn Company. Cloid Smith was a stockholder and director of the company. When the Iowa Pop Corn Company was dissolved in 1926, the property was reacquired by the American Pop Corn Company. In the same year the partnership between the father and son was dissolved, and the American Pop Corn Company was incorporated.[26]

The American Pop Corn Company's first pound carton was constructed of cardboard and displayed a bright green Jolly Time label.

However, cardboard boxes admitted air, which dried out the popcorn or increased the moisture content depending on the humidity. One potential solution was to seal the popcorn in glass jars, which Jolly Time did in 1920. The good news was that the kernels in the airtight package did not lose or gain moisture until opened; the bad news was that glass was expensive and breakage was high. Smith approached the American Can Company in Chicago, and a revolutionary solution resulted in 1924—popcorn hermetically sealed in a can. It was purportedly the forerunner of the modern beer can. The following year the American Pop Corn Company introduced this new creation to the market and conducted an extensive advertising campaign stressing the value of packaging popcorn in hermetically sealed cans.[27]

The introduction of the metal container in 1925 sparked an increase in the sale of packaged popcorn, requiring an expanded sales force. In addition to selling popcorn, the American Pop Corn Company also offered a full line of popcorn supplies, including popping oil, salt, cartons, and glassine bags. Vendors could buy everything they needed from one supplier. The American Pop Corn Company developed a network of food brokers to distribute Jolly Time to grocers and wholesalers. A monthly newsletter called the *Jolly Time Booster* targeted popcorn machine operators.[28]

A national network of brokers also made it possible for the American Pop Corn Company to advertise nationally. In the fall of 1925 Jolly Time advertisements appeared in *Good Housekeeping;* in 1929 they were placed in *Hollands Magazine, Liberty Magazine, Modern Priscilla,* and the *Saturday Evening Post.* Jolly Time advertisements were also published in metropolitan newspapers across the country. By 1929 a total of 162 newspapers carried promotions during the fall and winter season in the United States and Canada. This promotion made 1929 a record-breaking year for Jolly Time. Sales increased nearly 20 percent above the previous year. A subsequent promotion offered an electric popper for a dollar to Jolly Time users. The booklet that accompanied the popper offered directions for using the popper, games for children, and recipes for making popcorn balls, cheese snacks, chocolate popcorn, and fudge and caramel corn.[29]

The American Pop Corn Company soon claimed to be the largest seller of popcorn. In addition to Jolly Time, the company also marketed other brands, including Crown White, Little Wonder, Magic Pop, Jiffy, American Beauty, Thunderbolt, and South American. In 1939 the company decided to use only the Jolly Time brand name—a policy that was not changed until 1988 when it released its environmentally friendly American's Best Pop Corn, followed in 1995 by a microwavable low-fat version, which were grown without chemical pesticides.[30]

Many other popcorn processors sprouted before World War II. One successful operation was started by Reverend Ira E. Weaver of the Church of the Brethren, who first grew popcorn in 1927 to supplement his income. Weaver planted ten acres. Like other early processors, Weaver and his sons harvested, shucked, and bagged the popcorn by hand. He sold his popcorn in a horse-drawn wagon to neighbors and nearby markets. Based in Van Buren, Indiana, the Weaver Popcorn Company grew steadily.[31]

A few years after Jacob A. McCarty graduated from Purdue University in 1915, he became the first agricultural agent for Vanderburgh County, Indiana. In 1921 he launched a business that eventually was named the J. A. McCarty Seed Company. It sold agricultural equipment and seeds. About 1935 McCarty began growing and processing the yellow variety of South American popcorn on a small scale. At first some of his popcorn seeds ended up as poultry feed. As yellow popcorn came into demand by theater owners, McCarty increased his acreage. During the winter of 1938–1939 the company purchased a grain elevator from General Foods near Evansville, Indiana, and converted it into a popcorn processing plant. By 1940 McCarty heavily concentrated on popcorn. By the time America entered World War II, the J. A. McCarty Seed Company was an important popcorn processor.[32]

Another processor that would rise in importance after World War II was launched in 1935 by W. Hoover Brown of Marion, Ohio. When the federal government attempted to raise commodity prices by limiting the amount of acreage under cultivation, popcorn was not regulated. Brown decided to raise and market popcorn. He purchased seed from the Robinson Popcorn Company in Cleveland. As fate would have it, popcorn was in short supply in 1935, and Brown made a considerable profit. This success encouraged him to move into popcorn in a bigger way the following year. He converted an abandoned one-room schoolhouse into a processing plant, where the popcorn was dried, shelled, cleaned, bagged, and stored. W. Hoover Brown's son, George Brown, worked in the building during the summer, scooping up popcorn ears and placing them in a hopper. Years later he reported that "the dust and heat in the summertime was frightening." The Browns' first crib held 100 tons of popcorn. Later cribs were constructed with 150-ton capacities. Hoover Brown named his new popcorn company Wyandot Popcorn Company after the Wyandot Indians and Wyandot County.[33]

Processors performed a variety of functions. They usually contracted with farmers to produce popcorn and sometimes also grew it themselves. They stored the popcorn until the moisture was right for processing. Processing was a complex series of tasks. Popcorn ears were run along a broad sorting belt where moldy ears or those badly damaged were removed by hand. The ears were then run through a sheller to separate the kernels from the cobs and chaff. A fan blasted away light materials. A gravity separator excluded light or damaged kernels. Another machine polished the kernels. The cobs and kernels were often fumigated to kill insects and their eggs. Finally, the kernels were packaged.[34]

While the Albert Dickinson Company survived World War II, it played a progressively less important part in the popcorn industry.[35] Conversely, the American Pop Corn Company, the Wyandot Popcorn Company, the Blevins Popcorn Company, the Weaver Popcorn Company, the Central Popcorn Company, and the J. A. McCarty Seed Company thrived during World War II. After the war these companies emerged as America's leading popcorn producers.

Vendors

Vendors sold popcorn and popcorn products at public gatherings by the 1840s. Popcorn balls were peddled by street hawkers in Boston by the wagon loads. One entrepreneurial seller, Daniel Fobes, decided to use maple syrup rather than the more costly molasses as the binding force for his popcorn balls. During the presidential election of 1848 he sold his product at political rallies for Zachary Taylor and Millard Fillmore. He expanded his business through a series of partnerships and an ever-increasing sale of candy products. The firm Fobes founded was one of the three components that made up the New England Confectionary Company (NECCO). The company still survives today as does its popular NECCO Wafers. Hanging on the wall of the president's office in Cambridge, Massachusetts, is a painting of Daniel Fobes selling popcorn balls.[36]

During the 1850s many reports of popcorn vendors appeared in travelogues and newspaper accounts. British traveler James Johnston observed that "Boys with baskets attend upon the cars at the stopping-places, selling it at so much a quart." Another writer in the *New York Tribune* reported that he had barely made it onto a train from Buffalo "after flattening out an apple-boy and a pop-corn peddler." According to Robert Trall, popped corn was available in fruit stands "everywhere" by 1854. So many "pop-corn men" and "pop-corn merchants" hustled on the streets of America that Mortimer Thomson lampooned them in his *Doesticks' Letters.*"[37]

After the Civil War some popcorn vendors became more organized. The G. L. Meservy Pop Corn Manufacturer of Omaha, Nebraska, supplied fresh popcorn throughout the city and offered to fill orders from anyplace in the country. Popcorn vendors at fairs, circuses, and expositions attracted crowds to their stands. By the 1890s popcorn vendors prowled the streets with steam-driven popcorn wagons throughout America. One example was E. J. Harvey, a Civil War veteran. In 1886 Harvey rigged up a popcorn wagon and stationed it on a street in Charles City, Iowa. He constructed the popper of galvanized iron. A gas stove heated the popper, which was hung by a brass chain from the ceiling. Children watched the popping process and then purchased nickel bags. The children grew into adults, and their children also enjoyed the sight and taste. By 1908 Harvey's expanded business sold popcorn made from two and a half tons of unpopped kernels. When Harvey left the business, George Wyatt took possession. Wyatt shifted to electric poppers, "with the white kernels dancing around inside a big glass box like myriads of little white popcorn fairies." Although the proprietors have changed as has their equipment, popcorn vendors are still operating on the streets of Charles City today.[38]

Popcorn vendors were by no means poor. In 1907 the *Chicago Tribune* reported that sympathy was wasted on the popcorn man. While most people thought of a vendor "as an unfortunate individual, aged or decrepit, cut off from the legitimate lines of trade, and barely eking out a scanty living," the average popcorn man cleared about $150 per week. It was a poor stand, the *Chicago Tribune* reported, that did "not take in $8 to $10 a day." Many people started off as popcorn vendors and proceeded to other endeavors. About 1910 Daniel K. Ludwig sold popcorn at the Big Pavilion, his father's dance hall in Saugatuck, Michigan. After he left Michigan, Ludwig became a shipping magnate who built ships and tankers and was owner of the American-Hawaiian Company. In 1976 he was declared the world's richest man and hailed as the "Popcorn Millionaire."[39]

As automobiles began to clog the streets of America, many cities passed laws licensing street vendors to prevent congestion. The result was that many popcorn vendors were required to move indoors. One unusual pre–World War II popcorn store was that of Ernest Clair Brown of Wheaton, Illinois. Brown's place of business was three and one-half feet wide by thirty-one feet in depth. It was leased space in a building between a grocery store and Woolworth's. Brown appropriately christened his business the "In-Between Popcorn Store," which was founded on January 6, 1921. He worked from 2:00 p.m. to midnight every day, with the sole exceptions of Thanksgiving and Christmas. His dedication paid off, and he made a financial success of his popcorn store. His peak year was 1931. Due to the effects of the Depression, his business dropped in 1932 and 1933, but sales increased throughout the rest of the 1930s. Brown's store survived World War II; his best year was 1946, when he sold fifteen tons of popcorn and cleared $10,000. He claimed that the secret of his popcorn's success was an ingredient in the cottonseed oil he used to pop the corn. Business thrived in the postwar climate, and in 1958 he sold $15,000 worth of popcorn. On warm Sundays at least fifty people waited in line in front of his narrow shop to buy his popcorn. When interviewed by the *Chicago Daily News* in May 1959, he estimated that his shop had served one hundred thousand customers and sold over 132 tons of popcorn. Less than three months after the interview, he died at age eighty-eight.[40] His popcorn shop survived and continues to thrive today.

By the early twentieth century popcorn confections had multiplied exponentially. A grocer reported that consumption was large in rural areas and was growing yearly in cities. When asked to estimate probable sales of popcorn, he replied that his own trade had increased dramatically, and he assumed "that others have the same experience." Sales of popcorn confections had particularly taken off. Another grocer reported that there was "a large sale of this class of confectionery on trains and in all neighborhoods in cities where children congregate." His assessment of the reasons for its popularity was that purchasers received "more bulk for their money when they buy pop corn confections, consequently they buy liberally of it."[41]

Prepared Popcorn Products

Many popcorn products were developed during the latter nineteenth century. Grocers in Philadelphia, Boston, and Chicago carried two commercial popcorn products: Snowdrift and Snowflake, which were manufactured by Frederick Weschelman of Chicago. They were simply ground popcorn in half-pound boxes. These products were eaten as a "breakfast or supper dish, with milk and sugar, or without sweetening." Within a few years Chicago grocery stores sold popped corn and popcorn products. Popcorn flour was used for a variety of purposes, including as cake flour and as a filler to give body to commercial medicine drops and in chocolate candy confections.[42]

Elizabeth Grinnell described the process of popping corn for conversion to flour. She reported that Nebraska farmers dug a hole in the ground. Corncobs were tossed in the hole and set afire. When the fire was hot enough, green corn leaves were tossed on the coals and a flattened oil drum was placed on top. Popcorn kernels were strewn on the drum, and more green leaves were piled on the corn, and finally dirt was heaped on top of the leaves. After a few minutes, popping sounded from the subterranean depths. After twenty minutes the dirt was scraped off and a pile of popped corn was revealed beneath the top layer of steaming leaves. According to Grinnell, the popcorn was cream colored and had a fantastic smell. She sniffed and longed "for a means of conveying the perfume to other parts and other times." Likewise, the flavor of the popcorn was "marvelous." The mass was sent to the mills where it was ground into meal.[43] This method of preparing popcorn flour was already archaic when Grinnell described it. Commercial poppers of the day could produce more popcorn in a shorter period of time with much less effort.

Popcorn bricks were purportedly invented by George Washington Hall of Evansville, Wisconsin. He loved the circus and ran off to join it in his youth. During the winter time he sold popcorn in New York. He claimed to have invented popcorn bricks sometime before 1866. By the 1880s popcorn bricks were manufactured by the Garden City Pop Corn Works, owned initially by A. E. Jacobs. Jacobs advertised that his popcorn products were "manufactured from the best material" and were "put up in the most attractive form." The company's products were warranted to preserve their shape and flavor and were guaranteed not to fall to pieces as "the cheaper class of goods" invariably did. Jacobs made three different types of products: Garden City Sealed Bricks, Garden City Sealed Prize Bricks, and Chimo Bricks. His company also produced one- and five-cent popcorn balls and sold them by the barrel to "privilege men at Circuses, Street Fairs, Carnivals and Picnics." Later new confections were added to the product line, Taffy Corn and Want-A-Bite. By the early twentieth century the company claimed to have the largest popcorn factory in the world.[44]

Only two recipes for popcorn bricks have been located. One was surprisingly preserved in the 1890 edition of the British *Skuse's Complete Confectioner.* Skuse's recipe called for mixing popcorn with boiled brown sugar and pressing it "immediately into oiled tins." When the bricks cooled, they were ready for sale. Some were cut into smaller pieces before selling. The second popcorn brick recipe that survived was employed by F. W. Rueckheim & Brother in Chicago. These bricks were composed of popcorn, corn syrup, and molasses compressed into a rectangular shape. The brothers started making their bricks under the Reliable brand name in 1872. The bricks were covered in colored tissue paper and sold at circuses and fairs. On their fiftieth anniversary the company still manufactured bricks. According to a company booklet, without popcorn bricks circuses and fairs would lose some of their nostalgic romance.[45]

Frederick W. Rueckheim had emigrated from Germany to Illinois in 1869 and worked on a farm. By the fall of 1871 Rueckheim had saved up two hundred dollars. When Chicago's Great Fire destroyed 17,450 buildings, Rueckheim headed into the city to assist in cleaning up debris and rebuilding. As soon as he arrived, he met William Brinkmeyer, whose popcorn stand had burned down during the fire. Brinkmeyer convinced Rueckheim to become a partner in the Popcorn Specialties business. They operated out of a room but soon prospered serving the workers reconstructing the damaged city. One year later Brinkmeyer sold his share in the partnership to Frederick Rueckheim, who in turn sent for his brother, Louis Rueckheim, in Germany. The popcorn operation was renamed F. W. Rueckheim & Brother. In the beginning the brothers were equipped with a single molasses kettle and one hand popper; they operated out of a back-room kitchen and sold their popcorn in paper bags.[46] All their confections were made by hand until 1884, when they shifted to steam-powered machinery. Like many other popcorn vendors, the Rueckheim brothers experimented with sugar-coated popcorn. They tested different sweeteners and tried a variety of combinations with marshmallows, nuts, and other products.

Chicago's Columbian Exposition held in 1893 was visited by an estimated twenty-seven million people. It was the harbinger of many changes in America. More than one million fair-goers rode George Washington Gale Ferris's big steel wheel, soon called the Ferris Wheel. It foreshadowed a new industry of mass entertainment. Caramel maker Milton S. Hershey, after seeing a German chocolate machine there, subsequently ordered one and started manufacturing the first chocolate candy bars in America. The Exposition was illuminated by lights invented by Thomas Edison.[47]

The smell of popcorn was also in the air at the Exposition. The *World's Fair Souvenir Cook Book* incorporated two popcorn recipes: one for popped corn and the other for "Crystalized Pop-Corn." The latter recipe was composed of sugar, butter, and popcorn. The Rueckheim brothers sold a confection similar to the crystallized popcorn recipe consisting of popcorn, molasses, and roasted nuts. During the Exposition they substituted less-expensive peanuts. After the Exposition, sales remained brisk. Frederick Rueckheim commented, "No matter how we try to plan for it, orders always exceed production." They continued to experiment with the ingredients for the product that remained unnamed.[48]

Before January 1896 Louis Rueckheim came up with an interesting combination of popcorn, molasses, and peanuts. The company told conflicting stories as to how this product acquired its name. One version claimed that it was the brainchild of one of the Rueckheims. Another version proclaimed that a customer tasted a sample and remarked, "This is a cracker-jack of a product." The story preferred by the company combined elements of its several other renditions with accompanying dialogue. While sampling and tasting the new confection, John Berg—a company salesman—purportedly exclaimed: "That's a cracker-jack." Frederick Rueckheim looked at him and said, "Why not call it by that name?" Berg responded, "I see no objection." Rueckheim's decisive reply was "That settles it then."[49]

The story is probably apocryphal. "Cracker jack" was a commonly used slang term that meant first-rate or excellent. The *Historical Dictionary of American Slang* lists its first published appearance as 1895, but references suggest that the term had been used during the 1880s. Other commercial manufacturers employed it in their product names. For instance, the Moline Plow Company of Moline, Illinois, manufactured a Cracker Jack Corn Planter about this time. A fertilizer was also named Cracker Jack, as were many other products. By 1897 cookbooks used the term "Cracker Jack" to refer to popcorn confections. Recipes for making Cracker Jack at home appeared in cookbooks during the late 1890s, although these early recipes rendered significantly different results from the commercial product manufactured by the Rueckheims.[50]

However the name was selected, the Rueckheims began using the term "Cracker Jack" on January 28, 1896, applying for a trademark on February 17, 1896. Thirty-six days later the trademark was issued. They launched promotional and marketing campaigns in Chicago and soon thereafter in New York and Philadelphia. Three different advertisements appeared in Philadelphia's *Grocery World* in its July 13, 1896, issue. These promotions announced that Cracker Jack was a new confection, not yet six months old, that "made the most instantaneous success of anything ever introduced." It was called the "1896 sensation." Also in the advertisements was the phrase "the more you eat the more you want." To meet the needs generated by this extensive promotional campaign, the company mass-produced four and one-half tons of Cracker Jack daily. From May 5 through June 1, 1896, fourteen railroad cars of Cracker Jack were sold in New York city. In Philadelphia four carloads were distributed during the first ten days of the product's promotional campaign. Cracker Jack was "The Greatest Seller of its Kind."[51]

Early Cracker Jack advertisements also guaranteed their product "to be fresh and crisp," which was a difficult promise to keep. Cracker Jack was sold in cardboard boxes, but the crispness was difficult to retain even under the best conditions. After a box was opened, moisture was impossible to keep out. Henry G. Eckstein, a former general superintendent of the N. K. Fairbanks Company and a friend of the Rueckheims in the Oakland Methodist Church, proposed that Cracker Jack be protected with a new packaging system to keep out moisture and maintain crispness. The Rueckheims agreed. In 1899 a wax-sealed package was developed, followed by a moisture-proof package in 1902. This triple-sealed package has usually been documented as Eckstein's innovation. In fact, Eckstein paid a German scientist five hundred dollars for teaching him the method of making wax paper. He improved the process, and his improvements made him a millionaire.[52]

The Rueckheims launched another national advertising campaign in the early twentieth century in *Billboard* especially to promote the new packaging. The advertisement promoted Cracker Jack as "A delicious Pop Corn Confection, packed in moisture proof packages, that keep it fresh for a long time. A QUICK SELLER for theatres, Parks, Picnics, Carnivals, etc. Retail at 5 cents. A MONEY MAKER for the concessionist."[53] Consumer sales soared, mainly due to the advertising and packaging changes. In recognition of Eckstein's role in this phenomenal success, the firm was renamed Rueckheim Brothers & Eckstein in 1903.

Cracker Jack was a successful confection in many different milieus. One was baseball stadiums. In 1908 lyricist Jack Norworth along with composer Albert von Tilzer immortalized the product in their song "Take Me Out to the Ball Game" with the lyrics "Buy me some peanuts and cracker-jack— / I don't care if I never get back."[54]

As previously mentioned, the company that makes Cracker Jack had started out manufacturing popcorn bricks. In 1904 an advertisement reported that the company made "a full line of five-cent PACKAGE CONFECTIONS and the famous RELIABLE POP CORN BRICK." Three years later Angelus Marshmallows, the firm's second most important product, received a trademark. Rueckheim Brothers & Eckstein sold hundreds of candy products under the name Reliable Confections, most of which did not survive for long. One confection was Hunky Dory. According to a recipe for "Hunky-Dories" in *St. Nicholas* magazine, the confection consisted of sweet chocolate, cream, popped corn, and pecans. Another was New Wrinkle, composed of popcorn, peanuts, coconut, sugar, corn syrup, and molasses. Yet another confection was Chums, a popcorn and caramel creation. In 1908 a prize was added to the Chums boxes as a test. In 1912 the company claimed that Chums was the "Biggest hit in Prize Popcorn Confections ever brought out." Chums prizes were forerunners of Cracker Jack toys.[55]

An advertisement for Cracker Jack in 1912 reported that "They Don't Stay Long on the Shelf!" Cracker Jack, claimed the advertisement, was the "Standard Popcorn Confection" by which all others were judged. The advertisement also announced that "A Valuable Premium Coupon" was attached to every package. From 1910 to 1913 coupons for premiums were affixed on and placed in Cracker Jack boxes. The coupons could be redeemed for over three hundred "varieties of handsome and useful articles, such as Watches, Jewelry, Silverware, Sporting Goods, Toys, Games, Sewing Machines and many other useful Household articles." In 1912 children's toys were inserted directly into every package. Two years later Cracker Jack advertisements reported that "over 500 varieties of handsome and useful articles" were to be found in the boxes.[56] The little sailor boy and his dog Bingo were first used in advertisements in 1916, and three years later they appeared on a Cracker Jack box. This picture was based on one showing Frederick Rueckheim's grandson with his dog. His grandson, Robert, died of pneumonia shortly after the package was introduced. The dog was named Bingo probably because of its connection with the winning cry in the game of the same name.

Several special-order Cracker Jack boxes were developed. A Saint Louis distributor was interested in boxes only with riddle and puzzle books, and boxes were stamped "Consignment St. Louis." Another Cracker Jack box was issued for the theater trade. A company memo issued in 1919 specifically directed that no "crickets" were to be placed in these boxes. Western states also had their own boxes for a short period with their own prizes. When reports came back to the company stating that some Cracker Jack boxes in Kentucky had been delivered without prizes, the officers of the company issued an edict that fulfilling their promise of a prize in each box was extremely important. Precautions were taken to avoid such problems, and inspectors were placed on the line to guarantee product quality standards.[57]

Throughout the early twentieth century the company expanded. A 1913 advertisement proclaimed that Cracker Jack was "**the world's famous confection.**" By 1918 the company generated three million dollars in sales. In a 1919 advertisement in *Saturday Evening Post* Cracker Jack was touted as "America's Famous Food Confection." To augment its Chicago operations, sales offices were established in Brooklyn, New York. Sales continued to increase. In 1922 the Rueckheim Brothers & Eckstein company celebrated its fiftieth anniversary by changing its name to the Cracker Jack Company. That same year the Rueckheims and Eckstein elected the vice presidents from among their families' next generation: Frederick Rueckheim Jr., Henry Eckstein Jr., and Fred Warren, son-in-law of Louis Rueckheim. Within four years the Cracker Jack Company sold more than 138 million boxes annually. The company realized its largest pre–World War II profit in 1928, which amounted to $716,659 before taxes.[58]

Cracker Jack has had many imitators and competitors. Alfred H. Shotwell, founder of the Shotwell Company in Chicago with an office in Brooklyn, was one of Cracker Jack's fiercest rivals. In 1904 Shotwell began producing Checkers, also a popcorn confection, with red and white checked boxes. Another of the Shotwell Company's confections was Spreading Like Wild Fire, which was advertised as "Cheap Delicious, Pure." Shotwell claimed to have "the largest exclusive popcorn factory in America." Like the Cracker Jack Company, the Shotwell Company grew its popcorn in Ord, Nebraska, and in Ida Grove and Odebolt, Iowa, from whence it was shipping eight million pounds of raw corn annually by 1916. Unlike other Cracker Jack competitors, the Shotwell Company was very successful. To eliminate the competition, the Cracker Jack Company bought Shotwell out in 1926.[59]

During the Depression the Cracker Jack Company sold raw popcorn kernels under the brand name Pop-It. In 1931 the company marketed cases of twenty-four packages along with twenty-four popcorn poppers. Larger-sized poppers could also be acquired along with larger-sized boxes of Pop-It at a greater price. Many Cracker Jack products were floundered during the Depression. Chums, for instance, were discontinued in January 1935 due to poor sales. Simultaneously the company also launched new products. Cracker Jack Brittle and fruit popcorn were introduced, as were chocolate-covered Cracker Jack and Jack and Jill french-fried popcorn.[60]

The original Cracker Jack and the acquired Checkers confections remained on the market throughout the Depression. To boost sales, the company began purchasing sophisticated prizes from Europe and Japan. In San Antonio, Texas, and on the West Coast, Japanese prizes affronted consumers. In 1936 the Cracker Jack Company made the decision to send only boxes with prizes made in America to these locations.[61]

A major reason for Cracker Jack profits was improved marketing and increasingly efficient operations. The Cracker Jack Company contracted with Iowa and Illinois farmers for steady supplies of popcorn. Elevators were constructed to store and cure the grain. Automatic machinery was installed to convey the kernels from the burlap bags through the popper and under the syrup bath. The product was automatically packaged into boxes. This automation permitted Cracker Jack to undersell its competition while still making a solid profit. Boxes retailed for a nickel. Packaging cost about two cents and the contents about one cent. The company sold packages to grocers and vendors for 3 1/4¢ cents, leaving a 1/4¢ profit per box. This may seem a small profit, but Cracker Jack sold millions of boxes per year. Cracker Jack's competitors charged 3.5 cents per box, which meant that grocers and vendors made a greater profit by selling Cracker Jack. This encouraged retailers to stock Cracker Jack rather than competing brands. By 1937 the Cracker Jack Company declared itself producer of "America's Oldest, Best Known and Most Popular Confection."[62]

Many other manufacturers of popcorn thrived during the first half of the twentieth century. Eustace Reynolds Knott of Boston began producing many popcorn products during the early twentieth century. According to Knott, by 1915 Americans were "buying more pop-corn than ever before." It was purchased in many ways ground and whole, in squares, bars, fritters. Knott believed that "pop-corn made on quality builds business," and they were extremely interested in increasing the consumption of popcorn. Knott survived through the 1930s. Other manufacturers of popcorn products emerged during the Depression. One caramel corn product was manufactured by Snacks, Inc., with offices in Chicago and Windsor, Canada. The company was founded by W. T. Hawkins. It also sold other snacks in the United States and Canada, including puffed cheese curls. By 1939 the total yearly sales of all candied popcorn products reached $2.4 million.[63]

Commercial Poppers

The Rueckheims were not the only ones interested in popcorn who were influenced by the 1893 Columbian Exposition. Andrew B. Olson of Kansas City attended the exposition and had his brother who lived in Chicago advertise "Olson's Imported Rotary Corn Popper." Olson had patented popcorn devices, but eventually went out of business.[64] Also in attendance at the exposition was Charles Cretors, who had launched the C. Cretors and Company in Chicago in 1885 at the age of thirty-two. According to the company's first letterhead, Cretors engaged in the manufacture of "Steam peanut, popcorn and coffee roasters, Also small engines for running coffee mills, Sewing Machines, Dental Lathes, Etc."

Cretors's initial inventions focused on steam-powered roasters. His No. 1 Roaster was twenty-two inches wide, thirty inches long, forty-six inches high and weighed 175 pounds. The machine could roast peanuts, coffee beans, chestnuts, or popcorn. The No. 2 machine was slightly smaller but was designed to be displayed in a grocery store window when it was operating. No. 3 and No. 4 were smaller models for inside use. These machines introduced a revolutionary way of popping corn. By lighting a gas boiler, steam was generated, which powered the engine to turn the agitator. The agitator stirred the popcorn mixed with a popping medium composed of one-third clarified butter and two-thirds lard. The steam condenser warmed the popcorn in the storage compartment. Attracting passersby was a little red-suited toy clown, who appeared to crank the machine. Initially sales of roasters were limited, but the company demonstrated slow, steady growth. In 1887 the company turned out thirty machines, generating revenue of $3,627.[65]

In time for the Chicago Exposition in 1893 Cretors introduced two new models. One, later dubbed the "Earn More," was targeted at grocery store owners. It was a compact twenty inches square and sixty-five inches high—an important factor for shopkeepers with limited floor space. Its large rear wheels enabled the owner to roll it outside during the day and inside at night or during inclement weather. With the same high rate of return on all Cretors models—purportedly seventy cents on every dollar of popcorn sold—the Earn More promised to be one of the most economical investments a storekeeper could make.

Cretors demonstrated his popcorn wagon at Chicago's Columbian Exposition. According to company lore, during the first two days of the Exposition sales were not impressive. On the third day Cretors hired someone to stand by his machine while he explored the Exposition. He examined other inventions and thought about why the crowds were more promising elsewhere. Cretors decided to give his popcorn away. He and his assistant, as the C. Cretors Company later claimed, shouted out: "Try the new taste sensation! Free! Popcorn popped in butter—a revolutionary new method just patented! Try a bag for free!"[66]

Customers descended upon his wagon immediately. The clown perched atop the popcorn popper cranked furiously. As the enticing smell of hot, buttered popcorn drifted down the Midway, the crowds grew larger, attracted as much by the novelty of the show put on by the steam engine and the little clown as by the popcorn. Cretors soon charged for his popcorn and thrived financially during the Exposition. The long lines at the Exposition convinced many to purchase his machine. One purchaser was H. Hummels, of Jersey City, New Jersey. According to an article in *Scientific American,* it was "light and strong, and weighing but 400 or 500 pounds, can be drawn readily by a boy or by a small pony to any picnic ground, fair, political rally, etc., and to many other places where a good business could be done for a day or two." The machine measured five feet in length and about two feet wide. It was constructed of metal with the exception of the popcorn case, which was made of hardwood and glass. The running gear was composed of three springs on the rear end and a strong *V* spring in front. The wheels were similar to rubber bicycle tires with spokes. The wagon held a peanut roaster and a corn popper, both run by steam power. The water tank held about four gallons. The water was pumped into the copper boiler. The boiler was heated by white gas, as were the peanut roaster and popcorn pan composed of sheet iron. The steam engine caused the roaster and corn popper to revolve. About one pint of rice corn was placed in the popper at a time. A shaft connected to the bottom of the pan revolved the rods, which stirred the rice popcorn to prevent burning. When popping, the flakes were prevented from flying out of the pan by a lid. When the popping ended, the operator turned off the gas, raised the lid, and dumped the contents of the pan into the storage area. He then tossed the next batch of unpopped kernels into the popper. To sweeten the popcorn, the operator stirred sugar syrup into the popped corn rapidly. Raw popcorn retailed at about five cents per pound, but after popping it sold for two to three times the retail cost.[67]

The wagon's advantage was that it was a completely self-contained unit: its owner transported it wherever he wanted. If sales were slow in one location, the owner simply moved the wagon to a location with better prospects. While previous vendors maintained stationary popcorn stands, the wagon created a new class of mobile vendors who traversed America's streets for almost a half-century. Likewise, popcorn wagons plied the streets of Canada. Kenneth Wells of Toronto reminisced years later that his first recollection of popcorn was a wagon pushed down the streets. "The sound of the steam whistle called the youngsters but it was the popcorn in the storage compartment by the gas that sold us." Wells recollected, "The corn was 'hot' and tasted good."[68]

Cretors's success convinced others to manufacture popcorn machines. The Kingery Manufacturing Company of Cincinnati actually predated C. Cretors Company in 1875. Like Cretors, Kingery's early focus was on manufacturing peanut roasters. In February 1896 Kingery patented a large stationary gas machine that was later converted for electrical use. It may not have been sold extensively until 1902. Two of Kingery's earliest machines were the Eureka Corn Fritters Mold and the Faultless Fritter Mold. Shortly after the turn of the century Kingery introduced a number of popcorn machines and wagons, some of which were powered by electricity. Their combination peanut roaster and popcorn popper possessed a seven-inch gong under the machine, operated by pulling a chain, to attract customers.[69]

Another early manufacturer was the Bartholomew Company of Peoria, Illinois, with offices in Cincinnati, Philadelphia, and Des Moines. The owner, John B. Bartholomew, was an inventor in Des Moines. His early inventions were peanut roasters and waffle machines. By the 1890s he was manufacturing popcorn machines.[70] Within a decade the Bartholomew Company marketed a full range of popcorn poppers and wagons, which varied in price. The lowest price for a wagon was $60 for The Boss on Wheels. The highest price was for The Stunner at $125. For those interested in The Stunner, the Bartholomew Company proclaimed that the profits would quickly cover the initial investment and then would assist the proprietor to "start a bank account or [swell] it if you already have one." Their Nickel Mint was so named because it made "nickels as fast as if you had minted them." The company also constructed a variety of smaller machines under the name The Popcorn King. The Columbia popper attracted customers by shooting flakes of popcorn that appeared to be snowflakes falling from the clouds. In addition, they manufactured commercial corn poppers, warmers, and display cases.

In their advertisements the Bartholomew Company emphasized two points. First, their machines produced money for their owners. With a Bartholomew machine proprietors could "secure and maintain a profitable little business," but they also could "make it a stepping stone to a better and greatly enlarged business." Second, their machines were safe:

they did not have steam engines, which reportedly exploded from time to time. This last message was an attack on their main competition, C. Cretors Company, which solely produced steam-powered machines.[71]

Dunbar & Company was incorporated in 1900. The proprietor, C. F. Dunbar, had been employed by Cretors in its early days. Dunbar had first been employed in the shop at Cretors, but he had worked his way up the ranks to chief machinist. His role had been central in the construction of each of Cretors's popcorn machines. In late 1899 Dunbar devised a rotary screen drum that popped corn without butter. When the corn was popped, an internal spiral screen automatically fed the raw kernels into the drum's outer screen for popping. The screen separated unpopped kernels for easy removal after the popping cycle was completed. Dunbar approached Charles Cretors with the idea, but Cretors was unimpressed. Dunbar resigned and started his own company featuring his "dry" popper. Dunbar's poppers resembled those of Cretors but had a lower price tag. Dunbar was a master in the industry and an innovator, both by merit of his invention and for an automatic buttering device.[72]

The Holcomb & Hoke Manufacturing Company, a diversified manufacturer based in Indianapolis, began producing popcorn machines in 1914. In the search for a name, someone said: "If oranges are Sunkist, popcorn is butter-kissed." That's what Holcomb & Hoke called its popper. Butter Kist machines were different than machines of other manufacturers: they popped the corn on hot plates without oil. Holcomb & Hoke's machines were dependable, but they were strictly for indoor use. J. I. Holcomb was so enamored of his popcorn machines that in 1915 he published a book, *Salesology of the Butter-Kist Popcorn Machine,* extolling all the techniques salesmen used to sell the machines. After just four years of manufacturing popcorn machines Holcomb boasted that the Butter-Kist poppers produced 120 million packages of popcorn annually. The company also manufactured several million bags and cartons that advertised Butter-Kist popcorn.[73]

Unlike Cretors and other manufacturers who produced machines for a separate, distinct business, Holcomb & Hoke manufactured machines primarily for stores and merchants, such as Hillman's, Snellenberger's, Wanamaker's, the Boston Store, and the Fair Store, as well as druggists and confectionery stores. The company also claimed to have sold scores of machines to "the Best Motion Picture houses all over the country," but little evidence has been uncovered to support this claim. They did successfully target soda fountains, which for six months of the year had limited sales. As Holcomb pointed out, even during the high season for soda fountains, eating popcorn created a thirst in customers, which in turn increased sales of sodas. He went even further, predicting that the "Butter-Kist Sundae" would be "one of the famous dishes in soda fountains." The sundae, according to Holcomb, was made with or without butter, without salt, but served with a dish of cream.[74]

Another distinct advantage was that by 1920 Holcomb & Hoke's poppers were primarily electric, although some gas-heated models were still available. None of Holcomb & Hoke's machines were steam-driven, which was viewed as a safety concern by many store owners. According to Holcomb & Hoke promotions, the Butter-Kist Pop Corn Machines were so popular that farmers were "raising a bumper yield of pop corn to supply enormous demand built up since we brought out the Butter-Kist pop corn machine and made the pop corn business a vital part of retail stores of all descriptions even in towns down to 300 population." An advertisement claimed that the machine "runs itself, stands anywhere, beautifies surroundings." The manufacturers believed that the machine also boosted business because the "magical motion makes people stop and look—cooking flavor brings trade from blocks around." Their machines fit into a space twenty-six inches by twelve inches and generated two to ten dollars daily, a handsome profit in 1918.[75]

Holcomb & Hoke advertisements embodied excellent marketing techniques emphasizing the profitability and productivity of the Butter-Kist machines. In their 1920 catalog Holcomb & Hoke claimed to have rescued the popcorn industry from the clutches of disreputable street vendors: "the class of men that run such places on the street is thrown around their popcorn carts with every gust of wind." Other Holcomb & Hoke advertisements championed their machine as a money-maker. On the cover of a catalog was the line "Every dollar's worth sold represents 60¢ profit."[76] However, despite all of their successful advertising and salesmanship, during the Depression the company discontinued making poppers.

Cretors neared the company's silver anniversary in 1909, when they achieved the high point in the company's sales volume for nearly a decade. Sales of $214,000 would not be surpassed until 1917, when they reached $243,000. The major reason for the downward shift was that Cretors's patents expired and several new competitors, such as Holcomb & Hoke, and Peerless companies moved in on the market. Peerless made one basic line of popcorn machines, as well as Peerless Fritter Mold machines.[77] Machines made by smaller companies were cheaper and sold to the lower end of the market. Individually Bartholomew, Dunbar, Peerless, Holcomb & Hoke, and Kingery were not serious competitors to Cretors, but collectively they made considerable inroads into the market.

During the 1930s one company did seriously challenge Cretors. It was run by Charles T. Manley, who hailed from Butte, Montana, but had studied electrical engineering at Purdue University in Indiana. Manley started in the popcorn business in 1922 when he was introduced to Julius Burch of Kansas City. Burch wanted a partner for the manufacture of popcorn machines designed for the carnival trade. The machines were portable, boxlike popcorn wagons. Burch and Manley incorporated under the name Burch Manufacturing Company. Manley promptly bought out Burch but did not change the company's name to Manley Company until 1939. In 1924 Burch moved to St. Louis and launched the Advanced Manufacturing Company, which also produced popcorn machines. The Advanced Manufacturing Company was later renamed the Star Manufacturing Company. Manley produced his first electric popcorn machine in 1925, but his business did not prove successful until the 1930s. During the Depression popcorn was a luxury that most Americans could still afford. The Depression also gave Manley some high-powered salesmen who, without the economic collapse, would have scorned the popcorn business.[78]

Manley was particularly successful in selling poppers to theaters. Unlike the Cretors models, which rested on legs, Manley's extended to the floor. In the days when popcorn machines were rolled in and out of establishments, the legs on the Cretors machines gave them more mobility. When theaters permanently located machines inside, models with legs were more trouble to clean under. Theaters preferred Manley's floor length design.[79]

Popcorn vendors were particularly concerned with popping expansion. As previously noted, vendors bought by weight but sold by volume. Anything that increased the volume improved profits. While much of the expansion was due to the variety popped, Manley asserted that the type of machine also contributed to increased expansion. The proper application of heat was a factor in increasing popcorn's volume. In the dry popper held over a burner, some kernels received the right amount of heat, but others only popped partially. Manley's machines used the wet-pop method by which the popcorn was popped in oil or melted fat. The oil evened the distribution of heat to the kernels and assured a more uniform explosion. Manley's method also added salt before popping, which permitted the flavor of salt and oil to permeate each kernel. Manley decided that coconut oil was the best popping medium, and he created a coconut-oil seasoning that was also sold to commercial customers. Manley's most important contribution was his shiny glass-and-chromium electric popcorn machine, which largely replaced the popcorn wagon as a source of popcorn vending. His popper moved concessions off the streets and into stores and other establishments.[80] Manley's electric popping machines were safe and easy to incorporate into movie theaters.

In homes popcorn was popped mainly over open fires or on stovetops. Stove popping was difficult as the temperature was variable in wood- or coal-burning stoves. As the twentieth century progressed, cooking over fireplaces declined. Gas ranges made it easier to modulate the heat and keep the smoky wood and coal odors away from the popped corn. A further change began with the electrification of the country. As electricity became widely available, first in cities and later in rural areas, electric poppers quickly became common in homes.

Electric poppers were first proposed for use in making commercial popcorn. William Bean of Gadsden, Alabama, for instance, patented an improved Electric Popcorn-Machine in 1907. It included an electric heater in the pan that popped the corn. A magazine article published the same year judged the electrical popper the most useful electrical household appliance then available. An electric popper could be plugged into the wall, and "children can pop corn on the parlor table all day without the slightest danger or harm." The results, claimed the promotion, were "far better than the old way of building a red hot fire in the kitchen range and suffering from the heat while popping corn."[81]

A host of electric poppers soon deluged the market. They were composed of a variety of metal, glass, and wood components. The National Stamping & Electrical Company of Chicago made a White Cross popper consisting of a tin pot with a wire sticking out of the side connected to the hotplate inside. A wire basket fit into the base, and a top stirrer was mounted through the handle. The Challenge Popcorn Popper was an early black-bodied popper with very short legs and a side stirrer knob. The Style #75 popper developed by the Dominion Electric Manufacturing Company of Minneapolis was a one-piece cylinder made of nickel. The popper made by Excel Electric Company of Muncie, Indiana, was also made of nickel. Its handles had little lock-down levers to keep the lid from blowing off during popping. It had vents in the top to let the steam escape. The popper constructed by Knapp Monarch, Belleville, Illinois, consisted of a steel body with a lock-down lid and a stirrer knob on top. The model of the Rapaport Brothers of Chicago had a square Bakelite base that stood on metal legs. The upper part was constructed of aluminum. Chrome handles agitated the popcorn.[82]

By the 1930s the electric corn popper was common enough to give a boost to the popcorn industry in the midst of the Depression. It was a lot easier to plug the popper into the wall and stir the kernels gently with a crank than to stand and shake a long metal pole over an open fire or on top of a stove. During the 1930s even hand cranking became unnecessary when automatic versions came equipped with built-in thermostats to ensure that the temperature did not rise beyond the proper popping point. Other improvements appeared in the appearance of the poppers. Some were elegantly decorated. The Berstead Manufacturing Company's Model #302 was constructed of a square chrome body enclosing a circular hotplate. A glass lid adorned the top. A large black knob on top was attached to the rod for stirring. The Knapp Monarch popper was composed of aluminum with domed glass lid and a glass knob standing on a heavy wire base. The Model #500 popper made by the Manning-Bowman Company of Meriden, Connecticut, consisted of a detachable aluminum container that sat atop a chrome hotplate. The first popper manufactured by the U.S. Manufacturing Corporation of Decatur, Illinois, was one unit with a knob holding the crank and legs composed of wood. A later popper featured a hotplate base with a detachable cord. U.S. Manufacturing Corporation's Model #10 came in several color combinations including tar and brown, cream and green, and red and ivory. These color schemes matched those of 1930s kitchens.[83]

For those unable to purchase electric corn poppers, they were easily constructed. Industrial arts programs in schools encouraged students to construct them in shop classes. R. B. Farr, a teacher at South Junior High, Everette, Washington, proudly announced that making electrical corn poppers was "very popular with the boys in the general shop." Other industrial arts teachers concurred. If one wanted to make them in the home, no problem. In 1934 *Popular Mechanics* offered step-by-step directions for constructing a popper at home.[84]

The Invention of Snack Food

Popped corn's early adoption as a snack food in mainstream America was eased because it followed in the footsteps of peanuts—America's first commercial snack food. Peanuts, a legume and not botanically a nut, originated in South America. Southerners cultivated peanuts during the eighteenth century mainly for the oil, which was used for heating, lighting, and cooking. Peanuts were sometimes consumed directly as a snack food in the South. Peanut cultivation and consumption slowly migrated northward, and peanuts were eaten in New York theaters at the dawn of the nineteenth century.

Peanuts, unlike fruit and other foods eaten by Americans between meals, needed to be processed before they could be consumed. In cities and towns peanuts were often sold by street vendors. The advantage of peanuts was that they were inexpensive, particularly when compared with types of sweets or desserts. Peanuts were looked down upon by many because of the shells and were considered a lower-class food. Popcorn followed a similar path. Popcorn had to be processed either by popping or by conversion into popcorn balls and other confections before it could be sold. Vendors who sold peanuts readily sold popcorn.

There were important differences between peanuts and popcorn as snack foods. Peanuts, unlike popcorn, had to be shelled. Peanuts were usually sold with shells on, and the consumer shelled them wherever he wanted to eat them. In the early nineteenth century Washington Irving complained about the cracking noise peanuts made when the shells were crushed, which disturbed theater performances, and the mess left by the shells. Subsequently, many lodged complaints because of the debris generated by peanut consumers. Vendors, particularly those inside theaters and other commercial establishments, preferred popcorn, which did not generate shells. Slowly popcorn began to outsell peanuts.

Almost all commercial snack foods in the American diet came on the market during the last century. A century ago there were no commercially manufactured chocolate bars, ice cream, Popsicles, potato chips, or corn chips. Many Americans considered eating food between meals to be unhealthy. Peanuts and popcorn were the first commercial snack foods. They were the groundbreaking foods that launched an industry.

Many advertising techniques were employed to sell popcorn during the late nineteenth century. This early handbill promoted "Excelsior" Popcorn circa 1876. From the Print and Picture Collection, The Free Library of Philadelphia. Photo by Will Brown.

I. L. Baker paid the excessively large sum of $8,000 for the exclusive popcorn concession throughout the grounds of the Philadelphia Centennial Exposition in 1876. This illustration, which appeared in *Frank Leslie's Illustrated Newspaper,* shows the booth he established in the Machinery Hall which demonstrated the process of manufacturing red and white popcorn balls. In this exhibit men and women roasted popcorn over a gas furnace, mixed it with sugar syrup in large bowls, pressed it into the popcorn-ball shape, piled baskets with the finished product, and sold them to visitors. From *Frank Leslie's Illustrated Newspaper* 153 (November 18, 1876): 179. Courtesy of the Print and Picture Collection, The Free Library of Philadelphia. Photo by Will Brown.

The magical, mysterious, and surprising explosion of the popcorn kernels was a child's delight. From the 1850s popcorn poetry aimed at children appeared in magazines and poetry collections. This poem, "Popcorn Children," was published in Elizabeth Gordon's *Mother Earth's Children: The Frolics of Fruits and Vegetables*. Photo by Lisa Kahane.

Popcorn was also considered a romantic product when popped over an indoor or outdoor fire. *Popping Corn,* a watercolor by Benjamin Russell, circa 1865, is the first known painting using popcorn as a theme. Used by permission of the New Bedford Whaling Museum, New Bedford, Massachusetts.

Holcomb and Hoke automated popper, 1915. Used by permission of the Wyandot Popcorn Museum, Marion, Ohio.

This array of packages of pop corn shows the variety of effort to attain top position in pop corn distribution before concentrating on the one big brand . . . Jolly Time Pop Corn in a nationally known package.

The American Pop Corn Company, makers of JOLLY TIME POP CORN, experimented extensively with popcorn packaging. JOLLY TIME POP CORN was the first to introduce the hermetically sealed metal container in 1925, which was purportedly the forerunner of the modern beer can. Photo courtesy of American Pop Corn Company, Sioux City, Iowa.

Electric poppers were manufactured shortly after the turn of the twentieth century. They did not become big sellers until major retail stores began offering them in their catalogs. This advertisement appeared in Sears Catalogue during the 1920s. Photo by Lisa Kahane.

Electric corn poppers made popping corn much more convenient. Electric poppers could be set up almost anywhere where there was a wall socket and did not require extensive shaking back and forth as did previous hand-held poppers. Illustration of the Universal Combination Table Stove and Corn Popper, circa 1920, sold by Landers, Frary & Clark. Photo by Lisa Kahane.

C. Cretors & Co. began manufacturing popcorn machines beginning in 1885. Subsequent models were handcarts, while others were horse drawn. In 1901 Cretors launched a "Self Propelled or Automobile" popcorn machine. At first sales were limited, but during the following decades thousands of motorized popcorn and peanut wagons were sold. The above "Automobile Machine" was manufactured about 1911. Photo of the Cretors popcorn truck during the 1920s. Courtesy of C. Cretors and Company.

Trade cards and glassine bags were other mechanisms of advertising popcorn. These photos illustrate ephemera from the Connecticut Pop Corn Co., Norwich, Connecticut, circa 1920s. Photo by Lisa Kahane.

This cover for a brochure advertising "Mose Skinner's Grand World's Jubilee and Humstrum Convulsion" was published in Boston in 1876. Mose Skinner had nothing to do with popcorn, but the inclusion of a popcorn sign and stand with crowds lined up suggests that by this date popcorn was used to sell other products and ideas. From the collection of Ronald Toth Jr., Rochester, New Hampshire. Photo by Lisa Kahane.

These popcorn seed packages circa 1930s illustrate three different popcorn varieties: South American Giant, Japanese Hulless, and Yellow Hybrid. Photo by Lisa Kahane.

A. B. OLSON,

PATENTEE AND MANUFACTURER OF THE

OLSON IMPROVED ROTARY CORN POPPER

PEANUT AND COFFEE ROASTERS.

218-20 East Missouri Ave. KANSAS CITY, MO.

These Corn Poppers Guaranteed to have no Equal.

The Invincible for Small Dealers.

No. 25. Price, $20.00.

Construction and style about the same as in No. 5, with half the capacity, and 1 double burner. Frame work mostly galvanized iron. Size of popping and peanut drums, 8x12 inches; size set up, 16x14 inches, 23 inches high. Includes same fixtures as in No. 5; weighs 25 pounds. Recommended to a trade of not over 500 five-cent (1-pound bags) packages per day of ten hours operation. Just the machine for small dealers.

These Roasters are not a new thing. They have been tried for three years with wonderful success.

—14—

Greatest "Wheel of Fortune" Out.

IN SUCCESSFUL USE FOR THREE YEARS.

No. 15. Price, $43.00.

Capacity, and fixtures furnished with No. 15 same as in No. 10, including mountings and torch. Size, at extreme points, when set up, 2 feet 7 inches by 2 feet 1 inch, standing 4 feet 4 inches high. (1) indicates corn catcher; (2) raw corn booth; (3) apartment for bags, salt, etc. Total weight, 90 pounds; when crated, 115 pounds.

—8—

A Revolution in Corn Poppers.

No. 5. Price, $30.00.

Includes one combined peanut and coffee drum, and one popping drum, size of each 8x15 inches. One scoop, one corn catcher, one waste pan, one burner shield, one main casing with gasoline attachments, and two double burners. Size of roaster, set up, 1 foot 4 inches by 1 foot 6 inches, at extreme points, 3 feet high; weight, 45 pounds, or 75 pounds, crated. Capacity, about ten barrels flake corn in ten hours.

—2—

Price of case No. 3.	$ 9.00
Price of mountings No. 2	11.00
Price of mountings No. 12	15.00

SKELETON MOUNTINGS No. 2. as shown in cut to the left has necessary height to operate the cylinder in a standing position.

No. 4 peanut warmer, No. 7 corn catcher, No. 6 extension drawer for exposing goods for sale, No. 8 glass case in which pop corn is buttered, sacked and kept crisp. Popping drum operated through door No. 5. The advantages of this outfit is that roaster can be operated without case or mountings, or roaster and case can be operated on a counter, table or box without mountings.

In the cut machine No. 10 is represented and makes the best combination.

The combination of case No. 3 and mountings No. 2 makes a very neat and light corn popping cart. Machines No. 5 10 and 25 can be used with it although in ordering, state what style machine you have or wanted.

SKELETON MOUNTINGS NO 12. Are the same as number 2 mountings, but heavier and are recommended to carry machine No, 35 Peerless, which is a heavier machine, and requires heavy wheels and axle.

Any changes made in the construction of my machines are made for the benefit of purchasers. Hence all orders are received subject to such changes.

No. 20, Price $60.00.

N. B. OLSON, MANAGER OF

Branch Office in

Chicago, Ills. IN THE **Prittie Pharmacy,**

57th ST. AND STONY ISLAND AVENUE.

Opposite First Entrance to World's Fair.

Many inventors manufactured popcorn devices during the 1880s and 1890s. One inventor, Andrew B. Olson of Kansas City, Missouri, created a means of feeding the corn into the screens and allowing only the corn that was popped to pass out through the exit, while the small or unpopped grains were ejected into an outside container. Olson installed his invention in a hand cart, which he advertised in the above flyer at the Chicago World's Fair in 1893.

Chapter 6

The Popcorn Boom

Motion Pictures

An extraordinary influence on popcorn's history was its shotgun wedding to movie theaters. Motion pictures were a creation of the late nineteenth century. Early systems created images that flickered on screens and in viewing devices. The most important system was the Kinetoscope developed by Thomas Edison and his associate William K. L. Dickson. They first demonstrated a projected motion picture image on October 6, 1889. The Kinetoscope was intended to be featured at the World's Columbian Exposition in Chicago, but the prototype was not completed in time. Edison, the master marketer, was soon promoting his new device to newspaper reporters and other influentials. The Kinetoscope and other systems caught on quickly, and movie parlors sprang up all over the country.

The first motion pictures did not portray a great deal of motion. Early films cannibalized plays from the theater and were filmed on indoor stages. A major advance was contributed in 1903 by Edwin S. Porter, whose *The Great Train Robbery* moved the industry outdoors and away from the studio stage. Early pictures were short and were considered primarily curiosities. David W. Griffith broke this trend in 1915 with the epic *Birth of a Nation,* which dramatically portrayed a Southern perspective on the Civil War and Reconstruction Era. The film ran three hours and was accompanied by a musical score for a full orchestra.

During the 1920s the motion picture industry had emerged with large studios and chains of theaters. Initially the movies were looked down upon by the culturally sophisticated who preferred "legitimate" theater and live concerts. However, when stage stars appeared on the silver screen, cinema was recognized as an art form in its own right. During the decade of the 1920s, 20,000 motion-picture theaters opened for business. By 1925 weekly attendance at movie theaters reached 25 million. But by 1926 the novelty faded, and the movie fad ebbed. Warner Bros., nearly bankrupt, invested in a new untried process called the Vitaphone, which added a sound dimension to film. On October 6, 1927, *The Jazz Singer* starring Al Jolson opened in New York and was an overwhelming success. By 1928, 1,300 movie theaters had installed expensive sound systems; a year later the number soared to 9,000. Paid admissions nearly doubled from 1927 to 1929. Despite the stock market crash, all major studios and theaters were converted to sound. Film became a driving social and cultural force in American life as Saturday night at the movies became a fixture in family entertainment.[1]

Sound rescued the motion picture industry from the jaws of the Depression. With sound, moviegoers were released from the all-absorbing attention required to read the silent-film titles while watching the on-screen action. With sound movies, patrons could thus carry on whispered conversations with their companions and munch quietly on snacks.[2] Freedom from the necessity to read titles also opened theaters up to a different class of Americans, many of whom were illiterate. By 1930 movie attendance reached 90 million patrons per week.

This huge audience was potentially a prime target for popcorn sales, but movie owners refused to sell it. To some owners, vending all concessions was an unnecessary nuisance or "beneath their dignity." In the rowdy burlesque days hawkers went through the aisles with baskets selling Cracker Jack and popcorn. Much of the popcorn was tossed in the air or strewn on the floors. In addition popcorn sellers were often slovenly dressed and did not always follow the most hygienic practices preferred by the middle classes who frequented theaters. These were not the images most owners wanted to cultivate for their upscale theaters. Other owners considered the profits on concession sales to be negligible compared with the trouble and expense of cleaning up spilled popcorn and scattered boxes and sacks. Many movie theaters had carpeted their lobbies with valuable rugs to emulate the grand theater lobbies. Operators were not interested in having their expensive carpets destroyed by spilled popped kernels, soda pop, and other confections. Finally, most theaters did not have outside vents. Early popcorn machines filled theaters with an unpleasant, penetrating smoky odor. Owners interested in selling popcorn were required to construct vents, which ran up the expenses and reduced profits. Even when owners were willing to do this, fire laws in some cities prevented the popping of corn without further extensive remodeling.[3] Until the 1930s most theater owners considered popcorn to be a liability rather than an asset.

Theater owners shifted their perspectives dramatically during the Depression. At five or ten cents a bag, popcorn was an affordable luxury for most Americans. Unlike most other confections, popcorn sales increased throughout the Depression. A major reason for this increase was the introduction of popcorn into movie theaters. At first independent concessionaires leased "lobby privileges" in theaters. Vendors paid about a dollar a day for the right to sell popcorn. As many theaters did not have lobby space and most did not want the popcorn or smoke inside, operators leased vendors space outside the theaters. This suited the vendors for they were able to sell both to movie patrons and passersby on the street. This was a lucrative business during the Depression. When an Oklahoma banker went bankrupt during the Depression, he set himself up with a popcorn machine in a little store near a theater. He made enough money in a few years to buy back three farms he had lost in the bank failure.[4]

Kemmons Wilson was not so lucky selling popcorn in a theater. In 1930 he left school at age seventeen to support his family when the Depression hit his hometown, Memphis, Tennessee. Wilson worked at odd jobs in a movie theater, where no snacks were offered for moviegoers. Wilson proposed to the manager that he place a popcorn machine out in front of the theater. The manager agreed, so Wilson went to the local hardware store and purchased a popcorn machine on credit for fifty dollars. His hunch about the untapped concession potential proved correct. Selling popcorn for a nickel a bag, he earned forty to fifty dollars per week. Unfortunately for Wilson, the theater manager only made twenty-five dollars. The manager snatched the job away from Wilson, but the story has a nice ending. Wilson told his mother that someday he was going to acquire a movie theater, and nobody was ever going to take his popcorn machine away from him. Kemmons Wilson, the future founder of Holiday Inn, did just that several years later.[5]

Soon popcorn entered the theater. In part this change was effected in a roundabout way by popcorn machine salesmen. As a matter of tactics, salesmen made special efforts to sell poppers to stores near theaters. When theater owners saw their customers entering with popcorn bags, they quickly saw the light. The salesmen then sold larger popcorn machines to the theater owners. In one Texas town a salesman sold a machine to a customer who had leased a small space directly beside the theater's entrance. The vendor paid the theater operator twenty-five dollars rent a month. The vendor sold popcorn to a large proportion of the theater's customers, grossing $530 the first week. A hundred pounds of popcorn kernels cost about ten dollars. When popped, it produced approximately one thousand 10¢ bags worth one hundred dollars. Even after other costs were deducted, this left a sizeable profit margin. The theater owner renounced the lease, took over the space, purchased a popper, and sold his own popcorn.[6]

Independent movie theaters were the first to capitulate to popcorn's financial allure. When a popcorn machine salesman approached an independent owner in Texas at the beginning of the Depression, the owner did not even bother to hear the sales pitch. He just bought a machine. The owner told the salesman: "I just took this theater over on a mortgage, because the man running it went broke. But the old fellow who used to have a popcorn wagon outside bought a house, a store and a farm." By the mid-1930s movie chains started to crumble. A salesman won an order for five machines from a circuit owner whose small daughter loved caramel corn. Another salesman sold fifty machines to a southern chain. The owners of a Dallas chain put poppers in eighty theaters, mainly for the children who flocked to the movies on Saturdays. Five of its best theaters, however, were considered "too classy to get into the popcorn business." In two years the theaters with the popcorn netted $190,000: the five without machines went into the red. As soon as other theater owners found out, they "started putting in poppers as fast as they could be obtained." One theater chain in a large city tried to avoid the expense of installing poppers in each theater by setting up central facilities for large-scale production by big machines. The popcorn was then distributed to theaters where warmers purportedly prevented loss of crispness. Needless to say, this did not succeed. Popcorn sold so well because of its aroma—the same smell that some theater owners had reportedly despised earlier. The aroma was maximized during the popping process. As soon as machines were placed in the lobbies, business picked up.[7]

Popcorn was progressively introduced into more theaters as tales of popcorn wealth circulated. R. J. McKenna, the general manager of a chain of sixty-six western theaters, was initially antipopcorn. As his profits fell during the Depression, he experimented with popcorn sales in some of his theaters. In 1938 his theaters lost money on the sale of admission tickets, but he claimed to have made nearly two hundred thousand dollars on the sale of popcorn. He cut the admission price from fifty to fifteen cents just to get more people into the theater to buy more popcorn. Another tale of riches involved the owners of a big theater chain in New York and New England who casually granted the popcorn concession to their wives. The ladies purportedly grossed five hundred thousand dollars a year.[8]

These experiences and stories, whether or not accurate, convinced more movie operators to examine the reality of popcorn profits. In 1938 Glen W. Dickson, operator of a theater chain in Missouri, Kansas, and Iowa, acquired a popcorn machine in payment for a debt he was owed. He sent the machine to one of his Missouri houses where it generated an impressive profit. It was so noteworthy that he began studying the possibilities of placing popcorn machines in the lobbies of all his theaters. Unfortunately, virtually all of his theaters required alterations to position the stands strategically. Ceiling fans were placed above the corn poppers, and exhaust fans vented the smoke. Despite these initial construction expenses, his investment was soon recovered, and his profits soared.[9]

Dickson made a conscious decision to focus specifically on popcorn because its profit margin was greater than that of any other snack. His lobby kiosks intentionally did not stock candy bars or other snack foods, requiring patrons to buy popcorn and thereby increasing his profits. His director for this program, Alberta Meinert, offered another reason for success: "We've found that an attractive seventeen-year-old girl who has been properly trained can sell twice as much popcorn as a middle aged woman." To control expenses, the managers required concession stand operators to account for the boxes and sacks. The net weekly profit on popcorn per theater, reported Meinert, was about 70 percent.[10]

Theater sales influenced the type of commercial popcorn grown. During the early twentieth century nearly all popcorn was of the white variety. Yellow corn was scarce; in 1923 it cost twice as much as white corn. However, popcorn machine operators preferred yellow popcorn. The yellow kernels had greater popping expansion, which increased the profits of the vendors. In addition, the golden-yellow flakes appeared freshly buttered to customers. Movie theater vendors increasingly requested yellow corn. When consumers went to the market, they demanded yellow corn because it tasted "just like the popcorn at the movies."[11]

Of course, not everyone was happy with movie popcorn. A bill was introduced into the Oregon legislature intending to outlaw popcorn in movie theaters. The originator was upset because of the noises people made while eating popcorn. When theater owners reported that 75 percent of their patrons ate popcorn, the bill was quietly forgotten.[12]

Radio

Another invention—radio—propelled popcorn to ever greater sales. The theoretical basis for twentieth-century radio rested on scientific discoveries dating back to the nineteenth century. James Maxwell provided the basic understanding of electromagnetism in his 1873 book

Treatise on Electricity and Magnetism. German scientist Heinrich Hertz generated and received radio waves fifteen years later. Using Hertz's idea, the Italian scientist Guglielmo Marconi experimented with radio waves to transmit dots and dashes. When he failed to interest the Italian government in sponsoring his work, Marconi moved to the United Kingdom in 1896, patented his inventions, and established the Wireless Telegraph and Signal Company. In 1901 he succeeded in transmitting the first radio signals across the Atlantic to Newfoundland, and six years later he succeeded in reaching the United States.

Three pioneers converted the work of Marconi into radio broadcasting. Reginald Fessenden converted Marconi's dots and dashes into continuous waves that could carry voice or music. In 1902 he patented the first radio system using Hertzian waves. Lee De Forest, considered by some to be the father of radio, invented the forerunner of the vacuum tube, which permitted easier reception and more amplification of sound. Charles David of San Jose, California, claimed to be the first "broadcaster" because he offered the first regular programming on radio. None of these early efforts was particularly successful, and all nongovernmental radio operations were closed after the United States entered World War I. Radio technology was sped up by the military, and by the war's end several companies saw the potential of radio and experimented at different locations. The first radio station was the experimental 8MK in Detroit, which began broadcasting in August 1920. It was quickly followed by Pittsburgh's KDKA, which began broadcasting in November 1920. Radio swiftly spread throughout the United States and many other countries. The number of receiving sets jumped from fifty thousand in 1921 to more than six hundred thousand in 1922.

Popcorn was a part of radio broadcasting early on and has been so ever since. For instance, KMA first broadcast in 1925 in Shenandoah, Iowa. The May family, who owned the station, were popcorn lovers. The owner's son, Edward May, claimed that he had eaten popcorn "every Sunday of his entire life." He ate it without salt or butter, claiming that "once a person trains his or her palate, plain popcorn can be delicious." Through the years the May family experimented with various popcorn recipes. KMA's program *Radio Homemakers* offered many cooking tips and recipes to Iowa housewives. Among them were ones for "Carameled Corn"; "Popcorn on the Grill," which used heavy-duty aluminum foil; "Pink Pearl Popcorn Balls," with red gelatin; and "Susan Christiansen's Grandmother's Gooey Popcorn," made with heavy cream.[13]

Earl May remembered one on-the-air popcorn incident. On his program one day May meant to say that his son went to the cupboard and found a sack of popcorn after hearing him mention popcorn, which

May thought was pretty good for an eighteen-month-old child. His words were: "I thought that was pretty good for an eighteen-year-old boy." The mail flooded in regarding his statement. One letter read: "May I extend my congratulations to you upon your eighteen-year-old son liking popcorn—mine likes girls." Another wrote: "I have a well-balanced boy. He likes both girls and popcorn." Earl May had many good laughs over his gaff, but the lesson he really learned was that many people listened to radio.[14]

From popcorn's standpoint, radio's immense power lay in its advertising potential. Products advertised on the radio sold. Radio advertising helped crown popcorn as a favorite American snack. During the 1930s the American Pop Corn Company sponsored a weekly radio program, the *Jolly Time Pop Corn Revue,* which featured an orchestra led by General Jolly Time and his Pop Corn Colonels. The program was broadcast over leading radio stations throughout America. The most frequently requested song was the show's theme song, "A Bowl of Popcorn, a Radio and You," composed by Paul Blakemore expressly for General Jolly Time and his Pop Corn Colonels. The lyrics were as follows:

> My Sweetie is marvelous company
> Where ever we happen to go
> When she's at a dance no one else has a chance
> And she's just as much fun at a show.
> But the evenings when she says,
> "Bring pop-corn
> Tonight you're a fire side beau."
> They're the evenings that I call, the best of them all.
> And I sing while the fire burns low.
> Just a bowl full of pop-corn
> A radio and you
> Just a chair by the fire place
> That's big enough for two
> Just a heart-full of happiness
> Not a care can break through
> With a bowl full of "Jolly Time Pop-Corn,"
> A radio and you
> Just a you[15]

The American Pop Corn Company was not the only popcorn company to advertise on the radio or to have a jingle, but it was among the earliest to do so. The Cracker Jack Company, for instance, did not advertise on radio until 1944, when it modestly sponsored "News of the Week" on seventeen radio stations. After World War II, Gwen Johnson wrote the music and lyrics for "The Cracker Jack Song."[16]

Popcorn Technology and Breeding

In the late 1930s two major innovations were introduced that revolutionized popcorn production after World War II. The first was the application of the mechanical harvester to popcorn. Until the late 1930s the harvesting of popcorn was done by hand. Hand harvesting required labor which meant higher expenses than growing other types of maize. Although combines successfully harvested field corn, popcorn kernels were small, and processors believed that mechanical harvesters would harm the kernels. Harvesting tests were conducted at the University of California at Davis utilizing mechanical combines. The results proved that the expenses of machine harvesting of popcorn were similar to those of other grains, and the costs were much lower than the labor expenses connected with hand picking the popcorn ears. The kernels were cleanly removed from the ears, and only 2 percent was wasted. With adjustments of the rollers, even this loss was eliminated. Initially growers believed that machine harvesting was possible only in regions where dry weather prevailed. During World War II the labor shortage in agriculture became severe, and mechanical harvesting of popcorn expanded. Special popcorn rollers were developed for harvesters, which greatly facilitated the operation. Mechanical harvesting was soon employed in all regions of the nation. By the early 1950s almost all commercial popcorn was mechanically harvested.[17]

The second major innovation was in the development of popcorn hybrids. During the early twentieth century considerable progress was made in improving productivity of dent corn through breeding hybrids at agricultural experimental stations. These programs also developed hybrids that were resistant to particular diseases and insects. During the 1920s and 1930s popcorn breeders at several experimental stations tried to match dent corn's progress. To produce hybrids, a family of popcorn was inbred for many generations. Only the best characteristics were kept, and the result was then crossed with another family, similarly inbred and selected. The resulting hybrid retained the best characteristics that the researcher was seeking. The process of hybridizing required hard physical labor. The corn stalks have to be detasseled, which required the removal of the tassels so the corn plants would not pollinate themselves. Detasselers go through the field and on specified rows remove the tassels so the plants receive pollen from an inbred popcorn variety in the next row, thereby creating cross-bred hybrid seed.[18]

Popcorn breeders sought to develop resistance to specific diseases, increase productivity, and improve popping expansion.[19] Expansion was important because popcorn was one of the few foods that was bought by weight but retailed by volume. An increase in the expansion of popcorn meant improved profit for retailers who sold popped corn or ready-to-eat popcorn products. In addition to increased profits, early breeding efforts demonstrated that high expansion and tenderness were connected: the greater the volume of the popped kernel, the more tender was the texture.

John Willier of the Bureau of Plant Industry in Washington, D.C., and later at the Agricultural Experiment Station in Manhattan, Kansas, developed inbred lines with a yellow pearl popcorn similar to Golden Queen. The hybrid initially produced an expansion of about nineteen times its original volume. Willier increased the popping expansion to twenty-six volumes in six years. The resulting strain was originally known as Sunburst, but its name was later changed to Supergold. It was distributed by the Kansas station. When the work was finished in 1931, the study found that hybrids were "much superior to the foundation material." This finding was surprising enough to be announced in *Scientific American.*[20]

H. E. Brewbaker of the Michigan Agricultural Experiment Station began inbreeding Michigan Pop, a selection of Japanese Hulless. The original lines were culled severely on the basis of agronomic characteristics. The remaining inbreds were combined with each other, and the single crosses were tested thoroughly for four years. The component inbreds were distributed in 1934, and small commercial acreage was grown in 1935 and 1936. In a similar experiment, H. K. Hayes of the Minnesota Agricultural Experiment Station used Japanese Hulless as a germplasm source, inbred it, and culled the results. All possible crosses were made, and one cross was selected as superior. It generated a 16 percent increase in yield and a 29 percent higher popping expansion than the Japanese Hulless. In 1934 the station released Minhybrid 250. Unfortunately, it was adapted only to the northern fringe of the Corn Belt and was not widely used by other agricultural experiment stations.[21] Some progress had been made in popping expansion.

At the Iowa Agricultural Experiment Station, J. C. Eldredge began inbreeding in 1928 with fifty ears of Japanese Hulless. Nine years later he had produced eighty-one hybrids. About one-fourth of them showed improvement in popping expansion, and almost 90 percent demonstrated a marked improvement in yield. At the Texas Agricultural Experiment Station, Paul Mangelsdorf attempted to combine the superior resistance to corn earworms with the popping ability of popcorn. Earworms devastated all varieties of maize, but breeding resistance in popcorn was particularly important because it was primarily a human food.[22]

Popcorn hybrids were also developed at Purdue University in Indiana. In 1938 the Agricultural Alumni Seed Improvement Association (usually referred to as "Ag Alumni") was created in Indiana. The nonprofit corporation was dedicated to providing top quality seeds to farmers and seedsmen throughout the nation. As breeders at Purdue University had experimented with popcorn varieties, popcorn seed became a major product distributed by Ag Alumni. The work continued during the war. The dissemination of the new hybrid seed expanded after the war's end. By the late 1940s these hybrids had completely replaced the open-pollinated varieties for commercial production. Under open pollination popcorn production was twelve hundred to fifteen hundred pounds per acre. By 1948 hybrid popcorn production potential was three thousand to four thousand pounds per acre.[23]

Popping through World War II

World War II rocked the popcorn industry along with every other aspect of American life. When the War Production Board issued directive L-65, all nonessential production was curtailed. Some argued that popcorn was not essential and that its cultivation should be proscribed. Others argued for price ceilings on popcorn to prevent inflation. Still others argued that the oil necessary for popping corn should be restricted. Just before World War II popcorn processors and manufacturers organized into two different trade associations. The Popcorn Processors Association (PPA) was mainly composed of those who processed raw popcorn, such as the Wyandot, Vogel, and Weaver popcorn companies, while the National Association of Popcorn Manufacturers (NAPM) consisted of those producing ready-to-eat popcorn, such as the Cracker Jack Company, and other snack food manufacturers and concessionaires.

An ad hoc group of processors and manufacturers—called the National Popcorn Association—was formed with Carl Erne as the president. The association sponsored the publication of a forty-two-page pamphlet titled *Popcorn is a Fighting Food!* The pamphlet maintained that a pound of popcorn contained "approximately twice as many food energy units as a pound of Round Steak, 2 1/2 times as many as a pound of Eggs, and 6 times as many units as a pound of Milk." It also reported that popcorn supplied roughage and was "a universally liked food" and "a moral builder." The pamphlet pointed out that women could easily bag popcorn, suggesting that the men needed for the war effort would not be required for this task. It concluded that popcorn was "an essential wartime food as well!" After due deliberation, the War Production Board indeed declared popcorn to be an essential product.[24]

Despite this declaration, the war harmed sectors of the popcorn industry. The most important challenge was the labor shortage that plagued the industry throughout the war. At first the selective service drafted young men, including many young farmers, indiscriminately. As soon as it became apparent that the loss of farmers meant a decrease in food production, deferments were granted to agricultural workers. Most Americans supported the war, and many farmers worked even harder to help win the war. This was particularly true of popcorn growers. Despite loss of farm workers, popcorn harvests increased throughout the war.

The war greatly disrupted world trade patterns. For the popcorn industry, the most important effect related to popping oil. Popping oil was unique in that it was never reused. The oil was absorbed by the popped kernels and contributed to its taste. The most commonly used popping oil before the war was coconut oil because it could stay hot for long periods of time without going rancid. Operators believed that it preserved the popcorn after popping. In addition, it was the most stable oil at room temperatures. It was ideal for use in popcorn warmers, where repeated heating caused rancidity in all other oils. Prior to the war the United States and Canada imported coconut oil from the Philippines and British colonies in Asia. After Pearl Harbor was attacked, the Philippines was occupied by the armies of Japan and imports were cut off. A scramble for alternative popping oils ensued. Shortening, lard, beef fat, and soybean oil proved unsuccessful. Peanut oil proved satisfactory and was used throughout the war by many Americans. After the war coconut oil was again imported from the Philippines, Malaya (today Malaysia), and Ceylon (today Sri Lanka), but it was difficult to reestablish coconut oil's previous market share. However, when the price of peanut oil increased after the war, the popcorn industry reverted almost entirely to coconut oil use.[25]

The disruption of trade posed other challenges to some popcorn manufacturers. Prior to the war the toys in the Cracker Jack boxes had been imported from other countries, including Germany and Japan. During the war the Cracker Jack Company at first eliminated the prizes in the boxes. However, soldiers complained about their absence, and soon prizes reappeared. Instead of the sophisticated whistles and miniature glass figures and animals that had delighted children previously, war-time prizes principally consisted of paper and tin gadgets, featuring patriotic symbols of pilots, commanders, aircraft, flags, and artillery. Perhaps the most unusual war-time prizes were paper propaganda cards. One included an effigy of a hanging Adolf Hitler.[26]

A more serious problem for the Cracker Jack Company was the disruption of sugar imports. During the war some sugar-producing areas, such as the Philippines, were cut off from America. While sugar was imported from Hawaii and the Caribbean, this required ships to transport the sugar to the mainland. During the early stages of the war ships were a scarce commodity, and priorities needed to be established. Simultaneously, the demand for sugar expanded as the military commanded vast quantities for its own use, and sugar was exported to the United Kingdom and other allies. The result of declining domestic supply and increased demand was civilian rationing. Popcorn confection manufacturers that required sugar were hard-pressed by the shortages. Most continued to produce some products for civilian consumption but mainly survived on military contracts such as manufacturing emergency rations for the navy and K rations for the army.[27]

While shortages hurt the sugar-based popcorn snacks, overall the lack of sugar was paradoxically the major factor in popcorn's rise to stardom during the war. As the rationing of sugar, chocolate, and other products took effect, the availability of candy and chocolate bars for civilians diminished. For many Americans, commercial candy could not be acquired at any price. Theaters were hit particularly hard by the sugar and chocolate shortages. With the plunge in concession sales, theater owners searched for substitutes. During the war popcorn was not rationed, and none was imported. Many theaters in major cities had not sold much popcorn prior to the war. Chicago theaters, for instance, had not even begun to install poppers in their lobbies until 1940. With the advent of war, theaters desperately needed to recoup their lost candy-concession revenues. Popcorn was the obvious alternative. Where possible, theaters introduced or expanded popcorn concessions. Americans were fully employed during the war, and most had some idle money in their pockets. Since movie patrons had few other choices, "popcorn sales went sky high."[28]

As concession stands at movie theaters dramatically boosted popcorn sales, a scramble commenced to locate poppers. William H. Beaudot, head of the A. B. C. Popcorn Company in Chicago, purchased fifty popcorn vending machines and placed them in theaters during 1942. Had Beaudot waited, the poppers would have been unavailable. When the War Production Board issued directive L-65, all non-war-related production was curtailed. The Cretors and Kingery Companies stopped manufacturing poppers and converted to war-related production. Cretors's strongest competitor, Manley, Inc., was more fortunate. Prior to the war, Manley had leased its machines to theaters and variety stores and operated the concessions itself. Also, Manley acquired a government contract to manufacture popcorn machines throughout the war for military bases and recreational centers for the armed services. With government contracts, leased machines, and concession stand businesses in place, Manley thrived during the war.[29]

Shortly after the war's end, Manley operated in many theaters and had fifteen hundred machines in chain stores alone. Manley's concession business emerged as a major part of its operations. One dime store in Detroit reportedly "sold 66,000 bags of popcorn in one month."[30] Unfortunately for the company, Charles Manley died in 1946. Although the family continued the business, it soon relinquished its commanding lead to other companies. The company limped along with reduced operations until it was liquidated decades later.

During 1942 and 1943 the popcorn crops had the highest yields ever recorded previously, but even these bumper crops were unable to keep up with demand. Escalating demand flipped popcorn into an inflationary cycle. Before the war farmers sold popcorn to processors for $34.40 per ton. By late 1943 the processors paid farmers $150 for the same quantity. The processors turned around and sold shelled popcorn for $360 per ton. In the summer of 1943 Fred Stegall of the Office of Price Administration (OPA) established a price structure for all food products. The goal was to set fair prices that would curtail inflation during wartime. Ceilings for popcorn were established at $73.60 per ton for growers and $150 for processors. The ceilings limited the profits of growers and processors but did not solve the supply problem. Civilian usage had burgeoned to three times what it had been previously, and no surplus existed to meet this demand. When the OPA announced that these ceilings would go into effect in three weeks, processors scrambled to buy popcorn at any price. By June 1944 popcorn sales to civilians drastically declined. Thousands of popcorn vendors closed down. Others acquired popcorn at prices well above the approved price ceiling. Some processors had hoarded raw popcorn and thrived by selling it on the black market. Honest processors turned down extra cash payments offered by desperate theater operators. The black market dissolved when the new harvest became available in late October, but the price controls remained in effect until after the war's end.[31]

After the War

Even before the end of the war, a popcorn craze struck parts of middle America. In Iowa the *Des Moines Register* reported on the opening of new shops that sold popcorn buttered, "carameled, cooked with cheese or french fried." Popcorn had become a major sideline in drugstores, candy kitchens, movie theaters, bars, and cocktail lounges. The new popcorn millennium had dawned.[32]

The popcorn craze strengthened existing popcorn processors. To meet increased demand, Wyandot Popcorn Company in Marion, Ohio, expanded. By 1945 Hoover Brown and his sons completed an automated loading device crib that would hold six hundred tons of popcorn and also built a large processing plant with five twelve-ton drying bins. The cribs had a middle storage area and two aisles. Each crib was hooked up to four oil-fired dryers. At first drying was completed in two to four days. This time period was gradually increased to two weeks, as fast drying decreased the popping ability of the corn. The shelling created a tremendous amount of dust and sanitation problems. Wyandot Popcorn Company had twelve small cribs, two large wooden cribs, and eleven steel silolike storage tanks. At the peak of ear harvest operations Wyandot could store forty-eight hundred tons of popcorn. Even this could not keep up with demand. Some farmers temporarily stored the popcorn on the cobs until room became available, and eventually Wyandot constructed shelled storage tanks to increase total capacity by drying and shelling during the harvest season.[33]

As new popcorn harvesting technology was adopted, harvesting popcorn on the ear was abandoned. The Browns concluded that shelling the popcorn in the field would be impractical in Ohio, since popcorn was harvested with too much moisture. Wyandot contracted with farmers in dryer areas in Nebraska and Kentucky, and the shelled popcorn was trucked to Marion for processing. This belief that only states such as Nebraska and Kentucky could produce field-shelled premium popcorn eventually proved to be wrong. Popcorn continued to be grown in Ohio, Indiana, Illinois, and Iowa.[34]

The American Pop Corn Company in Sioux City, Iowa, also thrived during the war. After the war the company experienced a decade of fantastic growth. In 1947 the company sold 250,000 cases of Jolly Time; by 1949 it sold more than 500,000. The postwar boom gave popcorn a boost which was unparalleled in its history. However, not all went smoothly for the American Pop Corn Company. Disaster struck in 1953. Heavy rainfall caused the Floyd River to inundate Sioux City in several feet of water. The American Pop Corn Company's storage cribs were flooded: all the popcorn was destroyed, and the cribs were severely damaged. Fortunately, the American Pop Corn Company survived this disaster, and within a few months its operations were back to normal.[35]

To keep the boom going, Jolly Time was advertised in as many as thirty-five different magazines during the 1950s. When sales leveled off, producers scrambled for new advertising channels. Jolly Time was advertised on *Arthur Godfrey Time* during 1956 and 1957, and on television Arthur Godfrey personally endorsed Jolly Time as "the world's best pop corn." Beginning in the fall of 1957, the American Pop Corn Company offered a Black Forest clock from Germany for only $1.50 accompanied by a Jolly Time lid or label. The company also added new packaging features, including polyethylene bags and a new zip-top can, which could be conveniently closed if only part of the popcorn were used. In 1959 Jolly Time introduced its twenty-ounce "Economy Size."[36]

Some popcorn-connected companies had been harmed by the war but quickly recovered after the war's end. The Cracker Jack Company survived its sugar, molasses, and toy problems. Looking forward to a revival in foreign trade after the war, a company vice president proclaimed, "If we could put a thousand different prizes in a thousand different boxes, it would make us quite content." Cracker Jack sales rebounded. By 1947 annual sales reached 100 million packages, worth more than $3,300,000. Sales were so good in 1948 that the company retired all long-term debentures. But all did not go smoothly for the company. In 1948 C. Carey Cloud, a major designer of Cracker Jack prizes, developed a series of figures representing different occupations. One was a sea captain with a pipe in his mouth. During the zenith of Cold War–McCarthyite hysteria, this prize evoked the image of Joseph Stalin to some observers. The company immediately stopped manufacturing the prize, but its image had been smeared.[37] Cloud, who had designed prizes and delighted children for twenty-five years, was unfortunately remembered for his sea captain.

Perhaps to repair the company's patriotic image, Cracker Jack engaged Jack Norworth, lyricist for the 1907 song "Take Me Out to the Ball Game," living in Laguna Beach, California. They gave him a solid gold Cracker Jack box and asked him to become the official spokesperson for Cracker Jack. To demonstrate the company's true American spirit, Norworth toured the country in a red, white, and blue car.[38]

When the war ended, the Kingery and C. Cretors Companies, which had stopped making popcorn machines during the war, tried to pick up the pieces of their lost businesses. Kingery was unable to do so and went out of business in 1947. The C. Cretors Company was more fortunate. Right after the war the company faced severe problems due to steel shortages. To get around this problem, Cretors produced the Super 60 popcorn machine, which was encased in a walnut cabinet. Although it was elegant, it was expensive to manufacture. As soon as the steel shortage eased, Cretors discontinued making machines with walnut cabinets.[39]

Three factors assisted Cretors in reestablishing its business. First, as few popcorn machines had been produced during the war, most commercial machines needed to be replaced. Second, the popcorn boom under way in postwar America provided a ready market for poppers. The final factor was Jim Blevins, one of the most successful of the postwar Cretors distributors. Blevins and Cretors set up a national sales organization. Blevins continued his special association with Cretors while he also established the Blevins Popcorn Company. It was headquartered in "Popcorn Village" just outside Nashville, Tennessee. Blevins engaged in a variety of promotional schemes that advertised popcorn. In 1949 he conducted a contest to demonstrate the best ways to sell popcorn in theaters. Hundreds of responses were received, and many ideas emerged from the contest. One contestant urged theater owners to place poppers near their box offices as more sales ensued if patrons still had their wallets out when they smelled the popcorn. The winning formula for success was "Ingenuity+Initiative+Sales 'Engineering'+Courtesy=Popcorn Merchandising."[40]

The heightened interest in popcorn during the war encouraged others to enter the popcorn fray. In 1943 Alexander Vogel and his son Art started selling processed corn. They had a one-thousand-acre contract with a popcorn processor, but after fulfilling their contract, they had problems collecting their commission. They decided to contract on their own. In 1945 they founded Vogel and Son (later changed to Vogel Popcorn Company) and built their first processing plant in Hamburg, Iowa. They used fertilizer to increase popcorn yields, which at the time was not a common practice. They also began to advertise nationally. During 1948 overproduction of popcorn caused the price of raw popcorn to drop drastically. Vogel, like most other large processors, barely survived. In 1949 the price of popcorn escalated, and Vogel Popcorn made profits.[41]

Another processing operation launched during the war was the Ramsey Popcorn Company. In 1939 Edward G. Sieg and his wife planted ten acres of popcorn using two mules named Rebecca and Kate. Initially they sold their popcorn to neighborhood grocery stores around Ramsey, Indiana. In 1945 they named their new company the Ramsey Popcorn Company. They began selling raw kernels under the brand name PURDU-POP in 1946. Its name was changed subsequently to Cousin Willie's, which featured the portrait of Wilfred Sieg, Edward Sieg's son, on the box. While the Ramsey Popcorn Company remained focused on the midwestern market, it became one of the largest regional popcorn processors in America.[42]

The J. A. McCarty Seed Company thrived during World War II. By the end of the war it was the largest popcorn processor in America. Jacob McCarty, by now a millionaire, built another large plant after the war to fulfill the needs of a rapidly expanding business. McCarty produced 43 million pounds of popcorn annually. As popcorn was in great demand after the war and supply was limited, the price for raw popcorn escalated. In 1947 a freeze drastically reduced the availability of popcorn. The J. A. McCarty Company was hit particularly hard. Farmers believed that it was more financially lucrative to abrogate the contracts with McCarty and sell their popcorn on the open market. To meet contractual agreements with his customers, McCarty bought popcorn on the open market at a higher price and sold it to his customers at the lower price that he had agreed upon prior to the freeze.[43]

In 1948 McCarty decided to guarantee enough popcorn to fulfill the needs of his booming business. He contracted with farmers for popcorn at one hundred dollars per ton, an unusually high price. When growers saw the price of popcorn escalating in 1947 and the hefty contracts offered by McCarty, they increased the amount of popcorn acreage planted in spring 1948. Also, farmers planted expanded acreage of popcorn hybrids and extensively applied fertilizers. The weather was extremely good, and the yield per acre improved almost 200 percent over the 1947 yields. The inevitable result was a huge overproduction of popcorn and a wild plunge in its price. This affected most of the popcorn processors, but it was disastrous for McCarty. Due to a huge overproduction of popcorn that year, the price ended up at thirty-five dollars per ton. So for every ton he purchased he lost sixty-five dollars. To meet his contractual obligations, McCarty signed notes to farmers and honorably paid them off during the next five years, but this was not the end of the troubles. In 1952 McCarty's popcorn storage elevator burned down. Orville Redenbacher, who had moved from Princeton Farms and had established Chester Redbow Seeds with Charles Bowman, helped McCarty by storing and drying his seeds. The J. A. McCarty Seed Company survived, but it never regained its prominent position. When Jacob McCarty died in 1960, the company was liquidated.[44]

Hoover Brown of Wyandot Popcorn was more cautious than McCarty in 1948. Brown contracted for popcorn at eighty-five dollars per ton. When the price dropped, he decided to hold the popcorn rather than sell it. In 1949 Wyandot grew no popcorn and sold what had been stored from the previous year's crop. But since the company was only able to sell at a loss, its strategy was not overwhelmingly successful; Wyandot barely survived. During 1948 Wyandot created Popped-Right Inc. to make prepopped popcorn for a theater chain. Popped-Right expanded into the caramel corn business and eventually branched out to include cheese puffs, corn pops, tortilla chips, and cheese fries. The company distributed the brand names Pop Wow, Munchmates, and Tender Delite. When raw popcorn prices escalated in the early 1950s, Wyandot again thrived.[45]

Weaver Popcorn in Van Buren, Indiana, was more successful than others in dealing with the deluge. The company sold its raw popcorn at a loss in 1948 and proceeded to plant again in 1949. Weaver overcame its losses and subsequently maintained a healthy business. It was a family-run operation that made quick decisions. Once decisions were finalized, the family stood by them, which was reassuring to farmers and customers. Weaver Popcorn insisted upon a high-quality product. The company contracted with farmers at a slightly higher price than did other processors and held farmers to stricter standards. If the raw product did not meet Weaver standards, it was rejected or greatly discounted. To support the continued quality of their product, the company invested heavily in a breeding program with good results. Weaver also aggressively held onto its best customers and often underbid other popcorn processors who tried to steal customers away. Finally, during periods of popcorn shortage the company selectively purchased popcorn processors. For instance, in 1988 Weaver acquired Consolidated Popcorn Company in Schaller, Iowa. Over the years these strategies helped Weaver Popcorn become the nation's largest popcorn processor.[46]

The National Oats Company, headquartered in Cedar Rapids, Iowa, entered into the popcorn business in 1955 when it purchased the Popcorn Growers and Distributors in Wall Lake, Iowa. National Oats later acquired part of the Blevins company and became a major player in the popcorn processing industry. National Oats popcorn was sold under the 3-Minute Town House label at Safeway grocery stores; its institutional sales used the Butterflake label. By 1968 National Oats claimed that the company's Wall Lake processing facility was the largest popcorn plant in the world. It did incorporate several innovative features. After shelling, the cobs were used in the boiler room to provide fuel for the factory. Other popcorn components were sold to make furfural—a liquid used in production of plastics and nylon.[47]

Popcorn has been employed for a variety of functions other than consumption. One use was as a packing material. Popcorn was lightweight, low cost, and resistant to shock and compression. During the 1950s a lamp company placed polybags over its lamps and packed them in popcorn. Popcorn was less expensive than alternative packing material, and it cut breakage and reduced labor expenses. Unfortunately, the Food and Drug Administration (FDA) became concerned about children eating the popcorn. The FDA was worried that the popcorn used as packing material could be boxed for consumption by shady operators. There was also concern that popcorn packing material might attract rodents and vermin in warehouses. In 1952 the FDA created tough standards for using popcorn as a packing material. Requirements stated that the popcorn must be inedible, mildew proofed, and dyed a repulsive color. By-Products Processing Laboratories of New York City and Winthrop Stearns, in cooperation with Union Carbide & Carbon Company, worked out a compound that denatured the popcorn to meet FDA standards.[48]

The warning required by the FDA did not deter Howard Walden, the author of *Native Inheritance: The Story of Corn in America*. Walden received some chinaware packed in a two-by-three-foot carton full of popcorn. He ate some of the corn and had no ill effects. He left the rest outside for the birds and squirrels, who eventually consumed it. Despite the stringent regulations passed by the FDA, popped popcorn continues to be used as a packing material. Many environmentalists believe biodegradable popcorn is preferable to other packing materials.[49]

Not everyone was satisfied with popcorn as a packing material. Jim O'Connor, the editor of *Living Single Magazine,* reported that while he was serving in Vietnam he received a package from his father filled with popcorn. When the package arrived, it was lopsided and torn. The popcorn was pulverized and spilling out of the package. He imagined a stream of popcorn bits and pieces from his father's home all the way to Vietnam. O'Connor concluded that "popped popcorn was a lousy packing material—but it did make me feel closer to home."[50]

Perhaps the most unusual use of popcorn was its purported employment by a Coast Guard commander who was anxious to clean up oil spills. Rather than release oil which would have harmed the environment, he decided to caste popcorn on the water. He ordered his men to clean it up. Unfortunately, the plan had a hitch: the seagulls beat the Coast Guard to the popcorn, or so the story goes.[51]

A Global Business

Before World War II popcorn had been grown commercially in South Africa, Southern Europe, and Argentina. During the war popcorn traveled overseas with the American armed services to lend "a homey touch to military life." Popcorn followed servicemen throughout the Pacific and Europe. In turn, servicemen introduced popcorn to civilian populations all over the world. Over fifty years after the war Helen Peacocke, today a successful British food writer, still remembered how an American major introduced her to popcorn in Oxford when she was but a few years old: "Oh that taste—I shall never forget it. Even the burnt ones at the bottom of the pan tasted good."[52]

After the war several American popcorn processors broke into European markets. In the United Kingdom consumers preferred a sweeter product. British popcorn promoters also sprang up: the Bard Brothers, for instance, produced caramel corn, as did the House of Clark in London. Weaver Popcorn was extremely successful in Scandinavia, as was Wyandot Popcorn Company to a lesser extent. Rather than caramel corn, Scandinavians preferred ready-to-eat popcorn that was slightly sweet. This was created by adding sugar to the oil while popping the corn, which produced a slight glaze to the popcorn.[53]

Popcorn was less successful in entering other European countries, sometimes for bizarre reasons. In 1950 the Milwabel Products Company introduced popcorn into Belgium in a small way. They used the trade name Poppies because the word *popcorn* had been trademarked in Belgium. Jim Blevins tried to develop a popcorn booth at the Brussels World Exposition in 1958. He failed because he could not use the word *popcorn* in the exhibit or in promotions. Another linguistic problem emerged later in France. The French Culture Ministry proposed banning the word *popcorn* because of its English origin. The proper French word, claimed the ministry, is *Mais soufflé,* which also just happened to be the brand name of a French popcorn marketer.[54]

After the war Canadian popcorn sales accelerated, paralleling those in the United States. In the Kitchener Memorial sports arena near Toronto, popcorn sales netted seventeen thousand dollars in forty-two months. Europeans and Asians who had been introduced to popcorn by the American military increased their demand. Non-Americans who had been introduced to popcorn by Americans wanted to maintain their popcorn options. Unfortunately, the global economy after the war was in disarray. Nations struggled to acquire essentials, and popcorn and poppers were not high enough priorities to warrant expenditures of scarce funds. This still did not stop their spread. Many national groups tried to barter goods for poppers. Australians, for instance, offered to trade tinned bait for popcorn machines. Belgians tried to swap razor steel for popcorn machines.[55]

Shortly after World War II, American soldiers brought popcorn into Korea. During the early 1950s some enterprising Koreans tried to sell popcorn in Japan. This effort failed because the popcorn was of poor quality, and the Koreans tried to market the popcorn using traditional Japanese methods. In 1955 Tokyo hosted the World's Fair. When Jim Blevins learned that the U.S. Department of Agriculture would have an exhibit, he convinced officials that popcorn should be demonstrated. The USDA supported the effort, and the C. Cretors Company was asked to set up the demonstration. Cretors hired Masutaka (Mike) Imai, a student from the University of Tokyo, to run the exhibit. This was a success, but an even greater success occurred when Blevins and Cretors again teamed up to exhibit popcorn at the International Trade Fair held in Tokyo on May 5–9, 1957. Blevins and Cretors distributed nearly a quarter of a million bags of freshly popped corn. After tasting this treat, children and adults alike proclaimed it *oishii* (delicious). A highlight of the exhibit was a "Popcorn Jamboree" held by eight Japanese Boy Scouts who competed to see who could pop the most corn from a single can. Katsunobu Nakamura won and received a popcorn-studded crown and a year's supply of popcorn. At the fair Blevins pointed out that a Japanese scientist, Kikunae Ikeda, had produced one of the most important popcorn flavoring ingredients—monosodium glutamate

(MSG), a chemical isolated from seaweed in 1908. The Japanese called it *ajinimoto,* which translates as "essence of taste." By the 1950s MSG was used in commercial popcorn and in a variety of other foods in America as a flavor enhancer. The Ajinimoto company, a major manufacturer of MSG, is one of the largest food companies in the world.[56]

This time Japan caught the popcorn craze. Mike Imai created the Mike Popcorn Company in Tokyo, which operated concessions in ball parks and department stores. Imai visited the United States and studied merchandising techniques. After returning to Japan he decided to sell only the best grade of popcorn and to market it as "an American snack food." This succeeded, and the Mike Popcorn Company prospered. PepsiCo bought the company, and Mike became a senior executive of PepsiCo Japan.[57]

The Heyday of Movie Popcorn

Despite general success in introducing popcorn to movie theaters during World War II, some larger movie chains, particularly those in large cities, did not install popcorn poppers until the late 1940s. In New York popcorn machines were seldom seen in theaters, primarily because of local building codes and regulations. Even when the codes changed, some theater chains, notably the Loew theaters in New York, refused to sell popcorn until the 1950s. Some theaters even required "that customers arriving with popcorn check it at the door."[58]

By 1945, however, almost half of the popcorn grown in America was consumed in theaters. In 1946 Homer Croy in an article in *Harper's Magazine* reported that the sale of popcorn in movie theaters had become so massive "that Fox Midwest Amusement Corporation, in Kansas City has about four thousand acres in popcorn; in addition, it has contracts with neighboring farmers." Croy visited a farm in Tarkio, Missouri, which had six hundred acres planted with popcorn designated for movie theaters. Croy dryly commented: "The crunching must be terrific."[59]

Annual popcorn sales in theaters reached over one million dollars. In some small, independent theaters popcorn paid the entire overhead. In some places it grossed more than admissions. One Kansas City theater manager discovered that the average expenditure of his patrons—primarily for dime boxes of popcorn—was eleven cents. "Of course," he explained, "we allow plenty of time in the break between shows for people to come out and get their second boxes." An Oklahoma City theater man confided that in six years he had netted eighty thousand dollars on popcorn. He advised theater proprietors: "Find a good popcorn location and build a theater around it." Comedian Fred Allen wisecracked on a radio show, "If they sold the popcorn outside, half the people wouldn't go into the theater in the first place." Another observer commented that theaters were really in the popcorn business: they were operated "so that folks will have a place to sit and munch."[60]

By 1949 movie fans were eating theaters out of the red, reported an article in *Life:* "The greatest single attraction in any U.S. motion picture theater last week was not Clark Gable, Jane Russell or even Danny Kaye. It was popcorn." Theater operators who once had viewed popcorn with suspicion did not mind the mess a bit. "Many of them frankly confessed," reported *Life,* "that this strange, national hunger had come to mean the difference between profit and loss." A typical small theater seating twelve hundred persons grossed from nine hundred to one thousand dollars a week on popcorn, of which 80 percent was profit. Furthermore, popcorn sales dramatically increased with movies aimed at children. The highest sales were counted during Abbott and Costello comedies, while the worst were generated with horror films. As baby boomers grew, so did their worship of movie stars. Just hours before Elvis Presley was inducted into the army in 1957, Jim Blevins, president of Blevins Popcorn Company, honored Presley for being the movie star who generated the highest popcorn sales. Presley won again in 1958, even though he made no new films while in the army. Bob Hope, a close second in 1958, triumphed the following year. He was also properly honored with fanfare by Jim Blevins in Popcorn Village.[61]

By 1949 surveys showed that 86 percent of the movie theaters in the United States sold popcorn. Six out of every ten patrons bought popcorn or other confections, resulting in an average expenditure of almost eight cents per theater patron. Two years later *Film Daily* conducted a survey which showed that 96 percent of the twenty-three thousand theaters in the country sold popcorn in their lobbies, netting $193 million. By 1950 farmers raised enough popcorn to fill about 2.4 billion bags. Even at a dime a bag, almost a quarter of a billion dollars would have been grossed, most of it by the movie theaters.[62]

Movie theaters not only sold popcorn in the lobbies, they advertised popcorn. The National Association of Popcorn Manufacturers credited theaters with hooking America on the popcorn taste habit. To promote sales of popcorn, the association produced an eight-minute color-sound film telling of the nutritive value of popcorn. Likewise, popcorn also appeared on-screen in films. In *White Heat,* a 1949 thriller, Buddy Gorman plays a popcorn vendor. The 1952 film *The Greatest Show on Earth,* starring Charlton Heston, features a tune titled "Popcorn and Lemonade." The 1985 *Real Genius* ends with a scene in which a laser beam from outer space explodes a twenty-foot package of popcorn and the house overflows with popped popcorn. In the 1994 film *Camp Nowhere* children make a popcorn omelet. There are two films named *Popcorn:* one is a 1970 musical starring Mick Jagger and the Rolling Stones, Jimi Hendrix, and the Bee Gees; the other is a 1991 horror film.[63]

A more sinister plot featuring popcorn surfaced with "subliminal advertising," which flashed messages on the screen for time intervals shorter than one-ninth of a second during the movie. These messages were not consciously perceived by viewers. Subliminal advertising was conducted in movie theaters at least by 1950, with limited results. In 1958 the United Artists Theaters in Los Angeles experimented for ten weeks. The directive "Buy Popcorn" was inserted in the last reel of each feature just before the final fadeout. The three-frame sequence consisted of one frame bearing the word *buy,* a blank second frame, and a third frame printed with the word *popcorn.*[64] Popcorn sales zoomed up, but more controlled experiments were necessary before subliminal advertising could claim complete success.

Using the tachiscope, a film projector with a high speed shutter patented by Precon Process and Equipment Corporation of New Orleans, experimenters took another stab at subliminal advertising in the 1960s. The tachiscope flashed messages superimposed over film in theaters or on television. These messages were invisible to the conscious mind. One six-week experiment with the machine involved 45,699 patrons who were exposed to the message "Hungry? Eat Popcorn." Popcorn sales increased 57.7 percent. While not all people were influenced, a statistically significant number of viewers obeyed subliminal commands to purchase popcorn. Subsequently, other tests of subliminal advertising proved ineffective when dealing with more complex issues, such as donating blood.[65]

In 1946 only about three hundred drive-in movie theaters existed in America. By 1958 this figure had dramatically expanded to over six thousand. As these theaters were designed from scratch, large cafeteria interiors were originally constructed to accommodate thousands of people during the eighteen-minute intermission. Popcorn poppers were important features of the concession stands at drive-ins. For Sue Spitler and Nao Hauser, future writers of *The Popcorn Lover's Book,* their first introduction to movie popcorn was at a drive-in during 1955. The movie was *The Seven Little Foys* starring Bob Hope and James Cagney, but the main attraction left in their memory was the advertisement showing two buttered-popcorn boxes that appeared on-screen before the show began. The speaker in the car blared out: "At the Snack Bar Now!" After that, their only desire was the jumbo family-size popcorn.[66]

Television

By 1950 there were twenty thousand movie theaters in America, and movie attendance reached ninety million per week. Just when popcorn was firmly ensconced in the lobbies, theater construction peaked and movie attendance dropped sharply. By 1956 theater attendance plunged by 24 percent. The total number of walk-in theaters declined by 17 percent. By 1960 weekly movie attendance had dropped to forty million. Six thousand theaters had closed by 1965. With more than 65 percent of popcorn sales occurring in theaters, popcorn processors were profoundly worried. The falloff in movie attendance posed a serious threat to a major segment of the popcorn business. Moreover, as movie houses closed by the thousands, popcorn machines were dumped on the market. Many potential buyers of new machines picked up used models at a fraction of the cost. Those making commercial popcorn poppers suffered as a consequence.[67]

Worried about waning popcorn sales at theaters, processors sent pollsters to question two hundred families around Chicago. They found that the culprit was television. Although television technology had been perfected by the late 1930s, monetary and technological demands during World War II stopped early experimentation. When the war ended, television burst on the scene. By 1956 forty million television sets were in American homes. By the end of the decade 86 percent of American homes possessed one. The motion picture industry suffered as more and more televisions were acquired and people stayed at home. Why should people pay for a film when they could watch free television? Many theaters went bankrupt.[68]

The decline in movie attendance and the decrease in theaters sent a shock wave through processors and makers of poppers. Popcorn processors recognized the threat and responded promptly. In 1952 the National Association of Popcorn Manufacturers, headed by A. B. C. Popcorn Company's president, William H. Beaudot, launched a public relations campaign to promote popcorn as a nutritious food. Among his plans were to produce an eight-minute color-sound film praising the nutritive value of popcorn and to distribute it to theaters throughout the country.[69]

The following year the Popcorn Processors Association (PPA) created the Popcorn Institute for the sole purpose of promoting popcorn. An estimated $4 million was spent on popcorn marketing. The Popcorn Institute worked out agreements with Coca-Cola, Morton Salt, and other companies to merge advertisements. Popcorn was good to eat with salt on it. Salted popcorn made one thirsty, and Coca-Cola was just the right thirst quencher.[70]

The popcorn industry weathered its crisis by following the movie patrons home and establishing popcorn as part of the television ritual. A *Time* magazine article reported that according to a survey 4 percent of television owners ate "hot, buttered, home-made popcorn every single night of the week." Another 10 percent ate it five or six nights a week, and a whopping 63 percent indulged in popcorn one to four nights a week. People went to movies once a week, but they watched television every night.[71] The Popcorn Institute, under the direction of William Smith, had been so successful that the PPA was eventually dissolved and merged into the Popcorn Institute.

In addition to serving as a substitute form of entertainment during which viewers consumed popcorn, television was a powerful tool to promote sales. During a baseball game in the late 1940s, two songwriters heard the cry "Buttered all over. Get your popcorn. Buttered all over." They decided to write a song based on the hawkers' call. The resulting "Popcorn Polka" was broadcast live on ABC's Breakfast Club in the spring of 1950. It probably would have faded away except that the executive director of the recently created National Association of Popcorn Manufacturers heard it. He decided to broadcast the song—and advertise popcorn—via the recently created national television networks. As television programs became highly visible, popcorn processors turned to the stars of the programs to promote their products. The American Pop Corn Company, for instance, used Ozzie, Harriet, David, and Ricky Nelson, the stars of ABC's *The Adventures of Ozzie and Harriet,* to promote Jolly Time in magazine advertisements in 1954. In a more direct manner television promoted particular popcorn products. For instance, Cracker Jack advertised on television in 1955 when it sponsored the CBS program *On Your Account.* Jolly Time was featured on *Let's Make a Deal, Wheel of Fortune, Jeopardy,* and *The Price Is Right.*[72]

Despite initial misgivings, the advent of television gave popcorn a boost almost unparalleled in the industry's history. Popcorn boomed. The average popcorn production from 1936 to 1947 was 170 million pounds. In 1950 popcorn production reached 242 million pounds. Within ten years it hit 332 million pounds. By 1965 production soared to 533 million pounds.[73]

Chapter 7

Pop Convenience

For many urban Americans who were exposed only to theater popcorn, popping corn at home was difficult to imagine. For others, popping corn at home was inconvenient and unpleasant. As Julie Polshek stated in 1949, anyone nostalgic for popping corn over the fire had forgotten the strong arms needed and the tired backs resulting from the good old way of popping it. Electric poppers were a great substitute. While they had been sold since the turn of the century, prior to World War II most rural areas did not have electricity. When the Rural Electrification Administration (REA) was established in 1935, only 10 percent of America's rural homes had access to electricity. Other Americans were unable to afford electrical poppers. Shortly after the war these conditions changed. Thanks to the work of the REA, 90 percent of rural residences had access to electricity. World War II produced wealth for many rural and urban Americans. Electric poppers became the in things in postwar America. An article in *House Beautiful* urged readers to gather cocktail-party guests around the electric popper because "everyone gets a kick out of the proceedings."[1]

Many electric poppers were manufactured during the 1950s and 1960s. In 1968 *Consumer Bulletin* examined the most common popping devices then available and offered a grim assessment. Of those they examined, only one did not pose serious safety problems. At that time only two types of poppers were in use: special hot oil poppers with their own heating elements; and pots placed on the stove. Many freestanding poppers did not have thermostats. If they were not unplugged immediately after the popping ceased, the popcorn burned and could potentially cause a fire. The burnt popcorn stains were difficult to clean because the heating element could not be immersed in water. One device that had a detachable inside bowl for easy cleaning exposed the cleaner to the heating element. Other devices had plugs that could easily come into contact with fingers and cause fatal injury. Because both types contained hot oil, *Consumer Bulletin* highly recommended that children be prevented from being near poppers.[2]

While electrical poppers were touted as an improvement, they were only marginally more convenient than popping with a pan or skillet over the stove. Popcorn and oil still needed to be measured out. The popper still scorched popcorn and had to be scoured. Popping with electrical poppers was unsafe for children, and some were potentially dangerous for adults.

TV Time Popcorn

The man who pioneered the convenience revolution in popcorn was Benjamin Banowitz of Chicago. In 1940 Banowitz was a theater owner. When many of his colleagues in the movie business were opposed to popcorn, he stood out as an innovator. Not only did he install popcorn machines in his theaters, but he also compared popcorn sales to those of other concession items. He was surprised to note that popcorn outsold all the nationally advertised confections and drinks. These snack-food and soda companies spent millions on promotion, but the popcorn machine churned out the profits. In 1948 he witnessed diminishing movie receipts while his popcorn receipts went up. He foresaw the impact of television on his theater business and concluded that it should be possible to sell popcorn to those watching television in the homes if the popcorn packaging were more convenient to use. What was needed was a product that was simple to use along with a strong advertising campaign to promote its use in the home, believed Banowitz.[3]

Banowitz engaged in frenetic experimentation. Unfortunately, when coconut oil and popcorn were mixed together, the two produced a soapy smell and taste after a few weeks. Finally Banowitz created a package with the unpopped popcorn in a hermetically sealed bag with the coconut oil and salt in a separate compartment. All the consumer had to do was place the oil and the contents of the flavorings pouch into the pan and turn on the heat. When the oil smoked, the kernels were poured in and popped on top of the stove. Banowitz sealed the popcorn and the pouch in a polyethylene bag, but he found that it was impossible to print on polyethylene, so he placed this bag in a cellophane wrapper. On the outside of the cellophane bag was the trademarked name of his new product, TV Time popcorn.[4]

Banowitz test-marketed his product in Pittsburgh for a year. He concluded that his TV Time popcorn, properly advertised, could create a new market. He decided to go national as quickly as possible. The company expended large sums of money on advertising. He spent over two million dollars on advertising in Philadelphia and New York alone. He acquired the rights to use the characters Mary Poppins and Peter Pan to help promote TV Time. By 1954 TV Time popcorn hit a bonanza. It was available in nineteen markets, and Banowitz hoped it would be available in seventy-five new ones within a year. He projected sales at 2.5 million packages per year and expected that sales would eventually increase to 35 million. However, Banowitz did not have pockets deep enough to pay for the promotional expenses plus the rapidly expanding costs associated with manufacturing and marketing. Within a year TV Time was almost bankrupt. Its creditors required that Banowitz step down as president. He later came back to the company in a different capacity and continued his creative approach to the popcorn business. TV Time survives today, although it is not a major player among popcorn processors.[5]

Jiffy Pop

Despite TV Time's failure, it triggered the revolution in convenience popcorn. Benjamin Colman of Berkley, Michigan, was convinced that a major reason inhibiting people from popping corn in their homes was "the greasy mess of pans that must be cleaned up after cooking." Along with Betty N. Robins, Colman patented a strong aluminum pan with thin, expandable aluminum-foil cover. Aluminum foil had been previously used for food preparation, particularly for frozen foods. Aluminum was also used as a cooking container, so all Colman really patented was the placement of a handle on the aluminum container and the expanding aluminum foil covering. Consumers placed the pan on the stove and shook it back and forth. As the popcorn popped, the aluminum foil top expanded into a large mushroom shape. After the popcorn was removed, the pan and the lid were tossed out. He assigned the patent to the Top-Pop Products Company of Detroit, Michigan. It was an unusual novelty that generated considerable interest among consumers. The first pop-in-the-pan food was marketed under the name E-Z Pop in 1954. Despite its promising E-Z Pop novelty, the Top-Pop Company did not survive. When Top-Pop Products Company was dissolved, the patents for E-Z Pop were sold to the Mitchell Chemical Company of Detroit, which in turn sold the rights to the Taylor-Reed Corporation of Stamford, Connecticut.[6]

Frederick Mennen, Betty Robins's brother-in-law, thought that E-Z Pop's expanding aluminum top was a great idea. Along with Robins, he experimented with E-Z Pop's aluminum package and saw several problems with the popping system. First, the handle was not strong enough to withstand the shaking necessary to pop the corn. Second, the aluminum-foil cover did not expand enough, allowing popped corn to burn. In 1955 Mennen patented an attachable wire handle for the aluminum packages. As a reference to his patent application Mennen cited Colman's earlier patents. In the same year Mennen and Robins also applied for a patent for a "spirally wound covering" for popcorn containers. Robins and Mennen split the patent application expenses. This spiral winding provided for much larger expansion of the top, thus making it less likely that the popped corn would burn. The first patent was quickly approved, but the second was not approved until December 1957. As soon as it was approved, Mennen purchased the rights to the patent from Betty Robins.[7]

In October 1959 the newly created Mennen Food Products Company launched Jiffy Pop from their corporate base in La Porte, Indiana. Jiffy Pop popped in its own expandable, disposable foil pan, generating a gallon of popcorn in three minutes. Mennen's national advertising campaign made Jiffy Pop an immediate sensation. It was marketed as a fun food that youngsters could easily prepare without creating a mess for parents to clean up. In 1960 Mennen made additional improvements to the package that permitted nearly twice as many packages to be stocked on grocers' shelves. This design change also permitted the creation of the "Popcorn Tree," which was "a unique point-of-sale display and the first known effort geared specifically to mass merchandise popcorn." Jiffy Pop sales exploded. By 1961 fifteen thousand packages of Jiffy Pop were pouring out of the plant in La Porte daily, but it was not enough to keep up with demand. An additional production facility was established in Culver City, California.[8]

The Taylor-Reed Corporation was not happy with Jiffy Pop's success and filed a patent infringement suit in South Bend, Indiana, on January 20, 1960. Mennen responded in February, stating that E-Z Pop had been discontinued because it was unsuccessful. Mennen believed that the revisions in Jiffy Pop made his product "different and a drastic improvement" over Taylor-Reed's product. Mennen pointed out that his changes had been approved by the U.S. Patent Office. In September 1960 Betty Robins sued Mennen claiming that he had obtained the other half of the business "through false representations." The Taylor-Reed case went to trial in January 1962, but the judgment was not issued immediately. Meanwhile, Mennen settled the case with Robins by agreeing to sell his business and split the assets. Robins received stock compensation. Mennen then sold Jiffy Pop to American Home Foods, based in New York City. At the time American Home Foods was a diversified giant with over half a billion dollars in annual sales. Its food line included Chef-Boy-Ar-Dee food products and Franklin Nuts, which subsequently launched Franklin Crunch 'N' Munch, a Cracker Jack competitor.[9]

As soon as American Home Products assumed control over Mennen Food Products Company, attorneys for Taylor-Reed requested that American Home Products be named as an additional defendant in their lawsuit. The court finally agreed and concluded that Mennen and the other defendants had infringed Colman's patent and found for the Taylor-Reed Corporation. The defendants were ordered to pay damages and were enjoined from further infringement on the patent controlled by Taylor-Reed. The defendants appealed the case, but the appeal was turned down.[10] Subsequently, American Home Products acquired the patent rights from Taylor-Reed and continued to produce Jiffy Pop. It was still a wise investment. Jiffy Pop continued to sell well throughout the 1960s and into the 1970s.

Jiffy Pop did much to promote home popping in the late 1950s and 1960s. This early convenience food was particularly loved by children, who could easily pop the corn on the stove with relative safety. Unlike many of the other fads of the era, Jiffy Pop survived and remains an icon of American popular culture. Its survival was in part related to its novelty value. It was also portable and disposable. By comparison with other brands, however, it was extremely expensive, and it required shaking. Even when it was shaken vigorously, said *Consumer Reports,* some of the popped kernels were burned. Another reason for its survival may have been nostalgia. In 1989 a report by Packaged Facts identified Jiffy Pop as a key factor in the development of the popcorn industry. Jiffy Pop made an indelible impression on the many baby-boom children who underwent their first brand name bonding experiences during this era. This dynamic boosted popcorn sales throughout the 1960s. It also contributed to Jiffy Pop's endurance almost forty years after its creation.[11]

Microwave Popcorn

The American Appliance Company, launched in 1922 in Cambridge, Massachusetts, first manufactured thermostats and then shifted to refrigerators. When its refrigerator business failed, the company decided to venture into radio technology. At that time radios were operated by large batteries that had to be replaced frequently. Al Spencer, an employee of the American Appliance Company, invented a tube that permitted radios to be plugged directly into the wall. The president of the company, Lawrence Marshall, asked employees what the name of the new invention should be. Miles Pennybacker suggested "raytheon" or the "ray of the gods." The name stuck. The Raytheon tube revolutionized the radio industry. A year later the company changed its name to the Raytheon Manufacturing Corporation. To assist in developing additional radio tubes, Al Spencer recommended that the company hire his younger brother Percy, who had dropped out of school in the eighth grade. Raytheon did so, and despite Percy's lack of formal education, it was a good decision. Percy Spencer turned out to be a genius.[12]

During the 1920s immense consumer demands for radios for home and automobile brought a surge that created the triode, a much-improved transmitting and receiving tube. In 1925 Albert W. Hull at the General Electric Research Laboratory invented the magnetron, which was intended to be a low-frequency alternative to the vacuum tube triode. Researchers in Europe and Japan adapted the magnetron to very high frequency power output. Investigations by RCA, the Marconi Company, and the British Electrical and Musical Industries brought refinements in the cathode ray tube, setting the stage for the infant television industry.

During the mid 1930s other scientists began experimenting with pulse radio waves that bounced off close objects, such as nearby ships and airplanes, and returned to a receiver. Based on military needs, the British government made sizeable investments in developing this technology, soon called radar. A serious problem facing early experimentation was the need for more powerful waves that could bounce off distant objects and were strong enough to return to the receiver. British physicists John Randall and Henry Boot of Birmingham University decided to place a cavity resonator around a cathode ray tube to boost the power.[13] On February 21, 1940, Randall and Boot discovered a revolutionary way to generate microwaves through cavity magnetrons.

As the battle for Britain raged, the war-strained British electronics industry was unable to develop and produce the quantity of magnetrons that the war effort required. The British government decided to share technological secrets with the United States, which at that time was not at war. American electronics companies—including General Electric and Raytheon Manufacturing Corporation of Waltham, Massachusetts—were approached to mass-produce them. British scientists visited Raytheon on a Friday during the summer of 1940. Percy Spencer asked to examine the top-secret magnetron at his home over the weekend. As the British scientists only had one prototype device, they refused to grant permission. Spencer flatly declined to help them. The British relented, which turned out to be a wise decision. By the following Monday,

Spencer had figured out how to mass-produce magnetrons. Using his methods, production was increased from seventeen tubes per week to twenty-six hundred per day. By the war's end Raytheon had produced 80 percent of all magnetrons in use by the Allied Forces. For his services Percy Spencer was awarded a Distinguished Service Medal, the navy's highest civilian honor.[14]

In 1942 Raytheon's income totaled $6 million. By 1944 total sales had increased to $173 million. Six months before the end of World War II, Raytheon's president, Lawrence Marshall, brought together senior employees to discuss how the company could be perpetuated when the war ended. If Raytheon were to survive in the postwar world, it would have to convert to commercial projects. At the time it was generally known that magnetrons generated heat when molecules reacted to the frequency of the microwaves and vibrated. Percy Spencer suggested using the magnetron to heat food.

After the war General Electric, Westinghouse, RCA, and Raytheon explored magnetron heating applications. At that time the scientific and professional prognosis for commercial microwave heating, particularly for food applications, was unpromising. Still, some scientists had high hopes and proceeded to take practical actions.[15] Manufacturers began exploring commercial application, particularly for industrial use. Only Raytheon's effort was directed toward the microwave oven.

According to Raytheon legend, Spencer discovered the heating properties of microwaves when a candy bar he had in his pocket promptly melted when he leaned in front of the microwave tube. Spencer reportedly sent out for a bag of popcorn and watched the kernels pop all over the lab. According to the story perpetuated by Don Murray in his article about Spencer in *Reader's Digest,* Spencer's discovery led to the birth of microwave ovens. According to the witness of Spencer's coworkers, the process was gradual and many individuals contributed to it.[16]

In late 1945 Spencer took Elmer J. Gorn, Raytheon's chief patent attorney, to the laboratory. Spencer picked up a kernel of popcorn and dropped it in front of the wave guide. It immediately popped. Spencer told Gorn that he could make a device that cooked "food faster and more efficiently than any conventional cooker" and then asked, "Do you think you can get me a patent on the idea?" After Spencer explained his idea more fully, Gorn agreed. Spencer's first patent application for heating food with microwaves was submitted in 1945. The patent described two parallel magnetrons heating food passing on a conveyor belt. Two years later William M. Hall and Fritz A. Gross, Spencer's coworkers, applied for a patent for a microwave heating device enclosed in an oven. It consisted of two microwave-generating magnetron tubes packed in a metallic box. The oven included a timer and a means of controlling power.[17]

Spencer's popcorn experiments had led him to examine how popcorn was popped. To illustrate his invention using electromagnetic energy, Spencer used unshelled popcorn on the cob. In the patent application Spencer described the usual method of popping corn, which involved husking and shelling the kernels from the cob. The kernels were then sold, and the cob was discarded. Frequently the kernels were stored as much as a year before they were used by the consumer. The consumer placed the kernels in a heat conducting, heat resistant closed container, which was then exposed to dry heat, such as an open gas flame. After exposure to heat for four or five minutes, the majority of the kernels popped. The popped kernels were then seasoned with salt and butter. Spencer believed there were several drawbacks to this method. First, shelling the corn required an additional operation and thus involved expense. Second, the separation of the kernels from the cob dried out the kernels, partly because they could no longer absorb moisture from the cob and partly because they were not stored in a sealed container. Third, the separated kernels lost their original flavor over time. Fourth, the usual method required a long time to pop the corn, as heat proceeded from the outside to the interior of the kernel by conduction. Fifth, many kernels did not pop, mainly due to the lack of internal moisture. Finally, the popcorn was handled many different times from ear to prepared popcorn, which, Spencer believed, was "rather unsanitary."[18]

A few months after Hall and Gross's application was submitted, Spencer applied for a patent application for a method of preparing food, specifically popcorn, in a "microwave oven." Spencer believed that his invention overcame the deficiencies inherent in the normal way of popping corn. He believed that popcorn could be popped in a microwave oven on the cob, which eliminated the need to shell the ears. The kernels could therefore remain on the cob until popped. Second, the microwaves heated from the inside outward. As water had a high rate of absorption of microwave energy, the moisture contained in the interior of the cob and the kernel was quickly heated. The result was that popcorn could be popped in twenty to forty-five seconds. Finally, he claimed that his microwave process was a much more sanitary way of preparing popcorn.[19]

Spencer's idea was to place an unshelled popcorn ear with butter and seasoning into a bag composed of material that was flexible and transparent to electromagnetic energy, such as waxed paper or plastic. The purpose of the bag was simply to contain the kernels that popped off the cob. The bag was placed on the bottom of the microwave oven, and the corn was popped. Spencer reported that some of the kernels popped off the cob but were contained in the bag. Other popped kernels remained attached to the cob but could be easily removed "by a light brushing or shaking of the cob." Spencer admitted that even with microwave energy there were still "a few kernels which contain insufficient moisture to explode," but these unpopped kernels remained attached to the inedible cob and could be easily discarded along with the cob. The popped kernels, already seasoned with butter and salt, were ready for consumption as soon as the popcorn package was removed from the oven.[20]

Spencer was in a position to propose that Raytheon exploit the discovery, and his participation was a key contribution. Specifically, he interested Raytheon's president Laurence Marshall. A prototype microwave oven was constructed, which cost an estimated one hundred thousand dollars, and was placed in Marshall's home in 1946. To demonstrate the prototype, Spencer popped kernels in the cavity. Marshall exuded enthusiasm as he "foresaw a complete revolution in furnishing piping-hot food to large volumes of people." Marshall ordered "engineers to develop an oven with inside trays on which cold sandwiches could be heated and served almost without interruption." A contest was held to name the new oven, and the winner was "Raydar Range." This was changed first to "Radar Range," and finally the two words were merged into "Radarange."[21]

The first commercial Radarange model was a free-standing white-enameled unit operating from 220 volts of electricity with an internal water-cooling system. The first Raytheon microwave oven was sold to a restaurant in Cleveland in 1947. The drop-down door was a potential nuisance in small kitchens. Subsequent Radaranges incorporated sliding vertical doors. With a price tag of three thousand dollars, microwave sales were mainly limited to restaurants, railroads, cruise ships, and vending-machine companies.[22] Despite Spencer's interest in utilizing microwaves for popping corn, his ideas were ignored. The cost of the oven was simply too high to justify buying one to pop corn.

During the 1950s development continued on the microwave oven. Raytheon dominated the field of commercial microwave ovens and heating applications. It was the only manufacturer of ovens for restaurants and was the principal magnetron manufacturer. Although Raytheon did not attempt to market Radaranges directly to consumers, it did license other firms, including Hotpoint, Westinghouse, Kelvinator, Whirlpool, and Tappan. Raytheon furnished power supplies, magnetrons, and basic-oven design data to each company. Other aspects were tailored by each firm according to its tastes. Tappan was the most persistent of these manufacturers. The Tappan Company began experimenting with a Radarange installed in its lab. Tappan engineers, who were experts in cooking, teamed up with the Raytheon microwave engineers. In January 1952 the Tappan Company developed the first domestic commercial Radarange. It was powered by a fourteen-hundred-watt to seventeen-hundred-watt magnetron that was water cooled and required plumbing connections. The magnetron and related components were located below the oven, and the entire structure stood five and a half feet high. It was a large and bulky device weighing 750 pounds.

This experimental unit was impractical for domestic use. What was needed was a magnetron requiring less power and a heat dislocation system that could replace the water-cooling mechanism. Tappan engineers designed a cabinet with an air-cooled system. Eventually the magnetron and related components were relocated behind the oven. Relocation of the magnetron, which had fed microwaves directly into the cavity, made a wave guide necessary. An aluminum duct and a rotating four-bladed fan were designed to distribute the microwaves uniformly throughout the oven cavity. In October 1955 Tappan introduced the first domestic microwave oven for the consumer market. Designed to fit a standard forty-inch range or for built-in use, the unit had a stainless steel exterior and aluminum oven cavity with a glass shelf. The oven featured two cooking speeds (five hundred or eight hundred watts), a browning element in the top of the oven, a twenty-one-minute oven timer, and a recipe card file drawer. It retailed for $1,295. The unit was marketed as an "electric range." Its advertised advantages were cooking speed, a cool oven, and a unique reheating capability.[23]

General Electric's Hotpoint division, which also had been researching microwave cooking, unveiled its electronic oven the following year. Both the Tappan and Hotpoint ovens generated unprecedented enthusiasm and interest in 1956, but sales were dismal. The price was still too high for the average consumer, and food processing techniques were not well understood. Few food processors took the technology seriously, and hence few foods were produced specially for microwave ovens. Looking back, Bob Decareau reported that it was "extremely doubtful if the microwave-oven business came close to breaking even during those first ten to fifteen years."[24]

Tappan continued to improve its microwave oven. By 1965 Tappan had introduced the first "microwave cooking center," with a microwave oven mounted above a conventional range. It still retailed for well over one thousand dollars, however. Despite these advances, an estimated ten thousand households in America owned microwave ovens in 1966. Plenty of observers anticipated high future sales of built-in and countertop models, but little evidence supported these rosy predictions.[25]

Two events turned around the microwave oven industry. The first was the invention by Keisha Ogura of the New Japan Radio Company—

40 percent of which was owned by Raytheon—of a compact, low-cost magnetron. The second was Raytheon's acquisition of Amana Refrigeration, Inc. George Forestner, Amana's president, was a microwave visionary. Amana appliance engineers teamed up with Raytheon experts to develop and design a household Radarange. In August 1967 Amana released its first microwave oven. It operated at 115 volts and sold for $495.The unit was well received, and Forestner predicted the company would sell fifty thousand Radaranges per year. The Amana RR-1 set off a revolution in microwave oven technology. Amana's success encouraged other appliance manufacturers to produce microwave ovens.[26]

Problems still had to be overcome before the microwave oven was generally accepted. Manufacturers needed to convince the public that microwave ovens were safe. This fear was unleashed by the Radiation Control for Health and Safety Act passed by Congress in 1968. While this act initially concerned radiation emitted by color television sets, it was later extended to include microwave ovens. On January 4, 1970, the U.S. Department of Health, Education and Welfare published the results of microwave oven radiation tests. Microwave ovens constructed before 1970 leaked microwaves. The Federal government developed new standards and required changes in the construction of ovens beginning on October 6, 1971.[27] These new regulations required design changes that resulted in safer microwave ovens. Public apprehension slowly abated. Today televisions reportedly emit more microwaves than do microwave ovens.

Another crucial challenge was to convince food processors to repackage their products. Foods packed in foil blocked microwaves and damaged ovens. Frozen foods contained too much water for microwave ovens. At first food processors were not interested in working with microwave oven manufacturers. The market was simply not big enough. By the 1970s, however, more than 10 percent of all American homes possessed microwave ovens and many ovens were in use in vending businesses. And the number was steadily improving. Major food processors quickly reversed direction and invested in food products that could be microwaved. Specialized cookware for microwave ovens was introduced by various companies. By 1975 microwave ovens sold over one million units annually and outsold gas ranges.[28]

Many problems specific to popcorn needed to be overcome before the marriage between popcorn and microwave ovens could be consummated. Despite Percy Spencer's experiment with popcorn on the cob in the microwave oven, this method was simply outdated by the 1960s. Popcorn on the cob had been discontinued by processors during the 1950s. Cobs were cumbersome to store and bulky to transport, and the shelled husks had to be disposed of. Spencer's process created a buttered mess that was difficult—and unsanitary—to remove from the cob. Alternately, shelled popcorn kernels did not couple well with microwave energy. The shelled kernels were small, and microwaves bounced back into the waveguide, heating the magnetrons and decreasing their life span. Finally, popcorn needed extremely high heat to pop. Most counter-top microwave ovens did not have the power to heat the popcorn high enough. These problems had to be overcome before the microwave oven influenced popcorn consumption.

One early attempt to overcome the problems of microwave popping was engineered by Amana. They produced a popcorn maker shaped in a *V* cone with a lid on the top. According to two engineers at the Raytheon New Products Center, the objective of their research had been to devise a method in which the largest percentage of kernels could be popped in a minimum amount of time. To pop corn microwave energy needed to be concentrated. The kernels were most receptive to microwave heating when they were clumped together. The *V* cone concentrated popcorn at one point, and a power concentrator was placed around the bottom of the cone. Amana's popcorn maker popped three quarts in three and a half minutes. Despite this optimistic direction, the popped corn at the top absorbed the microwaves and dried out, while many kernels at the bottom of the cone failed to explode.[29] Even with the *V* cone, most microwave ovens in America could not pop the corn due to lack of power. For popcorn to become a viable commercial microwave product, technological changes in microwave ovens were necessary and a new system of concentrating heat on the unpopped kernels needed to be developed.

Litton was the first microwave oven manufacturer to develop the technology that permitted efficient corn popping. In 1964 Litton acquired a small microwave manufacturer called Heat & Eat. Litton had previously manufactured commercial microwave ovens for restaurants. When its Atherton Division was transferred to Minneapolis, the company launched its Microwave Cooking Products Division, which targeted the home market. Litton's Model 500 used 115 volts and was compact. Its microwave ovens were installed on TWA planes in 1965, and Litton dominated the restaurant business by 1970. The company sold microwave ovens to the University of Minnesota, which used them to heat vended food for students.[30] When Litton began working on its 850 series of microwave ovens, popping corn was part of the design specifications. The technological problems relating to popping corn in a microwave oven were solved.

Litton's willingness to write popcorn into its design specifications was mainly due to the urging of James Watkins, an employee of Pillsbury, a Minneapolis-based consumer food giant. Pillsbury had been interested in microwave products mainly to service a vending businesses. In 1971 Pillsbury hired James D. Watkins, a graduate of the University of Minnesota, who had used the Litton microwave oven vending machines. Watkins was asked to evaluate Pillsbury's line of microwave products. Watkins surveyed University of Minnesota students and concluded that microwaved sandwiches and chicken were not popular but that popcorn was a tremendous success. Under the tutelage of Mike Harper, the director of research and development at Pillsbury, Watkins began developing microwave popcorn. Pillsbury's first microwave bag received a patent in mid 1976, and soon the company's new microwave popcorn (subsequently called The Original) was released. The Pillsbury research team had found that popcorn heated up more rapidly in oil. This provided two heating sources, internal and external, for popcorn. Coconut oil, the preferred popping medium, unfortunately turned to soap after a few weeks when combined with the popcorn at room temperature. Hence, early microwave popcorn was frozen.[31]

During this period Pillsbury suffered numerous shake-ups due, in part, to its successive mergers and acquisitions. Pillsbury, for instance, had acquired operations such as French's Potatoes, Burger King, Steak & Ale, Bennigan's, and Häagan-Dazs ice cream. Unfortunately, the restaurants counted lackluster sales during the 1970s. When Pillsbury purchased Green Giant, the company decided to let Green Giant handle microwave products and became reluctant to support its own line. Pillsbury failed to understand the importance of the superior packaging James Watkins's team had developed, which afforded better heat dispersal. As a consequence, Pillsbury squandered its early lead in microwave popcorn to others.[32]

Another problem faced by microwave popcorn makers was that the bags were unable to contain the liquid. At room temperature oil leaked from the bags. The Austin-Kane company of Topeka, Kansas, achieved the next breakthrough—shelf-stable microwave popcorn, Micro-Pop, which had a multilayered film package that kept moisture in and oxygen out.[33] Other companies engaged in making microwave popcorn, and several conducted research to improve microwave packages. In 1983 Wyandot came out with a triangular-shaped box with a metallic laminated bottom to generate high heat. This new box produced the highest percentage of kernels popped in any package. No previously produced popcorn worked as well in a six-hundred-watt microwave oven.

TV Times and Jiffy Pop were reflections of broader trends toward greater convenience in American cookery. In 1951 C. A. Swanson & Sons of Omaha began selling frozen potpies. Two years later Swanson introduced frozen TV dinners. The Campbell Soup Company gained control over Swanson in 1955 and expanded the number of frozen food items to sixty-five by 1972. The consumption of many easily prepared foods, such as cake mixes, expanded. In addition an explosion in the consumption of all snack foods engulfed America. During the 1950s and early 1960s fast-food chains, such as McDonald's, were launched. During the 1970s microwave foods were developing quickly, but challenges had to be overcome before the real revolution in convenience foods and methods of food preparation took place.

Chapter 8

Pop Mania

In 1988 Wyandot Popcorn Company claimed that it had produced enough popcorn to fill the Empire State Building thirty times over. It issued videocassettes of the original 1933 version of *King Kong* and gave its personnel "Popcorn Mania" T-shirts. *Mania* was the appropriate word to describe what was then under way in the popcorn world. Magazines reinforced the upward spiral of popcorn mania. In 1984 *Reader's Digest* ran an article titled "Popcorn! It's No Flash in the Pan," which held that popcorn "was the voice of the people," for it helped patrons "smile through broken hearts and bad movies." According to the article, popcorn was "the original mood elevator" but had recently become "the latest *nouvelle cuisine:* the rage, a gustatory obsession."[1] The popularity of popcorn exploded for a variety of reasons, but particularly because of the boosterlike efforts of Orville Redenbacher and Charles Bowman on behalf of their gourmet popping corn, and to the successful marriage of popcorn with microwave technology.

The Popcorn King

Before the 1950s popcorn was sold on regional and local levels. Until the 1970s it was considered a generic item, and quality was not a key factor in selling the product. It was promoted as an economical snack. High popability of all the kernels in a package was the main claim advertised to consumers. Orville Redenbacher and Charles Bowman single-handedly introduced the concept of "gourmet" popping corn, proving that consumers would pay more for a product that popped up "bigger, fluffier and more tender."[2]

Born in 1907 in Brazil, Indiana, Redenbacher grew up on a one-hundred-acre Indiana farm where his family popped corn over a pot-bellied stove. He was always interested in agriculture and even planted popcorn while he was growing up. He reported later in his life that he sold the kernels to grocery stores. While completing his B.S. in agriculture, Redenbacher studied agronomy and genetics at Purdue University and conducted research into popcorn about the time the first hybrids were developed. Upon graduation in 1928, he was hired as a vocational agricultural teacher, a position he held until May 1929. He was then employed as an assistant county agricultural agent and spent a year and nine months in Terre Haute, Indiana. When the county agent moved to Indianapolis, Redenbacher took over his position. He conducted a five-minute radio program beginning in 1930. He was the first county agent in the country to broadcast a radio program live from his office and the first to interview farmers in the field with a mobile unit.[3] He gained skills working with media that would later in his life prove extremely valuable.

Tony Hulman and the owners of the Indianapolis Speedway talked Redenbacher into managing a twelve-thousand-acre farm in Princeton, Indiana. Princeton Farms had evolved from a single coal mine opened in the early 1920s by Robert Smith, who owned the Deep Vein Coal Company. In 1924 Smith added King's Mine Station south of Princeton. While Smith's interest was mining underground, the above-ground operation was used for seed farming. Redenbacher commenced managing the farm in January 1940. In his first year at Princeton Farms he built a hybrid seed corn plant. During his second year he experimented with popcorn hybrids developed in the 1930s by Purdue researchers. He constructed another plant to process hybrid popcorn seed. During the first year of World War II, Princeton Farms was hit hard by the loss of thirty-eight workers drafted into the military, but Redenbacher overcame the labor shortage and continued to prosper. In 1944 he raised Purdue popcorn varieties P20, P22, and P32. He started work on Princeton Hybrids in 1946. Two years later he processed and sold popcorn in sealed containers under the Princeton Farms label, catering to the bulk popcorn seed market. Redenbacher increased the farm's operations and acreage. By 1949 Redenbacher was also a major producer of liquid fertilizer, which was distributed throughout northern Indiana. The Princeton Farms operations had grown by 50 percent and encompassed eighteen thousand acres either owned outright or under contract.[4]

Redenbacher's partner in the popcorn business, Charles Bowman, majored in agricultural education at Purdue University. His professional specialty was seed certification. Upon graduation in 1941

Bowman became the manager of the Agricultural Alumni Seed Improvement Association. The association played a major role in helping to multiply the new hybrids from inbreds and disseminate them into the hands of commercial firms or growers. Since Redenbacher's operation was one of the state's largest producers of hybrid seed corn, Bowman frequently visited Princeton Farms. Redenbacher and Bowman's relationship burgeoned into a close friendship. They occasionally discussed the possibility of owning their own seed company. When Bowman was offered one of the oldest seed companies in Indiana—the George F. Chester & Son Seed Company at Boone Grove—he approached Redenbacher, who agreed to form a partnership. Each man put up ten thousand dollars for the down payment, they negotiated a bank loan, and they established their new company. The Agricultural Alumni Seed Improvement Association would not release Bowman for seventeen months, so Redenbacher launched the effort.[5] Both Redenbacher and Bowman were satisfied with this arrangement. There was not enough money to pay two salaries and still expand the operation. But expand the operation Redenbacher and Bowman truly did. They built a new plant on U.S. Highway 30, two miles east of Valparaiso, Indiana.

While Redenbacher had previously developed and sold popcorn hybrids, what really got him into the popcorn seed business was the J. A. McCarty Seed Company. McCarty had purchased seed from Princeton Farms. When Redenbacher and Bowman started Chester Redbow Seeds, popcorn was part of their hybrid field seed operation. When McCarty's popcorn facility burned down in 1952, they helped McCarty by storing and drying some of his popcorn. Within a few years Redenbacher and Bowman sold popcorn seed throughout the United States and Canada, and they eventually sold to growers in Hungary, Israel, Argentina, Chile, and South Africa. They became the world's largest supplier of hybrid popcorn seed. They developed new hybrids, one of which was called Red Bow after the first three letters in Redenbacher's and Bowman's last names. Carl Hartman was hired to work full time on popcorn hybrids. Hartman hit on the idea of making a synthetic hybrid by planting a couple of acres with every conceivable popcorn variety and permitting open pollination. Hartman came up with a real hot shot in 1965, which was initially identified as Red Bow 65. When popped it expanded to nearly twice the size of commercial brands and left almost no unpopped kernels. For five years Redenbacher tried to sell his new hybrid to the major processors. Unfortunately, it cost more to harvest and yields were smaller. It was dried on the cob, which required more storage time and space. In fact it cost 50 percent more than leading popcorn brands. Processors, believing that consumers wanted economy and not popping expansion, refused to buy it. Redenbacher's response was characteristic: "They said people would not pay the higher price. I thought they were wrong, and I set out to prove it."[6]

To "prove it," Redenbacher literally sold Red Bow out of the trunk of his car. He traveled at first to local stores in northern Indiana, hawking his popcorn to anyone who would buy it. In 1970 Redenbacher quit producing popcorn seed for other processors and concentrated on selling Red Bow. If Red Bow were going to succeed, Redenbacher and Bowman needed professional advice on how to proceed. They visited Gerson, Howe & Johnson, a public relations firm located in the Hancock Building in Chicago, who convinced them to change the name from Red Bow to Orville Redenbacher's Gourmet Popping Corn. The agency argued that as the price was higher than prices of other popcorn, consumers needed to be convinced that Redenbacher's product was of a better quality than its competitors. As Redenbacher later stated, they did everything to increase the price of their popcorn. When other brands were sold in polyethylene bags or cardboard tubes, Redenbacher's was packaged in expensive vacuum-packed, quart-sized glass containers. Redenbacher and Bowman promoted it as "The World's Most Expensive Popcorn." The tide turned when Marshall Fields in Chicago and Churchill's in Toledo agreed to stock the popcorn in their gourmet food departments.[7] Redenbacher popped his corn on a table at Marshall Fields and distributed it to the media and the public. Soon other shops, such as Byerly's in Minneapolis, along with various midwestern gourmet grocery shops and supermarkets, fell in line. Gourmet popcorn began to command regional attention. With virtually no advertising, they had achieved their success through word-of-mouth promotion.

But Redenbacher and Bowman could not move beyond the region without additional assistance. In 1973 they teamed up with Blue Plate Foods to market their gourmet popcorn nationally. Blue Plate Foods was a subsidiary of Hunt-Wesson Foods based in Fullerton, California. Hunt-Wesson, in turn, was a division of BCI Holding Corporation, owned by Norton Simon. It was subsequently acquired by ConAgra, the food giant based in Saint Louis. This connection permitted national advertising and a widespread distribution system. For a kickoff, Hunt-Wesson and Redenbacher invited the press and food editors to Chicago's Gaslight Club, known for its scantily clad showgirls. Many members of the press showed up just to see the inside of the club. Scantily clad women were not to be seen, but the show entailed singing, dancing, and young cheerleaders spelling out "Orville." Redenbacher's gourmet popping corn received good reviews from the press.[8]

As part of the promotional campaign, Redenbacher appeared on *What's My Line, To Tell the Truth, New York AM,* and *Today.* Gourmet popcorn retailed at seventy-nine cents for fifteen ounces while their competitors sold for forty-nine to fifty-four cents for two-pound bags. Redenbacher's popcorn achieved a 4 percent market share by 1974. One reason for this success was Redenbacher's belief that his real competition was not other popcorn manufacturers but other snack foods. His gourmet popping corn may have been more expensive than other popcorn brands, but it was much less expensive than other snack foods. He stated: "You can fill a three-quart popper for about 11 cents. Compare that with the price of potato chips or pretzels."[9]

When Hunt-Wesson sold Blue Plate Foods in 1974, Redenbacher's gourmet popcorn was so successful that they kept the rights to it. On July 1, 1976, Orville Redenbacher's Gourmet Popping Corn business operations and property were sold to Hunt-Wesson. Hunt-Wesson was empowered to use the name Orville Redenbacher's Gourmet Popping Corn in perpetuity.[10] The actual amount of the buyout has been kept secret, but it was reportedly in excess of six million dollars. Despite the subsequent vast success of their product, neither partner ever regretted selling out.

Hunt-Wesson launched a massive advertising campaign for its newly acquired product, and Redenbacher began a new career as a television personality. He made hundreds of personal presentations a year and appeared in scores of television commercials. Redenbacher was one of America's most unlikely television stars. His bow tie, dark-framed spectacles, and midwestern accent convinced many that he was just a country hick. He described himself as "a funny looking farmer with a funny sounding name." The image worked. As one observer wrote, it called up "a sympathetic response from the inner nerd in all of us." Consumers easily recognized the glass jar and simple label adorned with Redenbacher's folksy image. It lent the product owned by a corporate giant a homey, small-town image. Redenbacher kept up a heavy advertising schedule. As he later commented: "The commercials have been fun, but it's hard work. It takes eight hours to make a 30–second commercial. But I've met a lot of interesting people and I've been able to do some things I never thought I could."[11]

Redenbacher and Bowman traveled constantly during the first few years of their contract with Hunt-Wesson. At the Rotary Club in Merrillville, Indiana, Bowman introduced Redenbacher as the "Popcorn King." Previously Redenbacher had been called the "Popcorn Kernel."[12] Everywhere Redenbacher traveled he carried with him little signs with sticky backs which said "I just met Orville Redenbacher." Whenever he met someone, he took out a sticker and affixed it to the other person. When he met women, he was known to place stickers on their chests.

Promotion paid off. Sales went from a 4 percent market share in 1974 to first place with 17.7 percent by 1979. In Canada, Redenbacher's gourmet popping corn went to number one in only two years. Despite the spectacular success, most processors believed that gourmet popcorn would be a short-lived phenomenon. They were wrong. By 1988 Redenbacher reached a 33 percent share in the unpopped popcorn category. The Redenbacher division marketed gourmet popping corn for regular and electric hot-air poppers and microwave ovens, and gourmet popping oil in regular and buttered flavors. Redenbacher is the exclusive supplier for Disneyland and Disney World leisure parks. In 1988 sales were estimated at roughly $258 million and the product was supported with the largest advertising budget of any of the popcorn packagers. Its advertising of all popcorn products totaled $37.5 million in 1988, which was double the figure in 1985. By the end of the 1980s Redenbacher remained the heaviest advertiser, particularly on network television, where 71 percent of their promotional budget was expended.[13]

Television contributed monumentally to popcorn mania, and not just through Orville Redenbacher's enduring television commercials or televised appearances. Networks and independent stations started broadcasting recently released movies. During the early 1980s conventional broadcasting was augmented, and in some cases replaced, by satellite, cable, and videocassette players. With the expansion of cable television into homes in America, more movies were shown on TV. With the advent of videocassette players, yet even more movies were screened at home. Many video stores sold popcorn to customers renting videos. VCRs were so important that in 1989 those responsible for Orville Redenbacher's Gourmet Popping Corn aimed a direct mail campaign at the thirty-five million owners. In 1997 *Snack World* still believed that the emerging trend was to "cross promotional aspects of popcorn and video rentals." Popcorn remained a high-impulse item that took up minimal shelf space and possessed a relatively long shelf life. There was "a lot of potential in secondary outlets like video stores, vending and kiosks."[14]

Redenbacher served as a goodwill ambassador to other countries promoting popcorn. In Israel, where popcorn was an export crop, Redenbacher received an award for saving the country's popcorn crop. However, Redenbacher's star began to fade in the mid-1990s. His contract for television commercials was not renewed in 1994. While lounging in a hot tub in his home in Coronado, California, Redenbacher suffered a heart attack and drowned on September 19, 1995.[15] Thus ended the life of one of the popcorn industry's most illustrious personalities. His gourmet popping corn stands as his shining legacy.

Gourmet Microwave Popcorn

In September 1978 James Watkins left Pillsbury and founded Golden Valley Microwave Foods in Hopkins, Minnesota. In 1980 Golden Valley introduced Act I, a frozen product which used soybean oil and a polyester bag. When Wyandot's triangular suscepter used for warming popcorn in the microwave was released, Watson took careful note. The suscepter was simply a panel laminated with several metallic layers which became extremely hot when exposed to microwaves. Watson greatly improved Wyandot's concept and incorporated the suscepter into an intergral component of the microwave popcorn bag known as Act II. The suscepter solved a major problem confronting microwave popcorn and it is an integral part of microwave popcorn packaging. Act II also solved another problem. Act II's grease-proof bag prevented leakage, which permitted the popcorn to be stored at room temperature. At first Act II was marketed solely to the vending trade. Golden Valley was too small to reach consumers directly. It was also undercapitalized and unable to generate the cash necessary for its operation. It had a negative net worth in 1986. During this time Watkins bartered popcorn from Vogel Popcorn in exchange for Golden Valley stock. Vogel took a risk—one that paid off handsomely.[16]

Golden Valley's success encouraged other processors to jump into the microwave popcorn business. Shelf-stable Orville Redenbacher's Gourmet Popping Corn for microwaves was first manufactured in the early 1980s and by 1986 laid claim to 41 percent of the microwave market.[17] The market for microwaveable popcorn jumped from $50 million to $150 million. Watkins conducted a blind taste test between his product and Redenbacher's. Watkins's won. Despite these results, Watkins realized that it would be impossible for Golden Valley to compete with Redenbacher's marketing juggernaut, so he approached General Mills, Inc. General Mills, another Minneapolis food giant, had been created in 1928 when the Washburn Crosby Company merged with other leading flour mills. The company was famous for its manufacture of Bisquick, Wheaties, Cheerios, and the Betty Crocker line of food products. Betty Crocker, a fictitious spokesperson, had been created in 1921 by an advertising manager of Washburn Crosby. Like Pillsbury, General Mills acquired other food manufacturers, such as Nature Valley health foods, and diversified into the restaurant trade by acquiring Red Lobster, Olive Garden, and York's Choice.

Watkins granted General Mills an exclusive license to sell shelf-stable microwave popping corn in grocery stores using Golden Valley's proprietary product and packaging technology. Golden Valley received a licensing fee for each popcorn bag and agreed not to compete in the grocery store business except in the freezer department. Conversely, General Mills did not compete against Golden Valley. When an agreed-upon sales level was reached, General Mills acquired exclusive rights to mass-merchandising outlets and discount chain stores. In January 1986 General Mills's Betty Crocker Pop Secret Microwave Popcorn made its debut. Pop Secret came in two flavors, natural and buttered. It required no refrigeration and popped in less than five minutes. Pop Secret soon ranked second to Orville Redenbacher in the microwave popcorn market. In 1988 General Mills reached the agreed-upon sales figure negotiated with Golden Valley and exchanged that right for free use of Golden Valley's packing technology. General Mills supported Pop Secret with an extensive advertising campaign. By 1989 Pop Secret had an 11.4 percent market share and ranked third among brands of microwave popcorn brands. In 1990 General Mills launched Pop Secret Light with 50 percent less fat than the original. The market for microwave popcorn shot sky high, and sales reached $240 million. Watkins's meteoric rise was just as remarkable as that of Orville Redenbacher. By 1988 Golden Valley's sales exceeded $110 million. In addition to Act I and Act II, the company introduced Express Pop and also sold microwave popcorn under private labels.[18]

Vogel Popcorn entered the microwave popcorn business in 1981 with a frozen product containing real butter.[19] By 1985, 85 percent of Vogel's raw corn sales were destined for microwave use. In 1987 Vogel Popcorn sold out to Golden Valley. Meanwhile, Mike Harper, who had originally encouraged Jim Watkins at Pillsbury, became the chairman of ConAgra. Due to this connection, Golden Valley began joint ventures with ConAgra in 1990. Within three years ConAgra acquired Golden Valley.

Popcorn Boutiques

Prior to World War II many popcorn shops had sprung up across America. The Karmelkorn & Nuts to You Shoppe in Washington Square, Indiana, had begun in 1929. By the 1980s it served such treats as cherry, chocolate, lemon, and orange popcorn; cheese corn; and sour cream and onion corn. In Chicago, Garrett Pop Corn Shops began operation in 1949 and initially sold only butter, caramel, cheese, and plain popcorn. By the early 1980s Garrett's business had tripled in just one decade, even though several competitors had launched popcorn operations close by. Local residents claim that Garrett's triple mix remains Chicago's tastiest popcorn. Currently Chicago has five Garrett shops. They sell special popcorn cans adorned with images of the Chicago Bulls, Cubs, White Sox, and Blackhawks as well as seasonal cans for Christmas. All can be acquired through the Internet.[20]

Wherever people congregated, popcorn appeared. As malls and other gathering places opened up, popcorn soon followed. Perhaps one of the unusual success stories was the Popcorn Shop at Dayton Airport that was launched in 1965. The popcorn became so famous that flight crews began calling Dayton the "popcorn stop" or the "popcorn airport." Airline attendants and flight deck officers proclaimed it to be the "finest popcorn in the United States" and scrambled to the shop during layovers to acquire some of the tasty product. Some flights were delayed as flight crews waited in line for their popcorn. Within a few years the shop sold twenty thousand pounds of popcorn a month, and new shops opened in other airports. Over thirty years later these shops are still in business.[21]

The late 1970s and early 1980s saw a great proliferation of popcorn boutiques. In Manhattan, Popcorn Paradise opened with a lobby designed after a movie theater. Actor Jack Klugman, who became interested in popcorn in 1980, challenged this operation. While on a diet, he found that popcorn was the answer to his craving for snacks. He launched Jack's Corn Crib and opened two outlets in Manhattan. He planned to develop a chain of a hundred more by 1985. Klugman tried to get his popcorn into the theaters, but his effort floundered.[22]

One man who succeeded was Charlie Bird, who had been an employee of the Mars Company. After his retirement in 1978, his wife, Marie Bird, asked him to make some chocolate popcorn. The result was so heavenly that Bird purchased a popcorn boutique named Corn Poppers in Dallas, Texas. During the first six months he experimented with popcorn flavors, such as chocolate-coated popcorn, which received an enthusiastic response. Then Bird developed an entire array of flavors: sour cream and onion, bacon, and jalapeño pepper. Eventually Bird developed sixty different recipes, incorporating popcorn into dishes with bacon, eggs, coffee, clam chowder, pizza, shrimp cocktail, lobster, and watermelon. After considerable initial success Bird began to franchise his operation. By 1983 Bird owned five stores and had franchised thirty-five others. He planned on doubling his operation within a year. These boutiques were small storefront operations in high-traffic areas. The initial start-up investment for a franchise was relatively small, from $15,000 to $40,000. Each franchisee gave a percentage of sales as an ongoing royalty fee. The materials needed were inexpensive. Unbuttered popcorn cost as low as 7 percent of the retail price. Personnel were essentially unskilled part-time help, which ensured a solid profit margin.[23]

Bird's stores were permitted to sell only "32 flavors," which was close to Baskin-Robbins's oft-advertised "31 flavors," but Bird claimed that he simply liked the ring of "32." By 1983 there was "a coast to coast explosion of popcorn coated in every conceivable flavor, from apple to yogurt cucumber." Not all popcorn boutiques survived, but those that did generated anywhere from $50,000 to $1 million per year in annual sales. Those who thrived did so by selling popcorn to impulse buyers on the street as well as to close-by corporate clients and mail-order customers. Today specialty popcorn shops account for a small but significant portion of sales of freshly popped corn. They also package their popcorn for sale to consumers and local businesses for later use.[24] Bird's model was soon copied by other franchises, and popcorn boutiques sprang up across the country. While this rage cooled off as the 1980s ended, popcorn boutiques still flourish in many cities.

Popcorn mania spawned the development of new popcorn companies. Paul Newman, for instance, inaugurated his own company—Newman's Own—in 1982, which intended to "create nutritious, all-natural versions of his favorite foods." Newman, a real lover of popcorn, reportedly carried his own brown bag of homemade popped popcorn into movie theaters. When asked if he really liked popcorn, with a genuine smile he reported that almost every night he sat in a chair with one hand holding a book and the other dipping into a bowl of popcorn. Newman popped his own corn, but he was famous for messing up the kitchen whenever he did so. Newman sought an easier and more convenient method of making popcorn to appease his family and keep the kitchen clean, or so the story goes. He spent two years searching for a popcorn that he would be proud to have associated with his company's motto "Nomen Vide, Optima Exspecta" (See the Name, Expect the Best). It was harvested from the top 20 percent of the special hybrid corn crop especially grown for Newman's Own. Today, Newman's Own produces Old Style Picture Show Popcorn. Newman's Own gives all profits to charity, or as the company's motto states, it engages in "Shameless Exploitation in Pursuit of the Common Good." Paul Newman donated $10 million to charity in 1996, representing 100 percent of his after-tax profits from his food company. His company's charitable contributions have totaled $100 million since 1982.[25]

Popcorn Celebrations

Along with popcorn mania came popcorn festivals. Some festivals predated the postwar period. North Loup, Nebraska, held the first popcorn festival in 1902 when a group of businessmen gathered to promote North Loup as a popcorn center in the United States. In the early days the leftover popcorn was dumped in the horse trough in the middle of the street. Today the traditional event has been modernized. At the hub of the 1997 celebration was the Volunteer Fire Department Hall, where the kitchen was especially designed for popping corn. For thirty-five years Chuck Lundstedt has been the chief popper. He supervises the popping in "Old Faithful," a gas-fueled machine that pops eight pounds of popcorn in under seven minutes. Other activities constituted selecting the Popcorn Queen and presenting the "1st Kernel Award." Twenty-five thousand bags of free popcorn were supplied by Mormac, a local popcorn company.[26]

Four thousand people attended the first Popcorn Day held in Schaller, Iowa, in 1951. This festival was presided over by a Popcorn Queen and included a parade with fifty floats celebrating Schaller history. The winning float in the parade was that sponsored by the Central Popcorn Company. It was built on an "Indian theme" and included a tepee. Local citizens dressed up like Indians and threw bags of popcorn to the crowd lining the street. The festival has been held ever since, although it has been renamed "Popcorn Days at Schaller." By the 1970s Schaller boasted four popcorn companies, and a sign outside the town proudly proclaimed it the "world pop corn capital."[27] By 1978 only two companies were left: the American Pop Corn Company and the Consolidated Popcorn Company. Consolidated sold out to Weaver Popcorn Company in 1988, and only the American Pop Corn Company still operates in Schaller. The community is proud of its heritage and has continued to celebrate its popcorn traditions.

Illinois and Indiana boast three popcorn festivals. Illinois's Ridgeway Popcorn Day celebration was launched in 1957 and has been held yearly ever since. The 1997 program sponsored a culinary fair, which offered awards for the best caramel popcorn and popcorn balls, and pronounced a popcorn "Champion." The first Van Buren Popcorn Festival was held in 1973. Brochures proclaim Van Buren, Indiana, to be "The Popcorn Center of the World." This festival has featured Children's Popcorn Olympics and a Popcorn Stage. The proceeds from the festival are donated to local charities or other local fund-raising projects. Valparaiso, Indiana, first hosted a Popcorn Festival beginning in 1979, with the first theme being "A Salute to Orville Redenbacher." Redenbacher and Charles Bowman had centered their popcorn operation near Valparaiso, but by 1979 they had sold the popcorn facility to Hunt-Wesson. Redenbacher had moved to California. An estimated thirty thousand to thirty-five thousand people show up annually for the festival. This festival has featured a Popcorn Walk, a Popcorn Talent Show, and a parade in Orville Redenbacher's honor.[28]

In Ohio the Marion Popcorn Festival honors Wyandot Popcorn Company and Popped-Right, Inc. The first festival was held in 1981. Fifty thousand people attended the first night's parade, and officials estimated that two hundred thousand attended some part of the festivities. Entertainment featured Henney Youngman, the Lettermen, and Ray Stevens. The following year's program starred free performances by

Helen Reddy and Guy Lombardo's Royal Canadians. It also boasted of a beauty pageant, a Popcorn Ball (dance), and a golf tournament. In subsequent years activities included the Popcorn 100 bike race, the Miss Teeny Pop contest, popcorn floats, and concessioners with plenty of popcorn.[29] The Marion festival quickly became the largest popcorn festival in America. The 1997 festival lasted three days and featured free entertainment, with nationally famous groups. The Thursday parade exceeded three hundred bands, floats, and majorette groups.

The Prepopped Surge

In 1970 Cracker Jack was enjoyed in 24,689,000 homes, or 41 percent of all American households. It retained its dominance in the ready-to-eat popcorn category for decades. Cracker Jack utilized twenty-five tons of popcorn per day and reportedly was the largest user of popcorn in the nation. The company had also expanded abroad. Cracker Jack was sold in the United Kingdom in 1897 and in Canada in 1901. Cracker Jack was sold in fifty-three countries by 1976.[30] Then its commanding lead slipped abroad and at home.

Local companies began manufacturing Cracker Jack–like snacks, and Cracker Jack sales abroad declined. By the end of the 1980s Cracker Jack was still the leader in the sweet popcorn field in America, but it was losing its market share to a pack of competitors. American Home Products, owners of Jiffy Pop, launched Franklin Crunch 'N' Munch in the 1970s. Fiddle Faddle and Screaming Yellow Zonkers, manufactured by Sandoz Nutrition, held third place. Like Cracker Jack and Franklin Crunch 'N' Munch, Sandoz's products were aimed at youthful consumers. Poppycock, its premium brand, sold at premium prices. By the early 1990s Franklin Crunch 'N' Munch had toppled Cracker Jack as the nation's number one ready-to-eat popcorn confection.[31]

For years Frito-Lay sold ready-to-eat cheese-flavored popcorn. In 1986 Smartfoods, Inc., located in Massachusetts, launched a gourmet ready-to-eat white cheddar cheese popcorn. Smartfoods had been founded by Andrew Meyers, whose real interest was to market a patented resealable plastic bag that he and Ken Martin had developed. The popcorn contents, developed by Annie Withey, generated more interest than the bag. Within two years sales had reached $12 million. Smartfoods had quickly became the leader in its field. One reason for its success was its advertising campaign. Smartfoods capitalized on two trends, New Wave and New Age. Its lack of preservatives and artificial colorings permitted its positioning as an "all-natural" product. The company gave away samples at sporting events, beach parties, and other youth-oriented events. Smartfoods's executives also contributed to the success. As a promotional stunt, Ken Martin wore huge Smartfoods bags on Vermont ski slopes and was featured in an issue of *Adweek's Marketing Week*. Success often breeds trouble, and so it was at Smartfoods. A power struggle ensued, and Meyers won control of the company. Martin and Withey left the company and created Annie's, Inc.[32]

Smartfoods's success revitalized sales of other prepopped popcorn products and encouraged others to develop new lines. Frito-Lay responded by introducing Chee*tos Cheddar Cheese Flavored Popcorn in 1988. For its advertising campaign the company relied on Chester Cheetah, a cartoon character targeted at children and young adults. Chee*tos differed from Smartfoods in that the former was yellow and the latter was white. Frito-Lay purchased Smartfoods in 1989 for $14.5 million. The Cape Cod Company, located in Hyannis, Massachusetts, and owned by Anheuser-Busch, also launched a white cheddar product. Its gourmet image and high price aimed for an upscale clientele. By the end of the 1980s Cape Cod popcorn was accessible to 70 percent of the country's population, and its manufacturing plant ran at maximum speed. Borden's Wise Foods offered cheese popcorn "made with premium white cheddar." Since the company reduced expenses by excluding flavorings and decreasing the amount of cheese, this product had a lower price than its competitors. In 1989 Ann Withey and Andrew Martin reemerged in the prepopped cheese category with their release of Annie's All Natural Popcorn & Real Wisconsin Cheddar Cheese. They employed a similar approach as they had with Smartfoods. Annie's claimed to contain no preservatives and used recyclable bags, and the company pledged to donate a percentage of its gross revenues to social and environmental causes.[33]

Pop Food Revival

Another effect of popcorn mania was the revival of popcorn cookery. Only one popcorn recipe was published in *Gourmet* prior to 1980. As popcorn acquired a "gourmet" image, the magazine finally decided to infuse some of its issues with recipes. In 1981 *Gourmet* published a popcorn recipe for "Nut Butter Crunch" with pecans and blanched whole almonds. The following year it published a recipe for popcorn balls. In February 1984 it weighed in with several more popcorn recipes, these calling for decidedly untraditional flavorings. The magazine recipes featured ingredients such as cheddar cheese, bacon, Middle Eastern and Oriental flavors, peanuts, Parmesan cheese, hot pepper, and sesame seeds. In October 1984 it promulgated another recipe for molasses popcorn balls.[34] While these recipes were neither original nor voluminous, *Gourmet* bestowed a kind legitimacy on the mania sweeping the nation.

After a sixty-year respite, popcorn cookbooks returned during the mid 1970s. In 1976 Carolyn Vosburg Hall published a cookbook for children, *I Love Popcorn.* The book featured twenty-five mainly traditional recipes along with information about popcorn. A couple of unusual recipes were Pizza Popcorn with Italian salad dressing, Hawaiian Popcorn Bars with pineapple, Beanut Butter Popcorn, the cookbook also featured tips for constructing popcorn sculptures, art, Easter eggs, and other decorations. In the same year Barbara Williams's *Cornzapoppin'! Popcorn Recipes and Party Ideas for All Occasions* was released. It included dozens of recipes for popcorn sculptures and for holidays and birthdays.[35] While these two cookbooks were not enshrined in the mainstream of American cookery, they did supply encouragement for cookbook authors who followed.

Published one year after Williams's and Hall's popcorn books, Larry Kusche's *Popcorn* was the first modern popcorn cookbook with gorgeous illustrations and hundreds of popcorn recipes. The book contained recipes for making salty, sweet, and flavored popcorn as well as for assembling traditional popcorn balls, bars, and candy. Kusche added new variations of the traditional popcorn ball, such as "Rum-Flavored," "Whiskey-Sour," "Russian Tea," "Sweet & Sour," "Cranberry," "Peanut Butter," and "Hawaiian." Kusche recommended serving popcorn dishes for breakfast, appetizers, entrées, and desserts. For campouts he suggested "Hobo Popcorn," with aluminum foil tied on a stick as a makeshift popper, and "Back Packer's Mix" with raisins, coconut, and sunflower seeds. He also presented recipes for using popcorn flour to make cottage-cheese bread, granola muffins, and honey buns. In addition to recipes, Kusche included a wide range of information about popcorn history, advice for selecting poppers, and instructions for making popcorn sculptures.[36]

Five popcorn cookbooks were published during the 1980s. In 1982 Connie Evener and MarSue Birtler's *Kernel Knowledge* included over seventy-five recipes interspersed with popcorn history, trivia, and art. While the material presented as history left much to be desired, recipes for such treats as tomato soup, meatloaf, and spinach salad were creative. All the profits from the sale of the cookbook went to a charity to help those unable to read. Two popcorn books were published in 1983. Robert Brucken's *Bang! The Explosive Popcorn Recipe Book* had more than 150 popcorn recipes, plus additional ones for making special butter to put on popcorn. Brucken's cookbook divided the recipes into popcorn dips, soups, side dishes, main dishes, breakfast dishes, breads, muffins and rolls, desserts, cookies, and other snacks. That same year Sue Spitler and Nao Hauser's *The Popcorn Lover's Book* included over 100 serving ideas. Spitler and Hauser featured recipes that mixed butter with chutney, cardamom, Cheddar cheese mix, herbs, chili, pesto, and fruit and combined salt with herbs, caraway seeds, and toasted sesame seeds and poured them over the popcorn. They also included alcoholic ingredients—bourbon and red wine—to add to popcorn along with many popcorn mixes, sweets, entrées, and decorations.[37]

By far the wildest popcorn cookbook was Diane Pfeifer's *For Popcorn Lovers Only,* published in 1987. Her chapter "Popping through the Ages" spotlighted "Aris-Pop-Le" with feta cheese; "Attila The Hun-Ey Crunch" with Rice Chex cereal; "Julius Caesar Salad" with olive oil and Parmesan cheese; "Marc Anthony Nibble" with marshmallow cream and peanut butter; "Cleo-Pop-Ra" with coconut; "Confucius Corn" with chow mein noodles and soy sauce; "Mona Lisa Pizza Corn" with olive oil, tomato paste, oregano, basil, thyme, and garlic powder; "Tarzan Banana Cream Pop" with mashed banana and instant vanilla pudding mix; and "The Godpopper" with garlic, olive oil, and Parmesan cheese. She also highlighted popcorn concoctions using traditional (or stereotypical) ingredients from Ireland, Germany, Africa, Russia, Japan, India, and China. Her recipes featured such unusual combinations as popcorn with bacon, horseradish, ranch dressing, piña colada mix, berry preserves, instant coffee, cumin, tahini, and ginger snaps.[38]

Two popcorn cookbooks were issued by the popcorn industry. Orville Redenbacher's *Popcorn Book,* published in 1984, was vintage Orville. It featured his own popcorn autobiography as well as recipes. Many recipes were purportedly created by family members, such as "Nina's Favorite Topping," composed of chili powder, paprika, and onion powder. He published recipes to appeal to the palates of college students, such as "College Corn Bowl" with chicken-flavored broth mix, poultry seasoning, and celery seeds. He also presented some unusual combinations mixing popcorn with whitefish or in a birthday pie along with strawberry-flavored gelatin and vanilla ice cream. Like others' before this, some of Redenbacher's recipes were flavored with purportedly ethnic ingredients from around the world: dry taco mix; soy sauce and ginger; and Italian herb dressing. Ursla Hotchner's *Newman's Own Gourmet Popcorn Recipes* consisted of unusual combinations of popcorn with polenta, sherry, Roquefort, pesto, schnitzel, spinach, buckwheat, strawberries, apples, peaches, and other fruit.[39]

Recently two new popcorn cookbooks were released. Frances Towner Giedt's *Popcorn!* featured sixty popcorn recipes. Her recipes contained new ethnic flavors in otherwise traditional popcorn treats, such as cumin, peppers, oregano, garlic, thyme, jalapeños, pecans, ginger, spaghetti sauce mix, and taco seasoning. Giedt also highlighted new variations on sweet recipes, starring bananas, butterscotch, toffee, key limes, and tutti-frutti. Gina Steer's *The Hoppin 'n' Poppin Popcorn Cookbook* was composed of sixty recipes featuring tuna, Gouda cheese, chili peppers, cut-up chicken breasts, yeast extract, sun-dried tomatoes, Jamaican hot pepper sauce, Thai chili peppers, garam masala, garlic, and olive oil. Steer's surprise recipes included "Smoothie Fruity Pops" with diced prunes, "Yankee Doodle Treat" with ice cream, and "Boozy Chocs" with chocolate and rum. The Internet is also a source for popcorn recipes. The Popcorn Institute's Web site alone features twenty-eight recipes with intriguing titles: "Yummy Yogurt Popcorn," "Tex-Mex Mix," "Popcorn Chipwiches," "Halloween Popcorn Logs," and "Boston Tea Party Popcorn."[40]

Popping Devices

The search for the ideal popper has been a continuously unfolding story. In hot-oil popping the kernels were coated in a thin layer of oil. Two drawbacks were apparent in this method: more oil was added to the product, and the diet; and the kernels often ended up tough and chewy. New popping devices emerged during the 1970s and 1980s to counteract these challenges. The most revolutionary was the hot-air popper introduced in the late 1970s. In hot-air popping the kernels were fed into a hopper and tossed about in hot air until they popped and were blown out of the popper into a surrounding container. For the best hot-air popping, specially graded kernels must be used. Hot-air poppers made it possible to pop corn without using oil, resulting in a healthier, and fluffier popcorn, which was, unfortunately, often tough, less crisp, dry, and tasteless. One observer commented that hot-air popped corn tasted like "polystyrene packing balls." The hot-air popping method expelled too much moisture. Corn popped this way also left "more particles stuck in the crevices of your teeth."[41]

Electric hot-air and hot-oil poppers made it possible for people to pop corn in their living rooms, and thus avoid missing any part of their favorite television shows or movies. These poppers were also easily transported and were used in places where microwaves or ovens were not available. College dormitories soon brimmed with electric hot-air poppers. *Consumer Reports* tested ten popping devices along with five major brands of popcorn and judged them on the duration of procedures, the expansion of the kernels, and the completeness of popping. The hot-air units included the Presto Popcorn Now Plus, which popped corn in two minutes, and a Sears Kenmore popper, both of which were highly rated. The hot-oil units included the West Bend Stir Crazy and another Sears Kenmore machine, both of which were also highly rated.[42]

According to the *Consumer Reports* panel of trained experts, the cooking method had more of an influence on taste than did the brand of popcorn. Their conclusion was that popcorn popped in a microwave was better than popcorn cooked in hot oil. Popcorn cooked in hot oil was less crisp and tougher than microwave popcorn. Hot-air poppers created the largest popped kernels, but they were tougher and less crisp than kernels popped using microwave or hot-oil methods. The major reason for the differences appears to be the way each method deals with the moisture in the kernels. Hot-air popping allows too much moisture to escape. Hot oil cooks the popcorn from the outside in, heating and drying the outside first. Microwave popping using oil heats the corn both from the inside and the outside simultaneously. The one microwave brand that failed miserably according to several criteria was Weight Watchers popcorn. As it was not popped in oil, its kernels tended to scorch.[43]

As barbecuing became an important pastime in suburban America, cookbooks recommended placing the unpopped kernels in aluminum foil and placing the bags over the grill. Needless to say, this often resulted in burned popcorn. Of course, it was still possible to pop corn on the stove. Most people used their own pans. Some companies manufactured poppers for use on the stove. The RSVP Perfect Popper, for instance, had a hand-cranked stirrer that circumvented the need for shaking. Both methods required cleaning up with hot soapy water. Many popping devices were on the market, and not all met basic performance criteria established by the Popcorn Institute. To encourage the development and marketing of proper poppers, the institute awarded a "Seal of Quality Performance" to poppers that successfully underwent "scientific laboratory testing and have proved to do the best popping job.[44]

For many consumers, microwave bags did not work well in their ovens. Rubbermaid created a bowl that was helpful, particularly for those whose ovens performed poorly with microwave bags. The bowl contained small holes at the top, which permitted butter to be melted on the popcorn. The device was also intended to be inverted and used as a bowl. Unfortunately, according to *Consumer Reports*, the unpopped kernels fell through the holes. The Goldstar popper worked the best and counted the fewest unpopped kernels.[45]

For concessionaires, the largest popcorn machine maker is Gold Medal Products in Cincinnati, Ohio. In 1989 its P-60, a light-duty commercial machine, sold for $487.50. The company president at the time was Bruce Evans, who reported heavy buying by video stores who sold to renters of videocassette movies. One such store recently installed a machine capable of popping five hundred pounds of popcorn a week. "I think he's got a popcorn store with videos on the side," Evans speculated.[46]

Perhaps the most interesting popping device was the industrial Flo-Thru machine made by C. Cretors & Company. George Brown was asked to assist in the creation of a new design based on technology and patents developed by Midland-Ross for the Cracker Jack Company, which popped kernels as they were suspended in hot air. Brown alerted Charles Cretors to the new invention. Cretors was licensed by Midland-Ross to produce the Flo-Thru machine. The advantage of the new machine was that it could handle a high volume without burning the popcorn. It was ideal for producers of ready-to-eat popcorn snacks. Cretors's Flo-Thru machine debuted on January 24, 1968, at the Potato Chip Institute International Convention in Miami held at the Americana Hotel. Unfortunately, the machine was not allowed in the building, so the demonstration was conducted in the parking lot. The machine had the capacity to pop one thousand pounds per hour. The visual image of popcorn piled high was memorable. By the mid-1970s Cretors was firmly established in the Flo-Thru machine business.[47]

Odds and Ends

Enthusiasts soon discovered ways of using popcorn other than for culinary purposes. In Kansas some placed charred popcorn kernels in corncob pipes and puffed on them. Small and broken popcorn kernels were recommended as a food for feeding poultry. In Nebraska, H. W. Furnas of Brownsville believed that the popcorn plant made an excellent fodder for animals. In fact, popcorn made good silage, and during the 1980s seed companies marketed popcorn hybrids designated specifically for that purpose.[48]

Popcorn mania popped up in a variety of guises. Percy Spencer's microwave popcorn on the cob, dubbed "The Pet Rock of Popcorn" by *Consumer Reports,* was actually produced by two commercial companies: Corny Brothers of Venice, Florida; and All Ears of Linden, New Jersey. Popcorn cobs packaged with bags were convenient for popping in the microwave. Both popped up decently, reported *Consumer Reports,* but left quite a few unpopped kernels. The publication also reported that popcorn on the cob was a little on the tough side because it was not popped in oil.[49]

Most popcorn enthusiasts were concerned with consuming popcorn. Others collected popcorn memorabilia. Of particular interest to collectors were popcorn machines and wagons. George Brown, former president of the Wyandot Popcorn Company, collected over fifty antique popcorn machines and wagons. With these as his base, he opened up the Wyandot Popcorn Museum in Marion, Ohio, in 1983. One enterprising company restored and reproduced antique popcorn machines and pull carts. For those unable to purchase the real or reconstructed wagons, Dick Sands of Beloit, Wisconsin, made scale models. For those unable to find model popcorn wagons, it was possible to go to the U.S. Postal Service and purchase a 16.7¢ stamp commemorating the first Cretors popcorn wagon.[50]

Others collected Cracker Jack prizes. Four major books have been published on Cracker Jack collectibles. The first, *Cracker Jack Collecting for Fun and Profit,* was self-published by James D. Russo in 1976. This fifty-two-page work included a brief history of Cracker Jack and an initial price for the prizes. The second, Alex Jaramillo's *Cracker Jack Prizes,* was mainly a description of the author's collection. Ravi Piña's *Crack Jack Collectibles* included a small price guide at the end. By far the most complete work was Larry White's *Cracker Jack Toys*. Prices for some of the toys range upward of $250. A mint set of the 1914 Cracker Jack baseball cards was estimated at $12,000. In 1987 a permanent Cracker Jack exhibit at the Ohio Center of Science and Industry in Columbus was opened with ten thousand Cracker Jack toys and other memorabilia. In 1993 the Cracker Jack Collector's Association was established through the efforts of Ann Brogeley of Philadelphia. The association publishes a newsletter, the *Prize Insider,* ten times a year and holds an annual conference where its two hundred members meet to sell, discuss, and exhibit Cracker Jack prizes. Two members are from France, and one is from Belgium. Alex Jaramillo, a spokesman for Cracker Jack during the early 1980s, collected over five thousand items. His collection, however, was dwarfed by that of Ronald Toth of Rochester, New Hampshire. When Toth last counted his toys in 1991, he possessed more than sixty thousand Cracker Jack prizes and related toys. Since then he has added another fifteen thousand. He has also amassed thousands of other Cracker Jack memorabilia totaling close to one hundred thousand items.[51]

While popcorn boomed during the 1950s and 1960s, it exploded during the 1970s and 1980s. In 1970 American farmers produced 353 million pounds of unpopped popcorn. Just as the effects of Redenbacher's revolutionary gourmet popcorn were beginning to influence the market, the harvest increased to 393 million pounds by 1975. By 1980 popcorn production was up to 586 million; by 1985 it had increased to 670 million pounds; and by 1991 it surpassed 956 million pounds.[52] Amazingly, popcorn production had lurched upward by almost 250 percent during the preceding decade and a half.

Chapter 9

The End of Popcorn?

Popcorn had undeniably been the "snack of the 1980s." Reviewing the popcorn industry during the early 1990s, a writer in *Snack Food* magazine reported that there were "fewer 'pops' and considerably more 'flops' in this once scorching category."[1] Perhaps this shift occurred because the popcorn industry grew so fast during the 1970s and 1980s that the market was oversaturated. Perhaps popcorn processors failed to appreciate signs that indicated warnings of challenges ahead. Perhaps the American consumer was fickle. Whatever the cause, popcorn sales slumped beginning in 1991 and demonstrated little real growth during the following six years. Today many popcorn processors and manufacturers believe that popcorn in America is a "mature" market with modest prospects for future growth.

A Healthy Snack?

During the 1980s Americans demanded fast, easily prepared, healthy foods—a role that popcorn fit nicely. In 1987 Joel Herskowitz proposed popcorn as a healthy alternative to other diet foods. He specifically claimed that the thought of having a bowl of popcorn later in the evening kept him from losing control and overeating during supper. His diet book featured a number of healthy and nutritious recipes, many with popcorn.[2]

Popcorn is unquestionably nutritious. Unpopped corn consists of approximately 71 percent carbohydrates, 14 percent water, 10.5 percent protein, 3 percent fat, and small amounts of minerals. One cup of plain popcorn contains only 27 calories. Popcorn without additives does not contain the bad things other snack foods are criticized for—salt, sugar, and chemical additives. It has been highly recommended by the National Cancer Institute as a "a high-fiber food to choose more often." The Illinois division of the American Cancer Society praised popcorn as one of the "eleven things that don't cause cancer." The American Heart Association has recommended it as "low in saturated fat and fairly low in calories." The American Dental Association recommended sugar-free popcorn as a food that does not promote tooth decay but does remove tartar from teeth.[3] These recommendations were all based on plain hot-air popped popcorn without additives.

However, most people do not consume popcorn without oil and additives. The Center for Science in the Public Interest (CSPI) issued a warning in 1988 about the high fat content of most microwave and prepared popcorns. Their message was that most microwave popcorn makers as well as ready-to-eat popcorn producers loaded their products with high levels of salt, saturated fats, artificial butter-flavor consisting of hydrogenated oils, saturated fats, artificial colorings, flavorings, and other preservatives. The first company to produce a low-fat and low-salt popcorn was Weight Watchers. A serving of Weight Watchers brand microwave popcorn contained 9 percent fat, 150 calories, and 8 milligrams sodium. Other manufacturers have followed suit. Redenbacher's Gourmet Light Microwave Popping Corn contained one-third less salt, one-third fewer calories, and two-thirds less fat than Redenbacher's regular popcorn. Other companies produced "light" popcorn: Deli Express, Wise Foods, and the Boston Popcorn Company.[4]

Despite these new products, the popcorn industry, swept up in a period of frenzied expansion, largely ignored the initial CSPI report. At the height of the popcorn slump in 1994, CSPI again appalled popcorn lovers when it revealed that theater popcorn cooked in coconut oil was extraordinarily high in saturated fat. Saturated fat raises blood cholesterol and increases the risk of heart disease. Specifically, CSPI proclaimed that a tub of movie theater popcorn which had been popped in coconut oil without imitation butter contained 80 grams of fat—more than six Big Macs. If imitation butter was added, fat was boosted to 130 grams or eight Big Macs.[5]

The report shocked theater owners even more than the general public, for more than half their revenues were produced by their food concessions. Some movie chains switched to oils low in saturated fats. After the CSPI report was issued, AMC Entertainment Inc., one of the largest U.S. movie chains, and the Toronto-based Cineplex Odeon started popping with canola oil. The same bucket popped in canola oil had one-sixth the amount of saturated fat. "It's very positive press," said Dwight More, president of the Canola Council of Canada. His euphoria was short-lived. A week later scientists at Howard University reported that hydrogenated canola oil was full of trans fatty acids that clogged arteries even faster than butter. When the host of the *Tonight Show,* Jay Leno, heard about the CSPI study, he quipped: "They released a big study about how bad movie-theater popcorn is for you. In fact, we went to the movies last night. The popcorn came in three sizes: medium, large, and 'Roger Ebert's Tub of Death.'"[6]

Popcorn's healthy image was tarnished. Processors blamed CSPI's study for the sharp tailspin in popcorn sales in 1994 and 1995. They complained that consumers were unable to discern the difference between movie popcorn and packaged popcorn. Hearing that one type of popcorn was not healthy, consumers assumed that all popcorn was not healthy. Even though the study had focused on popcorn sold in the movie theaters, sales of raw and microwave popcorn sharply declined. According to the 1995 A. C. Nielsen ratings, consumption of popped and unpopped corn was down 10.2 percent and 7.9 percent respectively. Others blamed the slump on new federal labeling laws. Alan Liverman, founder of the Boston Popcorn Company, concluded that the labeling laws were a major reason for the decline of other popcorn sales. The law required a shift from a one-half-ounce to a one-ounce serving size, thereby doubling the reported fat from three to six grams. In 1996 Boston Popcorn's sales declined by 32 percent. Liverman's assessment was contested by others. During this same time frame, sales of caramel corn rose by 9.2 percent. Darryl Thomas, director of marketing for Herr Foods Inc., concluded that the reason for the increased popularity of caramel corn was mandatory government labeling: "A lot of people have discovered that caramel corn is a low fat snack."[7]

In some ways the popcorn industry set itself up for the problems. On the one hand, the industry regularly proclaimed that raw popcorn was a healthy snack. On the other hand, the industry sold popcorn loaded with fat, salt, and calories. Popcorn without additives was tasteless. For years popcorn breeders bred out flavor. As Kenneth Ziegler pointed out, "present-day hybrids have very little flavor." Breeders have created popcorn hybrids that taste good only when popped in oil. Popcorn hybrids have been "selected for the absence of bad flavors or bad taste."[8] For many consumers, popcorn that flew out of hot-air poppers was tasteless. The popcorn that promoters and nutritionists recommended was not the same popcorn that most people ate. Most consumers preferred popcorn with oil and flavorings.

Virtually every popcorn maker except Weight Watchers flavored their microwave popcorn with fats or oils. These commonly included hydrogenated soybean oil, as well as cottonseed, coconut, corn, and palm oil. Butter was often used as well, though in many cases it was replaced by butter flavorings or margarine. Salt was another integral part of the popcorn experience, and it was invariably and generously added, except when it was deliberately reduced or excluded in no- or low-salt items. Sugars were used in candied products, usually in the form of brown sugar and corn syrup. Other additives included the entire range of natural flavorings found in other snack food products, including cheese, jalapeño peppers, dried onions and garlic, cinnamon, and much, much more. Also added were their chemical flavoring counterparts, plus preservatives and coloring agents. Other confections mixed popcorn with peanuts, walnuts, pecans, macadamia nuts, maple syrup, toffee, sesame seeds, shredded coconut, and all manner of foodstuffs.[9]

The popcorn industry's solution to these problems was to improve marketing. Mike Weaver, president of Weaver Popcorn, stated that "more promotion and total support of the entire industry" was needed to counter the CSPI report. The industry welcomed the government program that permitted popcorn processors to tax themselves to promote popcorn sales and research. Under the proposed rules, processors who handle more than four million pounds of popcorn per year would pay a mandatory fee of no more than 8¢ per hundred pounds of kernels. The fee would raise about $750,000 a year from about thirty processors.[10]

The Popcorn Processor's Shuffle

Past trends will likely have a major impact on popcorn's future. One trend is evident in the consolidation of the popcorn processing industry that began after World War II. In 1963 the Cracker Jack Company was sold to Borden, Inc. Borden, based in New York City, embarked on an acquisition drive that resulted in the purchase of twenty-three companies during the 1980s. With the acquisition of Laura Scudder's snack food company of Anaheim and the Snacktime Company in Indianapolis, Borden became the number two marketer of snack foods in the nation behind Frito-Lay, a subsidiary of PepsiCo.[11] Borden developed Cracker Jack Extra Fresh Gourmet Quality Popping Corn. In 1997 Borden sold Cracker Jack to Frito-Lay, which also marketed Chee*tos Cheddar Cheese Flavored Popcorn and Smartfoods popcorn.

In 1958 Central Popcorn Company in Schaller, Iowa, was divided in two. The Indiana component became the Wanberg Popcorn Company, which continues to exist today. Central Popcorn, later renamed Consolidated Popcorn, was sold to Weaver Popcorn in 1988.

The National Oats Company, which had purchased part of Blevins Popcorn Company and the Popcorn Growers and Supply Company, was sold to Curtice Burns in 1980. Curtice Burns was acquired by Pro-Fac and Agway. Several food lines within the company were combined, reorganized, and renamed Curtice Burns Foods.[12] In 1994 Agway sold its shares in Curtice Burns Foods and Pro-Fac, creating Agrilink Foods, which continues to manufacture small quantities of popcorn.

By the 1980s Wyandot Popcorn Company had become the nation's second largest processor of raw popcorn and one of the largest exporters of unpopped corn. In 1989 Wyandot Popcorn Company was sold to investors in Chicago. After a year they went bankrupt and the company reverted to the bank. Approximately a year later Wyandot was sold to Vogel Popcorn, a division of Golden Valley. Golden Valley is now owned by ConAgra. ConAgra had previously purchased Orville Redenbacher's Gourmet Popping Corn during the mid 1970s. Jiffy Pop was sold in 1962 to American Home Products. In 1996 American Home Products was acquired by Hicks, Muse, Tate and Furst, an investment firm, and its food industry management affiliate, C. Dean Metropoulos. Today Jiffy Pop and Franklin Crunch 'N' Munch are part of International Home Foods, Inc., of Parsippany, New Jersey.

The importance of these shifts are multifold. On the positive side, the large food giants, such as Pro-Fac, ConAgra, International Home Products, and Frito-Lay, have the funds to invest in national advertising and marketing. They also have a national system that can guarantee widespread distribution throughout America. On the negative side, giant corporate structures make decisions based almost entirely on profit margin and projected future growth. With popcorn currently in the doldrums, fast future growth is not predicted. One executive of a popcorn company owned by a major corporation reported that making an 8 percent annual profit was not enough to guarantee the investment in needed equipment. The popcorn field has largely grown due to individuals who made quick decisions and were willing to take risks. Likewise, in the past anyone with a good idea could easily test it out. This flexibility is now limited.

Research and Breeding

Research efforts have greatly contributed to popcorn's success. Prior to the 1930s popcorn expansion was about one to fifteen. Breeding programs at agricultural experiment stations during the 1930s directly produced the post–World War II hybrids permitting vast increases in popping expansion, improved resistance to disease, and increased productivity. Since the 1940s breeding and research have greatly contributed to the growth of the popcorn field. The subsequent breeding of seed companies and popcorn processors increased expansion even higher. Orville Redenbacher and Charles Bowman's research effort paid off handsomely with their Gourmet Popping Corn, which produced popping expansion as high as forty-four to one.

Research and breeding efforts have declined precipitously during the past three decades. While individuals, such as Kenneth Ziegler at Iowa State University, remain intensely interested in popcorn breeding, most major university breeding programs have been eliminated or greatly reduced. While a few companies continue their research efforts—American Pop Corn Company, Weaver Popcorn, Orville Redenbacher's Gourmet Popping Corn, and seed companies, for instance—other programs have been reduced or eliminated. Likewise, one observer estimated that there were only about ten to fifteen active popcorn breeders today.

New Technologies

From its inception as a mainstream food, popcorn's drive for snack stardom was greatly enhanced by piggybacking on technology originally devised for other purposes. The inventions of radios, movies, and television have all had unanticipated consequences for popcorn. Microwave technology, invented for purposes of detecting ships and planes, became one of the most important popcorn enhancers. Today, the number one use of microwave ovens is reheating food; the second highest use is for popping popcorn.

Two new technologies have emerged during the last ten years which are already influencing the popcorn industry. With cable, the impact of national television is quickly dissipating. Cable, on the other hand, permits very direct advertising to very narrow audiences. Popcorn manufacturers and processors have already established beachheads on the Internet, and it is likely that at least sales will benefit soon through use of the World Wide Web. Although the Web has not yet been fully utilized, it is beginning to make an impact. Popcorn processors and marketers have already developed Web sites, and more will soon follow. The Internet will likely help small companies, as it now has the ability to distribute their products throughout the world. A quick search turns up at least five hundred popcorn processors, manufacturers, and marketers. One company, for instance, is already selling popcorn grown and processed in South Africa.

The Global Marketplace

Another potential growth area is the global marketplace. Today the United States has five major export markets for popcorn: Canada, Japan, the United Kingdom, Germany, and Mexico. Canada consumes one-third of U.S. popcorn exports. Europeans see popcorn as a sweet snack, and most consume it in caramelized form. The Japanese have acquired a taste for snack food, and popcorn sales have risen steadily. The Japanese are extremely concerned with quality. As several observers have pointed out, the Japanese find the presence of unpopped kernels to be distasteful. Today three kinds of popcorn products are sold in Japan: ready-to-eat; ready-to-pop with flavors such as cheese, butter-soy sauce, oriental barbecue, salt, and seaweed; and unprocessed kernels, which are sold to bars, theaters, and snack shops. One reason for stunted popcorn sales is that microwave ovens in Japan have lower wattage. In addition, the directions on packages geared to American microwave ovens are confusing for the Japanese. Popcorn consumption in the United Kingdom takes place mainly at movie theaters, carnivals, and to a much lesser extent at home. Many observers believe that there is a potentially explosive market in the United Kingdom and other Western European countries.[13]

With the fall of the Soviet Empire and the end of the Cold War, popcorn processors began looking to Eastern Europe and Russia as potential popcorn markets. In 1993 Golden Valley Microwave Products was invited to present popcorn at the Kremlin during the Christmas season. This has led to the development of a small popcorn processing plant in Krasnodar, Russia. Popcorn remains a speculative gamble, but many observers believe in Russia's future as an emerging market. Other potential popcorn markets are Brazil and other nations in South America.[14]

With popcorn sales sluggish, with health concerns challenging both microwave and theater popcorn, with dizzying corporate takeovers regularly rocking the industry, and with research declining, some observers have wondered whether or not popcorn will survive. Reports of popcorn's demise are greatly exaggerated. New technological advancements, such as the Internet, may assist popcorn in its drive for continued stardom in the snack world. Popcorn may be a mature industry in America, but it has just begun to expand abroad. The reasons for its potential success abroad are the same ones that produced popcorn's success in North America. It is easily grown, inexpensive to buy, and accessible to most people. It is readily processed and almost effortlessly prepared for consumption. It is a healthy food. As American snack foods continue their rise in popularity around the world, popcorn will follow.[15] With the vast increase of microwave ovens in other countries, microwave popcorn will be a logical partner.

Whatever its future abroad, popcorn remains a significant food in the United States and Canada. Perhaps popcorn as a snack food has limited growth potential for the future. Popcorn as an ingredient in cooking has just been revived and may well point in different directions for the future. Its bland taste provides a good vehicle for all types of flavors and ingredients. Its culinary versatility permits integration with almost any cuisine. Its popping still enthralls observers, young and old. Its aroma is heavenly. Popcorn is America's gift to the world, and what a wonderful, fun-filled bequest it is.

Part II

Historical Recipes

Hundreds of popcorn recipes have been published in the United States. These recipes appeared in cookbooks, agricultural and horticultural journals, newspapers, popular magazines, popcorn processors' promotional pamphlets, and a host of other sources. The recipes in this section constitute a representative sample of those historical recipes published prior to 1924. Some were selected because they were typical, others because they were unusual. As a collection they reflect the diversity of popcorn recipes and demonstrate the variety of sources in which they appeared. Spelling, grammar, and directions in these recipes have been left in their original form.

Extensive experience was needed to perform even basic cooking functions prior to the twentieth century. Most cookbook authors assumed that readers already possessed basic knowledge and understanding and so often felt it was unnecessary to spell out every detail. The cook was expected to do what made sense rather than blindly follow the directions of a cookbook author who had no idea of specific cooking conditions, equipment, or the availability of ingredients in the case of any given cook.

These recipes are included solely because of their historical importance and are not intended as a source of recipes for the modern reader. However, most recipes may be the bases for experimentation with popcorn cookery. After some experience, do not hesitate to experiment and take up the challenges and joys of popcorn cookery.

1. Almond Nougat

Pop-Corn Almond Nougat

Take two cupfuls of white sugar, one-fourth cupful of water and one-fourth cupful of corn syrup. Melt over the fire until the sugar is dissolved, then stir in one cupful of chopped pop-corn and one-half cupful of chopped almonds. Boil to the hard rock stage, flavor with a little almond extract, and pour over the buttered pans in tin sheets. When cold break into pieces or cut into squares with a sharp knife.

Source: Mary M. Wright. *Candy-Making at Home; Two Hundred Ways to Make Candy with Home Flavor and Professional Finish.* Philadelphia: Penn Publishing Company, 1915. 130.

2. Balls

Pop Corn Balls

Boil honey, maple, or other sugar to the great thread; pop corn and stick the corn together in balls with the candy.

Source: E. F. Haskell. *The Housekeeper's Encyclopedia.* New York: D. Appleton and Company, 1861. 193.

Pop-Corn Balls

To six quarts of pop corn boil one pint of molasses about fifteen minutes; then put the corn into a large pan, pour the boiled molasses over it, and stir it briskly until thoroughly mixed. Then with clean hands make the balls of the desired size.

Source: [Lafcadio Hearn]. *La Cuisine Creole; A Collection of Culinary Recipes from Leading Chefs and Noted Creole Housewives, Who Have Made New Orleans Famous for its Cuisine.* New York: Will H. Colman, 1885. 241.

Pop Corn Ball

Pop the corn, throw aside all that is not opened nicely; put 1/2 bushel corn on the table or in a large pan; put a little water in a kettle with 1 lb. sugar and boil as for candy, until it becomes quite waxy in water when tried as for candy, then remove it from the fire and pour 6 or 7 tablespoonfuls of thick gum solution into it, made by pouring boiling hot water upon gum arabic over night or some hours before. Now pour the mixture upon different parts of the corn, until the corn is all saturated with the candy mixture. Press into balls with the hand; in doing this be quick, or it will set. White or brown sugar may be used.

Source: John D. Hounihan. *Bakers' and Confectioners' Guide and Treasure.* Staunton, Va.: Printed for the Author, 1877. 298.

Pop Corn Balls

The corn, being popped and salted, and kept as warm as possible, sprinkle over with a whisk broom a mixture composed of an ounce of gum arabic and a half pound of sugar, dissolved in two quarts of water and boiled a few minutes. Stir the corn with the hands or a paddle thoroughly; then mold into balls with the hands. This makes a good, white ball. If desired, a red tint may be given by sprinkling with a solution of carmine to the mixture, after it has been balled.

Source: *The Candy-Maker: A Practical Guide to the Manufacture of the Various Kinds of Plain and Fancy Cand.* New York: Jesse Haney & Co., 1878. 38–39.

Pop Corn Balls, No. 2

Pour over the warm popped and salted corn the boiled sugar or molasses, boiled to the thread; not to cover it but a little at a time, stirring the corn, which should be kept warm, until it is in a condition to stick together, when molded by the hands. No flavor should be added in this mixture, as the excellence of this commodity depends entirely upon the united flavor of the corn, salt, and the sugar or molasses.

Source: *The Candy-Maker: A Practical Guide to the Manufacture of the Various Kinds of Plain and Fancy Candy.* New York: Jesse Haney & Co., 1878. 39.

Pop-corn Balls

Add one ounce of white gum arabic to a half pint of water, and let it stand until dissolved. Strain, add one pound of refined sugar and boil until when cooled it becomes very thick, so much so as to be stirred with difficulty. To ascertain when it has reached this point, a little may be cooled in a saucer. A convenient quantity of the freshly-popped corn having been placed in a milk-pan, enough of the warm syrupy candy is poured on and mixed by stirring, to cause the kernels to adhere in a mass, portions of which may be formed into balls by pressing them into the proper shape with the hands. Ordinary molasses, or sugar house syrup may be used as well, by being boiled to the same degree, no gum being necessary with these materials. Corn cake is prepared in a similar manner. This mass, while warm, is put into tins and pressed by rollers into thin sheets, which are afterwards divided into small, square cakes.

Source: May Perrin Goff, ed. *The Household: A Cyclopëdia of Practical Hints for Modern Homes with a Full and Complete Treatise on Cookery.* Detroit: Detroit Free Press Co., 1881. 446.

Pop-corn Balls

Grind rather finely two quarts of popped corn, and stir it into a boiling syrup made of a cupful of white sugar and three tablespoonfuls of water. When partly cooled, form into balls, and roll them in pulverized sugar.

Source: E. H. Leland. *Farm Homes In-Doors and Out Doors.* New York: Orange Judd Company, 1881. 151.

Pop-Corn Balls

Take three large ears of pop-corn (rice is best). After popping, shake it down in pan so the unpopped corn will settle at the bottom; put nice white popped in a greased pan. For the candy, take one cup of molasses, one cup of light brown or white sugar, one tablespoonful of vinegar. Boil until it will harden in water. Pour on the corn. Stir with a spoon until thoroughly mixed; then mold into balls with the hand.

No flavor should be added to this mixture, as the excellence of this commodity depends entirely upon the united flavor of the corn, salt and the sugar or molasses.

Source: F. L. Gillette. *The White House Cookbook*. Chicago: L. P. Miller & Co., 1887. 403–404.

Pop-Corn Balls

Roast the corn berries over a smokeless fire in a corn-popper; keep shaking until every berry has burst; boil sufficient sugar and water to the degree of feather, 245; add to each 7-lbs. of syrup, four ounces of dissolved gum arabic; wet the popped corn in this syrup, and roll them in fine pulverized sugar until coated all over, then lay them aside; when dry, repeat the coating process in the same manner until they have taken desired thickness of sugar. Weigh or measure sufficient coated berries, according to size of ball required; moisten them with thin syrup, partly from the ball by hand, then put it into a squeezer (something like a lemon squeezer), and press tightly into shape. N.B.—The corn berries may be coated in a comfit pan like other seeds or almonds, then form into balls in the usual way.

Source: E. Skuse. *Skuse's Complete Confectioner: A Practical Guide to the Art of Sugar Boiling in All Its Branches*. London: W. J. Bush & Co., Ltd., [1890]. 53.

Popped Corn Balls

In making popped corn balls you can make four kinds of candy for it to suit taste in flavor. Some prefer molasses and others prefer sugar candy. If you use molasses, take two cupfuls of molasses, one cupful of brown sugar, one tablespoonful of vinegar, butter size of an egg. Boil this thick and soft, and pour over the corn while warm. This will take four quarts of popped corn. If you prefer maple syrup, take two cupfuls of syrup and add one cupful of maple sugar (or you can use all sugar and dissolve it in a little water.) Add to it one teaspoonful of vinegar and a small lump of butter and boil until soft enough to pour over the popped corn. Sugar candy is made by dissolving three tablespoonfuls of gum arabic in half a pint of water, then add two cupfuls of confectioners' sugar, and boil, stirring all the while. Try a little in a saucer; when cool and so stiff you can hardly stir it, it is done. Flavor with orange or rose and pour over the corn. Another nice sugar candy is to take four cupfuls of light brown sugar dissolved in half a pint of water, add to it one teaspoonful of vinegar, a small lump of butter, and one tablespoon of glycerine. Boil until thick. Try a few drops in cold water; when it makes a soft ball, it is done. Pop your corn nicely, salt it slightly, and put all the popped-out kernels into a large bowl. Pour the candy, while warm, over as much corn as will adhere nicely; then butter your hands and lift out a large spoonful and press into a ball. Continue this until all are done, putting them to harden in a cool place.

Source: Sarah J. Cutter. *Palatable Dishes: A Practical Guide to Good Living*. Buffalo: Peter, Paul & Bro., 1891. 715–16.

Syrup for Pop-corn Balls

Take one ounce of white gum arabic, pour over it half a pint of cold water, let stand until dissolved, then strain it and add one pound of confectioners' sugar. Boil until when cooled it becomes thick; so much so as to be stirred with difficulty. Cool a little in a saucer to ascertain when it has reached this point. Put in a milk pan a convenient quantity of fresh pop-corn and pour enough of the warm syrup candy to cause the corn to adhere in a mass. Mix by stirring, then form into balls by pressing a small portion into shape with the hands. To make pop-corn cakes, turn the mass of corn and syrup, while warm, into greased tins, then with a roller roll it down into thin sheets. When almost cold, cut into small square cakes, or into strips an inch wide.

Source: Sarah J. Cutter. *Palatable Dishes: A Practical Guide to Good Living*. Buffalo: Peter, Paul & Bro., 1891. 716.

Popcorn Balls

For this purpose the corn must be carefully popped and sorted and all the hard kernels removed. It is often chopped fine, or light fluffy kernels may be left as they are. The syrup to bind them together may be made of sugar or molasses and the addition of a small quantity of butter makes the balls more tender. Here less corn is used than for the sugared kernels, as it is desirable to have a greater proportion of syrup to hold the corn together instead of having each kernel distinct. If the corn is warm the syrup does not cool rapidly and the balls will keep in shape better. When the corn is chopped and mixed with the syrup, bars or cakes can be made instead of balls by packing the mixture in buttered pans. Syrup of any color or flavor may be used, and chopped nuts or grated coconut combined with the corn.

Source: Barbara Allen. "Christmas Confections," *American Kitchen Magazine* 4 (December 1895): 142–43.

Pop Corn Balls, No. 2

Boil together without stirring a pint of sugar, a fourth of a cupful of rain water, a tablespoonful of vinegar and a half teaspoonful of butter.

When the syrup will snap on being tested in water, pour it immediately over the corn and stir with the paddle for a minute or so. Then dip the hands into very cold water and press the pop corn into balls, dipping the hands in the water before forming each ball. In this way the balls may be shaped before the candy hardens on the corn. The above-named quantities are sufficient for a peck of popped corn, and will make ten balls. The corn must be carefully prepared and all imperfectly popped or scorched grains thrown out. The appearance of the balls may be greatly improved by cutting circular portions of bright colored tissue paper the size of a pie-plate, fringing the edges an inch deep all round, and placing one on each ball, pressing it carefully so it will stay. This will not only add to the beauty of the balls, but will also prevent them sticking to the hands. The balls should be placed in a cold room as soon as finished, as pop corn is likely to become tough if allowed to remain in a warm place.

Source: Wehman Brothers. *Wehman's Confectioner's Guide and Assistant: or, A Complete Instruction in the Art of Candy-Making. An Aid Both to the Professional and Amateur Candy-Maker.* New York: Wehman Brothers, c1905. 93–94.

Coney Island Pop Corn Balls

First pop corn—2 or 3 ears is sufficient. Syrup for pop corn balls: One cup granulated sugar, 1/2 cup water, 1 teaspoonful vinegar; then add 2 tablespoonfuls dark molasses and butter the size of a walnut, 1/2 teaspoonful salt and boil. Drop some of the candy into cold water and if brittle it is done. Then pour syrup on pop corn and stir and form into balls with the hands.

Source: Jennie A. Hansey and Ella M. Blackstone. *New Standard Domestic Science Cook-Book*. Chicago: Laird & Lee, 1908. 374–75.

To Make Popcorn Balls

Boil to the thread about 2 1/2 pounds of sugar with 3/4 pound of glucose and 1 pint of water. Place the popcorn in an earthenware bowl, pour the sirup over it, mix with 2 wooden paddles and form into balls with the wet hands.

Or boil 1/2 pint of molasses about 12 minutes to the stiff-ball degree. Place 2 quarts of popcorn in a wet earthenware bowl, pour the boiling molasses over it, mix with paddles, and roll with wet fingers.

Or for a better quality of popcorn balls for home use, add to the above a good-sized piece of butter or otherwise as desired.

Or boil to the hard snap 1 pint of sugar, 1/2 teaspoonful of butter, about 1/4 teacup of soft water. Have ready about 1 peck of freshly popped corn in a wet pan or tub, dip the boiling sirup over it, mix with wooden paddles, roll with the wet hands.

Source: Sidney Morse. *Household Discoveries; An Encyclopedia of Practical Recipes and Processes;* and *Mrs Curtis's Cook Book*. Petersburg, N.Y.: Success Co., 1908. 539.

Popcorn Balls

After the corn has been popped, take from the quantity any uncooked or partially cooked grains, being sure to have only fine, large, puffy ones. To one cup Karo Corn Syrup allow one tablespoon vinegar. Boil together until it hardens when dropped in cold water. When ready pour over the popcorn while hot. As soon as cool enough to handle, butter the hands well and form the mass into balls.

Source: Emma Churchman Hewitt. *Karo Cook Book.* New York: Corn Products Refining Company, 1909. 36.

Popcorn Balls

In making popcorn balls proceed exactly the same as you would in making crispettes, but only cook the batch to 240 degrees. You can make these in any style or flavors such as molasses, vanilla, strawberry, chocolate, etc. Popcorn balls should be sold at a price that will bring you in 20 cents a pound. Penny popcorn balls weigh 4 ounces each. If the popcorn balls are too sticky cook them to 245 degrees or 250 degrees in hot weather. If they become sticky after they have been made up use less glucose and more sugar, but not more than 3/4 sugar. In winter some people make popcorn balls, using 4 pounds of glucose and 2 pounds of sugar.

Source: *Copyrighted Secret Formulas and Instructions for the Manufacture of Crispettes and Other Popcorn Confections.* Chicago: C. E. Dellenbarger Co., Chicago, 1913. 23.

Molasses Pop-Corn Balls

Take one cupful of light brown sugar and one cupful of New Orleans molasses, half a cupful of water and boil to the hard ball stage, then add two tablespoonfuls of butter. Boil to the crack stage, then add a half teaspoonful of soda and pour over some freshly popped corn in a bowl. Stir until the syrup is evenly distributed over the corn, but be careful not to break the grains in doing so. Dip the hands in water, take a portion of the pop-corn up into the hands and press into nice even round balls.

Source: Mary M. Wright. *Candy-Making at Home; Two Hundred Ways to Make Candy with Home Flavor and Professional Finish.* Philadelphia: Penn Publishing Company, 1915. 124.

Chocolate Pop-Corn Balls

Pop some corn and pick out only the large crisp, tender grains. Place in a saucepan two cupfuls of granulated sugar, one-half cupful of water and one-fourth teaspoonful of cream of tartar. Boil until it spins a thread or forms a hard ball when dropped in cold water; then flavor with a teaspoonful of vanilla. Pour part of this sugar syrup over the pop-corn, stirring until the syrup is evenly distributed through the pop-corn;

while doing this let the remainder stand on the back of the stove. Form into tiny pop-corn balls with the fingers, boil the remaining syrup to the crack stage, then dip each ball into this, and place on paraffin paper until cool. When cool dip into melted sweet chocolate.

Source: Mary M. Wright. *Candy-Making at Home; Two Hundred Ways to Make Candy with Home Flavor and Professional Finish.* Philadelphia: Penn Publishing Company, 1915. 124–25.

Snow Pop-Corn Balls

Take two cupfuls of granulated sugar, one-half cupful of white corn syrup, one-half cupful of water and a pinch of cream of tartar. Boil to the soft ball stage, then flavor with a few drops of peppermint extract or a half teaspoonful of vanilla and pour over the stiffly beaten whites of two eggs. Beat up until light and it begins to harden, then stir in two cupfuls of crisp pop-corn grains. Dip the hands into corn-starch and mold while still warm into small balls. Roll each ball in cocoanut, and then wrap in paraffin paper to keep their shape until cold. Unwrap and heap on plate.

Source: Mary M. Wright. *Candy-Making at Home; Two Hundred Ways to Make Candy with Home Flavor and Professional Finish.* Philadelphia: Penn Publishing Company, 1915. 125–26.

Ice Pop-Corn Balls

Take two cupfuls of granulated sugar, one-half cupful of water and one-fourth teaspoonful of cream of tartar. Boil to the crack stage and pour over pop-corn in a bowl, stirring until the syrup is well mixed with the corn. Form into small balls in pulverized or finely chopped rock candy to simulate ice.

Source: Mary M. Wright. *Candy-Making at Home; Two Hundred Ways to Make Candy with Home Flavor and Professional Finish.*Philadelphia: Penn Publishing Company, 1915. 126.

Maple Corn Balls

3 quarts popped corn
1 cup maple syrup
1/2 cup sugar
1 tablespoon butter
1/2 teaspoon salt

Pop corn and pick over, discarding kernels that do not pop, and put in large kettle. Melt butter in saucepan, and add syrup and sugar. Bring to the boiling point, and let boil until mixture will become brittle when tried in cold water. Pour mixture gradually, while stirring constantly, over corn which has been sprinkled with salt. Shape into balls, using as little pressure as possible.

Source: Alice Bradley. *The Candy Cook Book.* Boston: Little, Brown, and Company, 1917. 187–88.

Chocolate Pop Corn Balls

1 cup sugar
2 squares chocolate
4 quarts popped corn, well salted
1/2 cup molasses
1/2 cup water
2 tablespoons butter
1 teaspoon vanilla

Boil the sugar, molasses and water together until it threads; add the chocolate broken into small pieces and the butter. Stir until the chocolate is melted. Pour over salted corn. Butter hands and make into small balls.

Source: Mary L. Wade. *The Book of Corn Cookery.* Chicago: A. C. McClurg and Co., 1917. 98.

Honey Pop Corn Balls

Boil one cupful of strained honey until it will form a soft ball when dropped into cold water. Have ready a good sized bowl of Nelson's corn, popped, pour the honey over it, mold the corn into balls and stand them on greased paper. A cupful of sugar and half a cupful of water may be boiled to a syrup and used in the same way.

Source: Mary Hamilton Talbott. *Pop Corn Recipes.* Grinnell, Iowa: Sam Nelson, Jr., Company, 1916. n.p.

Peanut and Popcorn Balls

1/2 teaspoon soda
1 pint syrup
2 tablespoons butter
1 teaspoon vinegar
3 quarts freshly popped corn
1 quart freshly roasted peanuts

Cook until the syrup hardens when a little is dropped in cold water; remove to back of stove; add the soda dissolved in a teaspoon of hot water; pour syrup over the corn and nuts, stirring until each kernel is well coated; mould into balls.

Source: George Washington Carver. *How to Grow the Peanut and 105 Ways of Preparing it for Human Consumption.* Tuskegee, Ala.: Experiment Station. *Bulletin #31.* June 1916 [1925]. Seventh edition, January 1940. 25.

Pop Corn Balls

5 pounds sugar
1 1/2 pints water

Cook to 238°, then remove from fire, color if desired, and stir in all of the pop corn the batch will stand. Now press the corn with your hands into the square of round balls, or place in molds if you have them. When working, dampen hands occasionally to prevent sticking.

Source: W. O. Rigby. *Rigby's Reliable Candy Teacher.* Twelfth edition. Topeka, Kans.: Rigby Publishing Company, 1918. 153.

Pop Corn Raisin Balls

When adding pop corn to the formula for Pop Corn Balls, also add 3 pounds of sun dried raisins mixing them in with the pop corn. This is a new piece and makes a good looking as well as a choice eating novelty.

Source: W. O. Rigby. *Rigby's Reliable Candy Teacher.* Twelfth edition. Topeka, Kans.: Rigby Publishing Company, 1918. 153.

Maple Popcorn Balls

3 quarts freshly popped corn
1 cup melted maple sugar
Salt
1/2 cup brown sugar
1 tablespoon butter or butterine

PROCESS: Carefully pick over popped corn, discarding all, unpopped kernels. Melt butter or butterine in a large, round-bottom, iron kettle (an old-fashioned type if one is available); a large granite kettle will serve the purpose. Add maple syrup and sugar; bring to boiling point and cook until mixture will crack when tested in cold water. Sprinkle corn with salt; pour candy slowly over prepared popped corn while stirring briskly. Shape with slightly buttered hands quickly and little pressure into balls. When cool wrap in waxed paper. To prepare maple syrup, shave or break in small pieces, then measure. To one cup sugar add one-half cup of water and cook until the consistency of syrup. This will be found more satisfactory than commercial maple syrup, notwithstanding the extra trouble.

Source: Elizabeth Hiller. *The Corn Cook Book.* War edition. New York: P. F. Volland Company, 1918. 119.

3. Bars or Squares

Pop-Corn Candy

Take a cup of molasses, and one and a half cups of brown sugar, a tablespoonful of vinegar and a lump of butter the size of an egg. Boil until thick. Chop two cups of popped corn rather fine, put it into the boiling candy, and pour it all on the buttered plates. Cut in squares to be eaten without pulling.

Source: [Lafcadio Hearn]. *La Cuisine Creole; A Collection of Culinary Recipes from Leading Chefs and Noted Creole Housewives, Who Have Made New Orleans Famous for its Cuisine.* New York: Will H. Colman, 1885. 238.

Pop-Corn Bars

Take two cups of sugar, one-half cupful of water and boil to the hard ball stage. Add vanilla flavoring or any desired flavoring. Crush some fresh pop-corn with a rolling pin, and stir into the syrup. When the corn has been perfectly mixed with the syrup press into a square or oblong buttered pan to the depth of about an inch, patting it smooth on top. When cool cut into bars with a very sharp knife.

Source: Mary M. Wright. *Candy-Making at Home; Two Hundred Ways to Make Candy with Home Flavor and Professional Finish*. Philadelphia: Penn Publishing Company, 1915. 128.

Maple Pop-Corn Bars

Cook two cupfuls of maple sugar and one cupful of cream to the hard ball stage. Beat up until it begins to turn creamy, then stir in a pint of large, crisp kernels. See that the syrup is well mixed through the corn. Turn into a square or oblong pan that has been well buttered and press until flat on top, but not hard enough to crush the kernels. If liked it can be shaped into bars with the hands, and there will not be so much danger of crushing the kernels. If shaped in a pan cut into bars with a sharp knife.

Source: Mary M. Wright. *Candy-Making at Home; Two Hundred Ways to Make Candy with Home Flavor and Professional Finish*. Philadelphia: Penn Publishing Company, 1915. 128–29.

Popcorn Bars

1 quart freshly popped corn
1 cup sugar
1/4 cup corn syrup
1/4 cup water
1 tablespoon butterine or butter
1 teaspoon salt

PROCESS: Carefully pick over fresh popped corn, discarding all unpopped kernels. Pass through meat-chopper, using coarse knife; sprinkle with salt. Into a kettle put sugar, prepared corn and water; cook until candy cracks when tested in cold water (about 270 degree F., on sugar thermometer). Add butter and cook until candy is very hard when again tested in cold water (ice-water is preferable). Add corn, stir until thoroughly blended. Return to range to warm slightly and pour on an oiled marble slab or an enameled tray and with a slightly oiled rolling-pin roll as thin as possible. (This operation must be done quickly.) Cut in bars or squares. If it becomes too hard to cut break in small pieces.

Source: Elizabeth Hiller. *The Corn Cook Book*. War edition. New York: P. F. Volland Company, 1918. 118.

Maple or Chocolate Pop Corn Squares

Boil together 2 pounds of brown sugar or maple sugar, a pint of new milk and a quarter of a teaspoonful of cream of tartar. When the sirup makes a soft ball in cold water, add 2 tablespoonfuls of butter substitute; stir it gently and remove from the stove; add a teaspoonful of vanilla or maple flavoring; set the pan in a vessel of cold water and beat until it begins to cool. Then pour into greased, straight-sided pans and strew thick with pop corn. While still soft cut into squares, but cut again in the same lines when cold. Wrap the pieces in waxed paper. Chocolate bars may be made by adding half a cake of bitter chocolate.

Source: T. A. Gagnon. *Tried and Tested Recipes. Mrs. T. A. Gagnon's Cook Book for Practical Housekeeping.* Grafton, N.D.: Grafton News and Times Print, 1919. 272.

Pop-Corn Squares

Cook 2 pounds of sugar, 1/2 pound glucose, 1/2 pint molasses, to 285 or 290 degrees. Take off the fire and when the ebullition ceases add 1/4 teaspoonful of soda and sufficient pop-corn; mix well and pour on oiled slab between bars. Cut in 10-cent sized squares and wrap in waxed paper.

Source: Paul Richards. *Candy for Dessert.* Chicago: Hotel Monthly Press, 1919. 57.

4. Best Evers

"Best Evers"

Four tablespoons of water boiled
With sugar, just one cup;
Cook till its bubbles big declare
That it is "waxing up";
When dropped in water cold it makes
A soft and sticky ball,
Now crush some popped or buttered corn
And slowly pour it all
Into the well-whipped white of egg,
And stir it constantly;
Then spread on wafers or saltines
To brown in oven, you see.
They surely are delicious bits
To eat with cream or ice!
The boys who "pop" and the girls who "cook"
Will find them always nice.

Source: Charlotte Brewster Jordan. "A Pop-Corn Frolic for Hallowe'en," *St. Nicholas* 36 (October 1909): 1115.

5. Biscuits

Pop-Corn Biscuits

Sift four teaspoonfuls of baking powder and one each of sugar and salt with one cupful and a half of white flour; add one cupful of fine-ground pop corn and mix with two rounding tablespoonfuls of shortening and a cupful and a half of water into a soft-dough. Roll out; cut into squares or rounds and bake on a griddle, turning as the cakes brown. Or bake in a quick oven. This will make twelve biscuits.

Source: Riley M. Fletcher-Berry. "Dressing Up Pop Corn," *Ladies' Home Journal* 34 (December 1917): 70.

6. Bricks

Pop-Corn Bricks

Process.—The corn berries are prepared as for balls; boil brown sugar in the proportion of 8-lbs. sugar and 2-lbs. molasses to ball, 250; pour the syrup over the corn and thoroughly mix them; press them immediately into oiled tins. The process should be done quickly, and the seeds pressed as tightly as possible; when cold, they are ready for sale, and may be cut to size with sharp knife.

Source: E. Skuse. *Skuse's Complete Confectioner: A Practical Guide to the Art of Sugar Boiling in All Its Branches.* London: W. J. Bush & Co., Ltd., [1890]. 54.

7. Brittle

Popcorn Brittle

Add a cup of chopped peanuts to about three quarts of fresh, perfectly popped corn. Put a cup each of white and brown sugar into a smooth skillet, put over the fire and stir constantly until melted to a syrup, add two tablespoons of molasses, a fourth of a cup of butter and pour over the corn as directed for sugared popcorn, stirring continually until the kernels separate.

Source: Amelia Sulzbacher. "Popcorn Dainties," *Good Housekeeping* 43 (October 1906): 422–23.

Pop-Corn Brittle

Take a cupful of granulated sugar, one cupful of browned sugar, one-half cupful of golden corn syrup and one-fourth cupful of water. Melt to a syrup, then boil to the hard ball stage, add one-fourth cupful of butter and boil until it begins to turn color or to the hard crack stage. Place in a bowl two quarts of freshly popped corn and one cupful chopped peanuts. Pour the syrup over the corn and stir until all the kernels and nuts are covered with it. If not to be so thick with popcorn and nuts use only a quart of pop-corn.

Source: Mary M. Wright. *Candy-Making at Home; Two Hundred Ways to Make Candy with Home Flavor and Professional Finish.* Philadelphia: Penn Publishing Company, 1915. 130–31.

Popcorn Brittle

3 cups brown sugar
1 cup N. O. molasses
1/2 teaspoon cream tartar
1/2 cup butter or butter substitute
2 teaspoons hot water
1 quart freshly popped corn

PROCESS: Boil the first three ingredients in an iron kettle to the "hard crack" degree (310 degrees F.), i.e., when a little of the syrup is dropped into ice water it will form a hard ball and when pressed between the teeth it will not stick, but will leave them clean and free from taffy; add butter and when it is well blended add popcorn; stir it well. Remove from range, add soda dissolved in hot water, stir briskly; when mixture begins to rise turn it on an oiled or butter marble slab or platter; spread thin and evenly; when cold break in small pieces.

Source: Elizabeth Hiller. *The Corn Cook Book*. War edition. New York: P. F. Volland Company, 1918. 118.

Pop Corn Brittle

Boil 3 cups brown sugar, spoonful cream of tartar in an iron kettle until a little syrup dropped into cold water forms a hard ball, and will not stick in the teeth. Melt 1/2 cup butter and add when blended 1 quart popped corn and stir well. Remove from the stove and add 2 teaspoonful soda previously dissolved in 2 tablespoonfuls hot water. Stir briskly and when mixture begins to rise turn it on an oiled or buttered platter. Spread thin and even, when cold break into small pieces.

Source: "Little Buster Hull-Less Pop Corn." Chicago: Albert Dickinson Co., 1921. Broadside.

8. Cakes

Pop-Corn Cakes

Pop Corn Cake is made by chopping the popped and salted corn to the required size, spreading it even in a pan, and pouring on it a thin hot syrup mixed thoroughly with the hand or a wooden paddle and leveled up to a thickness of one and a half to two inches. When cooled it is flattened out by pressure. For a small trade this could be done in a family cider press or a clothes wringer, set wide. It is a little difficult to chop the popped corn, and for manufacturers a machine is used, which does it rapidly.

Source: *The Candy-Maker: A Practical Guide to the Manufacture of the Various Kinds of Plain and Fancy Candy.* New York: Jesse Haney & Co., 1878. 38.

Pop-Corn Cakes

PROCESS.—Prepare the corn as for balls, and pack them closely into strong square tins slightly oiled of best quality; boil to crack, sufficient brown sugar and glucose for quantity required, and pour the hot syrup over the pop-corns, just enough to make them adhere. When cold, cut them up with sharp knife to size.

Source: E. Skuse. *Skuse's Complete Confectioner: A Practical Guide to the Art of Sugar Boiling in All Its Branches*. London: W. J. Bush & Co., Ltd., [1890]. 54.

Another old fashioned sweet which never fails of its welcome is the popcorn ball, or better still, because the ball is clumsy and sticky and quite as likely as not to leave molasses on checks and chin, try the corn cake, making it by the same recipe as usual but pressing the well mixed hot corn and molasses into deep buttered loaf pans. "Press it down and shake it together" if you want good solid cakes, and when you have done that, put another tin on top with a flatiron in it When the corn is cool, turn out and slice in thick slices. Corn should never be allowed to stand long before it is eaten as it becomes very tough and indigestible.

Source: *Good Housekeeping* 37 (December 1903): 587.

Popcorn Cakes

Have ready enough popped corn to fill a two-quart measure, salt it, and sift it through your fingers to remove all the loose salt and unpopped kernels. Now make a candy with a cupful (a short half pint) of molasses, half a cupful of brown (cane) sugar, a dessertspoonful of best vinegar, stir in as much of the corn as it will take up, then press the mixture into buttered or oiled tins, mark it out in cakes with a sharp knife, and leave till set.

Source: Horace Cox. *The "Queen" Cookery Books*. Volume VI: Sweets, Part 2. Third edition. London: "Queen" Office, 1904. 116.

Pop Corn Cake

Pop corn cake is make by chopping the popped and salted corn to the required size, spreading it even in a pan, and pouring on it a thin hot syrup; mixed thoroughly with the hand or a wooden paddle, and leveled up to a thickness of one and a half to two inches. When cooled it is flattened out by pressure. For a small trade this could be done in a family cider press or a clothes-wringer, set wide. It is a little difficult to chop the popped corn, and for manufacturers a machine is used, which does it rapidly.

Source: Wehman Brothers. *Wehman's Confectioner's Guide and Assistant: or, A Complete Instruction in the Art of Candy-Making. An Aid Both to the Professional and Amateur Candy-Maker.* New York: Wehman Brothers, c1905. 84.

Popcorn Cake

1 quart popped corn
1 cup water
1/4 cup corn syrup
1/4 cup water
2 tablespoons molasses
1 tablespoon butter
1 teaspoon salt

Pick over the popped corn, discarding all hard kernels, and finely chop the corn, or put through meat grinder, using coarse knife. Put sugar, corn syrup, and water in saucepan, stir until it boils, and cook 270° F., or until candy cracks when tried in cold water; add molasses and butter, and cook to 290° F., or until it is very hard when tried in water. Add corn, stir until well mixed, return to fire a moment to loosen it, then pour on buttered slab or tray, and roll with rolling pin as thin as possible. Cut in squares or break in small pieces. Molasses may be omitted.

Source: Alice Bradley. *The Candy Cook Book*. Boston: Little, Brown, and Company, 1917. 189.

Popcorn Griddle Cakes

1/2 cup (2 ozs.) flour
1/2 cup (2 ozs.) corn flour
2 cups (1 pint) unsweetened popcorn
2 teaspoons baking soda
1 teaspoon sugar
1/2 teaspoon salt
1 egg, beaten
1/2 cup (1 gill) milk
1/2 cup (1 gill) water

Sift into a bowl flours, baking powder, sugar and salt, add popcorn put through a food chopper, egg, milk and water. Beat lightly until smooth, and bake on a hot, greased griddle. Serve with sirup or honey, or the following spread: pour one pint molasses into a saucepan, add pinch salt and two tablespoons each butter substitute and vinegar, and boil three minutes.

Source: Marion Harris Neil. *The Thrift Cook Book*. Philadelphia: David McKay, 1919. 246.

9. Canapes

Cut bread into any shape and fry it in deep fat. Mix chopped olives and Nelson's corn (popped) with mayonnaise and spread on the fried bread.

Rub the yolks of hard-boiled eggs to a paste and add an equal quantity of sardines and Nelson's pop corn (popped and ground.) Moisten with lemon juice and serve on rounds of toast.

Source: Mary Hamilton Talbott. *Pop Corn Recipes.* Grinnell, Iowa: Sam Nelson, Jr., Company, 1916. n.p.

10. Candy

Molasses Candy

Boil a quart of molasses half an hour; add a tea-spoonful of saleratus, to make it stiff and brittle; boil it until it is stiff enough to pull; butter a dish, pour it in, and let it get cool; pull it in a cool place. You may add any kind of nuts, or popped corn.

Source: A. M. Collins. *The Great Western Cook Book.* New York: A. S. Barnes & Company, 1857. 128.

Crystalized Pop Corn

Put into an enameled kettle one cupful of white sugar, three tablespoonfuls of boiling water and one tablespoonful of butter, cut up into tiny bits. Boil it for ten minutes, then drop a little into cold water to see if it will candy. If it hardens quickly, throw in as much popped corn as the sugar will cover, take the kettle from the fire into a cool place, and stir it well until all the corn is well crystallized with sugar. Setting the kettle into a pan of ice or snow will cool the sugar more quickly. Stir the corn all the time so that it will absorb all the sugar, that each kernel of corn will be separate, and not in bunches. Halves of English walnuts, chestnuts, filberts and almonds can also be covered with sugar in this way, and prove very attractive.

Source: *Country Gentleman* 48 (December 20, 1883): 1029.

Crystalized Pop-Corn or Nuts

Put into an iron kettle one teaspoonful of butter, three ounces of water, one teacupful of white sugar. Boil until ready to candy. Throw into this three quarts of pop-corn. Stir briskly until well mixed. Remove the kettle from the fire and stir until cooled a little. Nuts may be used instead of corn.

Source: San Grael Society of the First Presbyterian Church. *The Web-Foot Cook Book.* Portland, Oreg.: W. B. Ayer, 1885. 191.

Pop-Corn Candy. No. 1

Put into an iron kettle one tablespoonful of butter, three tablespoonfuls of water and one cupful of white sugar; boil until ready to candy, then throw in three quarts nicely popped corn; stir vigorously until the sugar is evenly distributed over the corn; take the kettle from the fire and stir until it cools a little, and in this way you may have each kernel separate and all coated with sugar. Of course it must have your undivided attention from the first, to prevent scorching. Almonds, English walnuts, or, in fact, any nuts are delicious prepared in this way.

Source: F. L. Gillette. *The White House Cookbook*. Chicago: L. P. Miller & Co., 1887. 403.

Pop-Corn Candy. No. 2

Having popped your corn, salt it and keep it warm, sprinkle over with a whisk broom a mixture composed of an ounce of gum arabic and a half pound of sugar, dissolved in two quarts of water; boil all a few minutes. Stir the corn with the hands or large spoon thoroughly; then mold into balls with the hands.

Source: F. L. Gillette. *The White House Cookbook*. Chicago: L. P. Miller & Co., 1887. 403.

Crisped Candied Pop Corns

Pop sufficient corn to make four quarts, sift it and reject all the hard grains. Put two cupfuls of sugar, three cupfuls of New Orleans molasses and a half cupful of butter in a large saucepan over the fire, boil, stirring occasionally, until the mixture hardens when dropped into water. Pour this over the pop corn, mix thoroughly, and press into squares.

Source: S. T. Rorer. *Home Candy Making*. Philadelphia: Arnold and Company, 1889. 70.

Candied Pop-corn

Nuts of any kind can be prepared in the same way. Put into a small iron kettle one tablespoonful of butter, three tablespoonfuls of water, one tea-cupful of pulverized sugar, one teaspoonful of lemon juice. Boil until it is ready to candy then add three quarts of nicely popped corn, stir briskly until the candy is evenly distributed over the corn. Then take the kettle from the stove and stir until the corn is cooked a little, and you have each grain separate and crystalized with sugar, taking care that it does not burn. Spread the corn out on buttered paper, or waxed paper, until it is dried over and hardened.

Source: Sarah J. Cutter. *Palatable Dishes: A Practical Guide to Good Living*. Buffalo: Peter, Paul & Bro., 1891. 715.

Pop=corn Candy

1 Cupful of White Sugar.
1 Tablespoonful of Butter
3 Tablespoonfuls of Water
3 Quarts of Nicely Popped Corn.

Put the butter, water and sugar into a boiler, and boil till it begins to almost run to candy; then throw in the nicely popped corn; stir vigorously over fire and stir until the sugar is evenly distributed over the corn; then take the kettle from the fire and stir until it cools a little. In this way you will have each grain or kernel separate and coated with sugar. If you wish, pile it into mounds and roll into balls while still hot enough for the grains to adhere. These are put into dainty rolls of tissue paper and sold along the streets of New Orleans.

Source: The Picayune. *The Picayune Creole Cook Book*. Second edition. New Orleans: The Picayune, 1901. 377.

Crystallized Pop-Corn

Take two cupfuls of granulated sugar, two tablespoonfuls of white corn syrup and one-half cupful of cream and boil to the soft ball stage. Divide into four portions, pouring each portion on a buttered plate, and flavoring differently with strawberry, orange, maple and melted chocolate, respectively. Beat the portion on each plate until creamy, coloring the portion that is flavored with strawberry pink, the orange flavored with yellow. One portion may be left white if liked, or the amount of syrup may be doubled and divided into more portions. Place each kind of the mixture in cups or bowls. Select very large, crisp kernels of corn and dip one by one into different mixtures until all is used. Dry them on greased or waxed paper. One may use a hat pin to dip with. These grains may be used to decorate other sweets or may be served in little baskets or odd receptacles.

Source: Mary M. Wright. *Candy-Making at Home; Two Hundred Ways to Make Candy with Home Flavor and Professional Finish*. Philadelphia: Penn Publishing Company, 1915. 127–28.

11. Cereal

Pop-corn Cereal

Children delight in the novelty of this breakfast food. If you do not care for the whole grains run them through the food chopper and serve with cream and sugar, fruit juices or plain fruit. A few raisins or dates added makes the dish more appetizing. The corn may be popped at any time and reheated in the oven.

Source: May Belle Brooks. "Meals from the Corn-Popper; Attractive Dishes for the New Year's Table," *Good Housekeeping* 56 (January 1913): 119.

Popcorn Cereal

Pop corn may be served either as a hot or cold cereal. If the former way is desired, cover the popped kernels—and none pop better than Nelson's—with cold water and allow them to soak over night; then cook them in milk in the morning and serve with sugar and cream. A very tasty accompaniment to this may be made by washing some dates; cut them up and put them in a saucepan with just enough water to cover and allow them to simmer for five minutes, then drain and place around the hot pop corn, or mix them with it. Stewed apples, prunes, plumped raisins, fruit juice, or any kind of plain fruit also make a nice addition to pop corn served as a cereal.

An unusual but delicious way to serve Nelson's corn, popped, as a cereal is to combine it with cheese, one of the varieties which is mild in flavor and soft in texture. When popped corn is cooked, just before removing from the stove stir in a cupful of grated cheese and a little butter and salt, allow to melt and become blended with the pop corn, then serve. This is eaten without cream and sugar.

Source: Mary Hamilton Talbott. *Pop Corn Recipes*. Grinnell, Iowa: Sam Nelson, Jr., Company, 1916. n.p.

12. Cheese and Nuts

Pop Corn with Cheese and Nuts

Grind the pop corn and soak one cupful in a cupful of warm water overnight, or all morning, or cook it in a double boiler for thirty minutes or more. Add it to three-quarters of a cupful of cheese and half a cupful of crumbs, with three tablespoonfuls of cornstarch dissolved in the same amount of water. Season with onion, pepper and salt; place in a greased baking dish and bake in a quick oven until browned. Serve with tomato sauce.

For the nut combination one cupful of fine, dry, sifted pop-corn meal with the same measure of chopped nuts and crumbs, one beaten egg, two tablespoonfuls of cornstarch dissolved in two tablespoonfuls of cold water, and salt and pepper to taste. Add just enough more water to make into a loaf; place on a greased pan and bake until browned. Serve with tomato sauce.

Source: Riley M. Fletcher-Berry. "Dressing Up Pop Corn," *Ladies' Home Journal* 34 (December 1917): 70.

13. Chocolate-Covered Popcorn

Choc-o-Pop

Have ready a mixture made of one cupful of sugar, one half cupful of molasses and one cake of chocolate, cooked until it nearly crisps in cold water, keep warm. Pop corn enough to fill a three quart bowl, turn into a big pan and mix with the candy.

Source: Constance Wachtmeister and Kate Buffington Davis, eds. *Practical Vegetarian Cookery*. Minneapolis: Printers Electrotyping Co., 1897. 142.

Chocolate Sugared Popcorn

2 quarts popped corn
2 tablespoons butter
2 cups brown sugar
1/2 cup water
2 squares chocolate

Pick over the corn, discarding all hard kernels. Melt butter in saucepan, add sugar, water, and chocolate. Stir over fire until chocolate is melted and boil to 238°F., or until it will form a soft ball when tried in cold water. Pour over corn, and stir until every kernel is coated with sugar.

Source: Alice Bradley. *The Candy Cook Book*. Boston: Little, Brown, and Company, 1917. 190.

Chocolate Pop Corn

2 teacupfuls of white sugar
1/2 cup corn syrup
2 ounces of chocolate
1 cup water

Put these ingredients in to a kettle and cook until the sirup hardens when put in cold water. Pour over 4 quarts of crisp, freshly popped corn and stir well to insure the uniform coating of the kernels.

Source: Charles P. Hartley and John G. Willier. "Pop Corn for the Home," in *Farmers' Bulletin #553*. Washington, D.C.: Department of Agriculture, 1913. 13.

Chocolate Pop Corn

Cook together one cupful of sugar, a quarter of a cupful of syrup, half a cupful of water and two ounces of grated chocolate together until it hardens when dropped into cold water. Pour this over two quarts of Nelson's fluffy popped corn kernels, stir well with a fork in order to cover all the grains.

Source: Mary Hamilton Talbott. *Pop Corn Recipes*. Grinnell, Iowa: Sam Nelson, Jr., Company, 1916. n.p.

14. Cookies

Pop-Corn Fruit Cookies

Mix one cupful each of fine-ground popcorn, sugar and fine cut figs or other dried fruit with half a cupful each of shortening and milk and a beaten egg. Gradually add one cupful each of wheat flour and corn meal, into which one teaspoonful and a half of nutmeg and four teaspoonfuls of baking powder have been sifted. Roll one-third inch thick; cut out and bake in a moderate oven.

Source: Riley M. Fletcher-Berry. "Dressing Up Pop Corn," *Ladies' Home Journal* 34 (December 1917): 70.

Pop-Corn Cookies

Whites of two eggs, 2 tablespoonfuls melted butter, 1 cupful of pop corn, 1/2 cupful pulverized sugar, 1/4 teaspoonful of salt, 1 teaspoonful of vanilla. First beat the whites, adding sugar slowly; add pop corn finely chopped and mixed with butter, salt and flavoring. Drop with a teaspoon on a buttered bake sheet one inch apart. Spread with a spatula that has been dipped in cold water. Bake in a moderate oven for from 25 to 30 minutes.

Source: T. A. Gagnon. *Tried and Tested Recipes. Mrs. T. A. Gagnon's Cook Book for Practical Housekeeping*. Grafton, N.D.: Grafton News and Times Print, 1919. 158.

15. Corn-Nut Loaf

Corn-nut Loaf

Mix together one cupful of ground pop-corn, one cupful of soft stale bread crumbs and one cupful of broken nut meats; add salt and pepper to taste and a teaspoonful of sage. Bind together with two beaten eggs and enough cold water to hold the mixture together. Form into a loaf and bake on a greased pan in a hot oven three-fourths of an hour. Serve with brown or tomato sauce.

Source: May Belle Brooks. "Meals from the Corn-Popper; Attractive Dishes for the New Year's Table," *Good Housekeeping* 56 (January 1913): 119.

16. Cornlets, Kornettes, and Dusky Maidens

Kornettes

1 cup finely chopped popped corn
1/3 cup powdered sugar
a few grains of salt
1 tablespoon melted butter
1 teaspoon vanilla
white of one egg
chopped nuts

Beat the white of egg until stiff; add gradually the sugar. Stir the butter into the chopped corn. Combine the mixtures and add salt and vanilla. Drop by teaspoonfuls on a well-buttered tin sheet one inch apart. Dip a knife into cold water and shape into circular form. Sprinkle with finely chopped nuts—almonds or any other nuts. Bake in a slow oven until a delicate brown.

Source: Mary L. Wade. *The Book of Corn Cookery.* Chicago: A. C. McClurg and Co., 1917. 97.

Cornlets

Large Recipe	Small Recipe
Popped corn, chopped, 4 cups	Popped corn, chopped, 2 cups
Egg whites, 2	Egg white, 1
Light corn syrup, 1/2 cup	Brown sugar, 1/4 cup
Flour, 1/2 cup	Flour, 1/4 cup
Almonds, blanched and chopped, 1/4 cup	Almonds, blanched and chopped, 2 tablespoons

Beat the egg whites until stiff. Gradually fold in the sugar, syrup, flour, and chopped, popped corn.

Drop on a slightly buttered baking sheet or inverted pan, forming biscuits about one and three-fourths inches in diameter. Sprinkle the tops of the biscuits with chopped, blanched almonds.

Bake in a moderate oven (350° F.) For fifteen minutes.

Remove from baking sheet while still warm, because these cookies become very brittle when cold.

Source: May B. Van Arsdale, Day Monroe, and Mary I. Barber. *Our Candy Recipes*. New York: Macmillan Company, 1922. 177.

Dusky Maidens

Make cornlets, following directions given above. Do not sprinkle the tops of the cookies with almonds, as a smooth surface is desired. When the cookies have been removed from the pan and have become cool, draw faces on them with melted chocolate, using a tooth pick or a small brush.

A great deal of ingenuity can be exercised in the drawing of these faces, and the decorated cookies are appropriate for children's parties.

Source: May B. Van Arsdale, Day Monroe, and Mary I. Barber. *Our Candy Recipes*. New York: Macmillan Company, 1922. 177–78.

17. Cracker Jack

K. of G. Cracker Jack

Pop your corn and keep hot also prepare nut meats (peanuts), then put two cupfuls molasses, one of sugar and butter size of an egg into a pan and boil until it stings; have popcorn and peanuts well mixed in a pan and pour syrup as above over them; pack into square tins the size you want for popcorn and form into balls. Can be made the day previous.

Source: Emma Garman Krape, compiler. *The Globe Cook Book*. Freeport, Ill.: Journal Printing Company, February 22, 1901. 232–33.

Cracker Jack

Four quarts popped corn, one cup sugar, one-half cup syrup, one fourth teaspoonful cream tartar, 1 teaspoonful butter. Boil sugar, syrup, [c]ream of tartar and butter together for four minutes. Pour over the corn; mix well, and press firmly into two large bread pans. When cold, cut into squares. A cup or more of any kind of nuts mixed with the corn makes nut cracker jack. Mary Kurtzwell.

Source: The Ladies of Des Moines. *A Collection of Choice Recipes*. Des Moines, Iowa, 1903. Reprint. *Fifty Years of Prairie Cooking*. Introduction and Suggested Recipes by Louis Szathmáry. New York: Arno Press, 1973. 81.

Crackerjack

Put in a large pan 2 quarts of corn, measured after popping, and pour over it the following mixture: boil 1 cup of molasses, 1 cup of sugar and 1/2 cup of vinegar until it crisps when dropped in cold water; add 2 cups of shelled peanuts, stir well; when mixed pour into a shallow baking pan that has been lined with waxed paper and lay heavy weights on until firm. This is fine. —Mrs. W. M. Burns.

Source: Ladies of the First Presbyterian Church. *The First Presbyterian Cook Book*. Spokane, Wash.: The author, [circa 1910]. 95.

Cracker Jacks

Take 2 cups of sugar, 1 tablespoonful of vinegar, and enough water to cover the sugar. Boil till it will roll into a ball by putting it in water. Have the whites of 2 eggs beaten to a stiff froth, into which beat the syrup. Take Teacup full of any kind of nuts desired (black walnuts are good), roll and stir into the above. Spread on top of crackers and set in the oven to brown lightly. —*Sister J. W. Miller, Hereford, Tex.*

Source: *The Inglenook Cook Book*. New and revised edition, Choice Recipes Contributed by the Sisters of the Church of the Brethren, Subscribers and Friends of The Inglenook Magazine. Elgin, Ill.: Brethren Publishing House, 1911. 250–51.

Cracker Jack

1 cup sorghum
1 cup of sugar
1 cup water
1 teaspoon cream tartar
2 level teaspoons soda
10 pints of corn

Add the soda before pouring over the corn. Spread on a board and cut in squares. Mrs. S. W. peters.

Source: Sunshine Society of Crawfordsville High School. *Sunshine Cook Book*. Crawfordsville, Ind.: Journal Printing Co., 1913. 38.

18. Crisps and Crispettes

Pop Corn Crisp

Pop a lot of corn and set to one side; now put in kettle
4 pounds sugar,
2 pounds glucose,
Water to dissolve same.

Cook to 280° or 290°, then add 1/4 pint of dark molasses; stir good half a minute and set kettle off and add 1/4 pound butter and a teaspoonful of fine salt; now pour in all the corn you possibly can get in the kettle and stir it until all is well covered; now set the kettle on the fire, only for a half minute so as to warm the bottom of the kettle; now turn it all out on the slab and spread it out evenly, then with a smooth board press it very light; when cold cut in pieces to fit pans.

Source: Will O. Rigby. *Rigby's Reliable Candy Teacher.* Topeka, Kans.: W. O. Rigby, 1902. 61.

Corn Crisp

1 cup soft sugar
1/2 cup Orleans molasses
1/4 cup butter

Stir these into a large pan and let boil until it will harden when dropped into cold water. Add 1/2 teaspoon of soda and stir well. Into this mixture put 1 gallon popped corn, quickly, and stir rapidly. Remove from stove and turn on bread board and press together with the hands. Mrs. Hugh E. Johnson.

Source: Ladies of the Cosmos Society of the Bradley Methodist Episcopal Church. *Favorite Recipes.* Greenfield, Ind.: Greenfield Printing and Publishing Company, [1906]. 41.

Molasses Popcorn Crispettes

First, have your mixing tank hot so that the steam comes out of the vent, then put 2 1/2 pounds of popcorn into the heater tank, then cover the tank. Now get your copper kettle and put into it 1 pint of water, 3 pounds sugar and 3 pounds glucose, stir until the whole mass is pretty well dissolved, then cook to 280 degrees on the thermometer. Add 1/2 pint molasses and stir vigorously until the whole mass comes back to a boil and is foamy. A little experience right here is necessary:—If you do not leave the kettle on the fire long enough after you add the molasses your crispettes will be a little sticky, and on the other hand if you leave it on too long the syrup will get brittle on the popcorn before you have the crispettes all molded up. Now shut off the gas or remove the kettle from the fire entirely and add a heaping teaspoonful of baking soda, stir this well until it becomes thoroughly mixed with the syrup and pour on to the popcorn in the heater.

Source: *Copyrighted Secret Formulas and Instructions for the Manufacture of Crispettes and Other Popcorn Confections.* Chicago: C. E. Dellenbarger Co., Chicago, 1913. 18.

Chocolate Crispettes

These are made just the same as the Molasses Crispettes except that you do not add molasses. Cook to 265 degrees, add 4 ounces bitter chocolate, grated or cut up fine, stir it for one-half minute. Put out the fire and add a heaping teaspoonful of soda, stir until thoroughly mixed and then pour on to the popcorn.

Source: *Copyrighted Secret Formulas and Instructions for the Manufacture of Crispettes and Other Popcorn Confections.* Chicago: C. E. Dellenbarger Co., Chicago, 1913. 19.

Cherokee Crisp

Take two cupfuls of light brown sugar, one-fourth cupful of New Orleans molasses, and one-half cupful of water. Melt over the fire until all the sugar is dissolved, add two tablespoonfuls of butter. Sprinkle some salt over a quart of freshly popped corn in a bowl. Flavor the syrup with a teaspoonful of vanilla after it has reached the hard crack stage and pour over the corn. Turn out on a large platter or marble slab and work until a very thin sheet. When cold break into pieces.

Source: Mary M. Wright. *Candy-Making at Home; Two Hundred Ways to Make Candy with Home Flavor and Professional Finish.* Philadelphia: Penn Publishing Company, 1915. 129–30.

Popcorn Crisp

Place in kettle:
3 lbs. sugar.
1/2 lb. Glucose.
1 pt. water.
Set on fire and mix.

Cook to 300° and add 1/2 pt. Molasses and a piece of butter the size of a walnut. Stir good until the batch turns golden color and set on tub.

Add 2 lbs. popcorn and stir until thoroughly covered with the candy.

Spread out on greased slab and break apart for tray.

This can also be made up in 5-cent balls.

Source: William M. Bell, compiler. *The Pilot: An Authoritative Book on the Manufac-ture of Candies and Ice Creams.* Third edition. Chicago: Wm. M. Bell, 1918. 125–26.

Crispettes

For 4 quarts popped corn take 1 cup sugar, 2 tablespoonfuls molasses, 1 teaspoonful butter, 1/2 teaspoonful salt. Boil until a few drops harden in water. Pour over corn and mix thoroughly. Spread into deep pie-pan and cut into squares as desired. To keep fresh and crisp, wrap in wax paper.

Source: "Little Buster Hull-Less Pop Corn." Chicago: Albert Dickinson Co., 1921. Broadside.

Pop Corn Crisp

Large Recipe	Small Recipe
Granulated sugar, 1 1/2 cups	Granulated sugar, 3/4 cup
Brown sugar, 1 1/2 cups	Brown sugar, 3/4 cup
Dark corn syrup, 1/2 cup	Dark corn syrup, 1/4 cup
Water, 1/2 cup	Water, 1/4 cup
Butter, 2 tablespoons	Butter, 1 tablespoon
Salt, 1/2 teaspoon	Salt, 1/4 teaspoon
Popped corn, chopped, 1 1/2 cups	Popped corn, chopped, 3/4 cup

Put the sugars, water, and corn syrup into a saucepan and cook, stirring until the sugars are dissolved. Continue cooking, without stirring, until the candy reaches the temperature 300° F.

Remove from fire, ad the butter and the chopped, salted popped corn. Stir only enough to mix well. Too much stirring will cause the brittle to sugar. Turn quickly on a greased slab or on greased inverted pans or baking sheets. Do not scrape the saucepan, as this may cause the brittle to sugar.

Have enough pans to give space for the brittle to be poured out in very thin sheets.

Smooth out with a spatula. After about one-half minute take hold of the edges of the candy and lifting it slightly from the slab, pull it as thin as possible. If the candy is in a large sheet it may be necessary to cut off the thin pieces at the edges in order to pull the center.

Break into irregular pieces.

Cold water test when candy reaches 300° F.: brittle.

Yield (large recipe): weight—one and one-half pounds.

Source: May B. Van Arsdale, Day Monroe, and Mary I. Barber. *Our Candy Recipes.* New York: Macmillan Company, 1922. 170–71.

Amber Pop Corn

Follow the directions for pop corn crisp, using unchopped, popped corn.

Turn the cooked candy out on a greased slab or on greased inverted pans or baking sheets.

Pull the brittle into small pieces, having about five grains of popped corn stuck together to form each piece. Each grain should be well covered with this coating and there should not be spaces of clear candy between the grains of popped corn.

Source: May B. Van Arsdale, Day Monroe, and Mary I. Barber. *Our Candy Recipes*. New York: Macmillan Company, 1922. 171.

19. Custard

Pop Corn Custard

Heat one quart of milk in a double boiler, when warm stir in the beaten yolks of four eggs, four tablespoonsful of granulated sugar and a scant tablespoonful corn starch (mixed with a little cold water). When this thickens add three-fourths of a cupful of Nelson's corn after it is popped and ground, and a teaspoonful of almond extract. When cold cover with a meringue, made by whipping the whites of the eggs to a stiff froth and adding slowly eight teaspoonsful of powdered sugar and a few spoonsful of tart jelly, preferably currant.

Source: Mary Hamilton Talbott. *Pop Corn Recipes*. Grinnell, Iowa: Sam Nelson, Jr., Company, 1916. n.p.

20. Cutlet

Pop Corn Cutlet

Mix two cupsful of bread crumbs, two cupsful of popped and ground corn—Nelson's corn gives a nutty flavor—one cupful of milk or cream, two eggs, and salt and pepper to taste: mold into cutlet form, flour and fry in hot butter as you do veal cutlet. Garnish with chopped parsley and tomato sauce.

Source: Mary Hamilton Talbott. *Pop Corn Recipes*. Grinnell, Iowa: Sam Nelson, Jr., Company, 1916. n.p.

21. Dainties

Pop-Corn Dainty

Place in a saucepan two cupfuls of granulated sugar, one-half cupful of water and one-fourth teaspoonful of cream of tartar. Boil to a firm ball. Just before removing from the fire stir into the syrup a pint of popcorn that has been run through the food chopper. Pour over the stiffly beaten whites of two eggs, flavor with a teaspoonful of vanilla and beat up until light and foamy; then pour into greased pans, and cut into squares, or drop from a spoon on paraffin paper, and press a whole popcorn grain into the top of each. These are also nice if crystallized popcorn in different colors is used for decoration.

Source: Mary M. Wright. *Candy-Making at Home; Two Hundred Ways to Make Candy with Home Flavor and Professional Finish*. Philadelphia: Penn Publishing Company, 1915. 126–27.

Coffee Pop-Corn Dainties

Boil together a pint of brown sugar, half a pint of clear, strong coffee, and a tablespoonful of butter substitute until the soft-ball stage is reached. Then take from the fire; add the stiff whipped white of one egg and one cupful of chopped, fresh popped corn. Beat until creamy; turn into greased, straight-sided tin and, when partly cool, mark off into small squares.

Source: Riley M. Fletcher-Berry. "Dressing Up Pop Corn," *Ladies' Home Journal* 34 (December 1917): 70.

Coffee Pop Corn Dainties

Boil together a pint of brown sugar, 1/2 a pint of clear, strong coffee, and a tablespoonful of butter substitute until the soft ball stage is reached. Then take from the fire; add the stiff whipped white of 1 egg and 1 cupful of chopped, freshly popped corn. Beat until creamy; turn into a greased, straight-sided tin and, when partly cool, mark off into small squares.

Source: T. A. Gagnon. *Tried and Tested Recipes. Mrs. T. A. Gagnon's Cook Book for Practical Housekeeping.* Grafton, N.D.: Grafton News and Times Print, 1919. 272.

22. Dates Stuffed with Popcorn

Dates Stuffed with Pop Corn

Cut open the dates, remove the pits and fill the cavities with Nelson's corn, popped and ground, mixed with a little strained honey. Press the edges of the dates together and roll in confectioner's sugar.

Source: Mary Hamilton Talbott. *Pop Corn Recipes.* Grinnell, Iowa: Sam Nelson, Jr., Company, 1916. n.p.

23. Dressing

Dressing for Fowl

Take equal quantities of stale bread and popped corn and soak them in cold water until soft. Squeeze dry, add two eggs and season with salt, pepper, onions and celery to taste and a teaspoonful of sage. Put sufficient butter in a frying pan and when melted, turn in the dressing. Cook slowly for twenty minutes, stirring and turning often. Stuff the fowl at once. The dressing will not be soggy.

Source: May Belle Brooks. "Meals from the Corn-Popper; Attractive Dishes for the New Year's Table," *Good Housekeeping* 56 (January 1913): 119.

24. Flake

Pop Corn Flake

Place in kettle:
4 pounds light yellow sugar,
1/2 pound glucose,
1 pint molasses.

Cook to 290°; take off the fire and let set about half a minute, then stir into the batch about half a tablespoonful of soda and whatever amount of fresh pop corn you wish; then pour on well greased slab, and cut into large sheets.

Source: Will O. Rigby. *Rigby's Reliable Candy Teacher.* Topeka, Kans.: Rigby Publishing Company, 1902. 128.

25. Fritters

Popcorn Balls and Fritters

After the corn has been popped, take from the quantity any uncooked or partially cooked grains, being sure to have only fine, large, puffy ones. To one cup Karo allow one tablespoon vinegar. Boil together until it hardens when dropped in cold water. When ready pour over the popcorn while hot. As soon as cool enough to handle, butter the hands well and form the mass into balls. To make Popcorn Fritters, form the mass into flat, round cakes instead of balls.

Source: Emma Churchman Hewitt. *Corn Products Cook Book.* New York: Corn Products Refining Company, c1910. 38.

26. Fudge

Pop-Corn Fudge

Take two cupfuls of white sugar, one cupful of milk, two tablespoonfuls of butter and a pinch of salt. Boil to the soft ball stage. Flavor with a half teaspoonful of almond extract, then stir in one cupful of chopped pop-corn and one-half cupful of chopped peanuts or any nuts desired. Stir until creamy and pour out on buttered pans, and when cool cut into squares.

Source: Mary M. Wright. *Candy-Making at Home; Two Hundred Ways to Make Candy with Home Flavor and Professional Finish.* Philadelphia: Penn Publishing Company, 1915. 131.

Pop Corn Fudge

Boil together two cupsful of sugar, half a cupful of maple syrup, half a cupful of water and a third of a teaspoonful of salt until they will form a soft ball when dropped into cold water. Beat this slowly into the stiffly beaten whites of two eggs; when smooth, add two and one-half cupsful of corn, popped and ground—Nelson's gives the nutty flavor. Pour into buttered pans and mark when cool.

Source: Mary Hamilton Talbott. *Pop Corn Recipes.* Grinnell, Iowa: Sam Nelson, Jr., Company, 1916. n.p.

Peanut-Popcorn Fudge

Cook to the soft ball stage half a cupful each of peanut butter and milk, with two cupfuls and a half of sugar. Add a teaspoonful of butter substitute, a heaped cupful of coarsely chopped pop corn and a teaspoonful of vanilla flavoring. Beat until creamy and pour onto a greased platter to cool.

Source: Riley M. Fletcher-Berry. "Dressing Up Pop Corn," *Ladies' Home Journal* 34 (December 1917): 70.

Chocolate Pop Corn Fudge

Cook together a pint of sugar, 1/2 a pint of milk, 2 squares of bitter chocolate, a tablespoonful of butter substitute and a saltspoonful of salt, until the soft ball stage is reached. Then remove from the fire; add a teaspoonful of vanilla extract, with 1 cupful and a half of coarsely chopped pop corn. Stir until the mixture is creamy but still soft; pour into a greased pan and, when it hardens sufficiently, mark into squares.

Source: T. A. Gagnon. *Tried and Tested Recipes. Mrs. T. A. Gagnon's Cook Book for Practical Housekeeping*. Grafton, N.D.: Grafton News and Times Print, 1919. 272.

27. Hash

Pop Corn Hash

Chop fine some cold boiled potatoes and any other vegetables desired that may be on hand. Put them into a buttered frying pan, heat quickly and thoroughly, and salt to taste. Then add a large spoonful of ground, popped corn (Nelson's is the best for popping), for each person to be served. When heated thoroughly, dish and serve.

Source: Mary Hamilton Talbott. *Pop Corn Recipes*. Grinnell, Iowa: Sam Nelson, Jr., Company, 1916. n.p.

28. Hunky-Dories

"Hunky-Dories"

First grate a cake of chocolate sweet
Into a dish which stands
In pan of boiling water near.
When melting, it demands
A spoonful of the best rich cream;
Then quickly in it beat
Two cups of freshly popped white corn
And cup of pecan meat.
Stir briskly with a fork until
The syrup covers all;
Dip out on sheets of paper waxed,
And dry the nuggets small.

Source: Charlotte Brewster Jordan. "A Pop-Corn Frolic for Hallowe'en," *St. Nicholas* 36 (October 1909): 1114–15.

29. Ice Cream

Popcorn with Ice Cream

Have you ever tried eating popcorn with ice cream? It is delicious—seems to supply the little added something which is lacking. Of course, you do not butter or salt the corn. You will say that you have added one more delicious dessert to your menus. Serena.

Source: *Good Housekeeping Discovery Book No. 1.* New York: Phelps Publishing Co., 1905. 299.

30. Johnny Cakes

Johnny Cake

Large Recipe	Small Recipe
Popped corn, chopped before measuring, 1 1/2 cups	Popped corn, chopped before measuring, 3/4 cup
Shelled peanuts, 1/2 cup	Shelled peanuts 1/4 cup
Brown sugar, 1 1/2 cups	Brown sugar, 3/4 cup
Light corn syrup, 1/2 cup	Light corn syrup, 3/4 cup
Water, 3/4 cup	Water, 1/2 cup
Molasses, 2 tablespoons	Molasses, 1 tablespoon
Butter, 2 tablespoons	Butter, 1 tablespoon
Soda, 1/4 teaspoon	Soda, 1/8 teaspoon
Salt, 1/2 teaspoon	Salt, 1/4 teaspoon

Brown the peanuts in the oven and break them into pieces. Chop the popped corn in a chopping bowl. It should be quite coarse.

Put the sugar, corn syrup, and water into a saucepan and cook, stirring, until the sugar is dissolved. Continue cooking, until the temperature 270° F.

Remove from fire, add soda (free from lumps), and stir until it ceases to bubble. Add chopped, popped corn and nuts, mixed with the salt, and stir until well mixed. If using the large recipe have the corn warm. Turn into small, greased patty tins, making cakes one-fourth of an inch thick. On top of each little cake place a half peanut. When cold remove from the pans.

It is necessary to work rapidly when turning the mixture into the pans, as it hardens very quickly. If it begins to become hard it is better to set the saucepan of candy into a pan of hot water while dipping out the cakes.

Cold water test when the candy reaches 270° F.: hard, almost brittle.

Yield (large recipe): number of cakes—thirty-two (one and one-fourth inches in diameter and one-fourth of an inch thick.)

Source: May B. Van Arsdale, Day Monroe, and Mary I. Barber. *Our Candy Recipes.* New York: Macmillan Company, 1922. 172–73.

31. Lace

Pop Corn Lace

Large Recipe	Small Recipe
Butter, 2 tablespoons	Butter, 1 tablespoon
Sugar, 1 cup	Sugar, 1/2 cup
Popped corn, chopped, 2 cups	Popped corn, chopped, 1 cup
Baking powder, chopped, 2 cups	Baking powder, 1/8 teaspoon
Salt, 1/2 teaspoon	Salt, 1/4 teaspoon
Eggs, 2	Eggs, 1

Cream the butter. Add the sugar, well mixed with the baking powder and salt. Cream together. Add beaten egg and mix thoroughly. Add chopped, popped corn and stir well.

Drop by teaspoonfuls on greased baking sheet or inverted pan. As these cookies will spread in baking only a level teaspoonful should be allowed for each cookie and they should not be placed too close together. Flatten with a spatula before placing in the oven.

Bake in a moderate oven (350° F.), for about ten minutes. When done the cookies should be delicately brown and very thin and lace-like. Remove from baking sheet while still warm, because these cookies become very brittle when cold. If they become too crisp, the cookies may be returned to the oven to heat until they soften.

Yield (large recipe): fifty small cookies.

Source: May B. Van Arsdale, Day Monroe, and Mary I. Barber. *Our Candy Recipes.* New York: Macmillan Company, 1922. 176.

32. Macaroons

Pop-Corn Macaroons

Run some freshly popped corn through the food chopper, or else chop up with a knife until fine. To a cupful of these add an equal quantity of blanched almonds that have been pounded to a paste. Put these together in a bowl. Beat up whites of three eggs until stiff, then add about one-half a cupful of sugar and beat up for about five minutes. Mix the pop-corn and paste into this slowly until thoroughly blended. Drop from a spoon on oiled or buttered paper in a pan and sprinkle with powdered sugar. Bake in a moderate oven for about twenty minutes. The centers of these can be decorated with crystallized pop-corn.

Source: Mary M. Wright. *Candy-Making at Home; Two Hundred Ways to Make Candy with Home Flavor and Professional Finish.* Philadelphia: Penn Publishing Company, 1915. 129.

Pop Corn Macaroons

Mix half a cupful of popped and rolled corn (Nelson's is the best). And half a package of chopped raisins, one cupful of powdered sugar, the whites of two eggs and a tablespoonful of flour together and drop on greased brown paper by tablespoonsful and bake in a moderate oven until light brown.

Source: Mary Hamilton Talbott. *Pop Corn Recipes.* Grinnell, Iowa: Sam Nelson, Jr., Company, 1916. n.p.

Popped Corn Macaroons

3/4 cup finely chopped corn
3/4 tablespoon melted butter
White 1 egg
5 1/2 tablespoons sugar
1/4 teaspoon salt
1/2 teaspoon vanilla
Blanched and finely chopped almonds
Candied cherries

PROCESS: Add butter to corn; beat white of egg until stiff; add sugar gradually; continue beating. Add to first mixture; add salt and vanilla. Drop from tip of teaspoon on a well buttered baking sheet one and one-half inches apart. With the spoon shape in circles and flatten with a knife, first dipped in cold water. Sprinkle with chopped nut meats and press a shred of candied cherry in top of each macaroon. Bake in a slow oven until daintily browned.

Source: Elizabeth Hiller. *The Corn Cook Book.* War edition. New York: P. F. Volland Company, 1918. 117.

33. Marguerites

Popcorn Marguerites

Make a boiled frosting as for cake, usin[g] a cup of sugar and a tablespoon of vinegar for two whites of eggs. When the frosting is done, stir into it about three cups of fresh, perfect popcorn. Spread wafers, perfectly unsalted ones, thickly with the mixture, and bake until a delicate brown in a moderate oven. These are easily made and delicious.

Source: Amelia Sulzbacher. "Popcorn Dainties," *Good Housekeeping* 43 (October 1906): 422–23.

Pop Corn Marguerites

Make a paste of Nelson's corn, popped and ground, and chopped raisins, mixed with boiled icing. Spread on vanilla wafers or crackers and put in the oven long enough to brown.

Source: Mary Hamilton Talbott. *Pop Corn Recipes.* Grinnell, Iowa: Sam Nelson, Jr., Company, 1916. n.p.

34. Mock Violets

Mock Violets

Popcorn
Fondant
Violet color paste
Angelica

Select large, open kernels of corn that will resemble the shape of violets. Color fondant a rich violet shade, melt it over hot water, and dip kernels of corn one at a time in the melted fondant, attach fine stems of angelica, place on paraffin paper, and leave until dry. Serve as a bonbon or use as a garnish on a bed of spun sugar around a mold of ice cream.

Source: Alice Bradley. *The Candy Cook Book*. Boston: Little, Brown, and Company, 1917. 190–91.

35. Muffins

Pop-Corn Muffins

Sift four teaspoonfuls of baking powder, one teaspoonful of sugar with one cupful and a half of white flour; add three-quarters of a cupful of fine-ground pop corn, two tablespoonfuls of shortening and a cupful of milk or water with one egg. Or use one cupful each of flour and pop corn and the whites of two eggs. Bake for about twenty-five minutes in greased gem pans.

Source: Riley M. Fletcher-Berry. "Dressing Up Pop Corn," *Ladies' Home Journal* 34 (December 1917): 70.

36. Nests

Popcorn Nests

Make popcorn balls and shape into hollow nests. Line with fringed wax paper, and fill with salted nuts or candies for holiday dinner table.

Source: Alice Bradley. *The Candy Cook Book*. Boston: Little, Brown, and Company, 1917. 191.

37. Nuggets

Popcorn Nuggets

2 cups sugar
2/3 cup water
1/4 teaspoon cream of tartar
1/3 cup dark molasses
2 tablespoons butter
Few grains of salt
5 quarts popcorn

Put sugar, water, and cream of tartar in saucepan, bring to boiling point without stirring to 280° F., or until syrup will crack when tried in cold water. Remove thermometer, add molasses, butter, and salt, and boil, stirring constantly, until candy will become very brittle when tried in cold water, being careful that it does not burn. Have ready a pan containing popped corn free from any hard kernels; pour candy over it, mixing thoroughly. Spread lightly on a buttered marble slab or large platter, and when firm cut in pieces, or break up in little bunches of three to six kernels of corn.

Source: Alice Bradley. *The Candy Cook Book*. Boston: Little, Brown, and Company, 1917. 188.

38. Omelets

Pop-corn Omelet

Add one half cupful of milk to one cupful of ground pop-corn and let stand twenty minutes. Beat the whites and yolks of four eggs separately and add them with one teaspoonful of pepper to the other ingredients. Melt two tablespoonfuls of butter in an omelet pan, add the mixture and cook slowly for ten minutes. Place the pan in a moderate oven to finish cooking the top; fold over carefully and garnish with parsley and a sprinkling of pop-corn.

Source: May Belle Brooks. "Meals from the Corn-Popper; Attractive Dishes for the New Year's Table," *Good Housekeeping* 56 (January 1913): 119.

Pop Corn Omelet

—Nelson's pop corn makes a delicious addition to the breakfast omelet. Put enough popped corn through a meat grinder to make a cupful and add to it a quarter of a cupful of milk, allow it to soak a few minutes, then add two well-beaten eggs (whipped separately), half a teaspoonful of salt, and a few grains of paprika and a teaspoonful of chopped parsley. Melt one teaspoonful of butter in an omelet pan, turn in the mixture and cook with moderate heat until firm. Fold, turn out upon a hot platter and garnish with crisp bacon and a generous sprinkling of the unground popped corn.

Source: Mary Hamilton Talbott. *Pop Corn Recipes*. Grinnell, Iowa: Sam Nelson, Jr., Company, 1916. n.p.

39. Pie

Pop Corn Pie

Cream well together one large cupful of granulated sugar, one heaping tablespoonful of butter and when very light add the well-beaten yolks of three eggs, one cupful of molasses and one teaspoonful of grated nutmeg and lastly the stiffly whipped whites of the eggs. Put this mixture into pans lined with a rich crust; before removing from the oven cover the top thickly with the snowy kernels which come when Nelson's corn is popped.

Source: Mary Hamilton Talbott. *Pop Corn Recipes.* Grinnell, Iowa: Sam Nelson, Jr., Company, 1916. n.p.

40. Popcorn and Apples

Pop Corn and Baked Apples

Peel and core tart apples, scoop out the centers and fill with a mixture of Nelson's corn, popped and ground, chopped raisins and a little lemon peel. Place in a baking dish and pour over them half a cupful of water and dust with granulated sugar. Bake in a slow oven until tender, sprinkle with soft bread crumbs and sugar, bake ten minutes more and serve hot with cream or a thin custard.

Source: Mary Hamilton Talbott. *Pop Corn Recipes.* Grinnell, Iowa: Sam Nelson, Jr., Company, 1916. n.p.

41. Popcorn and Bacon

Pop Corn and Bacon

Just before the morning bacon, or sausage, is altogether cooked, add to the grease a generous handful of Nelson's corn when popped: allow it to brown and serve with the meat. It adds a delicious, nutty flavor.

Source: Mary Hamilton Talbott. *Pop Corn Recipes.* Grinnell, Iowa: Sam Nelson, Jr., Company, 1916. n.p.

42. Popcorn and Macaroni

Macaroni and Pop Corn

Cook one cupful of macaroni, broken into inch lengths, in boiling salted water until tender; drain and pour cold water through it to separate the pieces. Then add cream sauce made with four tablespoonsful of flour, the same quantity of butter, salt and pepper to taste, and a cupful of milk; add two cupsful of Nelson's corn, after it is popped and ground. Pour into a buttered baking dish, cover with buttered crumbs and a little grated cheese and bake until a golden brown.

Source: Mary Hamilton Talbott. *Pop Corn Recipes.* Grinnell, Iowa: Sam Nelson, Jr., Company, 1916. n.p.

43. Popcorn and Raisins

Quickly Prepared Desert

A dainty and easily prepared desert is made by soaking a cupful of raisins in warm water until they are well plumped, drain them and mix them with a cupful of Nelsons corn, after it is popped and ground. Serve with plain or whipped cream.

Source: Mary Hamilton Talbott. *Pop Corn Recipes.* Grinnell, Iowa: Sam Nelson, Jr., Company, 1916. n.p.

44. Popcorn and Vegetables

Parsnips and Pop Corn

Wash, scrape and slice thin two good-sized parsnips and cook them until perfectly tender in two quarts of water. When they are nearly done add a teaspoonful of salt and when altogether done a tablespoonful of flour mixed smooth with a little cold water. Stir well and let boil until the flour is cooked, then stir in half a cupful of popped and ground corn—Nelson's pop corn is the best that grows—let boil up once or twice, or until the corn is hot and serve.

Source: Mary Hamilton Talbott. *Pop Corn Recipes*. Grinnell, Iowa: Sam Nelson, Jr., Company, 1916. n.p.

Pop Corn with Turnips or Carrots

Mashed turnips or carrots can be made more tasty by stirring in a cupful of Nelson's corn, popped and ground.

Source: Mary Hamilton Talbott. *Pop Corn Recipes*. Grinnell, Iowa: Sam Nelson, Jr., Company, 1916. n.p.

Potato and Pop Corn Balls

Mix two cupsful of hot mashed potatoes, one teaspoonful of chopped onion, one tablespoonful of chopped parsley, two tablespoonsful of butter, salt and pepper to taste, then shape them into small balls, open the center and put in some popped corn—Nelson's makes the crisp and flaky grains—place on a buttered dish and cook in a moderate oven a quarter of an hour, sprinkle ground popped corn over them before removing from the oven, and serve alone or with tomato sauce.

Source: Mary Hamilton Talbott. *Pop Corn Recipes*. Grinnell, Iowa: Sam Nelson, Jr., Company, 1916. n.p.

Pop Corn with Peppers and Scalloped Dishes

In stuffing peppers to bake, substitute ground pop corn for half the white bread crumbs ordinarily used and sprinkle the corn on top instead of bread crumbs. With scalloped vegetables substitute one-half or two-thirds ground pop corn for the white bread crumbs necessary.

Source: Riley M. Fletcher-Berry. "Dressing Up Pop Corn," *Ladies' Home Journal* 34 (December 1917): 70.

45. Popping Corn (Directions)

Pop Corn

Put some nice fresh lard into a pan; when boiling, drop in the corn and cover tightly, to prevent it popping out of the pan; when done popping, remove the corn from the pan and put them into a colander to drain; have ready some nice steam syrup, heat it and flavour with either seville orange juice or lemon juice; when simmering drop in the corn; let it simmer for ten minutes; take it out in large lumps and lay on buttered dishes to cool.

Source: *Cookery as It Should Be.* Philadelphia: Willis P. Hazard, 1853. 296.

46. Puddings

Pop-Corn Pudding

Three pints of new milk; 2 eggs; 3 pints pop-corn; 1/2 teaspoonful of salt.—Every kernel of corn should be popped perfectly and have a white fleecy look. Eaten with a rich cream sauce, it is an excellent and delicious desert. Bake half an hour.—S. A. Cole, Gorham, N.Y.

Source: *Rural New Yorker* 9 (February 27, 1858): 95.

Pop Corn Pudding

One quart of milk; 1 cup sugar; 4 eggs; 1 quart pop corn; flavor with nutmeg or cinnamon—a little salt. Line your pudding dish with a paste prepared as for soda biscuit, pour in the above ingredients, place a few bits of butter on the top—bake nearly an hour in a moderate oven, stir it occasionally till it begins to thicken.—C.M.M. *Rochester, N.Y.* 1859.

Source: *Rural New Yorker* 10 (March 19, 1859): 95.

Corn Pudding

Put one quart of popped corn in a pudding-dish; stir into one quart of milk two teaspoonfuls of salt, and turn the milk on the corn. Bake twenty minutes. Serve with sugar and cream.

Source: Maria Parloa. *The Appledore Cook Book: Containing Practical Receipts for Plain and Rich Cooking,* 142. Boston: Graves and Ellis, 1872.

Popped Corn Pudding

Mrs. C. H. Crane, Ossawattomie.

One pint popped corn, three pounded crackers, one egg, salt and sugar to taste; soak the corn in one quart of milk three hours. Bake three-fourths of an hour.

Source: C. H. Cushing and B. Gray, compilers. *The Kansas Home Cook-Book.* Fifth thousand. Leavenworth, Kans.: Crew and Brothers, 1877. 183.

Pop Corn Pudding

Take a scant pint of pop corn which is ground and put up in boxes, or if not available, freshly popped corn, rolled fine, is just as good. Add to it three cups of new milk, one half cup sugar, two whole eggs and the yolk of another, well beaten. Bake in a pudding dish placed inside another filled with hot water, till the custard is set. Cover with a meringue made of the remaining white of egg, a teaspoonful of sugar, and a sprinkling of the pop corn.

Source: E. E. Kellogg. *Science in the Kitchen.* Battle Creek, Mich.: Health Publishing Company, 1892. 330.

Popcorn Pudding

Pop some corn nicely, then roll it as fine as you can. One pint of the corn to one quart of sweet milk; add a small piece of butter, one teaspoonful of salt, beat two eggs with enough sugar to sweeten the milk: mix all together. Bake twenty minutes.

Source: *Good Housekeeping* 21 (November 1895): 211.

Pop Corn Pudding

Pop some corn nicely, then roll it as fine as you can. One pint of the corn to a quart of sweet milk; add a small piece of butter, one teaspoon salt, beat two eggs with enough sugar to sweeten the milk; mix all together. Bake twenty minutes.

Source: *Housewife* 21 (August 1904): 12.

Corn Pudding

1/2 scalded milk.
1/4 cup popped corn.
1/2 egg
1 tablespoon brown sugar.
1/2 teaspoon butter.
Few grains salt.

Pick over corn, using the white part only, and roll or pound in mortar until finely divided. Add to milk and butter and let stand until milk is cool; then add sugar, egg slightly beaten, and salt. Turn into a buttered dish and bake in a slow oven until firm, stirring once during baking to prevent corn settling to bottom of dish. Serve with or without cream.

Source: Fannie Merritt Farmer. *Food and Cookery for the Sick and Convalescent.* Boston: Little, Brown, and Company, 1904. 175.

Pop-corn Pudding

Scald three cupfuls of milk and pour it over two cupfuls of popcorn which have been finely pounded or ground, and let stand one hour. Add three eggs slightly beaten, one-half cupful brown sugar, one tablespoonful of butter, three-fourths of a teaspoonful of salt and stir until smooth, then turn into a butter baking dish. Bake in a slow oven thirty-five minutes and serve hot with thin cream or maple syrup.

Source: May Belle Brooks. "Meals from the Corn-Popper; Attractive Dishes for the New Year's Table," *Good Housekeeping* 56 (January 1913): 119.

Pop Corn Cream Pudding

Soak a quarter of a box of gelatine in a quarter of a cupful of cold water. Make a custard of two cupsful of milk, three egg yolks, a third of a cupful of sugar and a third of a teaspoonful of salt; add the gelatine and strain into a pan set in cold water. Stir in two-thirds of a cupful of Nelson's corn, popped and ground, and a teaspoonful of almond extract, stirring until it begins to thicken. Then add the stiffly whipped whites of three eggs, mould and chill and serve garnished with the whole grains of popped corn. Whipped cream may be served with this pudding.

Source: Mary Hamilton Talbott. *Pop Corn Recipes*. Grinnell, Iowa: Sam Nelson, Jr., Company, 1916. n.p.

Prune and Pop Corn Pudding

Pick over and wash half a pound of prunes and soak them an hour in two cupsful of cold water, boil until soft and remove the stones, being careful to retain all the meat of the prunes; add to them one cupful of sugar, a small piece of stick cinnamon, one and a third cupsful of boiling water and let them simmer about ten minutes. Add one-third of a cupful of corn starch diluted with enough water to make it pour easily and cook five minutes. Remove the cinnamon, add a tablespoonful of lemon juice, the stiffly beaten whites of two eggs and half a cupful of Nelson's corn, after it is popped and ground, mould, chill and serve with plain or whipped cream.

Source: Mary Hamilton Talbott. *Pop Corn Recipes*. Grinnell, Iowa: Sam Nelson, Jr., Company, 1916. n.p.

Iroquois Popcorn Mush or Pudding

Popcorn, awe'sq"gwa,' is the basis of a number of dishes which are highly in favour. It is very commonly popped and eaten and is considered a great dainty, as well as a treat for visitors. It was formerly popped by throwing it on the hot coals in an open fire-place, stirring it quickly, then pulling it out as it popped.

For popcorn pudding, the corn is first popped, then pounded and sifted, and last of all boiled by adding to hot water until it thickens to the consistency required. This is eaten with syrup, sugar, and milk or cream, also with sour milk.

Source: F. W. Waugh. *Iroquis Foods and Food Preparation; Memoir 36; #12 Anthropological Series*. Ottawa: Government Printing Office, 1916. 94.

Pop Corn Pudding

2 quarts of popped corn
1/4 cup cracker crumbs
1/4 cup sugar
1/4 teaspoon salt
1 quart milk
2 eggs
1 teaspoon vanilla or lemon extract
1/2 tablespoon butter

Beat the eggs slightly and add milk, butter, sugar and salt. Mix together the corn and cracker crumbs and stir into milk. Let stand several hours. Add the flavoring. Bake in a quick oven one-half hour.

Source: Mary L. Wade. *The Book of Corn Cookery*. Chicago: A. C. McClurg and Co., 1917. 92–93.

Popped Corn Pudding

3 cups scalded milk
2 1/2 cups popped corn finely crushed
3 eggs slightly beaten
1/2 cup brown sugar
1 tablespoon butter
3/4 teaspoon salt
2/3 cup finely chopped pecan nut meats

PROCESS: Add scalded milk to prepared popped corn, let stand one hour. Add remaining ingredients in the order given. Turn mixture into a buttered baking dish and bake in a moderate oven until firm. Serve hot with Caramel Sauce or maple syrup or with sweetened cream. Measure popped corn after crushing.

Source: Elizabeth Hiller. *The Corn Cook Book*. War edition. New York: P. F. Volland Company, 1918. 106.

47. Roast

Pop Corn Roast

Mix together two cupsful of bread crumbs, one-half a cupful of chopped nut meats and of popped and ground corn—Nelson's Pop Corn for Popping—half a cupful each of hot water and one-half teaspoonful of tomato catsup, one and one-half teaspoonful of salt, one salt-spoonful of pepper and one beaten egg. When mixed thoroughly put into buttered mold and bake about an hour. Cover the first part of the time, then baste three times with hot butter. Turn into a hot dish, sprinkle with popped corn and serve with a brown sauce.

Source: Mary Hamilton Talbott. *Pop Corn Recipes*. Grinnell, Iowa: Sam Nelson, Jr., Company, 1916. n.p.

48. Rolls

Pop Corn Rolls

To one tablespoonful of butter and one teaspoonful of peanut butter add two and one-half tablespoonful of hot water. When the butters are melted stir into them one cupful of finely ground, popped corn (Nelson's corn always pops) and a small quantity of bread crumbs, enough to make a paste which can be molded with the hands into small cakes. Fry these in butter until a delicate brown and serve with tomato sauce. These make a dainty luncheon or super dish.

Source: Mary Hamilton Talbott. *Pop Corn Recipes*. Grinnell, Iowa: Sam Nelson, Jr., Company, 1916. n.p.

49. Salads

Salad

Cut bananas into halves, scoop out the centers of each and fill with Nelson's corn (after it is popped and ground), and serve on lettuce with mayonnaise dressing.

Mix together one cupful of chopped celery, one cupful of raisins and one cupful of popped and rolled corn (Nelson's gives a nutty taste) and serve on lettuce or any salad green with mayonnaise dressing.

Mix together one pint of apples cut into small match like pieces, half a pint of pop corn, after it is popped and rolled (Nelson's corn pops best), and the same quantity of chopped celery. Dress with boiled dressing and serve in apple cups or on lettuce leaves.

Cut into thin slices four good sized boiled white potatoes and add to them the crisp white portion of two bunches of celery, chopped, and two and one-half cupsful of Nelson's corn, after it has been popped and ground, sprinkle with salt and pepper, mix with half a pint of mayonnaise and just before serving cover the salad with half a pint of whipped cream.

Source: Mary Hamilton Talbott. *Pop Corn Recipes*. Grinnell, Iowa: Sam Nelson, Jr., Company, 1916. n.p.

Pop-Corn Savory Balls for Salads

Mold into balls one cupful each of ground pop corn and grated cheese; season with salt and paprika and bind with mayonnaise. Served with salads, the combination, makes an excellent and substantial food.

Source: Riley M. Fletcher-Berry. "Dressing Up Pop Corn," *Ladies' Home Journal* 34 (December 1917): 70.

Pop Corn with Salads and Desserts

Pop corn (whole) may be used with either fruit or vegetable salads, mixing it with them in quantity desired. Or the whole pop corn may be mixed with the sliced or cubed fruit and served with custard or milk and sugar. Pop corn in these combinations adds such substantial food value that less of other food will be required.

Source: Riley M. Fletcher-Berry. "Dressing Up Pop Corn," *Ladies' Home Journal* 34 (December 1917): 70.

50. Sandwiches

Pop-Corn Sandwiches

Make pop-corn in sheets three-eighths or one-half inches thick. Between two sheets put peanut butter, whole raisins, etc. The particular likes of your neighborhood may be catered to by the filling you put into these sandwiches. You can cut them into various sizes, even as small as a caramel if you wish.

Source: Eustace Reynolds Knott, *Knott's Pop-corn Book*. Boston: E. R. Knott Machine Company, 1915. 24.

Daphne Sandwiches

Mix ground pop-corn with just enough peanut butter or cream cheese to form a paste. Spread on a thin slice of buttered bread; lay a few stoned dates on top and cover with another slice of bread.

Source: May Belle Brooks. "Meals from the Corn-Popper; Attractive Dishes for the New Year's Table," *Good Housekeeping* 56 (January 1913): 119.

Sandwiches

Put half a pint of Nelson's corn, popped, through the grinder and mix it with six boned sardines, a little salt and pepper and enough tomato catsup, or strained tomato juice, to form a paste. Spread on hot buttered toast, sprinkle with grated cheese and serve at once.

Make a paste of cream cheese and Nelson's corn, popped and ground, and spread it on a slice of brown bread, cover the top with raisins, currants or chopped figs and cover this with another slice of buttered bread. This makes a wholesome sandwich for the lunch box.

For Sunday night supper when a light but nutritious bill of fare is wanted: Chop fine a cupful of raisins and mix them with a cupful of Nelson's corn, after it has been popped and rolled; blend this with the white of an egg, well whipped and seasoned with a pinch of salt. Spread between thin slices of buttered bread. Do not prepare until just before serving time.

A dainty sweet sandwich is made by mixing strained honey with Nelson's corn, popped and ground, and mashed ripe bananas and placing between slices of buttered bread.

Remove the stones from dates and fill the cavities with Neufchatel cheese into which ground, popped corn—Nelson's corn for popping—has been worked. Serve with salted crackers. This is a delicious novelty for luncheon.

Source: Mary Hamilton Talbott. *Pop Corn Recipes*. Grinnell, Iowa: Sam Nelson, Jr., Company, 1916. n.p.

Pop-Corn Cheese for Sandwiches

Grind fine some freshly popped corn and mix with half its measure of chopped sweet peppers. Season with salt; add a tablespoonful of butter substitute and set aside, pressed into a greased dish, until chilled; then spread between bread or crackers. Cottage cheese may be used instead of butter substitute and gherkins for peppers. Or ground pop corn may be mixed with dates, soften chopped figs or persimmon pulp.

Source: Riley M. Fletcher-Berry. "Dressing Up Pop Corn," *Ladies' Home Journal* 34 (December 1917): 70.

51. Scrapple

Pop Corn Scrapple

Add to one cupful of hominy and two cupsful of cornmeal enough boiling water to cook thoroughly in a double boiler until of the consistency for frying. Take from the fire and stir in two heaping cupsful of popped and ground corn—Nelson's corn makes crisp and flaky kernels—then pour into buttered pan and when cold slice and fry. This is especially good on a cold, snappy morning.

Source: Mary Hamilton Talbott. *Pop Corn Recipes*. Grinnell, Iowa: Sam Nelson, Jr., Company, 1916. n.p.

52. Smacks

Pop Corn Smacks

Beat stiff the white of 1 egg, adding a teaspoonful of salt. Meantime have mixed 1/2 a cupful each of powdered sugar and ground pop corn with a desertspoonful of flour. When the egg is stiff, add the pop corn mixture gradually, then drop by teaspoonfuls onto a greased paper and bake slowly until browned. This will make 12 smacks.

Source: T. A. Gagnon. *Tried and Tested Recipes. Mrs. T. A. Gagnon's Cook Book for Practical Housekeeping*. Grafton, N.D.: Grafton News and Times Print, 1919. 272.

53. Soups and Accompaniments

Clam and Corn Soup

1 can corn
2 cups water
1 slice onion
2 cups clam water
2 1/2 tablespoons butter
2 1/2 tablespoons flour
1/4 teaspoon salt
Few grains pepper
Few grains cayenne
1 cup cream
Popped corn

Chop canned corn, add water and onion, bring to boiling point and let simmer twenty minutes; then rub through a sieve and add clam water. Melt butter, add flour and pour on, gradually, while stirring constantly, hot mixture. Add seasoning and, just before serving, cream. Garnish with popped corn.

To obtain clam water:

Wash thoroughly and scrub two quarts of clams, put in a granite stew pan, add one-half cup cold water, cover closely, place on front range, and let cook until shells open. Remove clams and strain liquor through double cheese cloth.

Source: Fannie Merritt Farmer. *What to Have for Dinner*, 130. New York: Dodge Publishing Company, 1905.

Popped Corn for Chowders

When we serve corn chowder, we use popped corn with it in place of crackers; it is a pleasing novelty.

Source: *Good Housekeeping* 44 (March 1907): 358.

Pop-corn Soup

Scald one quart of milk in a double boiler with one can of corn. Press through a sieve and add salt, pepper and a tablespoonful of butter. Thicken with cracker crumbs and a handful of pop-corn. When serving, put one tablespoonful of whipped cream on each plate of soup with a few kernels of the pop-corn.

Source: May Belle Brooks. "Meals from the Corn-Popper; Attractive Dishes for the New Year's Table," *Good Housekeeping* 56 (January 1913): 119.

Soup

A very delicious soup may be made by cooking a can of peas in a quart of milk until soft, press through a sieve to remove outer covering of peas, add a tablespoonful of onion juice, a tablespoonful of butter, pepper and salt to taste, and a good handful of Nelson's corn when popped, mixed with a few bread crumbs. After this has cooked up well, serve and add a teaspoonful of whole, popped grains to each plateful of soup. Corn may be used instead of the peas, and an equally good soup will result.

Source: Mary Hamilton Talbott. *Pop Corn Recipes*. Grinnell, Iowa: Sam Nelson, Jr., Company, 1916. n.p.

Iroquois Popcorn Soup or Hominy

The meal is prepared in the same way as for the mush or pudding, but was described as being more like hominy, particularly the kind called ontsdu'wane's.

The soup can be prepared in two ways: first, by boiling the meal along with some such meat as venison or beef, adding salt to season. This kind is called u'ne'ga"gec' (On.). A second method is to make a sweet soup by adding maple sugar. This is cooled and eaten with milk. The Onondaga name given was uwenowe'da"gec.'

Source: F. W. Waugh. *Iroquis Foods and Food Preparation; Memoir 36; #12 Anthropological Series*. Ottawa: Government Printing Office, 1916. 94.

Pop-Corn Balls for Clear Soup

Beat an egg and season it highly with salt, paprika and minced parsley or a little grated lemon peel. Gradually work in sufficient fine ground pop corn, or equal portions of chopped pop corn, to make a stiff dough. Roll out in balls half an inch in diameter; drop into the kettle of soup; boil five minutes before serving.

Source: Riley M. Fletcher-Berry. "Dressing Up Pop Corn," *Ladies' Home Journal* 34 (December 1917): 70.

Soup Accompaniments and Garnishes

The accompaniments to soups may be varied. Hot crackers, either plain or toasted and buttered; croutons, whether fried or browned in the oven; pulled bread, or crusts of bread dried in a slow oven until very crisp; strips of hot toast; hot buttered popcorn, or cheese straws are all suitable. Sometimes the accompaniment is served in the soup, as little drop dumplings, or forcemeat balls, in any cream or stock soup; ravioli in a stock soup; or generous-sized dumplings in a chowder or stew.

Source: Ida C. Bailey Allen. *Mrs. Allen on Cooking, Menus, Service.* Garden City, N.Y.: Doubleday, Page & Company, 1924. 155.

54. Stuffings

Stuffing For Fowl or Meats

Soak in cold water half a loaf of crumbled bread and an equal bulk of Nelson's corn (after it is popped) until soft; squeeze and add a slice of onion, a tablespoonful of chopped parsley, salt and pepper to taste, and two well-beaten eggs. Put this in a pan with some butter and put in the oven long enough to brown slightly, stirring often, then use.

Source: Mary Hamilton Talbott. *Pop Corn Recipes.* Grinnell, Iowa: Sam Nelson, Jr., Company, 1916. n.p.

Stuffing for Onions

Cook together for five minutes one tablespoonful of bread crumbs, five tablespoonsful of ground, popped corn (Nelson's corn for popping), two tablespoonsful of butter, two tablespoonsful of chopped parsley, salt and pepper to taste and a dash of paprika. Take from the fire and add one beaten egg. Remove the centers from onions, fill with this mixture and bake.

Source: Mary Hamilton Talbott. *Pop Corn Recipes.* Grinnell, Iowa: Sam Nelson, Jr., Company, 1916. n.p.

55. Sugared Popcorn

Sugared Pop Corn

White.

Pop a lot of corn and set it one side; now put about 5 pounds of sugar in the kettle, with water to dissolve same, and cook to 238°; then set off and pour in all the corn you can stir without spilling out any with the paddle; stir all good; and while doing so have your helper sprinkle over it 1 pound more of dry sugar, and this will make more of a crystal on the corn; stir until it is well grained.

Source: Will O. Rigby. *Rigby's Reliable Candy Teacher.* Topeka, Kans.: W. O. Rigby, 1902. 127.

Sugared Pop Corn

2 pounds popped corn.
4 pounds sugar (diamond A)
1 1/2 pints water.
1/2 ounce vanilla extract.

Boil sugar to 232 degs. and add the vanilla. While the corn is yet warm from popping place in a "shake-pan" over a very slow fire; pour syrup over in very small quantities, and shake continually until the syrup grains, and the corn separate. Continue this until the syrup is used up, always being careful not to get the corn too wet, as that would cause it to lump.

For coloring pink make the same above, but use a few drops of brilliant rose, and one drachm of strawberry extract to be put in the syrup before pouring on corn.

If a "shake-pan" cannot be obtained, use an ordinary candy kettle and stir with wood paddle.

Source: *Confectioner's Journal* 35 (October 10, 1913): 25.

56. Tac-Tac

Maïs "Tac-Tac."

1 Pint of Louisiana Molasses.
3/4 Pound of Indian Corn (Parched).

Boil one pint of Louisiana molasses, and, as it comes to the boiling point, throw in about three-quarters of a pound of parched Indian corn, parched to a blossom; stir well, and then pour into little paper cases, about five or six inches in length, three in width and one and a half in depth. Let these cool before touching. This is another of the peculiar forms of candies sold by the old Creole negroes of New Orleans.

Source: *The Picayune. The Picayune Creole Cook Book.* Second edition. New Orleans: The Picayune, 1901. Facsimile edition. New York: Dover Publications, 1971. 377.

57. Taffy

Popcorn Sponge Taffy

Three pounds of brown or granulated sugar, one pound of glucose, one pint of water, one and one-half pints molasses, one pound of sifted popcorn.

Boil to the hard crack, or 295° Fahr. Take off the fire and add one teaspoonful soda, and stir in the popcorn. Put on the slab between the bars, level and let cool. Before it hardens cut in bars or squares.

Source: Paul Richards. *Paul Richards' Pastry Book.* Chicago: Hotel Monthly Press, [circa 1907]. 130.

58. Trifle

Pop Corn Trifle

Place cut up marshmallows in a dish set in boiling water and when they are melted cover saltines with about an inch of the mixture, then sprinkle over the top, very thick, Nelson's corn, popped and rolled; set in a moderate oven until a delicate brown.

Source: Mary Hamilton Talbott. *Pop Corn Recipes.* Grinnell, Iowa: Sam Nelson, Jr., Company, 1916. n.p.

59. Wafers

Pop Corn Wafers

Cream together half a cupful of granulated sugar and a quarter of a cupful of butter; add one tablespoonful of milk, one well-beaten egg, one-quarter of a teaspoonful of salt, and one cupful of pop corn, popped and ground,—Nelson's makes crisp and flaky kernels. Mix into this one and one-half cupsful of pastry flour into which one teaspoonful of baking powder has been sifted, and half a teaspoonful of almond extract. Roll thin, cut into small rounds, or fancy shapes and bake. These are nice for the afternoon tea table or the kiddies' lunch box.

Source: Mary Hamilton Talbott. *Pop Corn Recipes.* Grinnell, Iowa: Sam Nelson, Jr., Company, 1916. n.p.

Notes

Chapter 1: The Pop Heard 'Round the Americas

1. Jane Austin, *Standish of Standish: A Story of the Pilgrims* (Boston: Houghton, Mifflin and Co., 1889), 281.

2. Gail Damerow, "Homegrown Popcorn," *Mother Earth News* [issue 137] (April/May 1993): 42; Syd Spiegel, "Profits from Popcorn," *Popcorn-Concession Merchandiser* 11 (April 1956): 28–30; Syd Spiegel, "Why Do People Buy Popcorn?," *Concessionaire Merchandiser* 15 (April 1960): 6; Elizabeth Grinnell, "Nothing but Corn," *Table Talk* 8 (November 1898): 391; Gordon Morrison, "Popcorn," *Horticulture* 47 (October 1969): 21.

3. Laura Ingalls Wilder, *Farmer Boy* (New York: Harper & Brothers, 1933), 22; Solveig Paulson Russell, *Peanuts, Popcorn, Ice Cream, Candy and Soda Pop and How They Began* (Nashville and New York: Abingdon Press, 1970), 27–28; Rose Wyler, *Science Fun with Peanuts and Popcorn* (New York: Julian Messner, 1986), 43.

4. *The Popcorn Market* (New York: Packaged Facts, 1989), 2; Tomie de Paola, *The Popcorn Book* (New York: Holiday House, 1978), n.p.; "Highlights of Popcorn History," developed by the Popcorn Institute in Chicago; *Washington Star,* as quoted in Paul Dickson, *The Book of Thanksgiving* (New York: Perigee Book, 1995), 20; Patricia Linden, "Popcorn! It's No Flash in the Pan," *Reader's Digest* (Canadian ed.) 125 (November 1984): 118; *New York Times,* November 26, 1997, p. A27.

5. William Bradford [Samuel Eliot Morison, ed.], *Of Plymouth Plantation 1620–1647* (New York: Alfred A. Knopf, 1952), 90; letter to the author from James W. Baker, vice president and chief historian, Plimouth Plantation, dated May 8, 1996; Jamie Kageleiry and Christine Schultz, "Exploding the Popcorn Myth," *Yankee Magazine* 57 (February 1993): 27; Paul Dickson, *The Book of Thanksgiving* (New York: Perigee Book, 1995), 19–20.

6. E. Lewis Sturtevant, *Maize: An Attempt at Classification* (Rochester, N.Y.: Democrat and Chronicle Print, 1884), 1–4.

7. E. Lewis Sturtevant, "Varieties of Corn," *Bulletin #57* (Washington, D.C.: Office of Experiment Stations, Department of Agriculture, 1899), 12–18; Stanley A. Watson, "Structure and Composition," in Stanley A. Watson and Paul E. Ramstad, eds., *Corn Chemistry and Technology* (Saint Paul, Minn.: American Association of Cereal Chemists, 1987), 55.

8. Kenneth E. Ziegler and Bruce Ashman, "Popcorn," in Arnel R. Hallauer, ed., *Speciality Corns* (Boca Raton, Fla.: CRC Press, 1994), 195–96.

9. Samuel A. Matz, *Snack Food Technology,* 3rd ed. (New York: AVI Books/Van Nostrand Reinhold, 1993), 134; Ziegler and Ashman, "Popcorn," 191; Paul Weatherwax, *Indian Corn in Old America* (New York: Macmillan, 1954), 161, 164.

10. Paul C. Mangelsdorf, *Corn—Its Origin, Evolution and Improvement* (Cambridge, Mass.: Harvard University Press, 1974), vii–ix.

11. Paul C. Mangelsdorf, "Mystery of Corn: New Perspectives," *Proceedings of the American Philosophical Society* 127 (1983): 221; Paul C. Mangelsdorf and R. G. Reeves, *The Origin of Indian Corn and Its Relatives* (Texas Agricultural Experiment Station Bulletin #574, May 1939), 303, 306.

12. Edgar Anderson, "Popcorn," *Natural History* 56 (May 1947): 227.

13. Mangelsdorf, *Corn,* 151.

14. E. J. Wellhausen, L. M. Roberts, and E. Hernandez X. in collaboration with Paul C. Mangelsdorf, *Races of Maize in Mexico* (Cambridge: Bussey Institution of Harvard University, 1952), 19; Mangelsdorf, *Corn*, 167, 170–71, 174; Maj. M. Goodman, "The History and Evolution of Maize," in *CRC Critical Reviews in Plant Science*, vol. 7 (CRC Press, 1988), 200.

15. Bruce Benz, "Reconstructing Racial Phylogeny of Mexican Maize: Where Do We Stand?," in Sissel Johannessen and Christine A. Hastorf, eds., *Corn and Culture in the Prehistoric New World* (Boulder, Colo.: Westview Press, 1994), 166–67.

16. Mangelsdorf, *Corn*, 154.

17. Bruce Smith, "The Origins of Agriculture in the Americas," *Evolutionary Anthropology* 3 (1994/95): 174–85.

18. Paul C. Mangelsdorf, Herbert W. Dick, and Julián Cámara-Hernández, "Bat Cave Revisited," *Botanical Museum Leaflets*, Harvard University 22 (September 8, 1967): 1–31; Michael S. Berry, "The Age of Maize in the Greater Southwest: A Critical Review," in Richard I. Ford, ed., *Prehistoric Food Production in North America* (Ann Arbor: Museum of Anthropology, University of Michigan #75, 1985), 303; Austin Long, B. F. Benz, D. J. Donahue, A. J. T. Jull, and L. J. Toolin, "First Direct AMS Dates on Early Maize from Tehuacán, Mexico," *Radiocarbon* 31 (1989): 1039. Michael S. Berry, "The Age of Maize in the Greater Southwest: A Critical Review," in Richard I. Ford, ed., *Prehistoric Food Production in North America* (Ann Arbor: Museum of Anthropology, University of Michigan #75, 1985), 284.

19. Paul C. Mangelsdorf, "Mystery of Corn: New Perspectives," *Proceedings of the American Philosophical Society* 127 (1983): 216; Mangelsdorf, *Corn*, 49.

20. George W. Beadle, "Teosinte and the Origin of Maize," *Journal of Heredity* 30 (May 1939): 247; George W. Beadle, "The Ancestry of Corn," *Scientific American* 242 (January 1980): 116.

21. George W. Beadle, "The Mystery of Maize," *Field Museum of Natural History Bulletin #43* (November 1972): 10; Mangelsdorf, *Corn*, 49–50; Paul C. Mangelsdorf, "Mystery of Corn: New Perspectives," *Proceedings of the American Philosophical Society* 127(4) (1983): 235–36.

22. George W. Beadle, "The Ancestry of Corn," *Scientific American* 242 (January 1980): 112–19; Thomas Murrey, *Salads and Sauces* (New York: H. J. Hewitt, 1884), 258–59; *Burpee's Farm Annual; Garden, Farm & Flower Seeds* (Philadelphia: W. Atlee Burpee & Co., 1888), 79.

23. Major M. Goodman and Robert McK. Bird, "The Races of Maize IV: Tentative Grouping of 219 Latin American Races," *Economic Botany* 31 (April–June 1977): 209–10. Reports of maize pollen from Mexico City that purportedly date to eighty thousand years ago have been released and discussed. This claim appears in many popcorn "histories" promoted by popcorn processors. A reanalysis of these studies concluded that the pollen was really only about two thousand years old. Subsequent pollen studies in Oaxaca, Mexico, have suggested a date of ten thousand years ago for the Maydeae tribe of grasses as cultivars. See Paul B. Sears, "Fossil Maize Pollen in Mexico," *Science* 216 (May 28, 1982): 34; J. Schoenwetter and L. D. Smith, "Pollen Analysis of the Oaxaca Archaic," in K. V. Flannery, ed., *Guila Naquitz: Archaic Foraging and Early Agriculture in Oaxaca, Mexico* (Orlando, Fla.: Academic Press, 1986), 216. Hugh, Iltis, "From Teosinte to Maize: The Catastrophic Sexual Transmutation," *Science* 222 (November 25, 1983): 886–94. Needless to say, not all researchers agree that teosinte is the progenitor of maize. Mary Eubanks is one researcher who is still convinced that Paul Mangelsdorf

was right. See Mary Eubanks, "A Cross between Two Maize Relatives: *Tripsacum dactyloides* and *Zea diploperennis*," *Economic Botany* 49 (April–June 1995): 172–82; Catherine Dold, "The Corn War," *Discover* 18 (December 1997): 108–13.

24. Walton C. Galinat, "Domestication and Diffusion of Maize," in Richard I. Ford, ed., *Prehistoric Food Production in North America* (Ann Arbor: Museum of Anthropology, University of Michigan #75, 1985), 276–77.

25. Walton C. Galinat and James H. Gunnerson, "Spread of Eight-Rowed Maize from the Pre-historic Southwest," *Botanical Museum Leaflets,* Harvard University 20 (1963): 117–60; Walton C. Galinat and Robert G. Campbell, "The Diffusion of Eight-Rowed Maize from the Southwest to the Central Plains," *Massachusetts Agricultural Experiment Station Monograph Series 1* (Amherst: Massachusetts Agricultural Experiment Station, 1967), 1; Carlos M. Zevallos, Walton C. Galinat, Donald W. Lathrap, Earl R. Leng, Jorge G. Marcos, and Kathleen M. Klumpp, "The San Pablo Corn Kernel and Its Friends," *Science* 196 (April 22, 1977): 385–89; Walton C. Galinat, "Domestication and Diffusion of Maize," in Richard I. Ford, ed., *Prehistoric Food Production in North America* (Ann Arbor: Museum of Anthropology, University of Michigan #75, 1985), 277; Walton C. Galinat, "Maize: Gift from America's First Peoples," in Nelson Foster and Linda S. Cordell, eds., *Chilies to Chocolate: Food the Americas Gave the World* (Tucson: University of Arizona Press, 1992), 58–59.

26. Murdo J. MacLeod, *Spanish Central America: A Socioeconomic History 1520–1720* (Berkeley and Los Angeles: University of California Press, 1973), 215; John C. Super, *Food, Conquest, and Colonization in Sixteenth-Century Spanish America* (Albuquerque: University of New Mexico Press, 1988), 67.

27. John C. Super, *Food, Conquest, and Colonization in Sixteenth-Century Spanish America* (Albuquerque: University of New Mexico Press, 1988), 66.

28. Thomas H. Goodspeed, *Plant Hunters in the Andes* (Berkeley and Los Angeles: University of California Press, 1961), 226–28.

29. John Claudius Loudon, *Encyclopedia of Agriculture,* 7th ed. (London: Longmans, Green, and Co., 1871), 829; William D. Emerson, *History and Incidents of Indian Corn and Its Culture* (Cincinnati: Wrightson & Co., 1878), 157; David H. Timothy, Peña V. Bertulfo, and Ricardo E. Latcham in collaboration with William L. Brown and Edgar Anderson, *Races of Maize in Chile,* Publication 847 (Washington, D.C.: National Academy of Sciences—National Research Council, 1961), 11.

30. Garcilaso de la Vega, el Inca [translated by Harold V. Livermore], *Royal Commentaries of the Incas,* vol. 1 (Austin: University of Texas Press, 1966), 498–99; Bernabé Cobo, *Historia del Nuevo Mundo,* vol. 4 (Seville: E. Rasco, 1893), 173; Martin Dobrizhoffer, *Account of the Abipones, an Equestrian People of Paraguay,* vol. 1 (London: John Murray, 1822), 425; Félix de Azara, *Voyages dans l'Amérique Méridionale (1781–1801),* vol. 1 (Paris: Dentu, 1809), 147.

31. Oliver Dunn and James E. Kelley, *The Diario of Christopher Columbus's First Voyage to America 1492–1493. Abstracted by Fray Bartolome de las Casas* (Norman: University of Oklahoma Press, 1988), 89; Samuel Eliot Morison, *Journals and Other Documents on the Life and Voyages of Christopher Columbus* (New York: Limited Editions Club, 1963), 72, 235, 337, 344–46.

32. *Códice Florentino: El manuscrito 218–20 de la Colección Palatina,* vol. 1 (Florence: Guinti Barbèra, 1975), 27. For the translation, see Arthur Anderson and Charles E. Dibble, trans., *Florentine Codex: Book 1: The Gods,* part II, no. 14 (Santa Fe, N.M.: School for American Research and University of Utah, 1950), 16; Frances F. Berdan and Patricia Rieff Anawalt, eds., *The Essential Codex Mendoza* (Berkeley and Los Angeles: University of California Press, 1997), 148, Folio 57r.

33. Joseph de Acosta [Edward Grimston, trans.], *The Naturall and Morall Historie of the East and West Indies* (London: Printed by Val Sims for Edward Blount and Williams, 1604), 254–56; Juan de Torquemada, *Monarquía indiana,* vol. 2 (Mexico City, Mexico: Editorial Porrua, 1969), 264; Paul Weatherwax, *Indian Corn in Old America* (New York: Macmillan, 1954), 87–88.

34. Edgar Anderson, "Popcorn," *Natural History* 56 (May 1947): 230; Charles M. Rick and Edgar Anderson, "On Some Uses of Maize in the Sierra of Ancash," *Annals, Missouri Botanical Garden* 36 (November 1949): 409; Paul C. Mangelsdorf, "The Mystery of Corn," *Scientific American* 183 (July 1950): 23; Charles M. Rick and Edgar Anderson, "On Some Uses of Maize in the Sierra of Ancash," *Annals, Missouri Botanical Garden* 36 (November 1949): 411; David H. Timothy, Peña V. Bertulfo, and Ricardo E. Latcham in collaboration with William L. Brown and Edgar Anderson, *Races of Maize in Chile,* Publication #847 (Washington, D.C.: National Academy of Sciences—National Research Council, 1961), 16. Several secondary sources have reported that popcorn poppers were displayed at the Field Museum of Natural History in Chicago. A careful examination of museum records indicates that several Mochica accessions, initially cataloged as "dippers," were given the "corn popper" attribution by persons unknown. The dippers are not similar to corn poppers located at other Peruvian archaeological sites, as described by Rick and Anderson. The Field Museum has reverted to its original designation of "dipper." See Field Museum Accession 486, nos. 1168, 4798, 4544, 4545, and 4800–5. Copies of accession files attached in letter to the author from Janice B. Klein, Registrar, Department of Anthropology, Field Museum of Natural History, Chicago, dated October 27, 1997.

35. Edgar Anderson, "Popcorn," *Natural History* 56 (May 1947): 230; Edger Anderson, "Maiz Reventador," *Annals, Missouri Botanical Garden* 31 (September 1944): 311; Edger Anderson, "Field Studies of Guatemalan Maize," *Annals, Missouri Botanical Garden* 34 (November 1947): 447.

36. E.-A. Duchesne, *Traité du Maïs ou Blé de Turquie* (Paris: Madame Huzard, 1833); Matthieu Bonafous, "Note sur le Maïs a Bec, (Zea rostrata, seminibus mucronatis, Bonafous)," in Nicolas C. Seringe, *Descriptions et figures des Céréales Europpéennes* (Lyon: Société royale d'agriculture de Lyon, 1841), 97–98. Tereza Stratilesco writes: "At the back of the hearth the big oven, heated also, contains sometimes some big pumpkin and tomatoes baking, to be together, with the maize and corn, the refreshment of the assembly, to which are added the sweet-tasting *cucuo ei* or *cucurigi,* maize grains baked in a kettle with sand and some salt, by which process they split and spring into beautiful white flowers." See Tereza Stratilesco, *From Carpathian to Pindus: Pictures of Roumanian Country Life* (Boston: J. W. Luce, 1907), 364–65. Joel Barlow, *The Hasty Pudding: A Poem in Three Cantos* (New York: Printed for the Purchaser, 1796), np.

37. C. R. Stonor and Edgar Anderson, "Maize among the Hill Peoples of Assam," *Annals, Missouri Botanical Garden* 36 (September 1949): 355; Li Shih-chên, *Pê ts'ao Kung ma,* written 1578, published in 1590, as quoted in Walter T. Swingle, "Notes on Chinese Herbals and Other Works on Materia Medica," in *Report of Librarian of Congress for the Fiscal Year Ending June 30, 1932* (Washington, D.C.: Government Printing Office, 1932), 199–207; quoted material from p. 200.

38. Joseph Hooker, *Himalayan Journals,* 2nd ed., vol. 2 (London: John Murray, 1855), 96. Another edition was published in a single volume in 1905, and the popcorn statement appears in a footnote on p. 343.

39. Henry N. C. Stevenson, *The Economics of the Central Chin Tribes* (Bombay: Times of India Press, 1942), 111; C. R. Stonor and Edgar Anderson, "Maize among

the Hill Peoples of Assam," *Annals, Missouri Botanical Garden* 36 (September 1949): 367, 371–72; Edgar Anderson, "Popcorn," *Natural History* 56 (May 1947): 230.

40. *A Relation or Iournall of the Beginning and Proceeding of the English Plantation Setled at Plimoth in New England* (London: Iohn Bellamie, 1622); rpt. as *Journal of the Pilgrims at Plymouth* (New York: John Wiley, 1848), 46; Roger Williams, *A Key into the Language of America* (London: Printed by Gregory Dexter, 1643), 39–40.

41. Henry R. Schoolcraft, *Notes on the Iroquois* (New York: Bartlett & Welford, 1846), 11–12; Lewis H. Morgan, "Report of the Fabrics, Inventions, Implements and Utensils of the Iroquois," Appendix to *Fifth Annual Report of the University on the Condition of the State Cabinet and Natural History* (Albany: Richard H. Pease, 1852), 91–92; George H. Loskiel, *History of Missions of the United Brethren* (London: Brethren's Society for the Furtherance of the Gospel, 1794), 67.

42. "Journal of John Barnwell," *Virginia Magazine of History and Biography* 6 (July 1898): 50; John Lawson, *A New Voyage to Carolina* (London: Printed for the author, 1709), 59; Bernard Romans, *A Concise Natural History of East and West Florida,* facsimile of the 1775 edition with introduction by Rembert W. Pitchard (Gainesville: University of Florida Press, 1962), 67; Edwin Bryant, *What I Saw in California* (New York: D. Appleton & Company, 1848), 372; Frank Hamilton Cushing, *Zuñi Breadstuffs,* as in *Indian Notes and Monographs* 8 (1920); rpt. (New York: Museum of the American Indian/Heye Foundation, 1974), 265–66. Originally published in *The Millstone* 9 (January 1884) and *The Millstone* 10 (August 1885).

43. Fulmer Mood, "John Winthrop, Jr., on Indian Corn," *New England Quarterly* 10 (March 1937): 121–33, from a letter dated July 29, 1662, in the Royal Society, London. An abridged version of the original letter was published in the Royal Society's *Philosophical Transaction* (1678): 142.

44. Benjamin Franklin, "Observations on Mayz, or Indian Corn," undated (circa 1770), as in Albert Henry Smyth, ed., *The Writings of Benjamin Franklin,* vol. 5 (New York: Macmillan, 1906), 554–55. Franklin sent this description of maize to Cadet de Vaux in 1785. It was published in the *Journal de Paris,* April 17, 1785. The English version has been preserved at the Library of Congress. See Benjamin Franklin, *On the Art of Eating* (Princeton, N.J.: Princeton University Press for the American Philosophical Society, 1958), 66.

45. John G. E. Heckewelder, *History, Manners, and Customs of the Indian Nations Who Once Inhabited Pennsylvania and the Neighboring States,* rev. ed. (Philadelphia: Fund of the Historical Society of Pennsylvania, 1876), 195.

46. Benjamin Franklin, "Observations on Mayz, or Indian Corn," undated (circa 1770), as in Albert Henry Smyth, ed., *The Writings of Benjamin Franklin,* vol. 5 (New York: Macmillan, 1906), 554–55. The conclusion that the corn popped was flint corn is not original. Historians at Plimoth Plantation in Plymouth, Massachusetts, believe the same. See Frances Towner Giedt, *Popcorn!* (New York: Simon & Schuster, 1995), 52.

47. A. T. Erwin, "The Origin and History of Pop Corn, Zea Mays L. var. Indurata (Sturt.) Baily mut. Everta (Sturt.) Erwin," *Agronomy Journal* 41 (February 1949): 54.

48. M. R. Harrington, "Some Seneca Corn Foods and Their Preparation," *American Anthropologist* n.s. 10 (October–December 1908): 587; Arthur C. Parker, *Iroquois Uses of Maize and Other Food Plants,* Bulletin #482 (Albany, N.Y.: Education Department, November 1, 1910), 57–58, 78; F. W. Waugh, *Iroquois*

Foods and Food Preparation; Memoir 36; #12 Anthropological Series (Ottawa: Government Printing Office, 1916), 94.

49. Edward F. Castetter and Willis H. Bell, *Pima and Papago Agriculture* (Albuquerque: University of New Mexico Press, 1942), 84–85; Melvin Randolph Gilmore, "Uses of Plants by the Indians of the Missouri River Basin," *Annual Report #33* (1911/12) (Washington, D.C.: Smithsonian Institution, Bureau of American Ethnology, 1919), 67; A. F. Yeager, "Popcorn Pointers," *Circular 24* (Fargo, N. Dak.: Agricultural Experiment Station, 1924), 3.

Chapter 2: The Invention of Popcorn

1. *Memoirs of the Philadelphia Society for Promoting Agriculture* 1 (1808): Appendix 15–16; *Massachusetts Agricultural Repository* 4 (July 1817): 318; G. Thorburn, and Son, *Catalogue of Kitchen Garden, Herb, Flower, Tree, and Grass* (New York: Clayton & Van Norden, 1825), 8; George C. Barrett, *Catalogue of Kitchen Garden, Herb, Tree, Flower and Grass Seeds* (Boston: J. Ford, 1833), 12; Werner L. Janney and Asa More Janney, eds., *John Jay Janney's Virginia: An American Farm Lad's Life in the Early 19th Century* [1812–1907] (McLean, Va.: EPM Publications, 1978), 25.

2. *Memoirs of the Philadelphia Society for Promoting Agriculture* 1 (1808): Appendix 15–16; *Massachusetts Agricultural Repository* 4 (July 1817): 318.

3. *Natural History of New York,* part 5, Ebenezer Emmons, *Agriculture of New York,* vol. 2 (Albany: C. Van Benthuysen, 1849), 264; Paul C. Mangelsdorf, "Reconstructing the Ancestor of Corn," *Proceedings of the American Philosophical Society* 102 (October 20, 1958): 457; *Country Gentleman* 17 (January 24, 1861): 65; *Country Gentleman* 24 (November 10, 1864): 305; *Country Gentleman* 30 (October 31, 1867): 262.

4. *The Cultivator* n.s. 5 (April 1838): 43; Bradford Torrey, ed., *Writings of Henry David Thoreau; Journal,* vol. 1 (Boston and New York: Houghton Mifflin, 1906), 311; *Yale Literary Magazine* 8 (January 1843): 141; *Knickerbocker* 25 (March 1845): 199; John Russell Bartlett, *Dictionary of Americanisms: A Glossary of Words and Phrases Usually Regarded as Peculiar to the United States* (New York: Bartlett and Welford, 1848), 257.

5. Joel Barlow, *The Hasty-Pudding: A Poem, with a Memoir on Maize, or Indian Corn,* compiled by Daniel Jay Browne (New York: W. H. Graham, 1847), 51; J. H. Salisbury, "History and Chemical Investigation of Maize or Indian Corn," *Transactions of the New York Agricultural Society for 1848,* vol. 8 (Albany: Weed, Parsons & Co., 1849), 764; *Natural History of New York,* part 5, Ebenezer Emmons, *Agriculture of New York,* vol. 2 (Albany: C. Van Benthuysen, 1849), 264–65.

6. Susan Fenimore Cooper, *Rural Hours* (New York: G. P. Putnam, 1850), 388; *Country Gentleman* 24 (July 7, 1864): 21; Fearing Burr, *The Field and Garden of America* (Boston: J. E. Tilton and Company, 1863), 599; Fearing Burr, *The Field and Garden of America,* 2nd ed. (Boston: J. E. Tilton and Company, 1865), 587–88.

7. *Omaha Daily Herald,* January 10, 1869, p. 3; *Mrs. Goodfellow's Cookery as it Should Be; A New Manual of the Dinning-Room and Kitchen* (Philadelphia: T. B. Peterson & Brothers, 1865), 328; *Cassell's Dictionary of Cookery* (London: Cassell Petter & Galpin, c1870), 401; cover of *Mose Skinner's Grand World's Jubilee and Humstrum Convulsion* (Boston: New England Newspaper Company, 1872), pamphlet in the collection of Ronald Toth Jr., Rochester, N.H.; *American Cyclopedia,* vol. 11 (New York: D. Appleton and Company, 1875), 44; Charles Bernard, *Bernard's Half Century of Circus Reviews and Red Wagon Stories*

(Savannah: Commercial Litho. & Printing Co., 1930), 8; *Grocer's Companion and Merchant's Hand-book* (Boston: New England Grocer Office, 1883), 112–13; *Grocer's Regulator* 1 (April 1, 1886): 24.

8. J. S. Ingram, *Centennial Exposition* (Philadelphia: Hubbard Bros., 1876), 758; *Frank Leslie's Illustrated Newspaper* 153 (November 18, 1876): 179, 186; *Frank Leslie's Illustrated Historical Register of the Exposition 1876* (New York: Frank Leslie's Publishing House, 1877), 56, 210, 306; "Excelsior Pop Corn," advertisement in the trade card collection at the Free Library of Philadelphia.

9. *Harper's* 6 (May 1853): 853; John Russell Bartlett, *Dictionary of Americanisms: A Glossary of Words and Phrases Usually Regarded as Peculiar to the United States,* 2nd ed. (Boston: Little, Brown and Company, 1859), 332–33; Edgar Anderson and Hugh Cutler, "Methods of Corn Popping and Their Historical Significance," *Southwestern Journal of Anthropology* 6 (Autumn 1950): 306.

10. *Country Gentleman* 51 (December 2, 1886): 920; *Yale Literary Magazine* 8 (January 1843): 141.

11. Robert Thacher Trall, *The New Hydropathic Cook-book* (New York: Fowlers and Wells, 1854), 186; *Maysville Appeal,* April 4, 1860, p. 1.

12. *People and Patriot,* as reprinted in the *New York Times,* August 3, 1890, p. 14. According to Gary Miller and K. M. Scotty Mitchell, the first wire poppers were made by the Bromwell Brush and Wire Goods Company founded in Cincinnati in 1819. No primary source was located to support this assertion. See Gary Miller and K. M. Scotty Mitchell, *Price Guide to Collectible Kitchen Appliances* (Radnor, Pa.: Wallace-Homestead Book Company, 1991), 43.

13. *New York Times,* August 3, 1890, p. 14; Joel Barlow, *The Hasty-Pudding: A Poem, with a Memoir on Maize, or Indian Corn,* compiled by Daniel Jay Browne (New York: W. H. Graham, 1847), 51; U.S. Patent #92,939, issued July 27, 1869. One of Knowlton's poppers was given to the New Hampshire Antiquarian Society, but it evidently has been lost. My letter to the Antiquarian Society failed to receive a response. Linda Campbell Franklin, *America in the Kitchen from Hearth to Cookstove; An American Domestic History of Gadgets and Utensils Made or Used in America from 1700 to 1930; A Guide for Collectors* (Florence, Ala.: House of Collectibles, 1976), 61.

14. U.S. Patent #59,253, issued October 30, 1866; U.S. Patent #67,736, issued August 15, 1867; U.S. Patent #72,173, issued December 17, 1867; U.S. Patent #76,362, issued April 7, 1868; U.S. Patent #105,530, issued July 19, 1870; U.S. Patent #93,271, issued August 3, 1869.

15. U.S. Patent #149,700, issued April 14, 1874; *Catalogue 1892* (Cincinnati: Bromwell Brush and Wire Goods Company, 1892), 45.

16. U.S. Patent #240,066, issued April 12, 1881.

17. *Country Gentleman* 42 (June 7, 1877): 361; *Country Gentleman* 42 (June 14, 1877): 379; Edward H. Knight, *Knight's American Mechanical Dictionary,* vol. 3 (New York: Hurd and Houghton, 1876), 1764; The Bartholomew Co., *The Peanut and Pop Corn Problem Solved* (Peoria, Ill.: Bartholomew Company, [circa 1907]), 26–27.

18. *Grocer's Bulletin* 2 (July 1, 1881): 45; U.S. Patent #170.976, issued December 14, 1875; *Iron Age* 35 (January 15, 1885): 3; *Iron Age* 39 (January 13, 1887): 25; *Iron Age* 45 (January 9, 1890): 82.

19. *U.S. Stamping Co. Catalog,* 1886, as in Louise K. Lantz, *Old American Kitchenware, 1725–1925* (Camden and New York: Thomas Nelson / Hanover, Pa.: Everybodys Press, 1971), 266; *Sears, Roebuck and Co. Catalogue #105* (Chicago:

Sears, Roebuck and Co., 1897), 15, 141; *Sears, Roebuck & Co. Consumer's Guide* (Chicago: Sears, Roebuck and Co., 1901), 1028.

20. *Country Gentleman* 42 (June 7, 1877): 361; *Country Gentleman* 42 (July 5, 1877): 427.

21. *Country Gentleman* 42 (June 14, 1877): 379.

22. *Good Housekeeping* 43 (November 1906): 583.

23. *Country Gentleman* 4 (February 2, 1854): 78.

24. *Harper's* 6 (May 1853): 853; *Country Gentleman* 15 (January 19, 1860): 56.

25. *Popping Corn,* by Benjamin Russell, circa 1865, watercolor at the Old Dartmouth Historical Society, New Bedford, Mass.; John S. Barrows, "Popping Corn," as in *Good Housekeeping* 15 (December 1892): n.p.; Howard T. Walden, *Native Lnheritance: The Story of Corn in America* (New York: Harper & Row, 1966), 157; *Parents* 68 (February 1993): 120.

26. Kate Sanborn, *A Truthful Woman in Southern California* (New York: D. Appleton and Co., 1893), 129–30.

27. Joel Barlow, *The Hasty-Pudding: A Poem, with a Memoir on Maize, or Indian Corn,* compiled by Daniel Jay Browne (New York: W. H. Graham, 1847), 40.

28. James F. W. Johnston, *Notes on North America,* vol. 1 (Edinburgh: William Blackwood and Sons, 1851), 153–54; *The Horticulturist* n.s. 5 (November 1855): 525; Ella E. Kellogg, *Science in the Kitchen* (Battle Creek, Mich.: Health Publishing Company, 1892), 104; *New American Cyclopedia,* vol. 11 (New York: D. Appleton and Company, 1861), 88–89; *Century Dictionary,* vol. 4 (New York: Century Company, 1889), 4,620.

29. E. L. Sturtevant, "Varieties of Corn," in *Bulletin #57* (Washington, D.C.: Department of Agriculture, Office of Experiment Stations, 1899), 15; Henry Kraemer, "The Structure of the Corn Grain and Its Relation to Popping," *Science* n.s. 17 (May 1, 1903): 683–84.

30. William Brewer, *Report on the Cereal Production of the United States* (Washington, D.C.: Department of the Interior, U.S. Census Office, 1884), 483; M. I. Wilbert, "Why Pop Corn Pops," *American Journal of Pharmacy* 75 (February 1903): 77–79, 100; F. H. Storer, "Remarks on the 'Popping' of Indian Corn," Harvard University, *Bulletin Bussey Institution* 3, part 4 (1904): 77–79; Kraemer, "The Structure of the Corn Grain," 683–84; Paul Weatherwax, "The Popping of Corn," in *Proceedings of the Indiana Academy of Science for 1921* (Indianapolis: Wm. B. Burford, 1922), 149–53; John G. Willier and A. M. Brunson, "Factors Affecting the Popping Quality of Popcorn," *Journal of Agricultural Research* 35 (1927): 615–24; Arthur M. Brunson, "Popcorn," in G. F. Sprague, ed., *Corn and Corn Improvement* (New York: Academic Press, 1955), 426.

31. Roger M. Reeve and H. G. Walker Jr., "The Microscopic Structure of Popped Cereals," *Cereal Chemistry* 46 (May 1969): 227.

32. Ziegler and Ashman, "Popcorn," 189–216.

33. W. F. Tracy and W. C. Galinat, "Thickness and Cell Layer Number of the Pericarp of Sweet Corn and Some of Its Relatives," *Hort-Science* 22 (1987): 645; Samuel A. Matz, *Snack Food Technology* (Westport, Conn.: AVI, 1976), 116–17; Ziegler and Ashman, "Popcorn," 207.

34. "Popcorn and Popcorn Poppers," *Consumer Reports* 54 (June 1989): 362.

35. Matz, *Snack Food Technology,* 116; Ziegler and Ashman, "Popcorn," 207.

36. F. A. Behymer, "Popcorn Crop Major Business at Shawneetown; Newspaper Pays Tribute to George Atkins," *Popcorn Merchandiser* 4 (March 1950): 36–38; Peter Schieberle, "Primary Odorants in Popcorn," *Journal of Agricultural and Food Chemistry* 39 (June 1991): 1141.

37. Piet Vroon, *Smell: The Secret Seducer* (New York: Farrar, Straus and Giroux, 1997), 103–4.

38. Anna Lindlahr and Henry Lindlahr, *The Lindlahr Vegetarian Cook Book and A B C of Natural Dietics,* 15th ed. (Chicago: Lindlahr, 1922), 337; Ella E. Kellogg, *Science in the Kitchen* (Battle Creek, Mich.: Health Publishing Company, 1892), 104, 330; John Harvey Kellogg, *The New Dietetics: A Guide to Scientific Feeding in Health and Disease,* rev. ed. (Battle Creek, Mich.: Modern Medicine Publishing Co., 1927), 270.

39. William M. Evans, "Medicated Pop-Corn," U.S. Patent #306,612, issued November 19, 1889.

40. *American Grocer* 68 (November 26, 1902): 6; Amelia Sulzbacher, "Popcorn Dainties," *Good Housekeeping* 43 (October 1906): 422–23; Harvey Wiley, *Foods and Their Adulteration* (Philadelphia: P. Blakiston's Son & Co., 1907), 225–26.

41. *Confectioner's Gazette* 34 (October 12, 1912): 12; *American Cooking,* 30 (January 1926): 429; *C. Cretors & Co. The First Hundred Years: 1885–1985* (Chicago: C. Cretors, 1985), 100; "It's Good and Good For You," *Kernel* 2 (May 1939): 7.

Chapter 3: Popcorn Children

1. Susan Fenimore Cooper, *Rural Hours* (New York: G. P. Putnam, 1850), 388. *Bartlett's Familiar Quotations* attributes "Pop Goes the Weasel" to W. R. Mandale. The weasel was a hatter's tool, and "pop" meant to pawn or hock. The Eagle was a music hall on City Road in London.

2. *Harper's* 6 (May 1853): 853.

3. *American Cyclopedia,* vol. 11 (New York: D. Appleton and Company, 1875), 44; *Old Pop Corn* (New York: McLoughlin Bros., 1879), 1–8.

4. *Grocer's Companion and Merchant's Hand-book* (Boston: New England Grocer Office, 1883), 47; *Country Gentleman* 58 (January 26, 1893): 77; *American Grocer* 68 (November 26, 1902): 6; *Grocer's Criterion* 31 (March 28, 1904): 11.

5. *Country Gentleman* 4 (February 2, 1854): 78; Ralph Waldo Emerson, lecture on "Resources," delivered in Boston, December 1864–January 1865, as reprinted in *Letters and Social Aims* (Boston and New York: Houghton Mifflin & Company, 1904), 148; William D. Emerson, *History and Incidents of Indian Corn,* 157.

6. Willa Cather, *My Ántonia* (New York: Barnes & Noble, 1994), 60–61; Martin A. Pease, *The Blue Book on Home Candy Making; Secrets of Professional Candy Making* (Bloomington, Ill.: Martin A. Pease, 1923), 45; Barbara Allen, "Christmas Confections," *American Kitchen Magazine* 4 (December 1895): 142–43.

7. Charles P. Hartley and John G. Willier, "Pop Corn for the Home," in *Farmers' Bulletin #553* (Washington, D.C.: Department of Agriculture, 1913), 5, 7, 9, 12.

8. Clemence Haskin, "Father Pops the Corn; and Mother Prepares It with Variations," *American Home* 15 (December 1935): 44–46.

9. Ibid., 46.

10. Diane Pfeifer, *For Popcorn Lovers Only* (Marietta, Ga.: Strawberry Patch / Atlanta, Ga.: Marmac Publishing Company, 1987), 109; Giedt, *Popcorn!,* 48.

11. Alice Bradley, "A Pop-corn Christmas is More Patriotic than a Candy One," *Woman's Home Companion* 44 (December 1917): 34; K. M. Palmer, "Crops for Winter Fun," *House and Garden* 87 (February 1945): 104; Lynn Parsons, "Popcorn Fun," *Better Homes and Gardens* 25 (December 1946): 56.

12. American Pop Corn Company, *Having Fun with Pop Corn* (Sioux City, Iowa: American Pop Corn Company, n.d.), n.p.; Julie Polschek, "New Ways with

Old Fashioned Popcorn," *House Beautiful* 99 (December 1957): 108–11; Sue Spitler and Nao Hauser, *The Popcorn Lover's Book* (Chicago: Contemporary Books, 1983), 69–84; Syd Spiegel, "Profits from Popcorn," *Popcorn-Concession Merchandiser* 11 (April 1956): 29.

13. Carolyn Vosburg Hall and the *Farm Journal* editors, *I Love Popcorn* (Garden City, N.Y.: Doubleday & Co., 1976), 36, 40–44, 48–49; Barbara Williams, *Cornzapoppin'! Popcorn Recipes & Party Ideas for All Occasions* (New York: Holt, Rinehart and Winston, 1976), 138–43; Patricia Fox Sheinwold, *Jolly Time Party Book: Games, Puzzles, Recipes, and Creative Party Ideas for All Occasions* (Cambridge and New York: Dorison House Publishers, 1977), 31–55; Orville Redenbacher, *Orville Redenbacher's Popcorn Book* (New York: St. Martin's Press, 1984), 83–87; Giedt, *Popcorn!,* 72; "For a 'Green' Christmas, Reuse, Renew, and Recycle," *Christian Science Monitor,* December 17, 1996.

14. V. H. Hallock & Son, *Hallock's Famous Long Island Seeds* (Queens, N.Y., 1891), 17; *Official Gazette,* U.S. Trademark #20,592, registered January 12, 1892; *Official Gazette,* U.S. Trademark #23,250, registered June 27, 1893; *Official Gazette,* U.S. Trademark #53,380, registered June 5, 1906; American Pop Corn Company, *Jolly Time: An American Tradition Since 1914* (Sioux City, Iowa: American Pop Corn Company, 1994), 5, 10–11.

15. Sheinwold, *Jolly Time Party Book,* 31–55, 95–102; Larry Kusche, *Popcorn* (Tucson, Ariz.: HPBooks, 1977); Spitler and Hauser, *The Popcorn Lover's Book,* 69–84; Connie Evener and MarSue Birtler, *Kernel Knowledge; A Cornucopia of Popcorn History, Trivia, Arts and Crafts, and Over 75 Recipes* (Columbus, Ohio: The authors, 1982), 52–59; Howard T. Walden, *Native Inheritance: The Story of Corn in America* (New York: Harper & Row, 1966), 158.

16. Barbara Williams, *Cornzapoppin'!* 26–146; "Easter-Basket Treats," *Parents* 69 (April 1994): 146.

17. American Pop Corn Company, *Jolly Time,* 10–11; *The Good Housekeeping Cook Book,* 7th ed. (New York: International Readers League, 1944), 818; "As Much Fun to Make as to Eat . . . Popcorn Treats for Hallowe'en," *Sunset* 115 (October 1955): 132–33; Virginia Huffington, "New Trends for Popcorn Treats," *Better House and Garden* 35 (October 1957): 119–20; Sheinwold, *Jolly Time Party Book,* 77–83.

18. J. A. Riddlick, as quoted in F. Roy Johnson, *The Peanut Story* (Murfreesboro, N.C.: Johnson Publishing Co., 1964), 48; James F. W. Johnston, *Notes on North America,* vol. 1 (Edinburgh: William Blackwood and Sons, 1851), 151.

19. *Country Gentleman* 51 (December 2, 1886): 920.

20. *Country Gentleman* 63 (May 12, 1898): 376.

21. A. A. Berry Seed Co., *Catalogue* (Clarinda, Iowa, 1902), 38.

22. *Country Gentleman* 69 (November 24, 1904): 1087.

23. *Good Housekeeping* 39 (November 1904): 575.

24. American Pop Corn Company, *Having Fun with Pop Corn,* n.p.; Sheinwold, *Jolly Time Party Book,* 82–83; 93.

25. Allen Prescott, *The Wifesaver's Candy Recipes* (New York: Blue Ribbon Books, 1934), 37–38.

26. Kusche, *Popcorn,* 38.

27. Laura Ingalls Wilder, *Farmer Boy* (New York: Harper & Brothers, 1933), 22.

28. Carl Sandburg, *Rootabaga Stories* (New York: Harcourt, Brace and Company, 1922), 79–88; Carl Sandburg, *Rootabaga Country* (New York: Harcourt, Brace and Company, [1929]), 233–40.

29. Ruth Adams, *Mr. Picklepaw's Popcorn* (New York: Lothrop, Lee & Shepard, [1965]); Jane Hoober Peifer, *The Biggest Popcorn Party Ever in Center County* (Scottdale, Pa.: Herald Press, 1987); American Pop Corn Company, *Jolly Time,* 19.

30. Charlotte Brewster Jordan, "A Pop-Corn Frolic for Hallowe'en," *St. Nicholas* 36 (October 1909): 1114–15; Mildred Stapley, "The K. & A. Company," *St. Nicholas* 34 (May 1907): 612–15; Emily Arnold McCully, *Popcorn at the Palace* (San Diego: Browndeer Press, 1997); Earnest Elmo Calkins, *They Broke the Prairie* (New York: Charles Scribner's Sons, 1937), 157.

31. Nancy Byrd Turner, "A Song of Pop Corn," *St. Nicholas* 34 (November 1906): 119; Helen Ferris, ed., *Favorite Poems Old and New* (Garden City, N.Y.: Doubleday & Company, 1957), 45–46; Beatrice Schenk de Regniers, Eva Moore, Mary Michaels White, and Jan Carr, *Sing a Song of Popcorn* (New York: Scholastic Hardcover, 1988), 23.

32. *Good Housekeeping* 40 (February 1905): 191.

33. Elizabeth Gordon, *Mother Earth's Children: The Frolics of Fruits and Vegetables* (Chicago: P. F. Volland & Co., 1913), 95.

34. "How Indians Popped Corn," *St. Nicholas* 65 (June 1938): 41.

35. Jerry L. Hess, *Snack Food, A Bicentennial History* (New York: Harcourt Brace Jovanovich, [1976]), 204; *The Popcorn Market,* 45.

36. *Snack Food & Wholesale Bakery* 86 (November 1997): 23.

37. Hazel Krantz, *100 Pounds of Popcorn* (New York: Vanguard Press, 1961); Alice Low, *The Popcorn Shop* (New York: Scholastic, 1993); Mary Wilkins, *The Pot of Gold* as retold by Elton Greene, retitled *Princess Rosetta and the Popcorn Man* (New York: Lothrop, Lee & Shepard Co., c1971); Regniers et al., *Sing a Song of Popcorn,* 23; James Stevenson, *Popcorn* (New York: Greenwillow Books, 1998).

38. Dave Woodside, *What Makes Popcorn Pop?* (New York: Atheneum, 1980); Wyler, *Science Fun;* Phylliss Adams, *Popcorn Magic* (Cleveland: Modern Curriculum Press, 1987); Michael B. Leyden, "Start the Year with a Pop," *Teaching PreK-8* 23 (August/September 1992): 32; Doris R. Kimbrough and Robert R. Meglen, "A Simple Laboratory Experiment Using Popcorn to Illustrate Measurement Errors," *Journal of Chemical Education* 71 (June 1994): 518.

39. Kathleen V. Kudlinski, *Popcorn Plants* (Minneapolis: Lerner Publications Company, 1997); *Washington Post,* June 2, 1997, "Washington Business," p. 3.

40. *The Guinness Book of Records 1992* (New York: Facts on File, 1991), 190; *The Guinness Book of Records 1993* (New York: Facts on File, 1992), 204, 304; *The Guinness Book of Records 1994* (New York: Facts on File, 1993), 203; *The Guinness Book of Records 1996* (New York: Facts on File, 1995), 207; *The Guinness Book of Records 1997* (New York: Bantam Books, 1997), 415.

41. Stephen Nissenbaum, *The Battle for Christmas: A Social and Cultural History of Christmas that Shows How it Was Transformed from an Unruly Carnival Season into the Quintessential American Family Holiday* (New York: Alfred A. Knopf, 1996), 140, 169. Eric Hobsbawm and Terence Ranger, eds., *The Invention of Tradition* (New York: Cambridge University Press, 1983), 7.

42. K. M. Palmer, "Crops for winter Fun," *House and Garden* 87 (February 1945): 104.

Chapter 4: Pop Cookery

1. Catherine Esther Beecher, *Miss Beecher's Domestic Receipt Book* (New York: Harper & Brothers, 1846), 292.

2. *Par Excellence, Manual of Cookery* (Chicago: Published by the St. Agnes Guild of the Church of the Epiphany, 1888), 145; Board of Managers of the Masonic and Eastern Star Home, *The Eastern Star Cook Book* (Washington, D.C.: National Tribune Publishing Company, 1907), 89; *Confectioner's Journal* 35 (October 10, 1913): 25; Mary M. Wright, *Candy-Making at Home; Two Hundred Ways to Make Candy with Home Flavor and Professional Finish* (Philadelphia: Penn Publishing Company, 1915), 124–25.

3. E. F. Haskell, *The Housekeeper's Encyclopedia* (New York: D. Appleton and Company, 1861), 200; Maria Parloa, *The Appledore Cook Book: Containing Practical Receipts for Plain and Rich Cooking* (Boston: Graves and Ellis, 1872), 142.

4. Charlotte Brewster Jordan, "A Pop-Corn Frolic for Hallowe'en," *St. Nicholas* 36 (October 1909): 1114–15; Amelia Sulzbacher, "Popcorn Dainties," *Good Housekeeping* 43 (October 1906): 422–23; Riley M. Fletcher-Berry, "Dressing Up Pop Corn," *Ladies' Home Journal* 34 (December 1917): 70; Mary M. Wright, *Candy-Making at Home; Two Hundred Ways to Make Candy with Home Flavor and Professional Finish* (Philadelphia: Penn Publishing Company, 1915).

5. Alice Bradley, *The Candy Cook Book* (Boston: Little, Brown, and Company, 1917); Alice Bradley, *The Candy Cook Book* (Boston: Little, Brown, and Company, 1924); Alice Bradley, *The Candy Cook Book* (Boston: Little, Brown, and Company, 1929); Alice Bradley, "A Pop-corn Christmas is More Patriotic than a Candy One," *Woman's Home Companion* 44 (December 1917): 34.

6. May B. Van Arsdale, Day Monroe, and Mary I. Barber, *Our Candy Recipes* (New York: Macmillan, 1922), 164–81.

7. Alice Bradley, *The Candy Cook Book* (Boston: Little, Brown, and Company, 1917); Mary Hamilton Talbott, *Pop Corn Recipes* (Grinnell, Iowa: Sam Nelson, Jr., Company, 1916); Albert Dickinson Company, "Little Buster Hull-Less Pop Corn" (broadside) (Chicago: Albert Dickinson Co., 1921).

8. Fulmer Mood, "John Winthrop, Jr., on Indian Corn," *New England Quarterly* 10 (March 1937): 121–33, from a letter dated July 29, 1662, in the Royal Society, London. An abridged version of the original letter was published in the Royal Society's *Philosophical Transaction* in 1678, 142; Catharine Esther Beecher, *Miss Beecher's Domestic Receipt Book* (New York: Harper & Brothers, c1846), 292; Richard J. Hooker, *Food and Drink in America: A History* (Indianapolis and New York: Bobbs-Merrill Company, 1981), 40.

9. *Rural New Yorker* 9 (February 27, 1858): 95; *Rural New Yorker* 10 (March 19, 1859): 95; Maria Parloa, *The Appledore Cook Book: Containing Practical Receipts for Plain and Rich Cooking* (Boston: Graves and Ellis, 1872), 142; C. H. Cushing and B. Gray, comps., *The Kansas Home Cook-Book* fifth thousand (Leavenworth, Kans.: Crew and Brothers, 1877), 183.

10. *Working Farmer* 13 (April 1861): 75; *Working Farmer* 14 (May 1862): 108.

11. Ella E. Kellogg, *Science in the Kitchen* (Battle Creek, Mich.: Health Publishing Company, 1892), 330; Almeda Lambert, *Guide for Nut Cookery* (Battle Creek, Mich.: Joseph Lambert & Company, 1899), 152.

12. Fannie Merritt Farmer, *Food and Cookery for the Sick and Convalescent* (Boston: Little, Brown, and Company, 1904), 175; Mary Hamilton Talbott, *Pop Corn Recipes* (Grinnell, Iowa: Sam Nelson, Jr., Company, 1916), n.p.; F. W. Waugh, *Iroquis Foods and Food Preparation; Memoir 36; #12 Anthropological Series* (Ottawa: Government Printing Office, 1916), 94. Ida C. Bailey Allen, *Mrs. Allen on Cooking, Menus, Service* (Garden City, N.Y.: Doubleday, Page & Company, 1924), 797.

13. *The Housewife* 21 (August 1904): 12; Mary L. Wade, *The Book of Corn Cookery* (Chicago: A. C. McClurg and Co., 1917), 92–93; Elizabeth Hiller, *The*

Corn Cook Book, war ed. (New York: P. F. Volland Company, 1918), 106; "Pop Corn Flour: Chicago Bakers Substitute for Wheat," *Business Week* (August 24, 1946): 74, 76; "Popcorn Bread," *Popcorn Merchandiser* 1 (July 1946): 29.

14. *Country Gentleman* 51 (December 2, 1886): 920; Ella E. Kellogg, *Science in the Kitchen* (Battle Creek, Mich.: Health Publishing Company, 1892), 104; "Popcorn as a Breakfast Cereal," *Independent* 90 (May 19, 1917): 316.

15. May Belle Brooks, "Meals from the Corn-Popper; Attractive Dishes for the New Year's Table," *Good Housekeeping* 56 (January 1913): 119; Charles D. Woods and Harry Snyder, "Cereal Breakfast Foods," in *Farmers' Bulletin #249* (Washington, D.C.: U.S. Department of Agriculture, 1911), 26–27; Hartley and Willier, "Pop Corn for the Home," 11.

16. *American Cooking* 30 (January 1926): 429; Artemas Ward, *The Encyclopedia of Food* (New York: Baker and Taylor Co., 1923), 405; J. I. Holcomb, *Salesology of the Butter-Kist Popcorn Machine* (Indianapolis, Ind.: Holcomb and Hoke Manufacturing Company, 1915), 96–97.

17. Mary Hamilton Talbott, *Pop Corn Recipes* (Grinnell, Iowa: Sam Nelson, Jr., Company, 1916), n.p.; "Popcorn as a Breakfast Cereal," *Independent* 90 (May 19, 1917): 316.

18. C. M. Littlejohn, "Popcorn for Breakfast Food Widens Markets," *Kernel* 2 (November 1938): 16; Gary Miller and K. M. Scotty Mitchell, *Price Guide to Collectible Kitchen Appliances* (Radnor, Pa.: Wallace-Homestead Book Company, 1991), 43–44.

19. James Margedant, "Tri-State Farmers Turning Out an Explosive Crop—It's Popcorn," *Sunday Courier and Press,* January 18, 1942, p. D1; "Popcorn as a Breakfast Food," *Popcorn Merchandiser* 1 (April 1946): 20; Irving Steurer, "The Story of Hybrid Popcorn," *Popcorn Merchandiser* 1 (August 1946): 14, 18–19.

20. Hall et al., *I Love Popcorn,* 20; Kusche, *Popcorn,* 71–76; Redenbacher, *Orville Redenbacher's Popcorn Book,* 36; Len Sherman, *Popcorn King: How Orville Redenbacher and his Popcorn Charmed America* (Arlington, Tex.: Summit Publishing Group, 1996), 90–91; Kimbra Postlewaite, "Popped Out," *Snack Food* 85 (August 1996): 17.

21. E. F. Haskell, *The Housekeeper's Encyclopedia* (New York: D. Appleton and Company, 1861), 193; *Country Gentleman* 58 (January 26, 1893): 77.

22. John D. Hounihan, *Bakers' and Confectioners' Guide and Treasure* (Staunton, Va.: Printed for the author, 1877), 298; *The Candy-Maker: A Practical Guide to the Manufacture of the Various Kinds of Plain and Fancy Candy* (New York: Jesse Haney & Co., 1878), 38–39; [Lafcadio Hearn], *La Cuisine Creole; A Collection of Culinary Recipes from Leading Chefs and Noted Creole Housewives, Who Have Made New Orleans Famous for its Cuisine* (New York: Will H. Coleman, 1885), 241.

23. U.S. Patent #30,661, issued November 20, 1860; U.S. Patent #129,623, issued July 16, 1872; U.S. Patent #377,303, issued January 31, 1888; E. H. Leland, *Farm Homes In-Doors and Out Doors* (New York: Orange Judd Company, 1881), 151.

24. Sidney Morse, *Household Discoveries; An Encyclopedia of Practical Recipes and Processes; Mrs Curtis's Cook Book* (Petersburg, N.Y.: Success Co., 1908), 539; Ladies of the Westminster Presbyterian Church, *Cook Book of the Northwest* (Keokuk, Iowa: R. B. Ogden, 1875), 144; *Country Gentleman* 42 (June 7, 1877): 361; Gussie Thomas, "Popping Corn," *Country Gentleman* 42 (July 5, 1877): 427; *The New Home Made Cook Book* (New York: M. J. Ivers & Co., 1882), 48; Frances E. Owens, *Mrs. Owens' Cook Book, and Useful Hints for the*

Household (Chicago: Household Helps Publication Society, 1882), 293–94; Jane Warren, *The Economical Cook Book* (New York: Hurst, [1882]), as in Susan Williams, *Savory Suppers Fashionable Feasts: Dining in Victorian America* (Knoxville: University of Tennessee Press, 1996), 298; *The Successful Housekeeper; A Manual of Universal Application* (Harrisburg: Pennsylvania Publishing Co., 1883), 97; Lucy W. Bostwick, *Margery Daw in the Kitchen and What She Learned There,* 6th ed. (Auburn, N.Y.: By the author, 1885), 86; *La Cuisine Creole; A Collection of Culinary Recipes from Leading Chefs and Noted Creole Housewives, Who Have Made New Orleans Famous for its Cuisine,* 2nd ed. (New Orleans: F. F. Hansell & Bro., Ltd., 1885), 241; *Country Gentleman* 52 (January 13, 1887): 37; F. L. Gillette, *The White House Cookbook* (Chicago: L. P. Miller & Co., 1887), 403–4; *Par Excellence, Manual of Cookery* (Chicago: Published by the St. Agnes Guild of the Church of the Epiphany, 1888), 145; *Good Housekeeping* 8 (January 5, 1889): 117; S. T. Rorer, *Home Candy Making* (Philadelphia: Arnold and Company, 1889), 70–71; Sarah J. Cutter, *Palatable Dishes: A Practical Guide to Good Living* (Buffalo: Peter, Paul & Bro., 1891), 715–16; M. W. Ellsworth, *Queen of the Household; A Carefully Classified and Alphabetically Arranged Repository of Useful Information* (Detroit: Ellsworth & Brey, 1891), 134; *Grace Church Cook Book; One Thousand Tested Recipes* (Grand Rapids, Mich.: Eaton Printing & Binding Company, 1892), 284; Ladies Parish Aid Society, *Trinity Parish Cook Book; Choice and Tested Recipes Contributed by the Ladies of Trinity Church* (Wilmington, Del.: John Rogers' Press, 1892), 168; Jane Warren, *The Grand Union Cook Book,* part 2 (New York: Grand Union Tea Company, 189?), 94; *Country Gentleman* 58 (January 26, 1893): 77; Estelle W. Wilcox, *The New Dixie Cook-Book,* rev. and enl. ed. (Atlanta, Ga.: Dixie Cook-Book Publishing Co., c1889 [1893]), 141; J. Magie, *Milwaukee Cook Book* (Milwaukee, Wis.: Riverside Printing Co., 1894), 330; Grace Townsend, *Imperial Cook Book,* rev. ed. (Philadelphia: Elliott Publishing Co., 1894), 409; Barbara Allen, "Christmas Confections," *American Kitchen Magazine* 4 (December 1895): 142–43; David Chidlow et al., *The American Pure Food Cook Book and Household Economist* (Chicago: Geo. M. Hill Co., c1899), 229–30; Sarah Smith (Mrs. Fred) Journal, bark *John P. West,* 1882–84, Log 78, in the G. W. Blunt-White Library, Mystic Seaport Museum, Mystic, Conn., as cited in Sandra L. Oliver, *Saltwater Foodways: New Englanders and Their Food at Sea and Ashore, in the Nineteenth Century* (Mystic, Conn.: Mystic Seaport Museum, 1995), 279; *Grocer's Regulator* 1 (April 1, 1886): 24; Jennie A. Hansey and Ella M. Blackstone, *New Standard Domestic Science Cook-Book* (Chicago: Laird & Lee, 1908), 374–75.

25. Mary M. Wright, *Candy-Making at Home; Two Hundred Ways to Make Candy with Home Flavor and Professional Finish* (Philadelphia: Penn Publishing Company, 1915), 124–26; Mary Hamilton Talbott, *Pop Corn Recipes* (Grinnell, Iowa: Sam Nelson, Jr., Company, 1916), n.p.; Alice Bradley, *The Candy Cook Book* (Boston: Little, Brown, and Company, 1917), 187–88; Elizabeth Hiller, *The Corn Cook Book,* war ed. (New York: P. F. Volland Company, 1918), 119; George Washington Carver, *Bulletin #31:* "How to Grow the Peanut and 105 Ways of Preparing it for Human Consumption" (Tuskegee, Ala.: Tuskegee Institute Experiment Station, June 1916), 25; W. O. Rigby, *Rigby's Reliable Candy Teacher,* 12th ed. (Topeka, Kans.: Rigby Publishing Company, 1918), 153; "When You Entertain: Delectable Popcorn Confections and a Thanksgiving Guessing Game," *Woman's Home Companion* 59 (November 1932): 46; Clemence Haskin, "Father Pops the Corn; and Mother Prepares It with Variations," *American Home* 15 (December 1935): 53.

26. Edger Anderson, "Field Studies of Guatemalan Maize," *Annals, Missouri Botanical Garden* 34 (November 1947): 446; Edger Anderson, "Maiz Reventador," *Annals, Missouri Botanical Garden* 31 (September 1944): 311; *Cassell's Dictionary of Cookery* (London: Cassell Petter & Galpin, c1877), 401; E. Skuse, *Skuse's Complete Confectioner: A Practical Guide to the Art of Sugar Boiling in All Its Branches* (London: W. J. Bush & Co., [1890]), 53.

27. Elizabeth Mills, Marjorie Peck, Grace Roper, Margaret Salladin, and Mildred Wheeler, eds., *At the Sign of the Rolling Pin,* 2nd ed. (Middletown, N.Y.: Stivers Printing Company, 1916), 178.

28. *Country Gentleman* 58 (January 26, 1893): 77; *Good Housekeeping* 37 (December 1903): 587.

29. Undated promotional brochure from the American Pop Corn Company; "Popcorn Sales More Hype than Heat," *Snack Food* 81 (June 1992): M24.

30. Giedt, *Popcorn!,* 71; *The Guinness Book of Records 1996* (New York: Facts on File, 1995), 209; *The Guinness Book of Records 1997* (New York: Bantam Books, 1997), 415; John Ketzenberger, "Popcorn Ball Rolls Up National Tour," *Chronicle Tribune,* November 2, 1997.

31. E. F. Haskell, *The Housekeeper's Encyclopedia* (New York: D. Appleton and Company, 1861), 193; *The Candy-Maker: A Practical Guide to the Manufacture of the Various Kinds of Plain and Fancy Candy* (New York: Jesse Haney & Co., 1878), 38; Wehman Brothers, *Wehman's Confectioner's Guide and Assistant: or, A Complete Instruction in the Art of Candy-Making. An Aid Both to the Professional and Amateur Candy-Maker* (New York: Wehman Brothers, c1905), 84.

32. May Perrin Goff, ed., *The Household: A Cyclopëdia of Practical Hints for Modern Homes with a Full and Complete Treatise on Cookery* (Detroit: Detroit Free Press Co., 1881), 446; *Good Housekeeping* 37 (December 1903): 587; Alice Bradley, *The Candy Cook Book* (Boston: Little, Brown, and Company, 1917), 189; Marion Harris Neil, *The Thrift Cook Book* (Philadelphia: David McKay, 1919), 246.

33. Edger Anderson, "Maiz Reventador," *Annals, Missouri Botanical Garden* 31 (September 1944): 311; E. Skuse, *Skuse's Complete Confectioner: A Practical Guide to the Art of Sugar Boiling in All Its Branches* (London: W. J. Bush & Co., [1890]), 53–54; Horace Cox, *The "Queen" Cookery Books,* 3rd ed., vol. 6, part 2 (London: "Queen" Office, 1904), 116.

34. Packages from Konriko Brand Popcorn Cakes, Shoprite Caramel Popped Corn Cakes, and Quaker Strawberry Crunch Corn Cakes.

35. Will O. Rigby, *Rigby's Reliable Candy Teacher* (Topeka, Kans.: W. O. Rigby, 1902), 61; Ladies of the Cosmos Society of the Bradley Methodist Episcopal Church, *Favorite Recipes* (Greenfield, Ind.: Greenfield Printing and Publishing Company, [1906]), 41; U.S. Patent #567,836, issued September 15, 1896; *Billboard* 19 (January 26, 1907): 48; C. E. Dellenbarger Co., *Copyrighted Secret Formulas and Instructions for the Manufacture of Crispettes and Other Popcorn Confections* (Chicago: C. E. Dellenbarger Co., 1913), 18.

36. C. E. Dellenbarger Co., *Copyrighted Secret Formulas,* 19–20.

37. C. E. Dellenbarger Co., *Copyrighted Secret Formulas,* 20; Martin A. Pease, *The Blue Book on Home Candy Making; Secrets of Professional Candy Making* (Bloomington, Ill.: Martin A. Pease, 1923), 45; "Cracker Jack Recipe Book," typed manuscript in the possession of Andrew F. Smith, page 26; Mary M. Wright, *Candy-Making at Home; Two Hundred Ways to Make Candy with Home Flavor and Professional Finish* (Philadelphia: Penn Publishing Company, 1915), 129–30; William M. Bell, comp., *The Pilot: An Authoritative Book on the Manufacture of Candies and Ice Creams,* 3rd ed. (Chicago: Wm. M. Bell, 1918), 125–26; *The Art of*

Home Candy Making, 3rd rev. ed. (Canton, Ohio: Home Candy Makers, 1913), 57–58; Mary L. Wade, *The Book of Corn Cookery* (Chicago: A. C. McClurg and Co., 1917), 97–98; W. O. Rigby, *Rigby's Reliable Candy Teacher,* 12th ed. (Topeka, Kans.: Rigby Publishing Company, 1918), 153; Albert Dickinson Company, "Little Buster Hull-Less Pop Corn"; Martin A. Pease, *The Blue Book on Home Candy Making; Secrets of Professional Candy Making* (Bloomington, Ill.: Martin A. Pease, 1923), 45; Spindler-Burnett Bible Class, *The Lutheran Cook Book,* rev. and enl. ed. (Dayton, Ohio: First Lutheran Church, 1929), 113.

38. Eliza Ann McAuly, "Iowa to the 'Land of Gold,'" in Kenneth L. Holmes, ed., *Covered Wagon Women: Diaries and Letters of the Western Trails,* vol. 4 (Glendale, Calif.: Arthur H. Clark Company, 1985), 63; A. M. Collins, *The Great Western Cook Book* (New York: A. S. Barnes & Company, 1857), 128; Ladies of California, *California Recipe Book* (San Francisco: Cubry & Company, 1875), 53; San Grael Society of the First Presbyterian Church, *The Web-Foot Cook Book* (Portland, Oreg.: W. B. Ayer, 1885), 191; *Country Gentleman* 48 (December 20, 1883): 1029; Mary M. Wright, *Candy-Making at Home; Two Hundred Ways to Make Candy with Home Flavor and Professional Finish* (Philadelphia: Penn Publishing Company, 1915), 127–28.

39. *Official Gazette,* U.S. Trademark #10,735, issued November 20, 1883, p. 702; *The Picayune Creole Cook Book,* 2nd ed. (New Orleans: The Picayune, 1901), 377.

40. The Ladies of Des Moines, *A Collection of Choice Recipes* [Des Moines, 1903] reprinted in *Fifty Years of Prairie Cooking,* introduction and suggested recipes by Louis Szathmáry (New York: Arno Press, 1973), 81; Ladies of the First Presbyterian Church, *The First Presbyterian Cook Book* (Spokane, Wash.: Author, [circa 1910]), 95; Sunshine Society of Crawfordsville High School, *Sunshine Cook Book* (Crawfordsville, Ind.: Journal Printing Co., 1913), 38; Loyal Daughter Sunday School Class, *Cook Book* (Bader, Ill., 1926), 52; Mary B. Bookmeyer, *Candy and Candy-Making* (Peoria, Ill.: Manual Arts Press, 1929), 42; Parco Woman's Club, *Choice Recipes* (Parco, Wyo.: Parco Woman's Club, 1930), n.p.; Allen Prescott, *The Wifesaver's Candy Recipes* (New York: Blue Ribbon Books, 1934), 40; *Granddaughter's Inglenook Cookbook* (Elgin, Ill.: Brethren Publishing House, 1942), 68; Constance Wachtmeister and Kate Buffington Davis, eds., *Practical Vegetarian Cookery* (Minneapolis: Printers Electrotyping Co., 1897), 142.

41. Emma Garman Krape, comp., *The Globe Cook Book* (Freeport, Ill.: Journal Printing Company, February 22, 1901), 232–33; *The Inglenook Cook Book,* rev. ed. (Elgin, Ill.: Brethren Publishing House, 1911 [rpt., 1970]), 250–51.

42. Fannie Merritt Farmer, *What to Have for Dinner* (New York: Dodge Publishing Company, 1905), 130; Amelia Sulzbacher, "Popcorn Dainties," *Good Housekeeping* 43 (October 1906): 422–23; *Good Housekeeping* 44 (March 1907): 358; Poppy Cannon and Patricia Brooks, *The Presidents' Cookbook: Practical Receipts from George Washington to the Present* ([New York]: Funk & Wagnalls, 1968), 358–59.

43. Mary Hamilton Talbott, *Pop Corn Recipes* (Grinnell, Iowa: Sam Nelson, Jr., Company, 1916), n.p.; *American Cooking* 30 (January 1926): 429; K. M. Palmer, "Crops for Winter Fun," *House and Garden* 87 (February 1945): 104; Charles H. Baker, *The Gentleman's Companion; Volume I being an Exotic Cookery Book or, Around the World with Knife, Fork and Spoon* (New York: Derrydale, 1939), 25–26.

44. F. W. Waugh, *Iroquis Foods and Food Preparation; Memoir 36; #12 Anthropological Series* (Ottawa: Government Printing Office, 1916), 94.

45. Amelia Sulzbacher, "Popcorn Dainties," *Good Housekeeping* 43 (October 1906): 422–23; Mary Hamilton Talbott, *Pop Corn Recipes* (Grinnell, Iowa: Sam Nelson, Jr., Company, 1916), n.p.; Riley M. Fletcher-Berry, "Dressing Up Pop Corn," *Ladies' Home Journal* 34 (December 1917): 70.

46. "Hot Butter Popcorn!" *Better Homes and Gardens* 27 (December 1948): 82–83.

Chapter 5: Early Pop Pros

1. Fearing Burr, *The Field and Garden of America* (Boston: J. E. Tilton and Company, 1863), 599.

2. John Russell Bartlett, *Dictionary of Americanisms: A Glossary of Words and Phrases Usually Regarded as Peculiar to the United States* (New York: Bartlett and Welford, 1848), 257; J. H. Salisbury, "History and Chemical Investigation of Maize or Indian Corn," *Transactions of the New York Agricultural Society for 1848,* vol. 8 (Albany: Weed, Parsons & Co., 1849), 764; Ebenezer Emmons, *Agriculture of New York,* vol. 2 (Albany: C. Van Benthuysen, 1849), 264–65; F. G. Brieger, J. T. A. Gurgel, E. Paterniani, A. Blumenschein, and M. R. Alleoni, *Races of Maize in Brazil and Other Eastern South American Countries,* Publication #593 (Washington, D.C.: National Academy of Sciences—National Research Council, 1958), 141.

3. J. M. Thorburn & Co.'s *Annual Descriptive Catalogue of Vegetable and Agricultural Seeds. Garden, Field, Fruit and Other Seeds* (New York: Law & Job Printer, 1875), 11; Joel Barlow, *The Hasty-Pudding: A Poem, with a Memoir on Maize, or Indian Corn,* compiled by Daniel Jay Browne (New York: W. H. Graham, 1847), 48; *Valley Farmer* 4 (January 1852): 24; *Country Gentleman* 17 (January 24, 1861): 65; *Country Gentleman* 24 (November 10, 1864): 305; *Country Gentleman* 30 (October 31, 1867): 262.

4. Fearing Burr, *The Field and Garden of America* (Boston: J. E. Tilton and Company, 1863), 598–99.

5. *American Cyclopedia,* vol. 11 (New York: D. Appleton and Company, 1875), 44; William D. Emerson, *History and Incidents of Indian Corn,* 159; E. Lewis Sturtevant, *Third Annual Report of the Board of Control of the New York Agricultural Experiment Station for the Year 1884* (Albany, N.Y.: Weed, Parsons and Company, 1895), n.p.; Thomas J. Burrill and George W. McClure, "Pop Corn, Tests of Varieties," in *Bulletin #13* (Champaign: University of Illinois Agricultural Experiment Station, 1891), 443–47; E. L. Sturtevant, "Varieties of Corn," in *Bulletin #57,* (Washington, D.C.: Department of Agriculture, Office of Experiment Stations, 1899), 29–31; *Louisville Commercial,* as cited in the *Country Gentleman* 65 (June 7, 1900): 461.

6. W. W. Tracy, "List of American Varieties of Vegetables for the Years 1901 and 1902," in *Bulletin #21* (Washington, D.C.: Department of Agriculture, Bureau of Plant Industry, 1903), 149–51.

7. Fearing Burr, *The Field and Garden of America* (Boston: J. E. Tilton and Company, 1863), 600; Burrill and McClure, "Pop Corn, Tests of Varieties," *Bulletin # 13* (Champaign: University of Illinois Agricultural Experiment Station, 1891), 445; *Grocer's Criterion* 18 (August 17, 1891): 14; *Burpee's Seeds Catalogue* (Philadelphia: W. Atlee Burpee & Co., 1888), 44.

8. Ziegler and Ashman, "Popcorn," 191.

9. F. G. Brieger, J. T. A. Gurgel, E. Paterniani, A. Blumenschein, and M. R. Alleoni, *The Races of Maize in Brazil and Other Eastern South American Countries* (Washington, D.C.: National Academy of Science—National Research Council Publication 593, 1958), 121; Arthur M. Brunson, "Popcorn Breeding," in *Yearbook*

of Agriculture 1937 (Washington, D.C.: Department of Agriculture, 1937), 396; "Hatful of Popcorn Worth $2,500," *Kernel* 2 (May 1939): 11.

10. *Country Gentleman* 40 (November 4, 1875): 696; *Country Gentleman* 52 (March 24, 1887): 233.

11. *Grocer's Criterion* 31 (March 28, 1904): 11; Charles D. Chapman & Co., *History of Knox County, Illinois* (Chicago: Blakeley, Brown & Marsh, 1878), 440–41.

12. William H. Hart, *History of Sac County* (Indianapolis: B. F. Bowen & Co., 1914), 101; Mrs. Charles Magnuson, "The Little Brother of the Tall Corn," at the Ida County Historical Society, Ida Grove, Iowa, p. 31–32; William H. Hart, *History of Sac County* (Indianapolis: B. F. Bowen & Co., 1914), 227; *Forty-sixth Annual Report of the Board of Directors of the Iowa State Agricultural Society for the year 1899* (Des Moines: F. R. Conway, 1899), 205.

13. William H. Hart, *History of Sac County* (Indianapolis: B. F. Bowen & Co., 1914), 227.

14. "Shortage of Popcorn Production," *American Agriculturist,* as reprinted in *Confectioner's Gazette* 34 (October 12, 1912): 20; Brunson, "Popcorn Breeding," 396; Mrs. Charles Magnuson, "The Little Brother of the Tall Corn," undated papers at the Ida County Historical Society in Iowa, p. 31–32.

15. Brunson, "Popcorn Breeding," 396.

16. *Grocer's Bulletin* 3 (February 8, 1882): 145; advertisements appear in back page of every issue of the *Grocer's Criterion,* from January to June 1882; *Prairie Farmer* 55 (February 3, 1883): 79; *Prairie Farmer* 56 (January 5, 1884): 15; *Grocer's Regulator* 1 (July 22, 1886): 12; *Grocer's Criterion* 15 (February 27, 1888): 6; photocopy of the bill of sale in the possession of the author.

17. *Official Gazette,* U.S. Trademark #20,592, registered January 12, 1892; *Official Gazette,* U.S. Trademark #22,343, registered January 17, 1893; *Official Gazette,* U.S. Trademark #23,250, registered June 27, 1893; Al Bergevin, *Food and Drink Containers and their Prices* (Radnor, Pa.: Wallace-Homestead, 1988), 212.

18. Mary Ann Anderson, letter to "Around the Town" in Grinnell, Iowa, dated December 2, 1996; Nelson Family file at the Grinnell Historical Society, Grinnell, Iowa.

19. Mary Hamilton Talbott, *Pop Corn Recipes* (Grinnell, Iowa: Sam Nelson, Jr., Company, 1916), n.p.

20. Unidentified obituaries for Sam Nelson Jr., July 7, 1916, from the archives of the Grinnell Historical Museum, Grinnell, Iowa.

21. Robert F. Ware, interview, December 9, 1997; George Brown, interview, December 9, 1997; "August J. Fisher [*sic*] 1895–1969," obituary circulated by the Popcorn Institute, February 28, 1969; "Carl W. Erne 1888–1968," obituary circulated by the Popcorn Institute, 1968.

22. Betty Bailey et al., *Schaller Centennial Book* (Schaller, Iowa: History Book Committee, 1983), 208–10; *Concessionaire Merchandiser* 13 (September 1958): 13.

23. American Pop Corn Company, *Jolly Time,* 4–5.

24. American Pop Corn Company, *Jolly Time,* 6–7; copy of letter to Christopher Thurber Grocery Company from the American Pop Corn Company dated April 22, 1915, from the archives of the American Pop Corn Company.

25. American Pop Corn Company, *Jolly Time,* 7–8; "Pop Corn That Pops," advertisement 1916, from the archives of the American Pop Corn Company.

26. American Pop Corn Company, *Jolly Time,* 9–10.

27. Ibid., 10–11.

28. Ibid., 12.

29. *Jolly Time: An American Tradition Since 1914* (Sious City, Iowa: American Pop Corn Company, 1994), 15–17; American Pop Corn Company, "Having Fun with Pop Corn" (Sious City, Iowa: American Pop Corn Company, n.d.), n.p.

30. "American's Best Environmentally Friendly," *Snack World* 52 (January 1995): 12.

31. Richard S. Simmons, "Kernel Kingdom," *Indianapolis Star Magazine,* February 19, 1984, pp. 10–11.

32. *Indianapolis Sunday Star,* January 25, 1942, part 2, p. 32; James A. McCarty, interview, December 12, 1997.

33. George K. Brown, "How the Popcorn Business Started," unpublished paper in the Wyandot Popcorn Museum, Marion, Ohio, dated July 15, 1987.

34. J. C. Eldredge and W. I. Thomas, "Popcorn . . . Its Production, Processing and Utilization," in *Bulletin #P127* (Ames: Iowa State University of Science and Technology, Agricultural and Home Economics Experiment Station, 1959), 12.

35. George Brown, interview, November 28, 1997.

36. Louis Untermeyer, *A Century of Candymaking 1847–1947; The Story of the Origin and Growth of New England Confectionary Company* (Boston: Barta Press, 1947), 12.

37. James F. W. Johnston, *Notes on North America,* vol. 1 (Edinburgh: William Blackwood and Sons, 1851), 151; *New York Tribune,* January 14, 1858; Robert Thacher Trall, *The New Hydropathic Cook-book* (New York: Fowlers and Wells, 1854), 186; Q. K. Philander Doesticks [pseud. for Mortimer Thomson], *Doesticks' Letters and What He Says* (Philadelphia: T. B. Peterson and Brother, 1855), 78, 257.

38. *Omaha Daily Herald,* January 10, 1869, p. 3; J. S. Ingram, *Centennial Exposition* (Philadelphia: Hubbard Bros., 1876), 758; Charles Bernard, *Bernard's Half Century of Circus Reviews and Red Wagon Stories* (Savannah: Commercial Litho. & Printing Co., 1930), 8; *Pomona (California) Progress,* February 12, 1891; *Scientific American* 71 (December 29, 1894): 405; *Charles City Intelligencer,* December 14, 1926; "Still Poppin' After All These Years!," *Floyd County Heritage* 25 (October 1996): 1–3.

39. *Chicago Tribune,* September 27, 1907; Kit Lane, *The Popcorn Millionaire and Other Tales of Saugatuck* (Douglas, Mich.: Pavilion Press, c1991), 52.

40. "A Modern Store and Only 4 Feet Wide," *Kernel* 2 (February 1939): 3; Dale Morrison, "Popcorn Artistry Pays Off; Keeps Recipe a Secret," *Chicago Daily News,* May 27, 1959, p. W2; *Wheaton Leader,* August 20, 1959, p. 4.

41. *Grocer's Criterion* 31 (March 28, 1904): 11.

42. Artemas Ward, *The Grocers' Hand-Book and Directory for 1883* (Philadelphia: Philadelphia Grocer Publishing Co., 1882), 165; *Grocer's Companion and Merchant's Hand-book* (Boston: New England Grocer Office, 1883), 112–13; Mrs. Charles Magnuson, "The Little Brother of the Tall Corn," undated papers at the Ida County Historical Society in Iowa, p. 33.

43. Elizabeth Grinnell, "Nothing but Corn," *Table Talk* 8 (November 1898): 391.

44. *Grocer's Criterion* 8 (May 16, 1881): 23; *Grocer's Criterion* 12 (January 5, 1885): 33; *Grocer's Criterion* 18 (August 17, 1891): 14; *Billboard* 16 (April 2, 1904): 25; *Billboard* 19 (January 12, 1907): 2. *New York Clipper,* October 5, 1912, p. 4.

45. E. Skuse, *Skuse's Complete Confectioner: A Practical Guide to the Art of Sugar Boiling in All Its Branches* (London: W. J. Bush & Co., [1890]), 54; Cracker Jack Recipe Book, typed manuscript, page 18 copy in possession of the author; *Fifty Years* (Chicago: Cracker Jack Company, 1922), n.p.

46. Donald L. Miller, *City of the Century; The Epic of Chicago and the Making of America* (New York: Simon & Schuster, 1996), 159; *Fifty Years,* n.p.; "The More

You Eat," *Fortune* 35 (June 1947): 144; Alex Jaramillo, *Cracker Jack Prizes* (New York: Abbeville Press, 1989), 8.

47. Donald L. Miller, *City of the Century; The Epic of Chicago and the Making of America* (New York: Simon & Schuster, 1996), 488–505; "The More You Eat," *Fortune* 35 (June 1947): 144.

48. *The "Home Queen" World's Fair Souvenir Cook Book* (Chicago: Geo. F. Cram Publishing Co., 1893), 551; Jaramillo, *Cracker Jack Prizes,* 8.

49. "The More You Eat," *Fortune* 35 (June 1947): 144; *Fifty Years,* n.p.; "How 'Cracker Jack' Was Given Its Name" [broadside]) (Chicago: Cracker Jack Company, c1950); "Information from the Cracker Jack History Book #1—to 1954," in the collection of Harriet Joyce, DeBary, Fla., dated 1982.

50. *Ohio Agricultural Report, Fair Exhibits, Ohio State Fair* (Columbus, Ohio, 1897), 33; Ronald Toth Jr., interview, December 13, 1997.

51. Undated photocopied material on Cracker Jack, supplied by Forest Wanberg Jr., former vice president for operations of Borden's Cracker Jack division; *Official Gazette,* U.S. Trademark #28,016, registered March 24, 1896; *Grocery World* 22 (July 13, 1896): 8, 23, 25.

52. Henry Eckstein's diary, in the collection of Ronald Toth Jr, Rochester, N.H.

53. *Billboard* 14 (August 9, 1902): 28.

54. Jack Norworth and Albert von Tilzer, "Take Me Out To the Ball Game," 1908.

55. *Billboard* 16 (April 23, 1904): 25; undated photocopied material on Cracker Jack, supplied by Forest Wanberg Jr., former vice president for operations of Borden's Cracker Jack division; *Billboard* 19 (February 9, 1907): 51; Charlotte Brewster Jordan, "A Pop-Corn Frolic for Hallowe'en," *St. Nicholas* 36 (October 1909): 1114–15; Cracker Jack Recipe Book, typed manuscript, page 26, copy in possession of the author; *Confectioner's Gazette* 34 (October 12, 1912): 12.

56. *Confectioner's Gazette* 34 (October 12, 1912): 12; *Confectioner's Gazette* 35 (February 10, 1914): 10.

57. Cracker Jack Recipe Book, typed manuscript, pages 9, 17, 18, copy in possession of the author.

58. *Confectioner's Gazette* 34 (June 10, 1913): 11; *Saturday Evening Post* 192 (June 7, 1919): 102; Jaramillo, *Cracker Jack Prizes,* 11–12; *Confectioner's Gazette* 35 (February 10, 1914): 10; *Fifty Years,* n.p.; *Grocer's Criterion* 31 (July 4, 1904): 52; *Confectioner's Gazette* 34 (October 12, 1912): 12; Ravi Piña, *Cracker Jack Collectibles with Price Guide* (Atglen, Pa.: Schiffer Publishing, 1995); undated photocopied material on Cracker Jack, supplied by Forest Wanberg Jr., former vice president for operations of Borden's Cracker Jack division.

59. *Billboard* 16 (April 2, 1904): 24; *Billboard* 28 (July 22, 1916): 29; *Arthur Advertiser,* July 20, 1917; Ronald Toth Jr., interview, December 8, 1997; letter addressed "To the Trade," signed by F. W. Rueckheim, president, The Cracker Jack Company, dated August 9, 1926, in the collection of Harriet Joyce, DeBarry, Fla.

60. "Information from the Cracker Jack History Book #1—to 1954," at the Cracker Jack archives in Chicago in 1982 in the collection of Harriet Joyce; Hess, *Snack Food,* 204.

61. "Information from the Cracker Jack History Book #1—to 1954," at the Cracker Jack archives in Chicago in 1982 in the collection of Harriet Joyce.

62. *Billboard* 49 (April 16, 1937): 94; "The More You Eat," *Fortune* 35 (June 1947): 144.

63. Ibid. Eustace Reynolds Knott, *Knott's Pop-corn Book* (Boston: E. R. Knott Machine Company, 1915), 3, 10; E. R. Knott, *Knott's Pop Corn Book* 3d ed. (Sharon, Mass.:E. R. Knott Co., 1936), 2.

64. *Olson's Improved Rotary Corn Popper* (Kansas City, Mo.: A. B. Olson, 1893), np; U.S. Patent No. 428,626, issued May 27, 1890.

65. *C. Cretors & Co. The First Hundred Years: 1885–1985* (Chicago: C. Cretors, 1985), 7, 133.

66. Ibid., 1–2.

67. *Scientific American* 71 (December 29, 1894): 405.

68. *C. Cretors & Co. The First Hundred Years: 1885–1985* (Chicago: C. Cretors, 1985), 13, 17; "Canadians Report on Third Annual IPA Regional Popcorn-Concession Conference," *Popcorn Merchandiser* 9 (May 1954): 2.

69. J. S. Ingram, *Centennial Exposition* (Philadelphia: Hubbard Bros., 1876), 758; *Scientific American* 71 (December 29, 1894): 405; *C. Cretors & Co., The First Hundred Years: 1885–1985* (Chicago: C. Cretors & Co., 1985); *Billboard* 14 (March 15, 1902): n.p., 24; *Kingery Manufacturing Company Catalogue* (Cincinnati, Ohio: Kingery Manufacturing Co., [1907]), 37, 39–47.

70. U.S. Patent #428,876, issued May 27, 1890, filed by J. B. Bartholomew.

71. *Billboard* 14 (May 3, 1902): 17; Will O. Rigby, *Rigby's Reliable Candy Teacher* (Topeka, Kans.: W. O. Rigby, 1902), n.p.; The Bartholomew Co., *The Peanut and Pop Corn Problem Solved.*

72. *C. Cretors & Co. The First Hundred Years: 1885–1985* (Chicago: C. Cretors, 1985), 44–45.

73. Lynn Hopper, "Old Popcorn Popper Is Bit of Movie Palace Nostalgia," *Indianapolis Star,* October 19, 1980, section 7, p. 10; Holcomb, *Salesology* (1915), 137.

74. Holcomb, *Salesology* (1915), 96–97; J. I. Holcomb, *Salesology of the Butter-Kist Popcorn Machine* (Indianapolis, Ind.: Holcomb and Hoke Manufacturing Company, 1917), 167, 191.

75. *Saturday Evening Post,* 191 (August 24, 1918): 46; Holcomb, *Salesology* (1917), 157, 161.

76. *C. Cretors & Co. The First Hundred Years: 1885–1985* (Chicago: C. Cretors, 1985), 46, 50–51.

77. *C. Cretors & Co. The First Hundred Years: 1885–1985* (Chicago: C. Cretors, 1985), 43, 55, 46; *Kingery Manufacturing Company Catalogue,* 37.

78. Arthur Bartlett, "Popcorn Crazy," *Saturday Evening Post* 221 (May 21, 1949): 36.

79. *C. Cretors & Co. The First Hundred Years: 1885–1985* (Chicago: C. Cretors, 1985), 91–92.

80. Arthur Bartlett, "Popcorn Crazy," *Saturday Evening Post* 221 (May 21, 1949): 36, 144.

81. U.S. Patent #870,155, issued November 5, 1907; Gary Miller and K. M. Scotty Mitchell, *Price Guide to Collectible Kitchen Appliances* (Radnor, Pa.: Wallace-Homestead Book Company, 1991), 43–44.

82. Gary Miller and K. M. Scotty Mitchell, *Price Guide to Collectible Kitchen Appliances* (Radnor, Pa.: Wallace-Homestead Book Company, 1991), 55–57.

83. Ibid., 55–58.

84. R. B. Farr, "Electric Pop-Corn Popper," *Industrial Arts and Vocational Education* 18 (September 1929): 358; B. H. Rowley, "Electric Corn Popper," *Industrial Arts and Vocational Education* 20 (April 1931): 149–50; "Homemade Electric Corn Popper," *Popular Mechanics* 61 (January 1934): 136.

Chapter 6: The Popcorn Boom

1. Roger Kahle and Robert E. A. Lee, *Popcorn and Parable: A New Look at the Movies* (Minneapolis: Augsburg Publishing House, 1971), 9–15.

2. Richard J. Hooker, *Food and Drink in America: A History* (Indianapolis and New York: Bobbs-Merrill Company, 1981), 328.

3. Arthur Bartlett, "Popcorn Crazy," *Saturday Evening Post* 221 (May 21, 1949): 36; *Saturday Evening Post* 191 (August 24, 1918): 46; *Boxoffice* 50 (February 1, 1947): 26; Benjamin Banowitz, "Producing a Popcorn and Oil Combination," *Popcorn Merchandiser* 9 (July 1954): 12; Steve McQueeny, "How the Glen W. Dickson Theatre Circuit Found New Profits in Lobby Shops," *Better Theatre,* (March 4, 1939,) as reprinted in *Kernel* 2 (March–April 1939): 3.

4. Steve McQueeny, "How the Glen W. Dickson Theatre Circuit Found New Profits in Lobby Shops," *Better Theatre,* (March 4, 1939,) as reprinted in *Kernel* 2 (March–April 1939): 3; Arthur Bartlett, "Popcorn Crazy," *Saturday Evening Post* 221 (May 21, 1949): 36.

5. Kemmons Wilson, *Half Luck and Half Brains: The Kemmons Wilson Holiday Inn Story* (Memphis, Tenn.: Hambleton-Hill Publishing, 1996), 15–16.

6. Arthur Bartlett, "Popcorn Crazy," *Saturday Evening Post* 221 (May 21, 1949): 36.

7. Arthur Bartlett, "Popcorn Crazy," *Saturday Evening Post* 221 (May 21, 1949): 112; F. A. Behymer, "Popcorn Crop Major Business at Shawneetown; Newspaper Pays Tribute to George Atkins," *Popcorn Merchandiser* 4 (March 1950): 36–38.

8. Arthur Bartlett, "Popcorn Crazy," *Saturday Evening Post* 221 (May 21, 1949): 112.

9. Steve McQueeny, "How the Glen W. Dickson Theatre Circuit Found New Profits in Lobby Shops," *Better Theatre,* (March 4, 1939,) as reprinted in *Kernel* 2 (March–April 1939): 3.

10. Ibid., 3–4.

11. American Pop Corn Company, *Jolly Time,* 13–15.

12. *Boxoffice* 54 (May 7, 1949): 37.

13. Evelyn Birkby, *Neighboring on the Air; Cooking with the KMA Radio Homemakers* (Iowa City: University of Iowa Press, 1991), 10–11, 68, 312.

14. Ibid., 10–11.

15. *A Bowl of Pop Corn, A Radio and You* (Sioux City, Iowa: American Pop Corn Company, 1930). Reprinted with permission.

16. Gwen Johnson, "The Cracker Jack Song" (Hollywood, Calif.: Cine-Mart Music Publishers, 1946), in the collection of Harriet Joyce, DeBarry, Fla.; James D. Russo, *Cracker Jack Collecting for Fun and Profit* (N.p.: Printed for the author, 1976), 15.

17. William W. Mackie, "Modern Methods of Producing Popcorn," *California Cultivator* 88 (April 5, 1941): 21; Arthur M. Brunson and Dwayne L. Richardson, "Popcorn," in *Farmers' Bulletin #1679,* rev. ed. (Washington, D.C.: Department of Agriculture, 1958), 7.

18. Brunson and Richardson, "Popcorn," 3; *Yearbook of Agriculture 1937* (Washington, D.C.: Department of Agriculture, 1937), 131–32; Sherman, *Popcorn King,* 35.

19. *Yearbook of Agriculture 1937* (Washington, D.C.: Department of Agriculture, 1937), 131–32.

20. "New Pop Corn Variety Pops to a Greater Size," *Scientific American* 147 (July 1932): 48; Brunson, "Popcorn Breeding," 399–401.

21. Brunson, "Popcorn Breeding," 399–400; *Yearbook of Agriculture 1937* (Washington, D.C.: U.S. Department of Agriculture, 1937), 131–32.

22. Brunson, "Popcorn Breeding," 404.

23. Agricultural Alumni Seed Improvement Association Web Site: http://www.agalumniseed.com; Brunson, "Popcorn," 423–24; From the *St. Louis Post-Dispatch,* F. A. Behymer, "Popcorn Crop Major Business at Shawneetown; Newspaper Pays Tribute to George Atkins," *Popcorn Merchandiser* 4 (March 1950): 38.

24. National Popcorn Association, *Popcorn Is a Fighting Food!* (Schaller, Iowa: National Popcorn Association, [1942]), n.p.; Robert F. Ware, interview, December 9, 1997.

25. Wales Newby, "Popping Oil—The Proper One for Your Popcorn," *Popcorn Merchandiser* 9 (July 1954): 20; "Canadians Report on Third Annual IPA Regional Popcorn-Concession Conference," *Popcorn Merchandiser* 9 (May 1954): 6.

26. Ronald Toth Jr., interview, Rochester, N.H., December 13, 1997; collection of Harriet Joyce, DeBarry, Fla.

27. Advertising brochure for the Cracker Jack Company in the collection of Harriet Joyce, DeBarry, Fla.

28. Homer Croy, "You Wouldn't Know the Old Farm Now," *Harper's* 193 (October 1946): 311; Clarence O. Grogan, O. V. Singleton, and M. S. Zuber, "Popcorn Culture in Missouri," in *Bulletin #718* (Columbia: University of Missouri/Agricultural Experiment Station, 1958), 3; *Popcorn Merchandiser* 9 (July 1954): 12; Charles G. Manley, "Pop Corn Sales Resistance—How to Turn it into Profit," *Boxoffice* 49 (August 17, 1946): 26.

29. *Chicago Tribune,* as in the *Popcorn Merchandiser* 7 (February 1952): 24; *C. Cretors & Co. The First Hundred Years: 1885–1985* (Chicago: C. Cretors, 1985), 86–87.

30. Arthur Bartlett, "Popcorn Crazy," *Saturday Evening Post* 221 (May 21, 1949): 36.

31. "Pop Goes the Corn," *Time Magazine* 46 (November 19, 1945): 88; "Now Its Popcorn; Latest Wartime Shortage," *Business Week* (June 17, 1944): 66.

32. *Des Moines Register,* January 2, 1945, as in the clipping file of the Iowa Historical Society Library, Des Moines; "Pop Goes the Corn," *Time Magazine* 46 (November 19, 1945): 88.

33. George K. Brown, "How the Popcorn Business Started," unpublished paper in the Wyandot Popcorn Museum, Marion, Ohio, dated July 15, 1987.

34. Ibid.

35. American Pop Corn Company, *Jolly Time,* 26–27.

36. Ibid., 16, 27–30.

37. "The More You Eat," *Fortune* 35 (June 1947): 144; Hess, *Snack Food,* 204; Deidre Waz, "Not Surprisingly, Prizes Reflect Century's Wide-Ranging Trends," *MassBay Antiques* (September 1993): 3.

38. Cracker Jack advertising brochure in the collection of Harriet Joyce, DeBarry, Fla.; Jaramillo, *Cracker Jack Prizes,* 18.

39. *C. Cretors & Co. The First Hundred Years: 1885–1985* (Chicago: C. Cretors, 1985), 105–6.

40. *Boxoffice* 49 (May 11, 1946): 36; *Boxoffice* 54 (May 7, 1949): Modern Theatre section, 25–26.

41. *Boxoffice* 48 (November 10, 1945): 58; Art Vogel, interview, September 26, 1997.

42. "Edward G. Sieg, 1898–1967," obituary notice issued by the Popcorn Institute, May 15, 1967; Snack Food Association, *Fifty Years: A Foundation for the Future* (Alexandria, Va.: Snack Food Association, 1987), 251; *Boxoffice* 49 (November 16, 1946): 59; "Willie in the Pop Behind the Corn," *Indianapolis Star,*

July 23, 1990, p. C4; Kimbra Postlewaite, "Popped Out," *Snack Food* 85 (August 1996): 17.

43. "1948 Popcorn Production a Near Record" [broadside] (Washington, D.C.: U.S. Department of Agriculture, Bureau of Agricultural Economics, December 20, 1948); George Brown, interview, December 9, 1997; Robert F. Ware, interview, December 9, 1997; James A. McCarty, interview, December 12, 1997.

44. "1948 Popcorn Production a Near Record" [broadside] (Washington, D.C.: U.S. Department of Agriculture, Bureau of Agricultural Economics, December 20, 1948); George Brown, interview, December 9, 1997; Robert F. Ware, interview, December 9, 1997; James A. McCarty, interview, December 12, 1997.

45. Hess, *Snack Food,* 207; George Brown, interview, December 9, 1997.

46. Robert F. Ware, interview, December 9, 1997.

47. Robert F. Ware, interview, December 9, 1997; George Brown, interview, December 9, 1997; "August J. Fisher 1895–1969," obituary circulated by the Popcorn Institute, February 28, 1969; "Carl W. Erne 1888–1968," obituary circulated by the Popcorn Institute, 1968; James R. McGuire, "Wall Lake: Home of Andy Williams and Largest Popcorn Plant in World," *Des Moines Register,* December 22, 1968, p. F2 as in the clipping file of the Iowa Historical Society Library, Des Moines.

48. Herbert Gettelfinger, interview, August 1, 1997; "Popcorn as a Packing Material," *Business Week* (April 12, 1952): 156.

49. Howard T. Walden, *Native Inheritance: The Story of Corn in America* (New York: Harper & Row, 1966), 156, 158; Myrtie Barker, "Popcorn is Big Business," *Indianapolis News,* November 17, 1971, p. 25; *Times* (London), April 12, 1991, p. 12; *Times* (London), September 4, 1992, p. 23; Alexandra Hardy, "For a 'Green' Christmas, Reuse, Renew, and Recycle," *Christian Science Monitor,* December 17, 1996, 14.

50. Evener and Birtler, *Kernel Knowledge,* 6.

51. Ibid., 47.

52. Joseph Burtt-Davy, *Maize: Its History, Cultivation, Handling, and Uses* (New York: Longmans, Green and Co., 1914), 326; J. C. Eldredge and P. J. Lyerly, "Popcorn in Iowa," in *Iowa Station Bulletin P54* (Ames: Iowa Agricultural Experiment Station, 1943), 755; "Pop Goes the Corn," *Time Magazine* 46 (November 19, 1945): 88; "Now Its Popcorn; Latest Wartime Shortage," *Business Week* (June 17, 1944): 66; Helen Peacocke, letter to author dated July 21, 1997.

53. George Brown, interview, December 9, 1997.

54. "Belgium Goes into Popcorn Business," *Popcorn Merchandiser* 5 (October 1950): 22; Lucy Howard and Gregory Cerio, "Get a Life," *Newsweek* 123 (March 28, 1994): 7.

55. Syd Spiegel, "Profits from Popcorn," *Popcorn-Concession Merchandiser* 11 (April 1956): 28; Arthur Bartlett, "Popcorn Crazy," *Saturday Evening Post* 221 (May 21, 1949): 36.

56. *Popcorn-Concession Merchandiser* 12 (August 1957): 21–22.

57. Masutaka "Mike" Imai, "Merchandising Popcorn in Japan," *Concessionaire Merchandiser* 16 (February 1962): 4–5; *C. Cretors & Co. The First Hundred Years: 1885–1985* (Chicago: C. Cretors, 1985), 116.

58. Arthur Bartlett, "Popcorn Crazy," *Saturday Evening Post* 221 (May 21, 1949): 141.

59. *Iowa Year Book of Agriculture 1945* (Des Moines: State of Iowa, 1945), 652–53; Homer Croy, "You Wouldn't Know the Old Farm Now," *Harper's* 193 (October 1946): 311.

60. Herb Owens, "Popcorn, Not Tall Corn, in Sac County; And it Brings $120 an Acre," *Des Moines Tribune,* November 28, 1948, as in the clipping file of the Iowa Historical Society Library, Des Moines; Arthur Bartlett, "Popcorn Crazy," *Saturday Evening Post* 221 (May 21, 1949): 36, 42; F. A. Behymer, "Popcorn Crop Major Business at Shawneetown; Newspaper Pays Tribute to George Atkins," *Popcorn Merchandiser* 4 (March 1950): 36–38.

61. "Popcorn Bonanza: Fans Are Eating Movie Exhibitors Out of the Red," *Life* 27 (July 25, 1949): 41; "Presley Also Good as a Popcorn Seller," *Popcorn-Concession Merchandiser* 13 (May 1958): 18; *Concessionaire Merchandiser* 13 (June 1958): 10; *Concessionaire Merchandiser* 14 (May 1959): 6.

62. *Film Daily,* as cited in *Advertising Age* 22 (December 24, 1951): 43; From the *St. Louis Post-Dispatch,* F. A. Behymer, "Popcorn Crop Major Business at Shawneetown; Newspaper Pays Tribute to George Atkins," *Popcorn Merchandiser* 4 (March 1950): 36–38, 42.

63. *Advertising Age* 22 (December 24, 1951): 43; Giedt, *Popcorn!,* 104–5.

64. "Los Angeles UA Houses Try Homemade Subliminal System," *Popcorn-Concession Merchandiser* 13 (March 1958): 28–29.

65. Wilson Bryan Key, *Subliminal Seduction* (New York: Penguin Books USA, 1974), 22–23; U.S. Patent #3,060,795, issued October 30, 1962; "'Subliminals' Ride Again, But No Sale," *Popcorn-Concession Merchandiser* 13 (April 1958): 16.

66. Rita Reif, "Drive-In Theatre Extends Horizon," *Popcorn Merchandiser* 13 (February 1958): 9; Spitler and Hauser, *The Popcorn Lover's Book,* 10–11.

67. "Theatre Receipts Drop 12 Per Cent in Seven Years," *Popcorn Concession Merchandiser* 11 (July 1956): 5; *C. Cretors & Co. The First Hundred Years: 1885–1985* (Chicago: C. Cretors, 1985), 110.

68. Connie Harder, "Popcorn—an Iowa Success Story," *Iowa REC News* (July 1961): 17; Richard L. Shayon, "The Popcorn Millennium," *Saturday Review* 40 (January 5, 1957): 28; Roger Kahle and Robert E. A. Lee, *Popcorn and Parable: A New Look at The Movies* (Minneapolis: Augsburg Publishing House, 1971), 16–17.

69. *Advertising Age* 22 (December 24, 1951): 43; *Chicago Tribune,* as in the *Popcorn Merchandiser* 7 (February 1952): 24, 37.

70. Ziegler and Ashman, "Popcorn," 191.

71. "Home Invasion," *Time Magazine* 56 (November 13, 1950): 85; Connie Harder, "Popcorn—an Iowa Success Story," *Iowa REC News* (July 1961): 17.

72. "Pop-Corn Polka Featured on Nation-Wide Broadcast," *Popcorn Merchandiser* 5 (May 1950): 6; *Saturday Evening Post,* October 20, 1954, from the files of The American Pop Corn Company; Hess, *Snack Food,* 205; Russo, *Cracker Jack Collecting,* 16; American Pop Corn Company, *Jolly Time,* 33, 44.

73. Kenneth E. Ziegler, "Popcorn Production as an Alternative Seed and Commodity Crop," in J. S. Burris, ed., *Proceedings of the Eleventh Seed Technology Conference* (Ames: Iowa State University, 1989), 114; Richard L. Shayon, "The Popcorn Millennium," *Saturday Review* 40 (January 5, 1957): 28; "Popcorn Production" (Washington, D.C.: United States Department of Agriculture, Bureau of Agricultural Economics, December 21, 1949); "Popcorn Production 1951" (Washington, D.C.: United States Department of Agriculture, Bureau of Agricultural Economics, December 1951); "1960 Popcorn Production up 15 Percent" (Washington, D.C.: United States Department of Agriculture, December 1960); "1965 Popcorn Production up 46 Percent" (Washington, D.C.: United States Department of Agriculture, Statistical Reporting Service, December 20, 1965).

Chapter 7: Pop Convenience

1. Julie Polshek, "Corn Popping is More Fun than Ever," *House Beautiful* 91 (April 1949): 195–96; "Cocktails and Popcorn were Made for Each Other," *House Beautiful* 91 (November 1949): 314.

2. "Electric Corn Poppers for *Zea Mays everta,*" *Consumer Bulletin* 51 (November 1968): 35–38.

3. Benjamin Banowitz, "Producing a Popcorn and Oil Combination," *Popcorn Merchandiser* 9 (July 1954): 12.

4. Interview with Orville Redenbacher by George Brown, August 3, 1981, at Coronado, Calif., in the Wyandot Popcorn Museum, Marion, Ohio; Phil Hanna, "Popcorn Profits Rescue Movie Man," *Chicago Daily News,* as reprinted in *Popcorn Merchandiser* 9 (August 1954): 20.

5. Benjamin Banowitz, "Producing a Popcorn and Oil Combination," *Popcorn Merchandiser* 9 (July 1954): 14–19; Phil S. Hanna, "Purdue's the Cradle of a Popcorn King," *Indianapolis Times,* August 9, 1954, p. 11; interview with Orville Redenbacher by George Brown, August 3, 1981, at Coronado, Calif., in the Wyandot Popcorn Museum, Marion, Ohio; George Brown, interview, November 28, 1997.

6. U.S. Patent #2,673,805 and #2,673,806, issued March 30, 1954; *Concessionaire Merchandiser* 16 (October 1961): 6.

7. U.S. Patent #2,791,350, issued May 7, 1957; *La Porte Herald-Argus,* May 28, 1962, clipping in the La Porte Historical Society, La Porte, Ind.

8. *The History of Jiffy Pop,* prepared by Consumer Affairs, International Home Foods, Inc., November 21, 1997; *La Porte Herald-Argus,* May 28, 1962, clipping in the La Porte Historical Society, La Porte, Ind.

9. Notes of interview of Frederick Mennen by Phillip Elasky, March 4, 1981, at the Wyandot Popcorn Museum, Marion, Ohio; *La Porte Herald-Argus,* January 5, 1961, and May 28, 1962, clippings in the La Porte Historical Society, La Porte, Ind.

10. "Findings of Fact, Conclusions of Law, and Judgement," in Civil Cases No. 2682 and 2821, Taylor-Reed Corporation vs Mennen Food Products, Inc., American Home Products Corporation, and Frederick C. Mennen, at the National Archives, Great Lakes Region.

11. *The Popcorn Market,* 3, 49; "Popcorn and Popcorn Poppers," *Consumer Reports* 54 (June 1989): 356–57.

12. American Portrait, "The Spirit of Raytheon; A History of the Company," video from the Raytheon Manufacturing Corporation's archives.

13. Robert Buderi, *The Invention that Changed the World: How A Small Group of Radar Pioneers Won the Second World War and Launched a Technological Revolution* (New York: Simon & Schuster, 1997), 85–90.

14. Robert Buderi, *The Invention that Changed the World: How A Small Group of Radar Pioneers Won the Second World War and Launched a Technological Revolution* (New York: Simon & Schuster, 1997), 82–83, 89; Charles R. Buffler, *Microwave Cooking and Processing: Engineering Fundamentals for the Food Scientist* (New York: AVI Books/Van Nostrand Reinhold, 1993), 14; American Portrait, "The Spirit of Raytheon, A History of the Company," video from the Raytheon Manufacturing Corporation's archives.

15. John Osepchuk, "A History of Microwave Applications," *IEEE Transactions on Microwave Theory and Technique* 32 (September 1984): 1203.

16. *Missile Messenger,* as cited in Otto J. Scott, *The Creative Ordeal: The Story

of Raytheon (New York: Atheneum, 1974), 180; John Osepchuk, "A History of Microwave Applications," *IEEE Transactions on Microwave Theory and Technique* 32 (September 1984): 1204.

17. Elmer J. Gorn, Chief Patent Attorney, Raytheon Company, "Micro Wave Cooking—The Story of a Man and His Invention," about 1970, unpublished paper in the Raytheon Company Archives, p. 3; Percy Spencer, U.S. Patent #2,480,629, issued October 8, 1945; William M. Hall and Fritz A. Gross, U.S. Patent #2,500,676 registered to Raytheon Manufacturing Corporation, applied for January 14, 1947, issued March 14, 1950.

18. Percy Spencer, U.S. Patent #2,480,679 registered to Raytheon Manufacturing Corporation, applied for March 29, 1947, issued August 30, 1949, 1.

19. Ibid., 1–2.

20. Percy Spencer, U.S. Patent #2,495,479 registered to the Raytheon Manufacturing Corporation, applied for March 29, 1947, issued August 30, 1949, 2–3.

21. John Osepchuk, "A History of Microwave Applications," *IEEE Transactions on Microwave Theory and Technique* 32 (September 1984): 1204; Charles W. Behrens, "The Development of the Microwave Oven," *Appliance Manufacturer,* 24 (November 1976): 72; Norman Krim, Raytheon Historian, interview, August 14, 1997.

22. Charles W. Behrens, "The Development of the Microwave Oven," *Appliance Manufacturer,* 24 (November 1976): 72; John Osepchuk, "A History of Microwave Applications," *IEEE Transactions on Microwave Theory and Technique* 32 (September 1984): 1205, 1207; American Portrait, "The Microwave Oven," video from the Raytheon Manufacturing Corporation's archives.

23. Charles W. Behrens, "The Development of the Microwave Oven," *Appliance Manufacturer* 24 (November 1976): 72.

24. John Osepchuk, "A History of Microwave Applications," *IEEE Transactions on Microwave Theory and Technique* 32 (September 1984): 1208.

25. Ibid., 1211.

26. Charles W. Behrens, "The Development of the Microwave Oven," *Appliance Manufacturer,* 24 (November 1976): 72; Robert Buderi, *The Invention that Changed the World: How a Small Group of Radar Pioneers Won the Second World War and Launched a Technological Revolution* (New York: Simon & Schuster, 1997), 256.

27. Tadashi Sasaki and Yoshihiro Kase, "Growth of the Microwave Oven Industry in Japan," *Journal of Microwave Power* 6 (December 1971): 283.

28. John Osepchuk, "A History of Microwave Applications," *IEEE Transactions on Microwave Theory and Technique* 32 (September 1984): 1211; Susan Strasser, *Never Done: A History of American Housework* (New York: Pantheon Books, 1982), 277; Wayne R. Tinga, "Microwave Ovens—History and Future," *Transactions of the International Microwave Power Institute* 6 (1976): 3.

29. Robert F. Bowen, "Symposium Presentations Describe Innovations in Microwave Cooking," *Microwave World* 1 (September/October 1980): 15; James D. Watkins, interview, September 15, 1997.

30. John Osepchuk, "A History of Microwave Applications," *IEEE Transactions on Microwave Theory and Technique* 32 (September 1984): 1211.

31. U.S. Patent #3,973,045, issued August 3, 1976, and U.S. Patent No. 4,219,573, issued August 26, 1980; James D. Watkins, interview, September 15, 1997.

32. *The Popcorn Market,* 63.

33. Ibid., 56.

Chapter 8: Pop Mania

1. Patricia Linden, "Popcorn! It's No Flash in the Pan," *Reader's Digest* (Canadian ed.) 125 (November 1984): 117.

2. *The Popcorn Market,* 3, 48–49.

3. "Orville Redenbacher," *U.S. News and World Report* 119 (October 2, 1995): 24; Don Vorhees, *Why Does Popcorn Pop? and 201 Other Fascinating Facts about Food* (New York: Citadel Press Books, 1995), 56; Thomas S. England, "The King of Pop, Orville Redenbacher was Popcorn's Own Kernel Sanders," *People* 45 (October 2, 1995): 139; Michael Lafavore, "Garden Gourmet Popcorn," *Organic Gardening* 30 (October 1983): 28–29; Redenbacher, *Orville Redenbacher's Popcorn Book,* 14–15; interview with Orville Redenbacher by George Brown, August 3, 1981, at Coronado, Calif., in the Wyandot Popcorn Museum, Marion, Ohio.

4. Frances E. Hughes, "Poppin' in Indiana," *Indianapolis Star Magazine,* October 6, 1963, pp. 46–49; Sherman, *Popcorn King,* 33–35; interview with Orville Redenbacher by George Brown, August 3, 1981, at Coronado, Calif., in the Wyandot Popcorn Museum, Marion, Ohio.

5. "Things Are Popping in Indiana," *Star Magazine,* February 3, 1957, pp. 6, 8; Sherman, *Popcorn King,* 36–37; interview with Orville Redenbacher by George Brown, August 3, 1981, at Coronado, Calif., in the Wyandot Popcorn Museum, Marion, Ohio.

6. Interview with Orville Redenbacher by George Brown, August 3, 1981, at Coronado, Calif., in the Wyandot Popcorn Museum, Marion, Ohio; Michael Lafavore, "Garden Gourmet Popcorn," *Organic Gardening* 30 (October 1983): 30.

7. Interview with Orville Redenbacher by George Brown, August 3, 1981, at Coronado, Calif., in the Wyandot Popcorn Museum, Marion, Ohio.

8. Charles F. Bowman, letter to author, July 15, 1997.

9. Dale Burgess, "Popcorn King Proclaims His Product Not Cheap," *Indianapolis News,* November 13, 1974, p. 5.

10. Thomas S. England, "The King of Pop, Orville Redenbacher was Popcorn's Own Kernel Sanders," *People* 45 (October 2, 1995): 139.

11. Robert McG. Thomas Jr., "Orville Redenbacher, Famous for His Popcorn, Is Dead at 88," *New York Times,* September 20, 1995, p. D20; Redenbacher, *Orville Redenbacher's Popcorn Book,* 14–16; Gail Collins, "Our Inner Nerd," *New York Times Magazine,* December 31, 1995, p. 23; Dan Carpenter, "Orville's Popcorn Empire Still Growing," *Indianapolis Star,* September 6, 1980, p. 26.

12. Charles F. Bowman, letter to author, July 15, 1997.

13. Interview with Orville Redenbacher by George Brown, August 3, 1981, at Coronado, Calif., in the Wyandot Popcorn Museum, Marion, Ohio; *The Popcorn Market,* 49–51, 9, 57–58, 82, 98.

14. *The Popcorn Market,* 98; "1997 Snack Food Association State of the Snack Food Industry Report," *Snack World* 54 (June 1997): 11.

15. Redenbacher, *Orville Redenbacher's Popcorn Book; Facts on File,* September 21, 1995, p. 708.

16. Speech by James D. Watkins given at the Corn Tech Seminar, November 2, 1988.

17. *The Popcorn Market,* 57.

18. James D. Watkins, interview, September 15, 1997; *The Popcorn Market,* 38–39, 59.

19. *Food Business* (March 20, 1989): 32.

20. Bonnie Britton, "Flavored Popcorn? Try It and See," *Indianapolis Star,* April 10, 1983, pp. H1, H6; "A Familiar Munch Goes Gourmet," *Time* 126 (March 14, 1983): 79; Steph McGrath, letter to the author, November 5, 1997; see also Web Site: http://www.garrettpopcorn.com/index.html#Home.

21. *Dayton Daily News,* February 29, 1976; George Theodore, "Popcorn Lovers Unite," *Happenings* (Akron, Ohio), April 1976.

22. "A Familiar Munch Goes Gourmet," *Time* 126 (March 14, 1983): 79.

23. Patricia Linden, "Popcorn! It's No Flash in the Pan," *Reader's Digest* (Canadian ed.) 125 (November 1984): 118; "A Familiar Munch Goes Gourmet," *Time* 126 (March 14, 1983): 79; *The Popcorn Market,* 52–53, 125.

24. Bonnie Britton, "Flavored Popcorn? Try It and See," *Indianapolis Star,* April 10, 1983, pp. H1, H6; *The Popcorn Market,* 9, 70–71.

25. Comment to the author, June 13, 1995, at Corcoran in Washington, D.C.; promotional material for Newman's Own.

26. *Omaha World-Herald,* August 21, 1997; various brochures and clippings supplied by Mormac Co., North Loup, Nebr.

27. Betty Bailey et al., *Schaller Centennial Book* (Schaller, Iowa: History Book Committee, 1983), 214–16; "Popcorn Days at Schaller," *Des Moines Register,* July 23, 1973, p. B3, as in the Historical Society of Iowa Library, clipping file.

28. *Popcorn Day Popper 1997* (Ridgeway, Ill., 1997); "Valparaiso Popcorn Festival History," photocopied material supplied by the Greater Valparaiso Chamber of Commerce.

29. Evener and Birtler, *Kernel Knowledge,* 34; *Marion Popcorn Festival 10th Anniversary Souvenir Magazine* (Marion, Ohio: Marion Popcorn Festival, 1990).

30. Russo, *Cracker Jack Collecting,* 17; Hess, *Snack Food,* 204.

31. *The Popcorn Market,* 43; "Popcorn Sales More Hype than Heat," *Snack Food* 81 (June 1992): p. M27; *Snack World* 51 (June 1994): 93; "1997 Snack Food Association State of the Snack Food Industry Report," *Snack World* 54 (June 1997): 12.

32. *The Popcorn Market,* 4.

33. Ibid., 46–47, 66.

34. *Gourmet* 21 (November 1961): 37; *Gourmet* 41 (December 1981): 228; *Gourmet* 42 (December 1982): 150; *Gourmet* 44 (February 1984): 168; *Gourmet* 44 (October 1984): 224.

35. Hall et al., *I Love Popcorn;* Barbara Williams, *Cornzapoppin'!*

36. Kusche, *Popcorn.*

37. Evener and Birtler, *Kernel Knowledge;* Robert T. Brucken, *Bang! The Explosive Popcorn Recipe Book* (New York: Ballantine Books, 1983); Spitler and Hauser, *The Popcorn Lover's Book.*

38. Pfeifer, *For Popcorn Lovers Only.*

39. Redenbacher, *Orville Redenbacher's Popcorn Book;* Ursla Hotchner, *Newman's Own Gourmet Popcorn Recipes* (Westport, Conn.: Newman's Own Inc., [1988]).

40. Giedt, *Popcorn!;* Gina Steer, *The Hoppin 'n' Poppin Popcorn Cookbook* (Edison, N.J.: Chartwell Books, 1995), 14–79; Popcorn Institute Web site: http://www.popcorn.org/mpindex.htm.

41. *The Popcorn Market,* 5–6; Kenneth Pins, "In Pursuit of Good Taste with Researcher at ISU," *Des Moines Register,* September 4, 1986, p. B1; "Popcorn and Popcorn Poppers," *Consumer Reports* 54 (June 1989): 355–56.

42. "Popcorn and Popcorn Poppers," *Consumer Reports* 54 (June 1989): 362.

43. Ibid., 355–56.

44. "The Popcorn Institute Seal of Quality Performance," undated sheet published and distributed by the Popcorn Institute in Chicago. For an updated list of quality poppers see the Popcorn Institute Web Site: http://www.popcorn.org/mpindex.htm

45. "Popcorn and Popcorn Poppers," *Consumer Reports* 54 (June 1989): 362.

46. *The Popcorn Market,* 117.

47. *C. Cretors & Co. The First Hundred Years: 1885–1985* (Chicago: C. Cretors, 1985), 123–28.

48. Elizabeth Grinnell, "Nothing but Corn," *Table Talk* 8 (November 1898): 391; Edward Enfield, *Indian Corn; Its Value, Culture, and Uses* (New York: D. Appleton and Company, 1866), 66; *Country Gentleman* 17 (January 24, 1861): 65; *Country Gentleman* 24 (November 10, 1864): 305; *Country Gentleman* 30 (October 31, 1867): 262; "Maybe You Can Plant Popcorn for Silage; Loop-hole in Feed Grain Program," *Farm Journal* 87 (June 1963): 31; Ziegler, "Popcorn Production," 118.

49. "Wesley Friesen's Improbable Dream: Popcorn-on-the-Cob is Now an Amazing Success," *People Weekly* 30 (August 1, 1988): 96; "Popcorn and Popcorn Poppers," *Consumer Reports* 54 (June 1989): 357.

50. *Handcrafted Original Pullcarts* (Crestwood, Ill.: American Enterprises Antique Wagons & Carts, n.d.); Don Condon, "His Mini-Machines Are Made from Memories," *Reminisce* 6 (May/June 1996): 52–53; Dan Milliman, "16.7 Cent Popcorn Wagon Added to Transportation Coils," *Stamps* 223 (June 25, 1988): 878.

51. Russo, *Cracker Jack Collecting.* Jaramillo, *Cracker Jack Prizes,* 15; Larry White, *Cracker Jack Toys: The Complete, Unofficial Guide for Collectors* (Atglen, Pa.: Schiffer Publishing, 1997). An earlier edition of White's book was published with the title *The Cracker Jack Price and Collector's Guide* ([Maynard, Mass.?]: Beagle Press, 1995). Roberta Bowen, ed., *The Prize Insider,* Cracker Jack Collector's Association, interview, December 6, 1997; Scott Green, "A Cracker Jack Collector," *Toy World* (October 1996): 73; Kate Carey, "Local Man has 60,000 Prizes," *Foster's Daily Democrat,* April 20, 1996, pp. 1, 20; Ronald Toth Jr., interview, December 13, 1997; Ravi Piña, *Cracker Jack Collectibles with Price Guide* (Atglen, Pa.: Schiffer Publishing, Ltd., 1995).

52. "Popcorn Industry Fact Sheet; Sales (unpopped popcorn)," produced by the Popcorn Institute, Chicago, 1994.

Chapter 9: The End of Popcorn?

1. "Popcorn," *Snack Food* 83 (June 1994): 91.

2. Joel Herskowitz, *The Popcorn Plus Diet* (New York: Pharos Books, 1987), 13. Unfortunately, the recipes could have been more carefully selected. One titled "Cajun Popcorn" originally appearing in Paul Prudhomme's *Louisiana Kitchen,* contains no popcorn but does include shrimp. "Popcorn" in the title of the recipe refers to the way the shrimp is prepared for the dish. See Paul Prudhomme, *Paul Prudhomme's Louisiana Kitchen* (New York: William Morrow & Co., 1984), 281–82.

3. "A Familiar Munch Goes Gourmet," *Time* 126 (March 14, 1983): 79; Deborah J. Thomas, *Popcorn: Foreign Markets and U.S. Opportunities. Occasional Paper #19* (Lexington: Center for Agricultural Export Development, University of Kentucky, 1992), 18.

4. *The Popcorn Market,* 22, 68–69.

5. "Popcorn: Oil in a Day's Work," *Nutrition Action HealthLetter* 21 (May 1994): 9.

6. Terry Johnson, "Then There's the Popcorn Factor," *Alberta Report* 21 (May 30, 1994): 12; "Time Out," *TV Guide* 42 (May 21, 1994): 55.

7. Kimbra Postlewaite, "Popped Out," *Snack Food* 85 (August 1996): 16; Jeff Swiatek, "Popcorn Has Lost Its Pop," *Indianapolis Star and News,* April 29, 1997, from Star/News On-Line; *Snack Food* 85 (August 1996): pp. SI38–SI40.

8. Ziegler and Ashman, "Popcorn," 208.

9. *The Popcorn Market,* 7.

10. Jeff Swiatek, "Popcorn Has Lost Its Pop," *Indianapolis Star and News,* April 29, 1997, from Star/News On-Line.

11. *The Popcorn Market,* 62.

12. Jane Stokes Lange, "A History for the 30th Anniversary Board of Directors Meeting," Curtice Burns Foods, Inc., November 5, 1991.

13. *The Popcorn Market,* 33–34, 88; Thomas, *Popcorn,* 4–5, 9, 14, 18.

14. James D. Watkins, interview, September 16, 1997; "Global Popping," *Snack Food and Wholesale Baker* 87 (April 1998): 16.

15. "A Familiar Munch Goes Gourmet," *Time* 126 (March 14, 1983): 79; Thomas, *Popcorn,* 18.

Select Bibliography and Resources

General Works on Snack Food

Booth, R. Gordon, ed. *Snack Food.* New York: AVI/Van Nostrand Reinhold, 1990.

Hess, Jerry L. *Snack Food, A Bicentennial History.* New York: Harcourt Brace Jovanovich, 1976.

Matz, Samuel. *Snack Food Technology.* Westport, Conn.: AVI, 1976; second edition, 1981; third edition, AVI Books/Van Nostrand Reinhold, 1993.

Snack Food Association. *Fifty Years: A Foundation for the Future.* Alexandria, Va.: Snack Food Association, 1987.

General Works on Maize

The Book of Corn. New York and Chicago: Orange Judd Company, 1903.

Browne, J. D. *A Memoir on Maize, or Indian Corn* combined with Joel Barlow, *The Hasty-Pudding: A Poem.* New York: W. H. Graham, 1847.

Browne, Porter A. *An Essay on Corn.* Philadelphia: J. Thompson, 1837.

Burtt-Davy, Joseph. *Maize: Its History, Cultivation, Handling, and Uses.* New York: Longmans, Green and Co., 1914.

Butler, Eva L. "Algonkian Culture and Use of Maize in Southern New England," *Bulletin of the Archaeological Society of Connecticut* 22 (December 1948): 1–39.

Elting, Mary, and Michael Folsom. *The Mysterious Grain.* Philadelphia and New York: J. B. Lippincott Company, 1967.

Emerson, William D. *History and Incidents of Indian Corn and Its Culture.* Cincinnati: Wrightson & Co., 1878.

Enfield, Edward. *Indian Corn; Its Value, Culture, and Uses.* New York: D. Appleton and Company, 1866.

Johannessen, Sissel, and Christine A. Hastorf, eds. *Corn and Culture in the Prehistoric New World.* Boulder: Westview Press, 1994.

Longone, Janice B. *Mother Maize and King Corn: The Persistence of Corn in the American Ethos.* Ann Arbor: William L. Clements Library, University of Michigan, n.d.

Mangelsdorf, Paul. *Corn—Its Origin, Evolution and Improvement.* Cambridge, Mass.: Harvard University Press, 1974.

Murphy, Charles J. *American Indian Corn (Maize) A Cheap, Wholesome, and Nutritious Food 150 Ways to Prepare and Cook It.* New York and London: G. P. Putnam's Sons, 1917.

Parker, Arthur C. *Iroquois Uses of Maize and Other Food Plants.* Albany, N.Y.: Education Department Bulletin #482, November 1, 1910, 57–58, 78.

Sprague, G. F., ed. *Corn and Corn Improvement.* New York: Academic Press, 1955. Second revised edition, Madison, Wis.: American Society of Agronomy, 1977.

Sprague, G. F., and J. W. Dudley, eds. *Corn and Corn Improvement.* Third edition. Madison, Wis.: American Society for Agronomy, 1988.

Popcorn Books, Cookbooks, and Pamphlets

American Pop Corn Company. *Jolly Time: An American Tradition Since 1914.* Sioux City, Iowa: American Pop Corn Company, 1994.

Brucken, Robert T. *Bang! The Explosive Popcorn Recipe Book.* New York: Ballantine Books, 1983.

C. E. Dellenbarger Co. *Copyrighted Secret Formulas and Instructions for the*

Manufacture of Crispettes and Other Popcorn Confections. Chicago: C. E. Dellenbarger Co., 1913.
The Cracker Jack Company; Operating Committee Minutes, September 29, 1924–October 30, 1925. Rochester, N.H.: Ron Toth, Jr., 1997.
Evener, Connie, and MarSue Birtler. *Kernel Knowledge; A Cornucopia of Popcorn History, Trivia, Arts and Crafts, and Over 75 Recipes.* Columbus, Ohio: The authors, 1982.
Fifty Years. Chicago: Cracker Jack Company, 1922.
Giedt, Frances Towner. *Popcorn!* New York: Simon & Schuster, 1995.
Hall, Carolyn Vosburg, et al. *I Love Popcorn.* Garden City, N.Y.: Doubleday & Co., 1976.
Herskowitz, Joel. *The Popcorn Plus Diet.* New York: Pharos Books, 1987.
Holcomb, J. I. *Salesology of the Butter-Kist Popcorn Machine.* Indianapolis, Ind.: Holcomb and Hoke Manufacturing Company, [1915].
Holcomb, J. I. *Salesology of the Butter-Kist Popcorn Machine.* Indianapolis, Ind.: Holcomb and Hoke Manufacturing Company, 1917.
Hotchner, Ursla. *Newman's Own Gourmet Popcorn Recipes.* Westport, Conn.: Newman's Own, [1988].
Jaramillo, Alex. *Cracker Jack Prizes.* New York: Abbeville Press, 1989.
Knott, Eustace Reynolds. *Knott's Pop-corn Book.* Boston: E.R. Knott Machine Company, 1915.
Knott, Eustace Reynolds. *Knott's Pop-corn Book.* Second edition. Boston: E. R. Knott Machine Company, [1920].
Knott, Eustace Reynolds. *Knott's Pop-corn Book.* Third edition. Sharon, Mass.: E. R. Knott Co., 1936.
Kusche, Larry. *Popcorn.* Tucson, Ariz.: HPBooks, 1977.
Pfeifer, Diane. *For Popcorn Lovers Only.* Marietta, Ga.: Strawberry Patch / Atlanta, Ga.: Marmac Publishing Company, 1987.
Piña, Ravi. *Cracker Jack Collectibles with Price Guide.* Atglen, Pa.: Schiffer Publishing, Ltd., 1995.
The Popcorn Market. New York: Packaged Facts, 1989.
Redenbacher, Orville. *Orville Redenbacher's Popcorn Book.* New York: St. Martin's Press, 1984.
Russo, James D. *Cracker Jack Collecting for Fun and Profit.* N.p.: The author, 1976.
Sheinwold, Patricia Fox. *Jolly Time Party Book: Games, Puzzles, Recipes, and Creative Party Ideas for All Occasions.* Cambridge, Mass. and New York: Dorison House Publishers, 1977.
Sherman, Len. *Popcorn King: How Orville Redenbacher and his Popcorn Charmed America.* Arlington, Tex.: Summit Publishing Group, 1996.
Spitler, Sue, and Nao Hauser. *The Popcorn Lover's Book.* Chicago: Contemporary Books, 1983.
Steer, Gina. *The Hoppin 'n' Poppin Popcorn Cookbook.* Edison, N.J.: Chartwell Books, 1995.
White, Larry. *Cracker Jack Toys: The Complete, Unofficial Guide for Collectors.* Atglen, Pa.: Schiffer Publishing, 1997.
Williams, Barbara. *Cornzapoppin'! Popcorn Recipes & Party Ideas for All Occasions.* New York: Holt, Rinehart and Winston, 1976.

Historical Catalogs and Advertising Brochures

Advance Mfg. Co. *15000 Other Merchants Have Chosen Advance Light Lunch and Popcorn Equipment.* St. Louis, Mo.: Advance Mfg. Co., [circa 1936].

Albert Dickinson Company. *Little Buster Hull-Less Pop Corn.* Chicago: Albert Dickinson Co., 1921.

American Pop Corn Company. *Advertising that Gets Results for Operators of Pop Corn Machines.* Sioux City, Iowa: American Pop Corn Company, n.d.

———. *Having Fun with Pop Corn.* Sioux City, Iowa: American Pop Corn Company, n.d.

———. *Jolly Time: An American Tradition Since 1914.* Sioux City, Iowa: American Pop Corn Company, 1994.

———. *Popportunity.* Buffalo, N.Y.: American Pop Corn Company, 1929.

———. *Speed'er Order Blank and Complete Price List, Jolly Time.* Buffalo, N.Y.: American Pop Corn Company, n.d.

The Bartholomew Co. *The Peanut and Pop Corn Problem Solved.* Peoria, Ill.: Bartholomew Company, n.d. Reprint. Vestal, N.Y.: Vestal Press, 1985.

Borden Company. *The Cracker Jack Story.* [Columbus, Ohio: Borden Company, 1987].

C. Cretors & Co. *The Cash Rolls In When There's a Cretors in the Door.* Chicago: C. Cretors Co., n.d.

C. E. Dellenbarger Co. *Catalogue No. 14 of Kettle Pop Corn Machines and Peanut Roasters.* Chicago: C. E. Dellenbarger Co., [circa 1912].

C. E. Dellenbarger Co. *Catalogue No. 15B Crispette and Pop Corn Ball Machines: The Only Self-Stripping Crispette Machines Manufactured.* Chicago: C. E. Dellenbarger, n.d.

C. E. Dellenbarger Co. *Supplement to Catalogues Nos. 14 and 15 of Pop Corn, Peanut, Candy and Crispette Machinery.* Chicago: C. E. Dellenbarger Co., n.d.

Dunbar & Co. *Steam Operated Popcorn Wagons & Poppers and Peanut Roasters 1927 Catalog.* Chicago: Dunbar & Co., 1927. Reprint. New York: Vestal Press, n.d.

Kingery Manufacturing Company. *Catalogue No. 59, Kingery Peanut and Popcorn Machines, Good Values for Nearly Half a Century, Daily Money Makers.* Cincinnati: Kingery Manufacturing Company, [1927]. Reprint. Vestal, N.Y.: Vestal Press, 1985.

Kingery Manufacturing Company Catalogue. Cincinnati: Kingery Manufacturing Co., [1907].

Syracuse Pop Corn Machine and Supply Co. [Price List]. Syracuse, N.Y.: Syracuse Pop Corn Machine and Supply Co., 1927.

Agricultural Bulletins, Chapters, Circulars, and Journal Articles

Ashman, R. B. *Popcorn.* Purdue University, Cooperative Extension Service, Plant Disease Control, Bulletin BP-4, 1983.

Brunson, Arthur M. "Popcorn." In *Corn and Corn Improvement,* edited by G. F. Sprague (423–44). New York: Academic Press, 1955.

———. "Popcorn Breeding." In *Yearbook of Agriculture 1937* (395–404). Washington, D.C.: Department of Agriculture, 1937.

Brunson, Arthur M., and Carl W. Bower. "Pop Corn," *Farmers' Bulletin #1679.* Washington D.C.: Department of Agriculture, 1931. Revised as "Popcorn," *Farmers' Bulletin #1679.* Washington, D.C.: Department of Agriculture, 1958.

Burrill, Thomas J., and George W. McClure. "Pop Corn, Tests of Varieties." In *Bulletin #13* (443–47). Champaign: University of Illinois Agricultural Experiment Station, 1891.

Carr, R. H., and E. F. Ripley. "What Puts 'Pop' in Pop Corn?" In *Proceedings of the Indiana Academy of Science for 1920* (261–69). Indianapolis: Wm. B. Burford, 1921.

Dofing, S. M., A. M. Thomas-Compton, and J. S. Buck. "Genotype X Popping Method Interaction for Expansion Volume in Popcorn," *Crop Science* 30 (January–February 1990): 62–65.

Duncan, J. R. "Culture and Uses of Popcorn," *Circular Bulletin #148*. East Lansing: Michigan Agricultural Experiment Station, 1934.

Eldredge, J. C., and P. J. Lyerly. "Popcorn in Iowa." In *Iowa Station Bulletin P54* (753–78). Ames: Iowa Agricultural Experiment Station, 1943.

Eldredge, J. C., and W. I. Thomas. "Popcorn ... Its Production, Processing and Utilization," *Bulletin P127*. Ames: Iowa State University of Science and Technology, Agricultural and Home Economics Experiment Station, 1959.

Erwin, A. T. "The Origin and History of Pop Corn, Zea Mays L. var. Indurata (Sturt.) Baily mut. Everta (Sturt.) Erwin," *Agronomy Journal* 41 (February 1949): 53–56.

Grogan, Clarence O., O. V. Singleton, and M. S. Zuber. "Popcorn Culture in Missouri," *Bulletin #718*. Columbia: University of Missouri/Agricultural Experiment Station, 1958.

Halsted, Byron D. "A List of Popcorns Grown in 1905." In *26th Annual Report 1904/05* (442–47). New Brunswick: New Jersey State Agricultural Experiment Station, 1906.

Hartley, Charles P., and John G. Willier. "Pop Corn for the Home," *Farmers' Bulletin #553*. Washington, D.C.: Department of Agriculture, 1913.

———. "Pop Corn for the Market," *Farmers' Bulletin #554*. Washington, D.C.: Department of Agriculture, 1913.

Hosney, R. C., K. Zeleznak, and A. Abdelrahman. "Mechanism of Popcorn Popping," *Journal of Cereal Science* 1 (January 1983): 43–52.

Kraemer, Henry. "The Structure of the Corn Grain and Its Relation to Popping," *Science* n.s. 17 (May 1, 1903): 683–84.

Mackie, William W. "Modern Methods of Producing Popcorn," *California Cultivator* 88 (April 5, 1941): 20–21.

Pordesimo, L. O., R. C. Anantheswaran, and P. J. Mattern. "Quantification of Horny and Floury Endosperm in Popcorn and their Effects on Popping Performance in a Microwave Oven," *Journal of Cereal Sciences* 14 (September 1991): 189–98.

Reeve, Roger M., and H. G. Walker Jr. "The Microscopic Structure of Popped Cereals," *Cereal Chemistry* 46 (May 1969): 227–41.

Schieberle, Peter. "Primary Odorants in Popcorn," *Journal of Agricultural and Food Chemistry* 39 (June 1991): 1141–44.

Smith, Glenn M., and Arthur M. Brunson. "Hybrid Popcorn in Indiana," *Bulletin #510*. Lafayette, Ind.: Purdue University Agricultural Experiment Station, 1946.

Smith, Jared G. "Field Experiments for 1889," *Bulletin #12*. Lincoln, Nebr.: Agricultural Experiment Station, 1890.

Song, A., and S. R. Eckhoff. "Optimum Popping Moisture Content for Popcorn Kernels of Different Sizes," *Cereal Chemistry* 71 (September/October 1994): 458–60.

Stewart, F. C. "The Relation of Age and Viability to the Popping of Popcorn," *Bulletin #672*. Ithaca: New York State Agricultural Experiment Station, July 1936.

Storer, F. H. "Remarks on the 'Popping' of Indian Corn," Harvard University, *Bulletin Bussey Institution,* volume 3, part 4 (1904): 74–79.

Thomas, Deborah J. *Popcorn: Foreign Markets and U.S. Opportunities. Occasional Paper #19*. Lexington: Center for Agricultural Export Development, University of Kentucky, 1992.

Walradt, John P., Robert C. Lindsay, and Leonard M. Libbey. "Popcorn Flavor: Identification of Volatile Compounds," *Journal of Agricultural and Food Chemistry* 18 (September/October 1970): 926–28.

Weatherwax, Paul. "The Popping of Corn." In *Proceedings of the Indiana Academy of Science for 1921* (149–53). Indianapolis: Wm. B. Burford, 1922.

Wilbert, M. I. "Why Pop Corn Pops," *American Journal of Pharmacy* 75 (February 1903): 77–79.

Willier, John G., and A. M. Brunson. "Factors Affecting the Popping Quality of Popcorn," *Journal of Agricultural Research* 35 (October 1, 1927): 615–24.

Yeager, A. F. "Popcorn Pointers," *Circular 24*. Fargo, N.Dak.: Agricultural Experiment Station, 1924.

Ziegler, Kenneth E. "Popcorn Production as an Alternative Seed and Commodity Crop." In *Proceedings of the Eleventh Seed Technology Conference,* edited by J. S. Burris (113–21). Ames: Iowa State University, 1989.

Ziegler, Kenneth, and Bruce Ashman. "Popcorn." In *Speciality Corns,* edited by Arnel R. Hallauer (189–216). Boca Raton, Fla.: CRC Press, 1994.

Children's Popcorn Books

Adams, Phylliss. *Popcorn Magic.* Cleveland: Modern Curriculum Press, 1987.

Adams, Ruth. *Mr. Picklepaw's Popcorn.* New York: Lothrop, Lee & Shepard, [1965].

Asch, Frank. *Popcorn: A Frank Asch Bear Story.* New York: Parent's Magazine Press, circa 1979.

Brucken, Robert T. *Bang! The Explosive Popcorn Recipe Book.* New York: Ballantine Books, 1983.

Krantz, Hazel. *100 Pounds of Popcorn.* New York: Vanguard Press, 1961.

Kudlinski, Kathleen V. *Popcorn Plants.* Minneapolis, Minn.: Lerner Publications Company, 1997.

Lemon, Julianne. *Popcorn and Peanuts.* Concord, Calif.: Nitty Gritty Productions, 1977.

Low, Alice. *The Popcorn Shop.* New York: Scholastic, 1993.

McCully, Emily Arnold. *Popcorn at the Palace.* San Diego: Browndeer Press, 1997.

Paola, Tomie de. *The Popcorn Book.* New York: Holiday House, 1978.

Peifer, Jane Hoober. *The Biggest Popcorn Party Ever in Center County.* Scottdale, Pa.: Herald Press, 1987.

Regniers, Beatrice Schenk de, Eva Moore, Mary Michaels White, and Jan Carr. *Sing a Song of Popcorn.* New York: Scholastic Hardcover, 1988.

Russell, Solveig Paulson. *Peanuts, Popcorn, Ice Cream, Candy and Soda Pop and How They Began.* Nashville and New York: Abingdon Press, 1970.

Selsam, Millicent E. *Popcorn.* New York: William Morrow and Co., 1976.

Stevenson, James. *Popcorn.* New York: Greenwillow Books, 1998.

Wilkins, Mary. *The Pot of Gold* [retold by Elton Greene]. Retitled *Princess Rosetta and the Popcorn Man.* New York: Lothrop, Lee & Shepard, circa 1971.

Woodside, Dave. *What Makes Popcorn Pop?* New York: Atheneum, 1980.

Wyler, Rose. *Science Fun with Peanuts and Popcorn.* New York: Julian Messner, 1986.

Selected Commercial Popcorn Businesses

American Pop Corn Company, Box 178, Sioux City, Iowa 51102; (712) 239-1232; Web site: http://www.jollytime.com

Ames Seed Farms, RR3—Iowa Acres, Ames, Iowa 50010; (515) 232-3648

Crookham Seed Co., P.O. Box 520, Caldweld, Idaho 83606; (208) 459-7451
Johnny's Selected Seeds, Foss Hill Road, Albion, Maine 04910; (207) 437-9294.
McCone Seed Company, RR 4, Squaw Valley, Ames, Iowa 50010; (515) 233-2482
Meade Seed Co., Laurel Meade, 201 W. 8th St., Pueblo, Colo. 81003; (719) 544-4511
Schlessman Seed Co., 11513 Star Rt., Milan, Ohio 44846; (419) 499-2572; E-mail: seedco@accnorwalk.com
Seeds Blum, Idaho City Stage, Boise, Idaho 83706; (208) 342-0858.
Southern Exposure Seed Exchange, P.O. Box 170, Earlysville, Va. 22936; (804) 973-4703.
Stokes Seeds, Inc., Box 548, Buffalo, N.Y. 14240; (416) 688-4300.

Other Resources

Agricultural Alumni Seed Improvement Association, Inc.; P.O. Box 158; Romney, Ind. 47981; 1-800-822-7134 or (765) 538-3145; E-mail: agalumni@agalumniseed.com; Web site: http://www.agalumniseed.com/
Cracker Jack Collection, The Center of Science and Industry, 280 East Broad St., Columbus, Ohio 43215; (614) 228-COSI; Web site: http://www.cosi.org
Cracker Jack Collector's Association, c/o Roberta Bowen, editor, *The Prize Insider,* 305 East Minton Drive, Tempe, Ariz. 85282; (602) 831-1402
Popcorn Institute, 401 N. Michigan Avenue, Chicago, Ill. 60611-4212; (312) 644-6610; Web site: http://www.popcorn.org/mpindex.htm
Seed Savers Exchange, 3076 North Winn Road, Decorah, Iowa 52101; (319) 382-5990
The Snack Food Association, 1711 King Street, Alexandria, Va. 22314; (703) 836-4500
Wyandot Popcorn Museum in Heritage Hall, 169 E. Church Street, Marion, Ohio 43302; (614) 387-HALL; Web site: http://www.popcorn.story.com and www.popcornmuseum.com

Index